ADVANCED PROPERTY

ADVANCED PROPERTY

Paul Butt LLB (Manchester), Solicitor
Alan Riley LLB (Leicester), Solicitor
Philip Rogers BSc, Solicitor (Hons)

JORDANS
1999

Published by
Jordan Publishing Limited
21 St Thomas Street
Bristol BS1 6JS

British Library Cataloguing-in-Publication Data
A catalogue record for this book is available from the British Library.

ISSN 1353–3584
ISBN 0 85308 533 1

Photoset by Pentacor PLC, High Wycombe, Buckinghamshire
Printed in Great Britain by Hobbs The Printers Ltd of Southampton

PREFACE

The aim of this book is to provide law students with a comprehensive introduction to three important areas of property law:

- town and country planning;
- commercial leases; and
- residential tenancies.

Although it is hoped that the book will provide a useful guide to trainee solicitors and others involved in this type of work, it is primarily intended to complement the Advanced Property Elective on the College of Law's Legal Practice Course. These electives are only undertaken once the compulsory Conveyancing and Property course has been completed and this book, therefore, contains a few references to the book accompanying that course.

In the interests of brevity, the masculine pronoun has been used throughout to include the feminine.

The law is stated as at 1 December 1998.

PAUL BUTT
ALAN RILEY
PHILIP ROGERS
The College of Law
Chester

CONTENTS

TABLE OF CASES

References in the right-hand column are to paragraph numbers.

TABLE OF STATUTES

References in the right-hand column are to paragraph numbers.

TABLE OF STATUTORY INSTRUMENTS

References in the right-hand column are to paragraph numbers.

ABBREVIATIONS

The following abbreviations are used throughout this book.

AGA	authorised guarantee agreement
BCN	breach of condition notice
CGT	capital gains tax
DCPNs	development control policy notes
DoE	Department of the Environment
EA	Environment Act 1995
EPA 1990	Environmental Protection Act 1990
GDPO	Town and Country Planning (General Development Procedure) Order 1995
GPDO	Town and Country Planning (General Permitted Development) Order 1995
HA 1985	Housing Act 1985
HA 1988	Housing Act 1988
HA 1996	Housing Act 1996
IA 1986	Insolvency Act 1986
LPA	local planning authority
LPA 1925	Law of Property Act 1925
LP(MP)A 1989	Law of Property (Miscellaneous Provisions) Act 1989
LRA	Land Reform Act 1967
LRHUDA	Leasehold Reform, Housing and Urban Development Act 1993
LTA 1927	Landlord and Tenant Act 1927
LTA 1954	Landlord and Tenant Act 1954
LTA 1985	Landlord and Tenant Act 1985
LTA 1987	Landlord and Tenant Act 1987
LTCA 1995	Landlord and Tenant (Covenants) Act 1995
OMRV	open market retail value
PCN	planning contravention notice
PEA 1977	Protection from Eviction Act 1977
PPGs	planning policy guidance
RA 1977	Rent Act 1977
SDO	special development order
SSE	Secretary of State for the Environment
TCPA 1990	Town and Country Planning Act 1990
UCO	Town and Country Planning (Use Classes) Order 1987
WO	Welsh Office

PART I

SITE ACQUISITIONS

Parts I and II of this Resource Book take the reader through the various stages of a commercial property transaction, from initial acquisition of a green field site to eventual disposal of the freehold reversion. In addition, the reader is taken in detail through the grant of a lease of business premises, the assignment of that lease and its termination. Part III of the book deals with the law relating to residential tenancies.

In this first part of the book, matters relevant to property development are considered. These include the acquisition of the site, the requirement for planning permission, environmental implications, the inter-relation of developers and members of the construction industry, and the funding of commercial development.

The procedure to be followed on the sale and purchase of a plot of vacant land for development purposes is essentially the same as that adopted in residential conveyancing. Apart from the matters specifically mentioned in this part of the book, the law and practice relating to the drafting of the contract of sale, the making of pre-contract enquiries and searches, deducing and investigating title, exchanging contracts, preparing and executing the purchase deed, pre-completion searches, completion and post-completion steps do not differ from the law and practice in relation to residential conveyancing. The Law Society's National Conveyancing Protocol does not apply to commercial transactions.

Chapter 1

THE NEED FOR PLANNING PERMISSION

Chapter 1 contents

1.1 INTRODUCTION

The principal purpose of planning law is to control the development or use of land in order to improve amenity. This control is mainly exercised by local planning authorities by reference to development plans which they prepare. It is important to bear in mind from the outset that the basic rule is that planning permission is required from the relevant local planning authority for any operational development or material change of use of land. Note, however, that no criminal offence is initially committed (as a general rule) if operational development or a material change of use is carried out without permission; and it is not necessary for an applicant for planning permission to have any interest in the land for which the permission is sought.

For the sake of brevity, the following abbreviations have been used:

DoE	Department of the Environment
GDPO	Town and Country Planning (General Development Procedure) Order 1995
GPDO	Town and Country Planning (General Permitted Development) Order 1995
JPL	Journal of Planning and Environmental Law
LPA	local planning authority (which the Act, and therefore the text, refers to throughout as a plural entity)
PPGs	planning policy guidance notes
SSE	Secretary of State for the Environment (including, where relevant, the Secretary of State for Wales).

1.2 SOURCES OF PLANNING LAW

1.2.1 Statutory provisions

The principal Act is the Town and Country Planning Act 1990 (the Act) as substantially amended by the Planning and Compensation Act 1991 (the 1991 Act). All references in Chapter 1–5 of this book to section numbers or 'the Act' are to the 1990 Act as amended unless the contrary is stated.

The Act contains the legislative framework for all planning matters except for listed buildings, conservation areas and hazardous substances.

Although the Act is very large, running to 337 sections and 17 schedules, it sets out only the main framework of the planning system. The majority of the detail (including procedural rules and regulations, prescribed forms and many more substantive matters) is provided by a vast body of delegated legislation.

1.2.2 Department of Environment (ie government) policy

The policies of the Department of the Environment (DoE) can be found in various publications and are nearly always of considerable importance as many planning matters are concerned with questions of policy.

There are two main sources which set out DoE policy, namely circulars and policy guidance notes.

DoE circulars

DoE circulars are usually issued in conjunction with a new Act, commencement order or statutory instrument. They are primarily meant for local planning authorities (LPAs) and their principal purpose is to explain the new provisions being introduced and give guidance on how the provisions should be applied in practice. Notwithstanding that they are written for LPAs, DoE circulars are a valuable source of guidance for practitioners in that they reveal how the LPA will, should or is likely to, deal with a particular matter. If an LPA fails to follow relevant advice in a circular, it will significantly increase the chances of success of any appeal against the LPA's decision.

Policy guidance notes

The guidance and policy statements contained in DoE circulars are gradually being replaced by guidance in policy guidance notes. Until the process is complete, however, circulars remain an important source.

1.2.3 Case-law

The primary importance of case-law in the context of planning is in defining the meaning or extent of statutory provisions, defining the limits of the many discretionary powers that are given to LPAs and the SSE, clarifying the status of policy guidance contained in circulars and PPGs, etc, and establishing which matters are questions of law and which are questions of fact or degree.

It is important to remember that, where a matter is a question of fact or degree, case-law will be of little help in deciding the matter in a particular case in practice because cases cannot be precedents on questions of fact. Further, the courts will not interfere with the decision of an LPA or the SSE on an appeal as regards a question of fact or degree unless the LPA or the SSE have misdirected themselves on the law or reached a totally unreasonable decision on the facts.

1.3 THE SECRETARY OF STATE FOR THE ENVIRONMENT

The SSE has three broad classes of function under the Planning Acts, namely legislative, administrative and quasi-judicial.

1.3.1 Legislative powers

The Acts contain many powers for the SSE to make orders, rules and regulations, usually by statutory instrument. Examples include the Town and Country Planning (Use Classes) Order, the Town and Country Planning (General Permitted Development) Order, the Town and Country Planning (General Development Procedure) Order and special development orders.

1.3.2 Administrative powers

These powers include the dissemination of policy guidance through the medium of circulars. He also has powers to 'call in' a wide variety of matters for his own consideration (such as development plans and applications for planning permission).

1.3.3 Quasi-judicial powers

The SSE is the person to whom one appeals in the first instance against most decisions of a planning authority; in particular, appeals lie to him in respect of a refusal of, or conditions imposed on, a planning permission or the service of an enforcement notice.

1.4 LOCAL PLANNING AUTHORITIES (ss 1–9 and Sch 1)

1.4.1 The general rule (s 1)

Subject to any express provision to the contrary (see **1.4.2**), all references in the Planning Acts to an LPA should be construed as a reference to both the relevant county planning authority and district planning authority. The county council is the county planning authority and the district council is the district planning authority.

The county planning authority
The county planning authority normally has exclusive jurisdiction over preparing the structure plan (see **1.5.1**), mineral planning, and development control and enforcement which relate to 'county matters'. 'County matters' are defined in Sch 1, para 1, as being concerned with minerals and operational development falling partly within and partly outside a national park.

The district planning authority
Subject to the exceptions mentioned below, the district planning authority has exclusive jurisdiction over preparation of the local plan, development control and enforcement which does not concern a county matter and hazardous substances.

1.4.2 Exceptions to the general rule

Unitary councils
Where unitary councils have been established, those councils will normally be the LPAs for all purposes.

Greater London and the metropolitan areas (s 1(2))
In these areas there is only one planning authority, namely the appropriate London borough council (the Common Council in the City of London) or metropolitan district council.

1.5 DEVELOPMENT PLANS (ss 10–54 and Sch 2)

1.5.1 What are they?

Outside Greater London and the metropolitan areas
In the majority of the country the development plan consists of the structure plan and any local plan(s) in force.

STRUCTURE PLAN (ss 31–35C)

The structure plan is prepared normally by the county planning authority for the whole of their area. It basically consists of a broad statement of the county planning authority's strategic planning policies for the area illustrated by such diagrams and other illustrations as are necessary to explain the proposals. It must deal in particular with conservation of beauty and amenity, improvement of the physical environment, management of traffic, and social and economic conditions. It must also take into account regional planning guidance from the SSE, national policies, resources and any other matters which the SSE may prescribe (by regulations) or direct.

LOCAL PLAN (ss 36–45)

The local plan is prepared normally by the district planning authority in general conformity with the structure plan. Each district planning authority was due to prepare a local plan for the whole of their area within 5 years from 10 February 1992. Although the date for implementation has now passed, many LPAs have not yet completed the adoption of their area-wide local plan. Until the new local plans have been made and adopted, the local plans which were in force on that date (and which did not have to cover the whole area but could be made for parts of the area or for particular types of development) will remain in force.

Local plans are much more detailed. They must deal with the same type of matters as structure plans and take into account the same guidance, but in greater depth. They must also contain a map and such other diagrams, illustrations, etc as may be prescribed and which the authority think desirable. In addition, they must contain a reasoned justification of the policies formulated by the plan.

In Greater London and the metropolitan areas

In these areas the development plan consists of a 'unitary development plan' (ss 12–16).

The responsibility for making and altering a unitary development plan is that of the relevant London borough or metropolitan district council. Despite its name, a unitary development plan is in two parts where Part I is the broad equivalent of a structure plan, and Part II is the equivalent of a local plan. These two parts have to deal with and take into account very similar matters to their ordinary development plan counterparts and must be illustrated and justified in a similar way.

1.5.2 The importance of the development plan

In various parts of the Planning Acts, regard is required to be had to the development plan and any other material considerations. By s 54A (introduced by the Planning and Compensation Act 1991):

> 'where, in making any determination under the Planning Acts, regard is to be had to the development plan, the determination shall be made in accordance with the plan unless material considerations indicate otherwise.'

This section therefore appears to make the provisions of a development plan effectively paramount in the majority of cases.

In *Loup and Others v Secretary of State for the Environment and Salisbury District Council* [1996] JPL 2, CA, the court explained that the effect of s 54A is to require a planning authority or the SSE to give priority to the provisions of the development plan and, if the proposed development does not comply with those provisions or some of them, to weigh against them other material considerations (such as relevant advice in PPGs, etc) which are in favour of the granting of permission.

The practical consequences of s 54A are that because there is now, in effect, largely a plan-led development system, developers will need to look very carefully at the development plan to see if it contains any policy on the development proposed; if it does so and the proposal is not in accordance with the plan, any planning application is unlikely to succeed in most cases.

Chapter 2

WHAT IS DEVELOPMENT?

Chapter 2 contents

2.1 THE BASIC RULE

The basic rule is to be found in s 57(1) which states that planning permission is required for the carrying out of any development of land. The term 'development' is defined in s 55(1) as: 'the carrying out of building, engineering, mining or other operations in, on, over or under land, or the making of any material change in the use of any buildings or other land'. It is important to realise at the outset that the term 'development' thus has two mutually exclusive parts to it, namely the carrying out of operations and the making of a material change of use.

2.1.1 Operations

Relevant definitions (ss 55(1A) and 336(1))
'Building operations' include demolition of buildings (see further below), rebuilding, structural alterations of, or additions to buildings, and other operations normally undertaken by a person carrying on business as a builder.

'Engineering operations' includes the formation or laying out of means of access to highways.

'Mining operations' and 'other operations' are not defined in the Act.

Operations not constituting development (s 55(2))
Works for the maintenance, improvement or other alteration of a building which affect only the interior of the building or which do not materially affect its external appearance and which do not provide additional space underground do not constitute development (s 55(2)(a)).

Demolition
The position as regards demolition is governed by the provisions of s 55(1A) and (2)(g) which state that the demolition of any description of building specified in a direction given by the SSE does not constitute development. The direction exempts demolition of the following:

(1) listed buildings;
(2) buildings in a conservation area;
(3) scheduled monuments;
(4) buildings other than dwelling houses or buildings adjoining dwelling houses;
(5) buildings not exceeding 50 cu m in volume.

(Note as regards the first three categories in the above list that, although planning permission is not required for demolition, consents under the legislation dealing with these types of buildings and structures will be needed, eg listed buildings consent.)

Thus, the control of demolition will apply mainly to that of dwelling houses and buildings adjoining dwelling houses. However, demolition of these buildings may be permitted development under the GPDO, Sch 2, Part 31 (see **2.2.2**).

2.1.2 Change of use

In order to constitute development, a change of use must be material. The Act does not define what is meant by 'material'.

Case-law

Case-law makes it clear that the question as to whether a change of use is material is one of fact and degree in each case. It follows, therefore, that the courts will not normally interfere with a planning decision on the question of the materiality of a particular change of use unless the decision is totally unreasonable on the facts, or the deciding body has misdirected itself as to the relevant law.

Note, however, the following general points decided by case-law:

(1) It is necessary to look at the change in the use of the relevant 'planning unit'. In many cases this will be the whole of the land concerned, ie the land in the same ownership and occupation. Occasionally, particularly with larger sites, a single unit of occupation may comprise two or more physically distinct and separate areas which are occupied for substantially different and unrelated purposes, in which case each area (with its own main or primary use) should be considered as a separate planning unit (see *Burdle v Secretary of State for the Environment* [1972] 3 All ER 240). In a mall-type development, it now seems that each shop unit will be a separate planning unit (*Church Commissioners for England v SSE* [1996] JPL 669).

(2) The use of a planning unit may involve various (and possibly fluctuating) ancillary uses which do not need planning permission provided that they remain ancillary to, and retain their connection with, the primary use. For instance, where produce grown on an agricultural unit is sold on a limited scale from the farmhouse, this retail use is ancillary to the primary agricultural use; however, the ancillary status is lost if, for example, produce is subsequently bought in for the purposes of resale (see *Wood v Secretary of State for the Environment* [1973] 1 WLR 707, HL).

Non-statutory guidance

As the courts will not normally interfere with decisions on questions of fact and degree, it will therefore be the SSE or one of his inspectors who will generally be the final arbiter of the question as to whether a particular change of use is material. Thus, their views in similar cases will be important and guidance can be found, in particular, in relevant DoE circulars, PPGs and in Ministerial Decisions such as those reported in the JPL.

Statutory provisions

CHANGES OF USE DECLARED TO BE MATERIAL

For the avoidance of doubt, s 55(3) and (5) declare the following to be material changes of use:

(1) the use as two or more separate dwelling houses of any building previously used as a single dwelling house;

(2) (generally) the deposit of refuse or waste materials;

CHANGES OF USE NOT CONSTITUTING DEVELOPMENT

These are set out in s 55(2) and include the following.

(1) The use of any building or other land within the curtilage of a dwelling house for any purpose incidental to the enjoyment of the dwelling house as such (s 55(2)(d)).

Factors to be considered in deciding whether the use is 'incidental to the enjoyment of the dwelling house as such' include the nature and scale of the use and whether it is one which could reasonably be expected to be carried out in or around the house for domestic needs or incidental to the personal enjoyment of the house by its occupants: see *Ministerial Decision* [1977] JPL 116. Thus, for example, in *Wallington v Secretary of State for the Environment* [1991] JPL 942, CA, the keeping of 44 dogs as pets was held not to be an incidental use. Note that enjoyment of the dwelling house must be distinguished from the enjoyment of the occupier (ie the test for enjoyment is objective, not subjective).

(2) The use of any land or buildings occupied with it for the purposes of agriculture or forestry (s 55(2)(e)).

(3) In the case of buildings or other land which are used for a purpose of any class specified in the Town and Country Planning (Use Classes) Order 1987, the use of the buildings or other land for any other purpose of the same class (s 55(2)(f)). This very important exemption is dealt with in more detail at **2.1.3**.

2.1.3 The Town and Country Planning (Use Classes) Order 1987

This order specifies 16 use classes for the purposes of s 55(2)(f). Thus, a change of use within any such class does not, prima facie, amount to development (but see 'UCO checklist' below).

The classes are divided into four main groups as follows:

(1) Group A: shopping area uses;
(2) Group B: other business and industrial uses;
(3) Group C: residential uses
(4) Group D: non-residential uses.

Note in particular the following seven use classes.

Class A1: shops
Use for all or any of the following purposes: retail sale of goods other than hot food; post office; ticket or travel agency; sale of cold food for consumption off the premises; hairdressing; direction of funerals; display of goods for sale. In all cases, however, the sale, display or service must be to visiting members of the public.

Class A2: financial and professional services
Use for the provision of financial services, professional services (other than health or medical services) or any other services (including use as a betting office) which it is appropriate to provide in a shopping area, where the services are provided principally to visiting members of the public.

Class A3: food and drink
Use for the sale of food or drink for consumption on the premises or of hot food for consumption off the premises.

Class B1: business
Use for all or any of the following purposes, namely as an office other than a use within Class A2, for research and development of products or processes, or for any industrial process, being a use which can be carried out in any residential area without detriment to the amenity of that area.

Class B2: general industrial
Use for the carrying out of an industrial process other than one falling within Class B1.

Class B8: storage or distribution
Use for storage or as a distribution centre.

Class C3: dwelling houses
Use as a dwelling house by a single person or by people living together as a family or by not more than six residents living together as a single household (including a household where care is provided for residents).

Exclusions

Nothing in the Use Classes Order permits use as a theatre, amusement arcade, launderette, garage or motor showroom, taxi or hire-car business, hostel, or scrapyard (art 3(6) of Use Classes Order).

Note also that not all uses come within the Use Classes Order. The courts have consistently held that there is no justification for stretching the meaning of the wording of the classes and that other uses will therefore be outside the terms of the Order.

Problems

Many of the above use classes are not without their problems. For example, is a sandwich bar which sells tea and coffee and a few hot pies, within Class A1 or Class A3? (For guidance, see Circular 13/87.)

Is a high street solicitor's office within Class A2 or Class B1? The crucial question here is whether the firm principally serves visiting members of the public. (In *Kalra v Secretary of State for the Environment* [1995] EGCS 163, [1996] JPL 850, CA, the Court of Appeal held that the introduction of an appointment system did not of itself prevent a solicitor's office falling within Class A2.

UCO checklist

Although a change of use within a class does not amount to development it does not necessarily follow that a change of use from one class to another will constitute development. Whether it will depends on the basic rule, ie is that change of use 'material'? However, *Palisade Developments v SSE* [1995] 69 P & CR 638, CA, suggests that it will be extremely rare for this not to be the case.

A change of use within a class may be accompanied by building operations which could amount to development in their own right (remember that development has two parts to it).

A change of use within a class may have been validly restricted by a condition attached to a previous planning permission, in which case permission will be needed to change to a use restricted by that condition.

2.2 PERMITTED DEVELOPMENT

Once it has been established that development is involved, then the basic rule is that planning permission will be required. However, it is not always necessary to make an express application for planning permission for the reasons given below.

2.2.1 Resumption of previous use

By s 57(2)–(6), certain changes of use do not require planning permission even though they may amount to development, for example, the resumption of a previous lawful use after service of an enforcement notice.

2.2.2 The Town and Country Planning (General Permitted Development) Order 1995

By ss 59–61, the SSE may provide by statutory instrument for the automatic grant of planning permission by means of development orders. The most important of these orders is the Town and Country Planning (General Permitted Development) Order 1995 (GPDO). This lists, in Sch 2, 31 broad categories of development for which planning permission is automatically granted, ie there is not normally any need to make an application for planning permission in these cases (but see 'GPDO checklist' below).

Note in particular the following six categories.

Part 1: development within the curtilage of a dwelling house
Part 1 is divided into classes as follows:

(1) Class A: the enlargement, improvement or other alteration of the dwelling house
(2) Classes B and C: additions or alterations to its roof
(3) Class D: the erection of a porch
(4) Class E: the provision within the curtilage of the dwelling house of any building, enclosure or pool for a purpose incidental to the enjoyment of the dwelling house as such, or the maintenance, improvement or alteration of such a building or enclosure
(5) Classes F and G: the provision of a hard surface or a container for the storage of domestic heating oil
(6) Class H: the installation, alteration or replacement of a satellite antenna.

All of these classes of permitted development (except for Class F) are, however, subject to certain restrictions, limitations or conditions (see below).

There may occasionally be problems in determining the extent of the curtilage of the dwelling house. It is a small area of land forming part of the land on which the house stands and used for the purposes of the enjoyment of the house. Its extent is a question of fact and degree in each case. It is not necessarily synonymous with 'garden'.

Restrictions on Class A development (enlargement, improvement, etc) include:

(1) a limit on the increase in the cubic content of the dwelling house;
(2) height;
(3) distance from highway;

(4) the area covered by all the buildings (other than the original dwelling house) within the curtilage must not exceed one half of the area of the curtilage excluding the area of the original dwelling house.

Restrictions on Class E development (the provision of buildings within the curtilage, etc) include the latter two restrictions above (ie distance from highway and area covered by buildings within the curtilage). Additional restrictions include:

(1) a height limit; and
(2) a volume and nearness to house restriction.

Note that for a dwelling house on 'article 1(5) land' (ie within a National Park, an area of outstanding natural beauty or conservation area) there are further restrictions.

Restrictions on Class H development (satellite antennae) include dish size, height and siting.

Part 2: minor operations
Part 2 permits:

(1) the erection, construction, maintenance, improvement or alteration of a gate, fence, wall or other means of enclosure (Class A);
(2) the construction of a means of access to a highway which is not a trunk or classified road (Class B);
(3) the painting of the exterior of a building (Class C).

In Class A, any gates, fences, etc must be for the purpose of enclosure. They must not exceed one metre in height if they adjoin a highway, or 2 metres in any other case.

In Class C, painting of the exterior is not permitted if it is for the purpose of advertisement, announcement or direction.

Part 3: changes of use
Part 3 permits certain changes of use within Classes A and B of the Use Classes Order as follows:

(1) from A3 (food and drink) to A2 (financial and professional services);
(2) from A2 to A1 (shops) provided the premises have a display window at ground level;
(3) from A3 directly to A1;
(4) from B8 (storage and distribution) to B1 (business) and vice versa;
(5) from B2 (general industrial) to B8 or B1.

Part 4: temporary buildings and uses
Part 4 permits:

(1) the provision of buildings, structures, plant, etc required temporarily in connection with authorised operations (Class A);
(2) the use of open land for any purpose for not more than 28 days in any calendar year of which not more than 14 days may be used for holding a market or motor racing/trials (Class B).

Class A rights are subject to conditions requiring removal of the buildings, etc or reinstatement of land at the end of the operations.

The right to revert to the previous use of the land after the expiry of the temporary use is permitted by s 57(2) (see **2.2.1**).

Part 6: agricultural buildings and operations

Part 6 permits (inter alia) the carrying out on agricultural land of certain operations (in particular the erection, extension or alteration of buildings or excavation or engineering operations) which are reasonably necessary for the purposes of agriculture on that unit. These are subject to many exceptions and conditions.

Part 31: demolition of buildings

Part 31 permits any building operation consisting of the demolition of a building except where the building has been made unsafe or uninhabitable by the fault of anyone who owns the relevant land or where it is practicable to secure health or safety by works of repair or temporary support. Because of the provisions of s 55(2)(g) (see **2.1.1**), this provision will only need to be applied in the case of demolition of a dwelling house or a building (exceeding 50 cu m) adjoining a dwelling house.

GPDO checklist

If the proposed development is permitted by the GPDO there should, prima facie, be no need to make an application for planning permission. However, before deciding, the following other matters should also be checked.

LIMITATIONS, ETC

Confirm that all the limitations, restrictions and conditions imposed by the GPDO will be complied with. There are two categories of these. First, there is a general one in art 3(5) which applies to all the Parts in Sch 2 and which states that (subject to limited exceptions) the making or altering of an access to a trunk or classified road, or any development which obstructs the view of road users so as to cause them danger, is not permitted. Secondly, there are specific limitations, conditions, etc in almost all of the Parts of Sch 2 which must be observed (see above).

If the limitations, etc are not complied with then, as a general rule, the whole development will be unauthorised and not merely the excess. This, though, is subject to the LPA's power to under-enforce if they think fit (see **5.8.7** for details of this). If the excess is de minimis it can be ignored.

CONDITIONS ON EXISTING PLANNING PERMISSION

Check any existing planning permission to see whether it contains a condition excluding or restricting relevant permitted development rights. Such conditions can be imposed in appropriate cases (see further **3.6**).

ARTICLE 4 DIRECTION

Ascertain by means of an appropriate enquiry of the local authority whether an art 4 direction is in force which may affect the proposed development.

GPDO, art 4, empowers the SSE or an LPA (usually with the SSE's approval) to make a direction removing from the classes of permitted development under the GPDO any development specified in the direction as regards the area of land specified in it.

The making of an art 4 direction will not affect the lawfulness of any permitted development commenced before the direction was made.

SPECIAL DEVELOPMENT ORDERS

Check whether the land is in an area covered by a special development order (SDO).

Some SDOs restrict the provisions of the GPDO which would otherwise apply in the relevant area; others (especially those made for urban development areas) confer wider permitted development rights. It is therefore important to be aware of what SDOs exist and, where relevant, their provisions.

2.3 PROBLEM CASES

2.3.1 General considerations

It will be seen from the above that there are many matters to be considered before one can properly decide whether a particular proposal amounts to development and, if so, whether it is permitted development or whether it needs an express grant of planning permission. Although in practice it will be obvious in many cases whether or not planning permission will be needed, in quite a few cases (especially those involving small-scale development proposals) there may be some considerable uncertainty as to whether a particular proposal amounts to development or whether it is permitted development. In such a case there are two main options, namely either to go ahead without permission (thereby risking enforcement action if it did need an express grant of permission) or to apply under s 192 to the LPA for a determination of the question.

2.3.2 Certificate of lawful use or development

Under s 192, any person who wishes to ascertain the lawfulness of any proposed use or development, can apply to the LPA for a Certificate of Lawful Use or Development.

If a certificate is granted, it will be conclusive as to the lawfulness of the use or operations described in it unless there was a material change, before the use was instituted or the operations were begun, in any of the matters relevant to the determination.

Chapter 3

APPLYING FOR PLANNING PERMISSION

3.1 INTRODUCTION

Solicitors are not often involved in the completing and submission of an application for planning permission as this is usually done by the client's architect or planning consultant. However, it is very important to know what the statutory requirements are as this may be crucial in later negotiations with the LPA or on an appeal in case the action previously taken was flawed.

3.2 PRELIMINARY STEPS

(1) Consider whether planning permission is required at all: ie do the proposals amount to development and, if so, are they permitted development (see **2.1** and **2.2**)?

(2) Assuming planning permission is needed, the next step is to visit the site if possible. A site visit can be very valuable as it may:

   (a) clarify the client's maps, diagrams and plans;
   (b) provide information about the immediate environment;
   (c) alert the solicitor to potential problems with the application.

(3) Obtain copies of the relevant parts of the development plan and any non-statutory plans which may affect the proposed development. This could be vital in many cases as, for the application to stand a chance of succeeding, the development proposed will usually have to be in accordance with the development plan (see s 54A at **3.5.1**).

(4) Investigate the title to the land concerned. This is necessary for two main reasons, namely to check whether the proposed development is in breach of an enforceable covenant affecting the land concerned and to identify any other 'owners' who will need to be given notice of the application (see further **3.4.4**).

(5) Obtain the relevant application form from the LPA. Note that each LPA produces its own form which can be obtained free of charge.

(6) Consider whether a pre-application discussion with the appropriate case officer might be beneficial. This is encouraged by the DoE in order to reduce uncertainty and delay in processing applications. Such discussions can be particularly helpful in the case of large-scale or potentially controversial development proposals to enable the developer to find out in what respects the proposals may not be acceptable and in what ways chances of success can be improved; it also enables the LPA to advise the developer of probable objections to the development which, if remedied, should lead to a quicker determination. Note that LPAs have no statutory duty to enter into such discussions (although recent research has shown that 93 per cent of LPAs do so regularly). It follows therefore that any advice, etc given in such discussions is merely informal and advisory and cannot bind the LPA ultimately. Note also that LPAs may not charge a fee for the time taken in such pre-application discussions.

3.3 FULL OR OUTLINE PERMISSION?

One final matter to consider before completing and submitting the application form is whether to apply in full for planning permission or whether to apply for outline permission.

3.3.1 General

By the GDPO, arts 3 and 4, where the application is for permission to erect a building, the applicant may, if he wishes, apply for outline permission. In such a case, the application merely has to contain a description of the proposed development sufficient to indicate its major features (eg for residential developments, the number and type of dwellings). A plan is also required of sufficient detail to identify the boundaries of the site and the nearest classified public highway. However, the application need not contain the considerable amount of detail that is required for a full application for permission.

3.3.2 The 'reserved matters'

If outline planning permission is granted it will be subject to a condition setting out certain matters for which the subsequent approval of the LPA is required. The only matters which can be so specified ('reserved matters') are defined in the GDPO, art 1(2), and the Town and Country Planning (Applications) Regulations 1988 as those concerned with siting, design, external appearance, means of access and landscaping of the development.

3.3.3 The effect of outline permission

The effect of outline planning permission is that the LPA are committed to allowing the development in principle subject to approval of any reserved matters. This is because it is the grant of the outline permission which constitutes the grant of planning permission for the proposed development, ie no further planning permission is required.

Accordingly, the LPA cannot revoke the outline permission except on payment of compensation (see revocation of planning permissions at **3.5.2**) nor can they impose additional conditions subsequently except as regards the reserved matters.

3.3.4 Approval of reserved matters

When an applicant comes to apply for approval of the reserved matters he is equally bound by the outline permission. If the application for approval of reserved matters includes additional development it will normally be invalid.

3.4 THE PROCEDURE

Procedure is governed mainly by ss 62 to 69, the GDPO and the Town and Country Planning (Applications) Regulations 1988.

3.4.1 What is submitted to whom?

The application form and such other documents, plans, drawings, etc as are needed to describe the proposed development should be submitted (usually in triplicate) to the district planning authority, London borough or metropolitan district council or unitary council (as the case may be).

The application must be accompanied by the appropriate fee and a GDPO art 7 certificate (see **3.4.2** and **3.4.3**).

3.4.2 The fee

The fees vary according to the type of application and the scale of development involved.

3.4.3 Art 7 certificate

The application must be accompanied by an Article 7 Certificate and an Agricultural Holdings Certificate.

The certificates have to be given to certify compliance with the GDPO, art 6, which requires the applicant, where he is not the sole owner of the land concerned, to notify or try to notify the owners of the land and any relevant agricultural tenant of the fact of the application for planning permission (see **3.4.4**).

If an inaccurate certificate is given, this may result in the quashing of any planning permission granted pursuant to it. There are also criminal sanctions.

3.4.4 Notification of persons by the applicant

By the GDPO, art 6, where the applicant is not the sole owner of the application site, he must give notice (in the form prescribed in the GDPO, Sch 2, Part I) to all persons who are 'owners' or 'tenants' of the land on the prescribed date.

'Giving notice' means serving the notice on every owner or tenant whose name and address is known to the applicant and where, after taking all reasonable steps to ascertain the names and addresses of such persons, the applicant cannot identify any such person, by advertising the notice in a local newspaper after the prescribed date.

'Owner' is defined by s 65(8) as meaning any person who owns the fee simple or a tenancy granted or extended for a term certain of which not less than 7 years remain unexpired.

'Tenant' is defined by the GDPO, art 6(6), as meaning the tenant of an agricultural holding any part of which is comprised in the application site.

'Prescribed date' is defined by the GDPO, art 6(5), as meaning the period of 21 days before the date of the application.

3.4.5 Action by the LPA

Entry in the planning register
By s 69, the LPA must enter certain particulars of the application in the register that they are required to keep by that section. The register is open to public inspection.

Notification
By the GDPO, art 8, the LPA must publicise the application. This publicity may consist of a site notice, notifying neighbours, or a local advertisement, depending upon the type of development proposed.

3.5 THE DECISION

3.5.1 General points

By s 70(1), the LPA may grant planning permission either unconditionally or subject to such conditions as they think fit or they may refuse planning permission.

In reaching their decision they must have regard to the provisions of the development plan if it is relevant to the application and to any other material considerations (see further, below). They must also take into account any representations received in response to the publicity of the application (see **3.4.5**) and certain other matters if the development affects a listed building or a conservation area.

'... have regard to ... the development plan ...'

This must be read in conjunction with s 54A which states that where regard is to be had to the development plan, any determination must be made in accordance with the plan unless material considerations indicate otherwise. Thus, if the proposed development is covered by the plan, the LPA's decision should be made in accordance with the plan unless there are material considerations to the contrary.

Policy guidance on s 54A can be found in PPG 1 where, in para 40, the SSE advises that: 'Applications which are not in accordance with relevant policies in the plan should not be allowed unless material considerations justify granting planning permission ... In all cases where the plan is relevant, it will be necessary to decide if the proposal is in accordance with the plan and then to take into account other material considerations'. The section does not, however, create a legitimate expectation that a particular application will or must be determined solely by reference to the development plan (see *Trustees of the Viscount Folkestone 1963 Settlement and Camden Homes Ltd v Secretary of State for the Environment and Salisbury District Council* [1995] JPL 502, QB).

Recently, however, there has been a spate of cases (see, for example, *St Albans District Council v Secretary of State for the Environment and Allied Breweries Ltd* [1993] JPL 374; *R v Canterbury City Council, Robert Brett & Sons, ex p Springimage Ltd* [1994] JPL 427; *Bylander Waddell Partnership v Secretary of State for the Environment and Harrow London Borough Council* [1994] JPL 440) which have suggested that 'material considerations to the contrary' can include advice in DoE circulars and PPGs.

The LPA, or the inspector or SSE on an appeal, do not have to refer expressly to s 54A in their decision. It is sufficient that the decision was reached in accordance with the section: see, eg, *Newham London Borough Council v Secretary of State for the Environment* [1995] EGCS 6, *Spelthorne Borough Council v Secretary of State for the Environment and Lawlor Land plc* [1995] JPL 412, and *North Yorkshire County Council v Secretary of State for the Environment and Griffin* [1996] JPL 32, CA.

Note that it seems that s 54A applies also to the determination of an application for approval of reserved matters pursuant to an outline planning permission (see *St George Developments Ltd and Kew Riverside Developments v Secretary of State for the Environment and Richmond upon Thames London Borough Council* [1996] JPL 35).

'... other material considerations'

For other considerations to be 'material', they must be relevant to the application and be planning considerations, ie relate to the use and development of land: see *Stringer v Minister of Housing and Local Government* [1971] 1 All ER 65. Note the following examples (which are not exhaustive) of matters which the courts have held to be capable of being 'material considerations':

(1) a development plan which is in the course of preparation (see, eg *Allen v Corporation of the City of London* [1981] JPL 685 and *Kissel v Secretary of State for the Environment and Another* [1994] JPL 819. The closer the new plan gets to adoption, the greater the weight that should be given to it;
(2) the protection of private interests in a proper case and, in exceptional circumstances, personal hardship (see, eg *Great Portland Estates plc v Westminster City Council* [1985] AC 661, HL);
(3) financial considerations involved in the proposed development (see, eg, *Sovmots v Secretary of State for the Environment* [1977] 1 QB 411);
(4) planning obligations (as to which, see **4.2**);
(5) retention of an existing use (see, eg, *London Residuary Body v Lambeth Borough Council* [1990] 2 All ER 309, HL);
(6) the previous planning history of the site;
(7) a real danger of setting an undesirable precedent (see, eg, *Anglia Building Society v Secretary of State for the Environment* [1984] JPL 175);
(8) planning policies of the DoE (as evidenced in circulars and PPGs), of other government departments where relevant (eg transport, energy, etc) and the LPA concerned (as evidenced in their own policy statements and non-statutory plans);
(9) racial discrimination (by s 19A of the Race Relations Act 1976 it is unlawful for an LPA to discriminate on racial grounds when exercising any of their planning functions);
(10) environmental considerations: likely environmental pollution from a proposed development is a material consideration. However, it is not the function of the planning system to duplicate statutory pollution controls (see *Gateshead Metropolitan Borough Council v Secretary of State for the Environment* [1995] JPL 432, CA; *Envirocor Waste Holdings v Secretary of State for the Environment* [1995] EGCS 60, QB; PPG 23).

The making of the decision

The decision should be made within 8 weeks of the submission of the application or such longer period as may have been agreed in writing with the applicant (GDPO, art 20). If no decision has been made in time the applicant can appeal to the SSE.

Procedure after the decision

After making the decision, the LPA must register it in their planning register (which they are required to keep by virtue of s 69: see **3.4.5** and also the GDPO, art 25(2)). In addition, the applicant must be given written notification of the decision and, where the decision is a planning permission subject to conditions or a refusal, written reasons (see the GDPO, art 22, and **3.5.4**).

It is the written notification which constitutes the grant of planning permission (see *R v West Oxfordshire District Council, ex p Pearce (CH) Homes* [1986] JPL 523).

3.5.2 Effect of planning permission

By s 75(1), without prejudice to the provisions of the Act on duration, revocation or modification (for all of which, see below), planning permission shall (except insofar as the permission otherwise provides) enure for the benefit of the land and of all persons for the time being interested in it.

Therefore, the benefit of planning permission runs with the land concerned and, prima facie, lasts forever, but see **3.5.3**. Note, however, that any conditions attached to the planning permission will also run, ie will burden the relevant land.

A grant of planning permission is effective for planning purposes only; it does not confer, for example, listed building consent, building regulation consent or any consent required under any other enactment, nor does it confer the right to break any enforceable covenant affecting the land.

Note also that planning permission is merely permissive; it does not have to be implemented and the LPA cannot compel implementation.

'... the permission otherwise provides'

Planning permission may be expressly granted for a limited period or be made personal to the applicant.

Once such a permission lapses the right to revert to the previous use of the land is permitted by s 57(2) (see **2.2.1**).

Revocation and modification of planning permissions

By s 97, the LPA may, if they think it expedient to do so, revoke or modify (to the extent they consider necessary) any planning permission provided they do so before the development authorised by the permission is completed.

Abandonment of planning permission

It follows from the provisions in s 75(1) that the doctrine of abandonment cannot apply to planning permissions. Note, however, that once a permission has been fully implemented its effect is spent, ie it does not authorise the re-carrying out of that development.

3.5.3 Duration

General

Although, prima facie, the benefit of a planning permission lasts forever, there are some important statutory time-limits governing the implementation of the permission which, if not observed, may terminate it. These are set out in ss 91 to 93 which provide that with ordinary permissions, development must be commenced within 5 years of the grant of permission.

With outline permissions, there are two time-limits. Application for approval of the reserved matters must be made within 3 years of the grant of the outline permission, and the development must be commenced within 5 years of the grant of the outline permission or 2 years of the approval of the reserved matters, whichever is the later. Note also that with all permissions, the LPA may substitute longer or shorter time-limits if they think it appropriate on planning grounds; if they do this, however, they must give their reasons for doing so in case the applicant should wish to appeal against this (see further paras 53–58 of DoE Circular 11/95).

The start and end of the period

If the time-limit expires without the development having been started, then the permission effectively lapses. Any further development will be unauthorised and subject to possible enforcement proceedings. Because of this, it is important to know two things, namely what is the effective date of the permission and when does development commence?

As regards the effective date of the permission, the Act provides no guidance; however, the case of *R v West Oxfordshire District Council, ex p Pearce (CH) Homes* [1986] JPL 523, established that this is the date which appears on the written notification to the applicant (ie it is not the date on which the decision was made by the LPA). This is, therefore, the starting date for the time-limit.

As regards the date when development commences, the Act defines this very carefully in s 56 which provides that development is taken to be begun on the earliest date on which any of the following operations begin to be carried out:

(1) any work of construction in the course of erection of a building;
(2) any work of demolition of a building;
(3) the digging of a trench for the foundations of a building;
(4) the laying of an underground main or pipe to the foundations;
(5) any operation in the course of laying out or constructing a road;
(6) any material change in the use of any land.

Renewal of a planning permission

What if a developer cannot start the development within the time-limit because of, for instance, financial problems? In such a case, the developer can apply for a renewal of the permission using a simplified procedure, but should do so before the original permission expires, otherwise the whole permission will lapse and a fresh application for planning permission will therefore have to be made.

Completion notice (ss 94–95)

What happens if a developer starts the development within the time-limit but the time-limit subsequently expires without the development having been completed? In such a case, if the LPA is of the opinion that the development will not be completed within a reasonable period, it may serve a completion notice on the owner and any occupier of the land stating that the permission will cease to have effect at the expiration of a further period specified in the notice (being not less than 12 months after the notice takes effect). The notice is subject to confirmation by the SSE. Any part of the development carried out before a confirmed completion notice takes effect is not affected.

3.5.4 Refusals and planning permissions subject to conditions

As stated at **3.5.1**, by s 70(1), an LPA may grant planning permission unconditionally or subject to such conditions as they think fit or they may refuse permission (permissions subject to conditions are dealt with in detail at **3.6**). In the latter two cases, the written notification of the decision must state clearly and precisely the full reasons for the conditions imposed or the refusal as the case may be. If full reasons are not given this will probably not invalidate the decision itself although the decision could be challenged by judicial review or dealt with by way of appeal.

There is also a general right of appeal to the SSE against a permission subject to conditions, a refusal and a 'deemed refusal' (ie where no decision is reached within the relevant period, as to which see **3.5.1**).

3.6 PLANNING PERMISSIONS SUBJECT TO CONDITIONS

3.6.1 General points

The power in s 70(1) for an LPA to impose such conditions as they think fit (see **3.5.1**) is supplemented by s 72(1) which provides that, without prejudice to the generality of s 70(1), conditions may be imposed on the grant of planning permission for the purpose of:

(1) regulating the development or use of any land under the control of the applicant (whether or not it is land in respect of which the application was made) or requiring the carrying out of works on any such land, so far as appears to the LPA to be expedient for the purposes of or in connection with the development authorised by the permission; or
(2) requiring the removal of any buildings or works authorised by the permission, or the discontinuance of any use of land so authorised, at the end of a specified period, and the carrying out of any works required for the reinstatement of land at the end of that period.

Whether an applicant has 'control' of the relevant land is a question of fact and degree in each case.

3.6.2 Judicial restrictions on the power

The general power to impose conditions in s 70(1) is not as wide or unfettered as it appears because over the years the courts have imposed restraints on it.

The leading case on the judicial control of the power is *Newbury District Council v Secretary of State for the Environment* [1981] AC 578, HL, where Viscount Dilhorne (at p 599) said:

> 'The conditions imposed must be for a planning purpose and not for any ulterior one and ... they must fairly and reasonably relate to the development permitted. Also they must not be so unreasonable that no reasonable planning authority could have imposed them.'

'Planning purpose'

There are many cases illustrating the first element of the above test (ie that conditions must be imposed for a planning purpose). For example, in *R v Hillingdon London Borough Council, ex p Royco Homes Ltd* [1974] 1 QB 720, outline permission for a residential development was granted subject to a condition that the dwellings should first be occupied by persons on the local authority's housing waiting list with security of tenure for 10 years. The court held that the principal purpose of the condition was to require the applicants to assume at their expense a significant part of the authority's statutory duties as a housing authority. The condition was therefore ultra vires.

'Fairly and reasonably related to the development permitted'

The second part of the test in *Newbury* is probably the most difficult one to understand and apply. In *Newbury* the facts were that planning permission was granted for a change of use of aircraft hangers to warehouses subject to a condition requiring removal of the hangers at the end of 10 years. The House of Lords held that, although this condition satisfied the first test in that the removal of unsightly old buildings was a proper planning purpose, the condition was not sufficiently related to the change of use permitted by the permission and was therefore void.

'Manifestly unreasonable'

The final part of the test in *Newbury* is that the condition must not be manifestly unreasonable in the sense that no reasonable LPA would have imposed the condition in question.

Under this element, a condition may not require the applicant to pay money or provide other consideration for the granting of planning permission (but see Chapter 4 where a similar practical result can be achieved by means of a planning obligation). Nor may a condition require the ceding of land owned by the applicant for public purposes (eg a highway) even if the applicant consents.

***General note on* Newbury**

It is important to bear in mind that the majority of conditions imposed by LPAs on planning permissions do not fall foul of the test in *Newbury*.

In the very few cases where a condition does fail, it will normally breach more than one of the elements in the test. This is because there are potentially considerable areas of overlap between the three elements in the test. This is illustrated by the *Ministerial Decision* noted at [1991] JPL 184 where a condition attached to a planning permission restricting car parking spaces on the land to residents of a specified London borough was held to be void on the grounds that it did not fulfil a proper planning purpose and that it was manifestly unreasonable. In reality, despite the three elements, there is just one basic test.

Severability of void conditions

If the condition in question is fundamental to the permission (ie if the permission would not have been granted without the condition) the court will not sever the offending condition. (Most conditions are considered to be fundamental to their permissions.) Thus, if the condition is quashed, the whole permission will fail, ie the applicant will be left with no permission at all. This is, therefore, an important point to bear in mind in deciding how to challenge a particular condition's validity (ie by way of application to the High Court for judicial review, or by appeal to the SSE). In most cases, it will be better to appeal to the SSE as, unlike the courts, he has power to grant the permission free from the offending condition or conditions if he thinks fit (see **3.6.3**). In addition, an application for judicial review must be made promptly, and in any event within 3 months of the decision (RSC Ord 53, r 4), whereas an appeal to the SSE must be made within 6 months (see **3.7**).

3.6.3 The Secretary of State's guidance

General points

The Annex to DoE Circular 11/95 gives detailed guidance to planning authorities on the imposition of conditions. It is, therefore, essential reading when considering whether or not to appeal against a permission subject to conditions.

The main starting point is para 14 of the Annex to the Circular, which sets out six criteria that conditions must satisfy, namely that they should only be imposed where they are:

(1) necessary (see further paras 15–17 of the Annex);
(2) relevant to planning (see paras 20–23);
(3) relevant to the development to be permitted (see paras 24 and 25);
(4) enforceable (see paras 26–29);

(5) precise (see paras 30–33); and
(6) reasonable in all other respects (see paras 34–42).

These basic principles (which are clearly based on the courts' criteria, see **3.6.2**) are expanded in paras 15 to 42, following which there are a further 78 paragraphs dealing with particular problem areas.

3.6.4 Section 73 and Section 73A applications

Section 73

Section 73 entitles a person to apply for planning permission to develop land without complying with conditions subject to which a previous planning permission was granted. Such an application must, though, be made before the previous permission expires.

The application merely has to be made in writing and give sufficient information to enable the LPA to identify the previous grant of planning permission and the condition or conditions in question (Town and Country Planning (Applications) Regulations 1988, reg 3).

The important feature of a s 73 application is that in determining the application, the planning authority may consider only the question of the conditions subject to which the permission should be granted and thus may only:

(1) grant unconditional permission;
(2) grant permission subject to different conditions; or
(3) refuse the application.

In the first two cases above, the applicant will then have the benefit of two permissions (ie the original one and the one obtained on the s 73 application). In cases (2) and (3), the applicant can appeal to the SSE in the usual way. Thus, whatever happens on the s 73 application, the applicant will retain the benefit of the original planning permission.

This procedure may be particularly useful in securing the removal of a condition restricting freedom of change of use within a class of the Use Classes Order 1987 or a condition restricting permitted development rights under the GPDO. Further, this is the only procedure available for challenging a condition where the time-limit for appealing has passed.

In *Allied London Property Investment Ltd v Secretary of State for the Environment* (1996) 72 P&CR 327, it was held that there is no distinction to be drawn between time and other conditions. Therefore, s 73 could be used to apply for, eg, an extension of time for applying for approval of reserved matters under an outline permission (instead of applying for a renewal of the outline permission – see **3.5.3**).

Section 73A

Section 73 applies only to applications for the removal, etc of a condition before it is breached. However, under s 73A an application may be made for planning permission for (inter alia) development carried out before the date of the application in breach of a condition subject to which planning permission was previously granted.

Permission for such development may be granted to have effect from the date on which the development was carried out thereby rendering it retrospectively lawful.

3.7 APPEALS AGAINST ADVERSE PLANNING DETERMINATIONS

Where an LPA have:

(1) refused to grant planning permission, or
(2) granted planning permission subject to conditions to which the applicant objects, or
(3) refused approval of reserved matters on an outline permission, or
(4) refused an application or granted a permission subject to conditions under s 73 or s 73A, or
(5) failed to notify their decision within the prescribed period (normally 8 weeks),

the applicant may appeal to the SSE within 6 months of the notice of the decision or failure to determine as the case may be (s 78, and the GDPO, arts 20 and 23).

3.7.1 Who may appeal?

Only the applicant may appeal; this is so even though the applicant may not be the owner of an interest in the land. Third parties have no right of appeal and neither does the owner of the freehold have an independent right of appeal.

3.7.2 Initial procedure (GDPO, art 23)

An appeal must be made on the form supplied by the SSE.

As well as setting out the grounds of appeal (see **3.9**), the appellant must also indicate whether he would like the appeal to be determined by the written representations procedure, or whether he wishes it to be heard by an inspector (see **3.8**).

The completed form together with all relevant documents must be sent to the Planning Inspectorate to reach them within the time-limit. Copies of the form must also be sent to the LPA together with copies of any documents sent to the Inspectorate which the LPA have not yet seen (GDPO, art 23(1)(b)).

3.8 TYPES OF APPEAL

As mentioned above, when filling in the appeal form the appellant must notify the SSE whether he wishes to proceed by way of written representations or to be heard by an inspector.

3.8.1 Written representations

Under the written representations procedure the appeal is decided, as its name suggests, almost entirely on the basis of written representations submitted to the Inspectorate by the appellant, the LPA and any other interested parties. No oral evidence is permitted and that includes evidence by way of video or audio tape; maps, plans and photographs are, however, acceptable and in many cases will be necessary. At some point before a decision is made, the inspector will visit the site either unaccompanied, if the site can be seen sufficiently well from a public road or place, or accompanied by the appellant or his representative and a representative from the LPA.

The procedure is governed by the Town and Country Planning (Appeals) (Written Representations Procedure) Regulations 1987 and is explained in DoE Circular 15/96 (for details see **3.9**). It is speedy and cost-effective and is recommended by the DoE for simpler or non-controversial cases. It is by far the most common appeal procedure accounting for about 80 per cent of current appeals. Because of its nature it also offers less scope for third parties to influence the eventual decision. Note, however, that the written representations procedure can only be used if the applicant requests it and the LPA agree.

3.8.2 Inquiry

The appellant and the LPA have the right to be heard by an inspector appointed by the SSE. If either requests an inquiry then, subject to the Inspectorate suggesting and both sides agreeing to a less formal hearing instead (see below), the Inspectorate will appoint a suitable inspector, arrange a date and notify interested parties.

The procedure is more formal and is governed by the Town and Country Planning (Inquiries Procedure) Rules 1992 or the Town and Country Planning (Determination by Inspectors) (Inquiries Procedure) Rules 1992 (as appropriate) and is explained in DoE Circular 15/96. The purpose of the Rules is to try to be as fair as possible to all parties, in particular by ensuring that the parties are in possession of all relevant information before the inquiry begins. Because it involves a public hearing for all interested parties and because the appellant will normally wish to be represented at the inquiry it is therefore a slower and much more costly procedure.

3.8.3 Hearing

Where the appellant has not opted for the written representations procedure the Inspectorate may, in an appropriate case, offer a hearing instead of a full inquiry; either side may also suggest a hearing. Both sides must agree to this more informal procedure before it can be used.

The procedure is governed by a code of practice set out in DoE Circular 15/96 a copy of which will be sent to the parties when they agree to a hearing. The procedure is intended to save time and money for the parties. In essence, it will be an informal hearing before an inspector who will try to stimulate a discussion on the main issues between the parties. It is not appropriate for complex or controversial appeals but where it is appropriate it is quicker and more cost-effective than an inquiry.

However, in *Dyason v SSE* [1998] EGCS 11, the Court of Appeal criticised the current procedure at informal hearings on the basis that the more relaxed atmosphere might not lead to a full and fair hearing of the matters in issue.

3.8.4 Factors influencing choice of forum

It is not possible to set out specific criteria upon which a decision can be reached as to the most appropriate forum for any given case in practice. As a general rule, however, the more important or larger the development and the more controversial it is, the more likely it is that an inquiry is the correct forum. In the 'Planning Appeals' booklet sent to appellants, the Inspectorate suggest the following considerations:

(1) that where the outcome of the appeal will depend on the planning merits of the appeal, the written representations procedure will normally be appropriate;

(2) that written representations are quicker and cheaper;
(3) that an inquiry will be necessary if there is considerable local interest or if the issues are likely to be complex;
(4) that at an inquiry the appellant can address the inspector personally and can challenge the evidence put forward by the LPA and any third parties;
(5) whether the decision is of sufficient importance to justify the additional costs and time involved in an inquiry;
(6) the possibility of costs being awarded (see **3.10**).

In addition, consideration should be given to the appellant's contractual obligations and the potential for third party influence at an inquiry.

3.9 THE PROCEDURES FOR APPEAL

3.9.1 Written representations

The procedure is set out in the 1987 Regulations referred to at **3.8.1**.

Statement of case

The appellant's statement of case must be set out in the appeal form. If this is not given or is considered to be inadequate, the appeal will be returned for full details to be given.

As a general guide, the statement should:

(1) start with quotations from planning policy guidance notes and DoE circulars which support the appellant's case;
(2) consider each of the reasons given (where relevant) for the refusal, etc and analyse and refute them, by logical argument. In this part, any precedent (ie showing that the LPA have granted a similar application) should be mentioned as should any policies of the LPA which contradict the LPA's reasons;
(3) justify the appellant's case. Here there should be a brief description of the development proposed together with additional plans, photographs, etc if desired. The local environment may be described (although the inspector will visit the site). Any policies from the structure or local plans which support the appellant's case should be quoted. Any special circumstances should be set out and any objections from third parties should be addressed;
(4) conclude (optionally) with a general policy statement in support of the appellant's case.

Outline of procedure up to the decision

Within 14 days of receipt of the appeal by the Inspectorate ('the starting date'), the LPA must complete and return a questionnaire. This must be accompanied by certain documents including the planning officer's report to committee (if available), any relevant committee minutes, and extracts from the relevant plans or policies of the LPA on which the decision was based. These will all be copied to the appellant by the LPA which must also indicate if they intend to provide a further written statement. If they do intend to do so, this must be provided within 28 days of the starting date.

The appellant must respond (if appropriate) to the LPA's questionnaire or further statement within 17 days of the date of that document or, if the appeal was against a non-determination by the LPA, must provide a full statement of case (as above) in that time. If the LPA wish to make further representations they must be submitted within 7 days of the appellant's response.

The time-limits set out above will only be extended in exceptional circumstances.

After the time for representations has expired, the Inspectorate will send all the appeal papers to an inspector who will subsequently visit the site. Unless the site can be seen clearly from a road or public land, the appellant will need to arrange access for the inspector. The inspector will be accompanied normally by the appellant or his representative and a representative of the LPA. No discussions concerning the appeal are allowed during the visit.

The decision

The inspector's decision will be based on the site visit and any written representations received in time; however, the inspector has a discretion to accept further documents out of time provided that he observes the rules of natural justice (see *Geha v Secretary of State for the Environment and Harrow London Borough Council* [1993] JPL B34).

The decision letter will be sent to the appellant's agent, if any, otherwise to the appellant. The date of the decision letter is the date from which time runs for any appeal against the inspector's decision (see **3.11**).

3.9.2 Inquiry

The procedure is governed by the Town and Country Planning (Inquiries Procedure) Rules 1992 (which only apply where the SSE causes the inquiry to be held before he determines the appeal) or the Town and Country Planning (Determination by Inspectors) (Inquiries Procedure) Rules 1992. These Rules are explained in DoE Circular 15/96.

The appeal form

In the appeal form it is not necessary or desirable to give a full statement of case. Full grounds of appeal must, however, be included. Thus, the appellant must, as before, consider each of the LPA's reasons and analyse and refute them briefly. The entire case should be summarised by describing the development proposed, the environment and any special needs or circumstances, and by referring to any appropriate parts of the structure and local plans and government policies. Any relevant previous decisions (whether by the LPA or on appeal) should be set out as being 'material considerations' and potential planning gain to the LPA should also be outlined.

It is important that the full grounds of appeal are stated and that nothing is omitted, as the appellant or his representative at the appeal will largely be bound by the grounds, and any omissions may cause adjournments and may have financial consequences (see **3.10**).

Procedure up to the inquiry

(1) The appellant and the LPA will be notified of the fact that an inquiry is to be held. The date of this notice is the 'relevant date'.
(2) The LPA must then immediately inform the SSE and the appellant of the name and address of any parties who made representations.
(3) Where the SSE is holding the inquiry prior to his determining the appeal, he may convene a pre-inquiry meeting between the main parties and the inspector

who will conduct the inquiry. This should only be used at this point for major inquiries (see also the code of practice 'Preparing for Major Inquiries in England and Wales'). The purpose is to allow the inspector to set a programme for the inquiry itself. The SSE will serve the parties with a statement of the matters about which he particularly wishes to be informed at the meeting and may require the parties to serve an outline statement within a specified time-limit before the meeting.

(4) Within a specified number of weeks (which varies according to the circumstances) from the relevant date, the appellant and the LPA must serve a statement of case on the other party, the SSE and any other statutory party. All statements of case must be served at least 4 weeks before the date of the inquiry. A statement of case should contain the full particulars of the case to be put by that party at the inquiry together with a list of relevant documents (see Circular 15/96, Annex 3). The SSE may require any other person to serve a statement and he or the inspector may require further information following service of a statement. If so required, any party must send a copy or extract of a document referred to in their statement to the person requesting this.
(5) The inspector may require a pre-inquiry meeting to be held. It is important to remember that the inquiry timetable and much of its procedure will be at his discretion.
(6) If an assessor is to be appointed (ie a technical expert to assist the inspector) all parties must be notified of his name and the matters on which he is to advise.
(7) Unless it is impracticable, the date fixed for the inquiry must not be later than 22 weeks from the relevant date or 8 weeks after the pre-inquiry meeting; otherwise the earliest practicable date must be used. The parties must be given at least 4 weeks' notice of the inquiry (unless they agree a shorter period).
(8) Proofs of the evidence to be given at the inquiry must be sent to the inspector not later than 3 weeks before the evidence is given unless a different timetable has been agreed. If the proof is more than 1,500 words long it must be accompanied by a summary. All statements and summaries must be circulated to interested parties.

For a list of who is entitled to attend the inquiry, see r 11 of the 1992 Rules. There are included in the list any LPAs (as defined in **1.4**) or parish or community council in whose area the appeal site is situated, any 'statutory party' (as defined in the GDPO, art 19) and any person who has served a statement of case.

Procedure at the inquiry

Except for certain minor matters laid down by the Rules, the procedure at the inquiry is entirely within the discretion of the inspector. However, a typical inquiry will proceed as follows.

(1) The inspector will take appearances (ie details of parties, witnesses, third parties, etc).
(2) The appellant makes opening submissions.
(3) The appellant's witnesses give evidence-in-chief by reading their proofs (or summaries where the proof is long). They can then be cross-examined, first by the LPA and then by any third parties (cross-examination is on the full proof, not the summary). The appellant may then re-examine.
(4) The LPA present their case but without an opening submission. Examination of witnesses is as for the appellant's case.
(5) Third parties give any evidence.

(6) The LPA give their closing submissions followed by the appellant.

Note that the inspector may ask questions at any point in the proceedings.

Following the inquiry there will normally be an accompanied site inspection where the inspector can be addressed only on matters of fact arising from the inquiry. (The inspector will often visit the appeal site and its surroundings on his own before the start of the inquiry.)

As to applications for costs, see **3.10**. See also 'Good Practice at Planning Inquiries' in DoE Circular 15/96 at Annex 5.

Procedure after the inquiry

The procedure outlined in (1) to (3) below is the one which applies in the overwhelming majority of cases where the appeal is to be decided by an inspector and not by the SSE.

(1) Any assessor appointed may submit a report on the matters on which he was asked to advise to the inspector.
(2) If, after the close of the inquiry, the inspector proposes to take into consideration any new evidence or matter of fact (not being a matter of government policy) which was not raised at the inquiry and which is material to his decision, he must not come to a decision without first notifying the persons who attended the inquiry of the new evidence or matter. He must then allow 3 weeks for further representations or a request to re-open the inquiry. The inspector must re-open the inquiry if asked to do so by the appellant or the LPA and may do so in any other case. If the inquiry is re-opened, the inspector must send a written statement of the new matters to all persons who were entitled to appear at the original inquiry. Thereafter, the inquiry procedure above is followed.
(3) All parties who were entitled to and did appear at the inquiry (and any other person who appeared and asked to be notified of the decision) will be sent written notification of the inspector's decision and the reasons for it. The appellant will also be sent a leaflet telling him how the decision might be challenged on appeal to the High Court (see **3.11**).

In the rare cases where the appeal decision is to be made by the SSE, the inspector will send his and any assessor's report to the SSE. If the SSE takes new evidence or material into account or disagrees with the inspector, he must follow the procedure in (2) above. The only other procedural difference is that if a copy of the inspector's report is not sent with the SSE's decision notice, the latter should be accompanied by a statement of the inspector's conclusions and recommendations.

3.9.3 Hearing

The procedure is governed by the 'Code of Practice for Hearings' a copy of which will be sent to the appellant when the Inspectorate or one of the parties suggests or requests a hearing. Note, however, that in *Dyason v SSE* [1998] EGCS 11, the Court of Appeal criticised the current procedure at informal hearings on the basis that the more relaxed atmosphere might not lead to a full and fair hearing of the matters in issue.

The parties agree to prepare and serve their full statements of case within 6 weeks of the letter from the Inspectorate confirming that a hearing will take place. In any event, the statements of case must be served at least 3 weeks before the hearing is due to begin.

At the hearing the inspector will lead an informal discussion on the main issues in the appeal. Evidence can be called but the parties waive their right to cross-examine or re-examine. Legal representation is discouraged. The appellant will normally be allowed to make a closing submission.

The procedure after the hearing is as for a full inquiry but with the word 'hearing' substituted for 'inquiry'.

3.10 COSTS IN APPEALS

By ss 320(2) and 322 the SSE is given the powers of s 250(5) of the Local Government Act 1972 to award costs in planning appeals. Inspectors may now exercise the SSE's powers. There is power to make an award in all cases, although at the moment the power is not yet in force for written representations cases.

Detailed guidance on the exercise of power to award costs is contained in Circular 8/93. The basic principle is that, unlike in civil cases, costs do not 'follow the event', ie normally, each party will bear their own costs. Costs may, however, be awarded against one party in favour of another where:

(a) a party has sought an award at the appropriate stage of the proceedings; and
(b) the party against whom costs are sought has behaved unreasonably; and
(c) this has caused the party seeking costs to incur or waste expense unnecessarily.

3.11 CHALLENGING THE APPEAL DECISION

By s 284, the validity of an appeal decision may not be challenged in any legal proceedings. However, by s 288, a 'person aggrieved' may question the decision by appeal to the High Court if the decision was not within the powers of the Act or if any relevant procedural requirements have not been complied with.

In certain limited cases, a challenge may alternatively be mounted by way of judicial review.

Chapter 4

PLANNING OBLIGATIONS

Chapter 4 contents

4.1 INTRODUCTION

A planning obligation (formerly a planning agreement) is a negotiating tool available to an LPA and a developer who is seeking planning permission. It is a legal instrument which offers a degree of flexibility to both parties which might not otherwise be available through the medium of a planning permission subject to conditions (see **3.6**).

4.2 PLANNING OBLIGATIONS (s 106)

4.2.1 The basic provision

Any person interested in land in the area of an LPA may, by agreement or otherwise, enter into a planning obligation which may:

(1) restrict the development or use of the land in a specified way; or
(2) may require specified operations or activities to be carried out in, on, over or under the land; or
(3) require the land to be used in a specified way; or
(4) require money to be paid to the LPA on a specified date or dates, or periodically (s 106(1)).

Note the following points:

(1) 'Person interested in land' means, if the section is to have its full effect (see enforceability at **4.2.3**), a person with a legal estate or interest in the land concerned and not, for example, a developer who merely has an option to purchase the land at the time the obligation is entered into.
(2) 'Agreement or otherwise' indicates that a planning obligation may be created either by agreement between the LPA and the developer or by means of a unilateral undertaking offered by the developer or a combination of both. (As to the potential use of unilateral undertakings, see **4.6**.)
(3) A planning obligation may impose both restrictive covenants (eg restricting the development or use of the land) and positive ones (eg requiring works to be done or money to be paid). These covenants will then be enforceable against successors in title of the developer (see **4.2.3**).
(4) A planning obligation may be unconditional or subject to conditions and may impose its restrictions and requirements either indefinitely or for a specified period. It may also provide that a person will only be bound by the obligation whilst he has an interest in the land (s 106(2) and (4)).

4.2.2 Formalities

A planning obligation must be made by a deed which states that it is a planning obligation for the purposes of s 106 and identifies the land and the parties concerned (including the interest of the developer). It is registrable by the LPA as a local land charge.

4.2.3 Enforceability

By s 106(3) and (4) a planning obligation is enforceable by the LPA against the original person interested ('developer') and any person deriving title from him but subject to the terms of the obligation (see **4.2.1**).

Note the following points:

(1) The obligation will only bind the interest or estate of the developer and those deriving title from him. It cannot bind a superior title. Thus, for example, if a tenant enters into a planning obligation, it cannot bind the landlord of that tenant; accordingly, if the lease subsequently comes to an end, the obligation will only bind the original covenantor.

(2) A planning obligation cannot bind parties who have rights in the land existing at the time the obligation is entered into unless they consent to be bound by it. Thus, for example, existing mortgagees of the land will not be bound (unless they consent) so that if they subsequently sell under their statutory power, the purchaser will take the land free from the obligation which will only be enforceable against the original covenantor.

4.2.4 Enforcement by the LPA

Section 106 provides three main methods of enforcement as follows:

(1) Injunction to restrain a breach of any restrictive covenant in the obligation (s 106(5)).

(2) By s 106(6) where there is a failure to carry out any operations required by a planning obligation the LPA may enter upon the land, carry out the operations and recover their expenses from the person or persons against whom the obligation is enforceable (see **4.2.3**).

(3) Any sums due under the planning obligation (including any expenses recoverable under s 106(6) above) may be charged on the land in accordance with regulations yet to be made (s 106(12)). Until regulations have been made, it is unclear whether such a charge will be registrable as a local land charge or as a private charge (and therefore registrable as a land charge or by notice, etc on the register of title).

4.3 'PLANNING GAIN'

4.3.1 Introduction

The main function of planning obligations is to allow the LPA and the developer to deal with issues that are necessary to be dealt with in order for a proposal to be acceptable, but which cannot be dealt with by condition, given the limitations (imposed by case-law etc) on the purposes for which conditions can be used. Planning obligations are not subject to such strict limitations and so can be used as a flexible means of solving any problems that a development proposal may cause.

The danger with this flexibility is that the use of planning obligations could be open to abuse. The fear was that developers would be tempted to offer inappropriate inducements to LPAs in order to obtain, or effectively 'buy', planning permission, and equally that LPAs would be tempted to draw up 'shopping lists', which they would expect developers to agree to pay for, in return for planning permission. This is sometimes referred to as planning gain and is clearly not in the public interest.

It is not surprising, therefore, that there is detailed policy and case-law guidance setting out what it is legitimate to include in a planning obligation. What follows is a summary of the key policy and case-law principles that govern this area.

4.3.2 SSE's advice – Circular 1/97

General policy

As a matter of policy, the Circular states that the use of planning obligations will be acceptable if they are:

> '(i) necessary to make a proposal acceptable in land use terms;
> (ii) relevant to planning;
> (iii) directly related to the proposed development;
> (iv) fairly and reasonably related in scale and kind to the proposed development;
> (v) reasonable in all other respects.'

Specific guidance

Paragraph B3 of Circular 1/97 states:

> 'Acceptable development should never be refused because an applicant is unwilling or unable to offer benefits. Unacceptable development should never be permitted because of unnecessary or unrelated benefits offered by the applicant. Those benefits that go beyond what is necessary should not affect the outcome of a planning decision.'

Paragraph B4 of Circular 1/97 states:

> '... local planning authorities and developers should place more emphasis on the overall quality of a development proposal than the number (or value) of planning benefits they can obtain or offer. Planning obligations ... may provide a means of ensuring high quality development. But good quality is an integral part of development and should be at the heart of all planning; the provision of add-on benefits should not be regarded as an acceptable alternative to such an integrated approach.'

Paragraph B9 states:

> 'In general it will be reasonable to seek ... a planning obligation if what is sought or offered:
>
> (i) is needed from a practical point of view to enable the development to go ahead and, in the case of financial payment, will meet or contribute towards the cost of providing such necessary facilities in the future;
> (ii) or is necessary from a planning point of view and is so directly related to the proposed development and to the use of the land after its completion that the development ought not to be permitted without it.'

Paragraph B12 states:

> '... a reasonable obligation would seek to restore facilities, resources and amenities equivalent to that existing before the development. Developers may reasonably be expected to pay for or contribute to the cost of infrastructure which would not have been necessary but for their development ... Developers should not be expected to pay for facilities which are needed solely in order to resolve existing deficiencies...'

Paragraph B20 states:

> '... if there is a choice between imposing conditions and entering into a planning obligation, the imposition of a condition which satisfies the policy tests in DoE

Circular 11/95 is preferable because it enables a developer to appeal to the Secretary of State.'

4.3.3 Case-law

There have recently been several cases concerned with the reasonableness of benefits contained in planning obligations and what weight should be given to them in deciding whether planning permission should be granted. The principal cases are *R v Plymouth City Council and Others ex p Plymouth & South Devon Co-operative Society Ltd* [1993] JPL B81, [1993] 36 EG 135, CA; *Tesco Stores Ltd v Secretary of State for the Environment and Others* [1995] JPL 581; [1995] EGCS 82, HL; and *Good and Another v Epping Forest District Council* [1994] JPL 372, [1993] EGCS 188, CA. These cases are authority for the following propositions:

(1) The tests in *Newbury* (see **3.6.2**) apply in determining whether the benefits offered in a planning obligation are material considerations to be taken into account when the LPA are deciding whether to grant planning permission. There is no requirement that the benefits offered also have to be necessary in the sense that they overcome what would otherwise be a planning objection to the development.

(2) If a benefit is a material consideration because it passes the tests in *Newbury*, the weight to be given to it is a matter of discretion (governed by policy considerations) for the LPA or SSE.

(3) The powers of LPAs under s 106 are not controlled by the nature and extent of the power to impose conditions under s 70(1). Thus, provided a benefit in a planning obligation satisfies s 106(1) (see above) and is not manifestly unreasonable, it is valid.

4.4 PRACTICAL POINTS

In view of the law and guidance above, the following points should be borne in mind when drafting and negotiating a planning obligation.

4.4.1 By the LPA

(1) It is important that the title to the land is thoroughly investigated before the LPA enters into the planning obligation. All parties with a legal interest in the land should be made parties to it including any persons with existing interests (such as a prior mortgagee); otherwise the obligation may not be enforceable against a successor in title to that interest.

(2) The future exercise of any of the LPA's statutory powers should not be fettered by the obligation. If this does occur and the obligation is later challenged in court, it could invalidate the planning obligation (see *Royal Borough of Windsor and Maidenhead v Brandrose Investments* [1983] 1 WLR 509, CA).

(3) The planning obligation should be executed either before, or simultaneously with, the grant of the planning permission otherwise the developer may have the benefit of the permission without being bound by the obligation.

(4) The timing of related infrastructure agreements should be carefully considered. It will normally be preferable, where possible, to have all related agreements (eg agreements under the Highways Act 1980) executed at the same time as the planning obligation.

(5) Consideration should be given as to whether the obligation ought, in the circumstances of the case, to provide that liability under the obligation will cease once the owner of the interest parts with it. In the absence of such a provision liability will continue against not only the original covenantor(s) but also against all subsequent successors in title to him (them).

(6) If there is a disagreement about the inclusion of a particular term in the planning obligation, the LPA should consider whether it is within the guidance contained in Circular 1/97. If it is doubtful, or may be considered excessive, the LPA may find that the developer will appeal and offer a unilateral undertaking on the appeal (see further **4.6**).

(7) Consideration should also be given as to whether a clause should be included providing for payment of the LPA's costs in connection with the negotiation, drafting and execution of the planning obligation. If there is no such clause the LPA will have to bear their own costs.

Costs paid?

4.4.2 By the developer

(1) The draft planning permission should be included in one of the schedules to the obligation so that it is clear from the terms of the obligation what conditions, etc will be attached to the planning permission.

(2) The developer should try to ensure that the terms of the obligation do not continue to bind after he has sold his interest to a successor. This is particularly important where positive covenants in the obligation are likely to continue well into the future.

(3) For the same reasons as for the LPA, it is important for the developer that the LPA do not fetter their statutory powers in the obligation. If there is such a fetter, the planning obligation may be challenged later by a third party.

(4) The developer should attempt to have a clause inserted to the effect that the planning obligation will be discharged or cease to have effect if the planning permission expires or is revoked or if planning permission is later granted for some other development which is incompatible with that originally granted.

(5) The obligation should not contain a covenant to comply with the conditions attached to the related planning permission (see para B20 of Circular 1/97 quoted at **4.3**). If there is such a covenant and the conditions on the planning permission are subsequently varied (under s 73 or s 73A, see **3.6.4**) or the permission lapses or is revoked, the conditions will continue to bind the land by virtue of the covenant in the planning obligation. (As an alternative, the obligation could contain a covenant to comply with the conditions originally imposed or as subsequently varied or removed and only insofar as the planning permission remains in effect.)

(6) Covenants should be avoided which impose obligations (in particular, positive ones) which take effect as soon as the planning obligation is executed (as opposed to when the planning permission is implemented). There may be a gap of quite a few months, if not a few years, between the developer obtaining the permission and being in a position to implement it.

4.5 MODIFICATION AND DISCHARGE OF PLANNING OBLIGATIONS (s 106A)

4.5.1 The power to modify or discharge

A planning obligation may be modified or discharged by either agreement between the LPA and the person(s) against whom it is then enforceable, or by application by such person to the LPA, or by appeal to the SSE.

Note that modification or discharge by agreement requires the participation of all persons against whom the obligation is then enforceable whereas an application to the LPA for modification or discharge can be made by any person against whom the obligation is enforceable. Any modification or discharge by agreement must be by deed (s 106A(2)).

4.5.2 Application for modification or discharge

A person against whom a planning obligation is enforceable may, at any time after the expiry of 5 years from the date of the planning obligation, apply to the LPA for the obligation to have effect subject to such modifications as may be specified in the application, or to be discharged (s 106A(3)–(4)).

4.5.3 Determination of application by the LPA

The LPA must notify the applicant of their decision within 8 weeks or such longer period as may be agreed in writing between the parties. Where the application is refused, the notification must state clearly and precisely the LPA's full reasons for their decision and tell the applicant of his rights of appeal (see below).

4.5.4 Appeal against determination (s 106B)

Where the LPA fail to reach a decision in the 8-week period or determine that the planning obligation shall continue to have effect without modification, the applicant may appeal to the SSE within 6 months of the date of the notice or deemed refusal, or such longer period as the SSE may allow.

The appeal procedure is closely modelled on that for ordinary planning appeals (see Chapter 3).

4.6 UNILATERAL UNDERTAKINGS

4.6.1 Introduction

By s 106(1) planning obligations may be entered into 'by agreement or otherwise'; 'or otherwise' indicates that a fully enforceable obligation may be offered unilaterally by the developer. The rules as to the contents and formalities of unilateral undertakings are the same as those that apply to ordinary planning obligations entered into by agreement except that the agreement of the LPA is not needed.

The reason for the introduction of the unilateral undertaking was 'to enable developers to break the stalemate when local planning authorities play for time or hold out for excessive gain . . . They should be particularly useful in clarifying the position at appeal' (Baroness Blatch quoted in Hansard, House of Lords, November 27, 1990, col 907).

4.6.2 DoE guidance

The SSE's guidance to LPAs on the use of unilateral undertakings is contained in paras B5 and B6 of Circular 1/97 which state that:

> 'It is reasonable to expect developers and LPAs to try to resolve any planning objections the authority may have to the development proposal by agreement, in accordance with this guidance. Where a developer considers that negotiations are being unneccessarily protracted or that unreasonable demands are being made, he may wish to enter into a planning obligation by making a unilateral undertaking ... The use of unilateral obligations is therefore expected to be principally, but not solely, at appeals, where there are planning objections which only a planning obligation can resolve, but the parties cannot reach agreement ... Such an undertaking should be in accordance with this guidance ... Undertakings should be relevant to planning and directly related to the needs created by the development proposal concerned.'

4.6.3 Practical effect

Thus, the normal course of events will be to attempt to reach an agreement first. If there is deadlock on this, the developer will then appeal to the SSE against the refusal or deemed refusal of planning permission. At the appeal the developer will offer a unilateral undertaking which, if it is considered appropriate by the inspector, may result in the developer obtaining planning permission. The unilateral undertaking will then become enforceable by the LPA.

Chapter 5

ENFORCEMENT OF PLANNING LAW

Chapter 5 contents

5.1 INTRODUCTION

In order to ensure that the planning controls set out in Part III of the Act (ss 55–106) are observed, LPAs are given wide powers of enforcement in Part VII (ss 171A–196). These powers are:

(1) a right of entry for certain enforcement purposes;
(2) service of a planning contravention notice to obtain information about a breach or suspected breach;
(3) service of a breach of condition notice to require compliance with a condition or limitation attached to a planning permission;
(4) the right to apply for an injunction to restrain any breach or threatened breach of planning control;
(5) service of an enforcement notice (sometimes followed by a stop notice) to secure compliance with planning controls.

Before looking at these powers in more detail, though, it is necessary to set out some basic definitions and time-limits which apply to enforcement generally and to consider certificates of lawful use or development which can provide immunity from enforcement action.

5.2 DEFINITIONS AND TIME-LIMITS

5.2.1 Definitions (s 171A)

For the purposes of the Act:

(1) A 'breach of planning control' occurs when development is carried out without the requisite planning permission or when any condition or limitation attached to a permission is not complied with.
(2) 'Taking enforcement action' means the issue of an enforcement notice or the service of a breach of condition notice.

5.2.2 Time-limits (s 171B)

The LPA can only take enforcement action if they do so within the appropriate time-limits. There are two of these:

(1) Where the breach of planning control consists of:

  (a) operational development carried out without planning permission; or
  (b) a change of use of any building to use as a single dwelling house;

  the LPA must take enforcement action within 4 years from the date on which the operations were substantially completed or the change of use occurred (as the case may be).

(2) With all other breaches (ie any material change of use other than to use as a single dwelling house and any breach of condition or limitation attached to a

planning permission) no enforcement action may be brought after the expiry of 10 years from the date of the breach.

Note as regards both of the above time-limits, the provisions of s 171B(4)(b) at **5.8.3**.

Once the relevant time-limit has passed, immunity is in effect given to the breach. It is therefore vital to check whether the relevant time-limit has passed and this in turn depends on the nature of the breach committed.

5.3 CERTIFICATES OF LAWFUL USE OR DEVELOPMENT (ss 191–192)

5.3.1 Preliminary definitions (s 191(2) and (3))

Uses and operations are 'lawful' if no enforcement action can be taken for any reason, including the expiry of the relevant time-limit (see **5.2.2**), and they are not in contravention of a current enforcement notice.

Breach of a condition or limitation attached to a permission is 'lawful' if the 10-year time-limit for taking enforcement action has expired and the breach is not in contravention of a current enforcement notice.

5.3.2 Existing development (s 191)

Any person who wishes to ascertain the lawfulness of any existing use or any operations which have been carried out or any other matter constituting a breach of condition or limitation may apply to the LPA specifying the land and describing the use, operations or other matter (s 191(1)). (Note that 'any person' may apply; so, for instance, a prospective purchaser of land could apply for such a certificate.)

Onus of proof

The onus of proof is on the applicant who must prove the lawfulness on a balance of probabilities. The planning merits of the case (ie whether or not the development is desirable) are irrelevant; the sole question in issue is whether or not the matters described in the application are lawful.

Issue of certificate (s 191(4))

If the LPA are satisfied of the lawfulness at the time of the application of the use, etc, they must issue a certificate. In any other case they must refuse one; note, though, that a refusal merely indicates that the matter has not been proved on a balance of probabilities.

Effect of certificate (s 191(6) and (7))

The lawfulness of any use, operations, etc for which a certificate is in force shall be conclusively presumed. Thus, no enforcement action may be brought in respect of the matters stated as lawful in the certificate.

5.3.3 Proposed development (s 192)

Any person who wishes to ascertain the lawfulness of any proposed use or operational development of land can apply to the LPA specifying the land and describing the use or operations in question.

Effect of certificate (s 192(4))
The lawfulness of any use or operations stated in the certificate shall be conclusively presumed unless there is a material change, before the proposed use or operations are started, in any of the matters relevant to the determination.

5.3.4 General provisions applying to certificates of lawful use or development

A certificate may be issued in respect of part only of the land or just some of the matters specified in the application (s 193(4)) or, with existing development, may be issued in terms which differ from those specified in the application (s 191(4)).

The LPA must enter prescribed details of any applications and decisions in their s 69 register (s 193(6)) and must notify the applicant of their decision within 8 weeks or such longer period as may be agreed in writing between the parties (GDPO, art 24).

Appeals (ss 195, 196 and 288)
The applicant can appeal to the SSE against a refusal, a refusal in part or a deemed refusal (ie where the LPA fail to determine the application within the relevant time). The time-limit is 6 months from the date of notification of the decision or the deemed refusal.

Further appeal lies to the High Court within 6 weeks of the decision of the SSE.

Offences (s 194)
It is an offence for any person to procure a particular decision on an application by knowingly or recklessly making a statement which is misleading or false in a material particular, or (with intent to deceive) using a document which is false or misleading in a material particular or withholding any material information.

If a statement was made or a document was used which was false or misleading in a material particular, or if any material information was withheld (whether or not this was done knowingly or recklessly or with intent to deceive), the LPA may revoke the certificate.

5.4 RIGHT OF ENTRY FOR ENFORCEMENT PURPOSES (ss 196A–196C)

5.4.1 Right of entry without a warrant (s 196A)

Any person duly authorised in writing by the LPA may enter any land at any reasonable hour without a warrant to:

(1) ascertain whether there is or has been any breach of planning control on that or any other land; or
(2) determine whether any enforcement power should be exercised and, if so, how; or
(3) ascertain whether there has been compliance with any enforcement power that has been exercised.

There must, however, be 'reasonable grounds' for doing so, ie entry must be the logical means of obtaining the information in question.

In addition to the general power above, a person duly authorised by the SSE, after consultation with the LPA, may similarly enter but only for the purpose of determining whether an enforcement notice should be issued.

In the case of a dwelling house (which includes any residential accommodation in, eg, a commercial building), 24 hours' notice of the intended entry must be given to the occupier. This requirement does not apply, however, to land or outbuildings in the curtilage of the house.

5.4.2 Power to enter under a warrant (s 196B)

A justice of the peace may issue a warrant to any person duly authorised as above for any of the purposes listed above if he is satisfied on sworn information in writing that:

(1) there are reasonable grounds for entering for the purpose in question; and
(2) admission has been refused, or it is reasonably apprehended that it will be refused, or it is an urgent case.

Entry is deemed to be refused if no reply is received within a reasonable time to a request for admission.

Entry under a warrant must be at a reasonable hour (except in cases of urgency) and must be within one month from the date of issue of the warrant. Each warrant authorises one entry only.

5.4.3 Restrictions and offences (s 196C)

The person entering the land must produce his authority and state the purpose of his entry, if requested, and may take with him such other persons as may be necessary (eg policeman, expert, etc). On leaving the land, if the owner or occupier is not then present, he must ensure that the land is as secured against trespassers as when he entered.

Anyone who wilfully obstructs a person exercising a lawful right of entry is guilty of an offence.

5.5 PLANNING CONTRAVENTION NOTICE (ss 171C–171D)

A planning contravention notice (PCN) (rather than the power of entry) is the principal power available to an LPA for obtaining information needed for enforcement purposes.

5.5.1 Contents of a PCN

There is no prescribed form of PCN although a model is suggested in the Appendix to Annex 1 of DoE Circular 21/91.

Section 171C states that a PCN may require the person on whom it is served to give any information specified in the notice in respect of any operations, use or activities being carried out on the land and any matter relating to conditions or limitations attached to an existing permission. In particular (and without prejudice to the generality of the above), it may require the person served, so far as he is able, to:

(1) state whether the land is being used as alleged in the notice or whether alleged operations or activities are or have been carried out;

(2) state when any use, operation or activity began;
(3) give particulars of any person known to use or have used the land for any purpose or to be carrying out or have carried out any operations or activities;
(4) give any information he holds about any relevant planning permission or to state why planning permission is not required;
(5) state his interest (if any) in the land and the name and address of any person he knows to have an interest in the land.

A PCN may also give notice of a time and place at which the LPA will consider:

(1) any offer from the person served to apply for planning permission or to refrain from operations or activities or to undertake remedial work; and
(2) any representations he may wish to make about the notice.

If the notice states this, the LPA must give him the opportunity to make the offer or representations at that time and place.

By s 171C(5), a PCN must warn the person served that if he fails to reply enforcement action may be taken and he may be deprived of compensation if a stop notice is served (see **5.10**).

5.5.2 The person served

A PCN may be served on anyone who is the owner or occupier of the land to which the notice relates or who has any other interest in it, or on anyone who is carrying out operations on the land or using it for any purpose (s 171C(1)).

It is an offence for any person served with a PCN to fail to reply to it within 21 days unless he has a reasonable excuse. The offence is a continuing one, even after conviction (s 171D(2)–(4)).

It is also an offence knowingly or recklessly to make a statement in a purported reply which is false or misleading in a material particular (s 171D(5)–(6)).

5.5.3 Effect of a PCN

Apart from the consequences mentioned above, service of a PCN does not affect the exercise of any other enforcement power available to the LPA.

5.6 BREACH OF CONDITION NOTICE (s 187A)

A breach of condition notice (BCN) is primarily intended as an alternative remedy to an enforcement notice where the LPA desire to secure compliance with conditions or limitations attached to an existing planning permission.

5.6.1 When and on whom a BCN may be served

Where there has been a breach of condition or limitation attached to an existing permission, the LPA may serve a BCN on any person who is carrying out or has carried out the development or on any person having control of the land. (Note that 'carrying out the development' is defined to include permitting another person to do so: s 187A(13).)

5.6.2 Contents of a BCN

The notice must specify the steps which the LPA consider ought to be taken or the activities which ought to cease in order to secure compliance with the conditions, etc specified in the notice. Where, however, a notice is served on a person who has control of the land but who is not carrying (or has not carried) out the development, it can only require compliance with any conditions regulating the use of the land.

The notice must also specify a period for compliance which must not be less than 28 days from the date of service of the notice.

5.6.3 Effect of a BCN

If the person served has not remedied the breach by the time specified in the notice (or by the time specified in any further notice served by the LPA), he is guilty of an offence: the offence is a continuing one. It is a defence, however, for the person served to prove that he took all reasonable measures to secure compliance with the notice or, if he was served as the person having control of the land, that he did not have control at the time he was served.

5.7 INJUNCTIONS (s 187B)

An LPA may apply to the High Court or county court for an injunction if they consider it necessary or expedient to restrain an actual or apprehended breach of planning control. They may do this whether or not they have used, or propose to use, any of their other enforcement powers under the Act.

This provision operates without prejudice to the power of a local authority (not just an LPA) to bring any proceedings under s 222 of the Local Government Act 1972 where they consider it expedient for the promotion or protection of the interests of the inhabitants in their area. Where an injunction is sought under this provision, the court is not limited merely to restraining a breach of planning control.

By s 187B(3), an injunction may be obtained against a person whose identity is unknown provided that the relevant rules of court are complied with. These rules are contained in RSC Ord 110 and CCR Ord 49, r 6, both of which require the LPA to identify to the best of their ability the person against whom the injunction is sought (by reference to, eg photographs of the person concerned or the registration number of any vehicle that may belong to that person).

Whether an injunction is granted and, if so, its terms, are entirely a matter for the discretion of the court as the remedy is an equitable one. Thus, an LPA will need to show not only that the remedy is expedient and necessary but also that they have taken into account all relevant considerations in coming to that decision, that there is a clear breach or a clear likelihood of a breach, and that the remedy is the most appropriate one in the circumstances of the case. (For good illustrations, see *Croydon London Borough Council v Gladden* [1994] JPL 723, CA, at p 729ff, *Harborough District Council v Wheatcroft & Son Ltd* [1996] JPL B128 and *Hambleton District Council v Bird* [1995] 3 PLR 8.)

5.8 ENFORCEMENT NOTICE (ss 172–182)

5.8.1 Introduction

As a general rule, there is no criminal liability for breaches of planning control. There are exceptions to this rule, for instance, where unauthorised works are done to a listed building, or where there is a breach of a tree preservation order or the display of an advertisement without consent. Subject to this, however, there is no criminal liability for a breach until a valid enforcement notice has been served, become effective and not complied with.

5.8.2 Issue of enforcement notice

By s 172(1), an LPA may issue an enforcement notice where it appears to them that there has been a breach of planning control and that it is expedient to issue the notice having regard to the provisions of their development plan and any other material considerations. Issue of an enforcement notice is the most commonly used method of enforcement.

Pre-requisites to issue

There must be an apparent breach of planning control and it must be expedient to issue an enforcement notice.

APPARENT BREACH OF PLANNING CONTROL

There is no duty on the LPA to satisfy themselves that there is a breach (see, eg, *Tidswell v Secretary of State for the Environment* [1977] JPL 104) although with the new powers now available to them, in particular the right to serve a PCN, it may be required to do some preliminary research before issuing an enforcement notice.

IT MUST BE EXPEDIENT TO ISSUE AN ENFORCEMENT NOTICE

The LPA should not automatically issue an enforcement notice whenever there appears to be a breach of planning control. They must consider their development plan and any other material considerations (which will include advice in circulars and PPGs).

In PPG 18 the DoE gives detailed guidance on this matter to LPAs. For example, in para 5 it states that enforcement action should always be commensurate with the breach to which it relates; thus, it will usually be inappropriate to take enforcement action against a trivial or technical breach which causes no harm to amenity in the locality. Another factor to consider is whether planning permission, if applied for, would be granted for the unauthorised development in question.

The decisive issue, therefore, is whether the breach would unacceptably affect public amenity or the existing use of the land which merits protection in the public interest.

Challenging the issue or failure to issue

A decision to issue an enforcement notice cannot be challenged unless the decision was arbitrary or capricious (see, eg, *Donovan v Secretary of State for the Environment* [1988] JPL 118).

Equally a decision not to issue an enforcement notice is not challengeable unless the decision is arbitrary or capricious (see *Perry v Stanborough (Developments) Ltd* [1978] JPL 36).

5.8.3 Time-limits

An enforcement notice must be issued (though not necessarily served) within the relevant time-limit as defined in s 171B (see **5.2.2**). Failure to do so will render the breach lawful.

However, by s 171B(4)(b), an LPA is not prevented from taking further enforcement action in respect of a breach of planning control if, during the 4 years prior to the new action being taken, the LPA have taken or purported to take enforcement action in respect of that breach. This would enable a LPA, for example, to serve another enforcement notice within 4 years of one which had been set aside on an appeal or one which had been withdrawn (see **5.8.8** and **5.10**).

5.8.4 Contents of an enforcement notice (s 173)

No statutory form is prescribed but the notice must comply with the following:

(1) It must state the matters alleged to constitute the breach of planning control in such a way as to enable the person served to know what those matters are, and must state the paragraph of s 171A(1) (development without permission or breach of condition/limitation: see **5.2.1**) within which, in the opinion of the LPA, the breach falls (s 173(1) and (2)).

(2) It must specify the steps to be taken or the activities to be discontinued in order to achieve wholly or partly the remedying of the breach or of any injury to amenity caused by the breach (s 173(3) and (4)). Examples of requirements that may be included are given in s 173(5)–(7) and include:

   (a) alteration or removal of buildings or works;
   (b) carrying out of any building or other operations;
   (c) cessation of any activity except to the extent permitted by the notice;
   (d) modification of the contour of any deposit of refuse or waste;
   (e) construction of a replacement building after unauthorised demolition.

(3) It must state the calendar date on which the notice is to take effect which must be at least 28 days from service of the notice (s 173(8)).

(4) It must state the period within which any steps specified in the notice are to be taken and may specify different periods for different steps (s 173(9)).

(5) It must state such additional matters as may be prescribed. These are set out in the Town and Country Planning (Enforcement Notices and Appeals) Regulations 1991, regs 3 and 4, which require that the notice:

   (a) states the reasons why the LPA considered it expedient to issue the enforcement notice. This is intended to enable appellants to direct their minds to relevant issues (see DoE Circular 21/91, Annex 2, para 12);
   (b) defines the precise boundaries of the site by reference to a plan or otherwise (ibid, para 13);
   (c) is accompanied by a copy or summary of ss 172–177, the booklet 'Enforcement Notice Appeals – A Guide to Procedure' and a copy of the recommended appeal form.

5.8.5 Service (s 172(2) and (3))

Persons to be served

The enforcement notice must be served on:

(1) the owner: this term is defined in s 336(1) as being the person (other than a mortgagee not in possession) who is entitled to receive a rack (ie full) rent or who would be so entitled if the land were let; and
(2) the occupier: this includes any person occupying by virtue of a lease or tenancy but may also extend to licensees if their occupation resembles that of a tenant (see *Stevens v Bromley London Borough Council* [1972] 2 WLR 605, CA); and
(3) any other person having an interest in the land, being an interest which, in the opinion of the LPA, is likely to be materially affected by the notice; this would include, in particular, known mortgagees.

Time for service

The notice must be served not more than 28 days after its issue and not less than 28 days before the date specified in the notice as the date on which it is to take effect. Failure to comply with these provisions is a ground for appeal to the SSE and, in general, is only challengeable in that way (s 285(1) and see *R v Greenwich London Borough Council, ex p Patel* [1985] JPL 851, CA; see also **5.10**).

5.8.6 Validity of notice

An error or defect in an enforcement notice may render it either a nullity or invalid.

Nullity

The notice will only be a nullity where there is a major defect on the face of it, for example, where it does not state what the alleged breach is, what must be done to put it right or on what date the notice takes effect. The notice will also be a nullity if it does not fairly and reasonably tell the recipient what he must do to remedy the breach.

If the notice is a nullity it is of no effect. This is therefore a complete defence to any prosecution brought for non-compliance with it. In addition, there is technically no right of appeal to the SSE under s 174 although, in practice, an appeal will normally be made at which the SSE may find as a preliminary issue that the notice is a nullity and that he therefore has no jurisdiction to hear the appeal. Any such finding may be challenged by the LPA by way of judicial review.

Invalidity

Other defects, errors or misdescriptions in an enforcement notice do not render it a nullity. In such a case, it can only be challenged by way of appeal under s 174 (see s 285 and **5.10**).

On a s 174 appeal, the SSE may correct such defects, etc, or vary the terms of the notice if he is satisfied that this will not cause injustice to either the appellant or the LPA (s 176(2)).

5.8.7 Effect of enforcement notice

An enforcement notice does not have to require restoration of the status quo, ie under-enforcement is possible. Where a notice could have required buildings or works to be removed or an activity to cease but does not do so and the notice is complied with, then planning permission is deemed to have been given under s 73A (see **3.6.4**) for those buildings, works or activities (s 173(11)).

Similarly, where an enforcement notice requires construction of a replacement building and is complied with, planning permission is deemed to have been given (s 173(12)).

Where a notice has become effective and has not been complied with, the then owner is guilty of an offence. In addition, the LPA may enter the land and take the steps required by the notice and recover their expenses of so doing (see **5.8.9**).

5.8.8 Variation and withdrawal (s 173A)

The LPA may withdraw or waive or relax any requirement of an enforcement notice whether or not it has become effective. If they do so they must immediately notify everyone who was served with the enforcement notice or who would have been served if it had been re-issued.

Note that the withdrawal of the notice (but not the waiver or relaxation of any requirement in it) does not affect the power of the LPA to issue a further enforcement notice in respect of the same breach.

5.8.9 Non-compliance with notice (ss 178–179)

Offences

Where the notice has become effective and any step required by the notice has not been taken or any activity required to cease is being carried on, the then owner is in breach and is liable on summary conviction to a fine of up to £20,000 or, on indictment, an unlimited amount. The court in assessing any fine must take into account any financial benefit or potential benefit accruing or likely to accrue as a result of the offence (s 179(1), (2), (8) and (9)). Note that the burden of proving ownership is on the prosecutor.

Any person (other than the owner) who has control of, or an interest in, the land must not carry on, or permit to be carried on, any activity required by the notice to cease. If he does so, he is guilty of an offence (s 179(4) and (5)).

Defences

It is a defence for the owner to show that he did everything he could be expected to do to secure compliance (s 179(3)).

It is also a defence for the person charged to show that he was not served with the enforcement notice, and that it was not entered in the s 188 register (in which LPAs are required to note all enforcement and stop notices), and that he did not know of the existence of the notice (s 179(7)).

It is no defence to show that the notice was defective because it failed to comply with s 173(2) (see **5.8.4**), although it would be a defence to show that the notice was a nullity (see **5.8.6**) or that the LPA exceeded their powers.

Action by the LPA

After any period for compliance with an enforcement notice has passed and the notice has not been fully complied with, the LPA, in addition to prosecuting, may enter the land and take any steps required by the notice. They may then recover any reasonable expenses incurred from the owner of the land at that time (s 178(1)).

Where the breach is a continuing one, the LPA may seek an injunction whether or not after any conviction (s 187B, see **5.7**).

5.9 STOP NOTICE (ss 183–187)

5.9.1 Introduction

As an enforcement notice cannot become effective earlier than 28 days after service and as its effect is suspended until final determination of any appeal (but subject to any court order to the contrary), it may be many months before the LPA can take steps to enforce it other than by way of an injunction. In the meantime local amenity may suffer detriment because of the continuing breach. Accordingly, the Act provides for the possibility of a stop notice to be served to bring activities in breach of planning control to an end before the enforcement notice takes effect.

5.9.2 Procedure

General

Where an LPA consider it expedient to prevent, before the expiry of the period for compliance, any activity specified in the enforcement notice they may serve a stop notice (s 183(1) and (2)). Details of this should be entered in the register of enforcement and stop notices kept under s 188.

Contents of the notice

The stop notice must refer to the enforcement notice and must have a copy of it annexed. It must also state the date on which it will take effect being at least 3 days and not more than 28 days after service of the notice; an earlier date may be specified if the LPA consider that there are special reasons and a statement of those reasons is served with the notice (s 184(1)–(3)).

Service

A stop notice may be served with the enforcement notice or subsequently but must be served before the enforcement notice takes effect (s 183(1) and (3)).

It must be served on any person who appears to have an interest in the land or to be engaged in any activity prohibited by the enforcement notice (s 183(6)).

Where a stop notice has been served, the LPA may also display a 'site notice' on the land concerned stating that a stop notice has been served, giving its details, and stating that any person contravening it may be prosecuted (see **5.9.4**).

5.9.3 Restrictions

A stop notice cannot prohibit the use of any building as a dwelling house or the carrying out of any activity which has been carried on for more than 4 years (whether continuously or not) unless, in the latter case, the activities consist of, or are incidental to, building, etc operations or the deposit of waste or refuse.

There is no appeal against the service of a stop notice.

5.9.4 Offences (s 187)

Any person who contravenes a stop notice (or causes or permits its contravention) after a site notice has been displayed or after he has been served with the stop notice is guilty of an offence which is punishable in the same way as for enforcement notices (including the taking into account of any financial benefit, see **5.8.9**).

It is a defence to prove that the stop notice was not served on him and that he did not know, and could not reasonably be expected to know, of its existence.

5.9.5 Withdrawal

By ss 183(7) and 184(7), the LPA may at any time withdraw a stop notice without prejudice to their power to serve another one. If they do withdraw a stop notice they must serve notice of this on everyone who was served with the original stop notice and, if a site notice was displayed, display a notice of withdrawal in place of the site notice. Compensation may then become payable (see **5.9.6**).

5.9.6 Compensation (s 186)

When payable

The LPA are liable to pay compensation in respect of any prohibition in a stop notice if:

(1) the enforcement notice is quashed on any ground other than that in s 174(2)(a) (see **5.10.1**); or
(2) the enforcement notice is varied other than under s 174(2)(a) so that the activity would no longer have fallen within the stop notice; or
(3) the enforcement notice is withdrawn otherwise than in consequence of a grant of planning permission or of permission to retain or continue the development without complying with a condition or limitation attached to a previous permission; or
(4) the stop notice is withdrawn.

No compensation is payable:

(1) if the enforcement notice is quashed or varied on the ground in s 174(2)(a); or
(2) in respect of any activity which, when the stop notice was in effect, constituted or contributed to a breach of planning control; or
(3) in respect of any loss or damage which could have been avoided if the claimant had provided the information when required to do so under s 171C (ie a PCN, see **5.5**), or s 330, or Local Government (Miscellaneous Provisions) Act 1976, s 16.

Amount and to whom payable

Compensation is payable to the person who, when the stop notice was first served, had an interest in or occupied the relevant land. The amount payable is that loss or damage which is directly attributable to the prohibition in the notice and can include any sum payable for breach of contract caused by compliance with the stop notice.

Any claim must be made within 12 months of the date compensation became payable (ie the date on which the enforcement notice was quashed, varied, etc). In the event of a dispute as to the amount, the matter must be referred to the Lands Tribunal.

5.10 APPEALS AGAINST ENFORCEMENT NOTICES (ss 174–177)

5.10.1 Grounds of appeal

Section 174(2) lists seven grounds of appeal as follows:

(a) Planning permission ought to be granted or any condition or limitation attached to an existing permission ought to be discharged (as the case may be) in respect of the matters alleged to be a breach of planning control in the enforcement notice.
(b) The matters alleged have not occurred.
(c) The matters, if they occurred, do not amount to a breach of planning control.
(d) No enforcement action could be taken at the date the notice was issued as regards the matters alleged in it (ie the LPA were out of time, see **5.2.2**).
(e) Copies of the enforcement notice were not served as required by s 172 (see **5.8.5**).
(f) The steps required by the notice or the activities required to cease exceed what is necessary to remedy any breach of planning control or injury to amenity (as the case may be).
(g) The period specified in the notice for the taking of steps, etc falls short of what should reasonably be allowed.

Note also the following points:

(1) Whether or not ground (a) is expressly made a ground of appeal, there is a deemed application for planning permission when a notice of appeal is lodged (s 177(5)).
(2) As regards ground (e), the SSE may disregard failure to serve any person if that failure has not caused substantial prejudice to that person or to the appellant (s 175(5)).
(3) Grounds (f) and (g) do not go to the validity of the enforcement notice and the SSE may vary the requirements of the original notice (s 176(1)).

5.10.2 Time-limit (s 174(3))

Written notice of appeal (which can be by letter, although the standard form supplied by the SSE is normally used) must be given to the SSE before the date on which the enforcement notice takes effect.

to SSE before date on which EN takes effect.

There is no power for the SSE or the court to extend the time-limit for appealing.

Note that if the notice is sent to the proper address by pre-paid post at such time that, in the ordinary course of post (2 working days in the case of first-class post), it would have been delivered before the enforcement notice takes effect, the appeal will be in time even if it is delayed in the post (s 174(3)(b)).

5.10.3 Who may appeal? (s 174(1) and (6))

Any person having an interest in the land (whether served with the enforcement notice or not) may appeal as may any person who was occupying the land under a licence at the time the notice was issued and continues to occupy the land when the appeal is brought.

5.10.4 Procedure

Documentation and fees to be submitted

By s 174(4), and reg 5 of the Town and Country Planning (Enforcement Notices and Appeals) Regulations 1991, the applicant may submit with the notice of appeal a statement in writing specifying the grounds on which he is appealing and stating briefly the facts in support of those grounds. If he does not submit this with the appeal he must do so within 14 days of being required to do so by notice from the SSE. It is important for the appellant to specify all the grounds on which he wishes to rely as amendments adding additional grounds are unlikely to be allowed subsequently.

As there is a deemed application for planning permission, whether or not the applicant also specifies ground (a), a fee is payable.

The fee is refundable in certain circumstances (eg if the appeal is allowed on grounds (b) to (e) or the enforcement notice is quashed or found to be invalid).

Appeal forum

The two main options are to proceed either by way of written representations or by public local inquiry. There is a right to a public local inquiry and, in practice, half of enforcement notice appeals are disposed of in this way. Written representations may be used if the appellant and the LPA agree; the DoE will suggest written representations where it thinks the circumstances of the case are appropriate.

Where the dispute is entirely concerned with the planning merits of the notice and the appeal, or the requirements and time for compliance in the notice, the matter may proceed by way of an informal hearing rather than a full public inquiry. An informal hearing is not appropriate where there is a dispute as to the evidence or a challenge on legal grounds.

The inquiry

The inspector determines the procedure at the inquiry. Broadly, though, the same procedure is followed as at an ordinary planning appeal inquiry (see **3.9.2**).

The persons entitled to appear are listed in r 12 of the Town and Country Planning (Enforcement) (Inquires Procedure) Rules 1992.

The onus of proof is on the appellant who has to prove that, on a balance of probabilities, there has been no breach of planning control, or as the case may be.

The SSE has power to correct any informality or defect, to quash or vary the enforcement notice, to grant planning permission for all or part of the unauthorised development, to discharge any condition or limitation, or to determine the purpose for which the land may be used.

Until the final determination or withdrawal of the appeal, the enforcement notice is of no effect. According to the Court of Appeal in *R v Kuxhaus* [1988] 2 WLR 1005, [1988] 2 All ER 705, CA, 'final determination' means when all rights of appeal have been exhausted, including appeals to the High Court under s 289. However, under s 289(4A) the High Court or Court of Appeal have power to order, if they think fit, that the notice shall have effect in whole or in part pending the final determination. Such an order may also require the LPA to give an undertaking as to damages.

The procedure after the inquiry is very similar to that applying to ordinary planning appeals (see **3.9.2**).

Written representations and informal hearings
As mentioned above, the DoE may suggest these alternatives in appropriate cases but they can only be used with the consent of both parties.

The procedure for both is closely modelled upon that for ordinary planning appeals (see **3.9**).

5.10.5 Costs

The SSE or his inspector has power to award costs in all cases, even where the appeal was by way of written representations or even where the inquiry was not held (ss 320 and 322).

5.10.6 Further appeals (s 289)

Further appeal to the High Court, but on a point of law only, lies against any decision made by the SSE in proceedings on an enforcement appeal. No such appeal lies, though, under s 289 if the SSE declined to entertain the appeal or set the enforcement notice aside as being a nullity; in these cases the appropriate way to proceed is by way of judicial review.

Leave of the court is required to bring the appeal and is governed by RSC Ord 94, rr 12 and 13. These require that the application for leave must be made within 28 days after notice of the decision was given to the appellant, although the court has power to extend the time-limit under the general jurisdiction in RSC Ord 3, r 5.

Chapter 6

THE PROBLEM OF CONTAMINATED LAND

6.1 INTRODUCTION

The definition of 'contaminated land' found in the Environment Act 1995 is:

> 'Any land which appears to [a] local authority to be in such a condition by reason of substances in, on or under the land that:
>
> (a) significant harm is being caused or there is a significant possibility of such harm being caused; or
> (b) pollution of controlled waters is being, or is likely to be caused ...'

'Harm' is defined as 'harm to the health of living organisms or other interference with the ecological systems of which they form part and, in the case of man, includes harm to his property'.

In determining whether any land is contaminated the local authority must act in accordance with guidance to be issued by the SSE.

Most contaminated land is located in industrialised urban areas and conurbations.

6.2 THE RISKS

The legal risks associated with contaminated land are:

(1) potential civil liability for damage caused by migrating pollution. In *Cambridge Water Co v Eastern Counties Leather Ltd* [1994] 2 WLR 53, the House of Lords decided that a defendant can be liable in nuisance if he brings onto his land any substance which may cause damage if it escaped. He will be liable for any damage caused without proof of fault or negligence, the only precondition to liability being that he must have been able reasonably to foresee the consequences of any escape, when he brought the substance onto his land. This means that a landowner could be liable for pollution damage following an escape even where he uses state-of-the art technology, and was not negligent in causing the escape;
(2) potential criminal liability for offences resulting from migrating pollution. For example, s 34 of the EPA 1990 imposes a duty of care to prevent the escape of waste from your control. Accordingly, any waste must be stored safely and securely;
(3) statutory liability for clean-up costs (see below);
(4) after-care and restoration provisions imposed by LPAs;
(5) planning constraints restricting the scope of development of contaminated land. For example, the GPDO requires the LPA to consult with the relevant waste disposal authority in respect of any application for planning permission within 250 metres of existing or past waste disposal sites; and
(6) s 157 of the EPA 1990 provides that where an offence is committed by a company and it can be proved that a director, manager, secretary or similar

officer of the company either consented, connived or was negligent, he as well as the company is guilty of an offence (see also s 158 of the EPA 1990).

These risks may mean heavy financial liabilities on the owner or occupier of the land. For example, s 78B of the Environment Act 1995 (when in force) will require local authorities to identify contaminated sites within their area. Having identified the contaminated land, the local authority (or sometimes the Environment Agency) shall serve a remediation notice on the 'appropriate person' requiring such clean-up works as they consider reasonable. The cost of this is likely to be considerable. In one case, a developer bought a site for residential development only to discover that the site had at one time been used as a gas mantle factory and was mildly radioactive; the clean-up costs exceeded £11 million. The 'appropriate person' to be served with a remediation notice is primarily the person(s) who caused or knowingly permitted the land to become contaminated (ie the original polluter). However, where that person cannot be found, after reasonable enquiry, the 'appropriate person' will be the 'owner or occupier'. Most commercial landlords will fall within the definition of owner and may be jointly liable with the tenant as occupier. Failure to comply with a remediation notice, without reasonable excuse, is a criminal offence. Moreover, in default of compliance with a remediation notice, the local authority have power to carry out the required works at the expense of the 'appropriate person'.

From a landlord's point of view, he will be anxious to ensure that if pollution is discovered during the term of the lease, he can require the tenant to carry out any necessary clean-up works under the provisions of the lease. Most modern commercial leases deal with environmental issues expressly but in the absence of express provisions are there any other lease terms upon which the landlord could rely to require the tenant to clean-up the site? It is doubtful whether clean-up works would fall within the tenant's repairing covenant unless the pollution caused some physical damage to the building (see **19.2.1**). However, the tenant's covenant to comply with the requirements of all statutory obligations (see **23.2**) may, depending on the exact form of wording used, be broad enough to extend to requirements under environmental law. Furthermore, if there is a service charge in the lease (see **27.5**) one of the items of expenditure recoverable from the tenant may include sums spent by the landlord on any necessary clean-up works. Even if this is not expressly mentioned in the list of services to be provided, the 'sweeping up' clause (see **27.5.1**) may be wide enough to embrace such work. It will be seen why such matters should be dealt with expressly in the lease.

6.3 STEPS TO TAKE TO REDUCE THE RISKS

There is no public list or register of sites which may be contaminated. However, s 78R of the Environment Act 1995 (when in force) will require local authorities to maintain a register containing particulars of remediation notices served by them. Furthermore, from time to time, the Environment Agency, on the basis of the information provided by the authorities, is required to publish a report on the state of contaminated land in its area. Notwithstanding these provisions, there is a very real danger of buying, in ignorance, a contaminated site at a price which does not reflect the cost of necessary clean-up works. Those involved in commercial property, therefore, must make their own careful enquiries to discover whether contamination may be a problem on the site they are buying, leasing or accepting as security for a loan. This may be done in a number of ways:

(1) a desk-top (or documentary) study. This involves:
- making specific enquiries of the various regulatory bodies such as local authorities and the Environment Agency to see if any pollution incidents have occurred on the site;
- making specific enquiries of the occupier;
- researching the previous planning history of the site;
- checking through the title deeds, including pre-registration documents. Such a check might indicate high risk property. For example, there may be information in old deeds and search certificates relating to previous uses of the land. While a long history of agricultural use may not raise much concern, a history of heavy industrial use will give greater cause for concern. Also, old plans attached to deeds can prove a useful source of information. For example, an old plan may indicate that the land has previously been used as (or is close to) an old quarry. In the same way old Ordnance Survey Maps may reveal useful information;

(2) undertaking a detailed physical survey of potentially contaminated sites. The desk-top study should establish the likelihood of contamination being present in which case a physical survey should be considered. This will be very expensive but the risks involved are great and the cost may, therefore, be justified.

6.4 CONTRACTUAL TERMS

In some cases, it may be possible to make the contract conditional on, for example, satisfactory site investigations; or on clean-up by the seller prior to completion; or on the buyer securing insurance cover against the risks of liability resulting from past contamination or pollution. Insurance will usually only be granted following an environmental risk assessment by consultants appointed by the insurer and may only cover third-party damage or injury rather than clean-up costs.

It may be possible to negotiate an indemnity from the seller against any future clean-up costs incurred or against damages which become payable as a result of past contamination or pollution. However, a seller will be unwilling to give such an indemnity unless he is convinced that the possibility of contamination is remote and the state of the market requires such an indemnity to be given. As an alternative, the buyer may seek a warranty from the seller that he has no knowledge of any pollution being present on site and that he has made full disclosure to the buyer of all relevant information. Alternatively, the buyer could seek a reduction in the purchase price to cover the likely clean-up costs. As always, much will depend on the relative bargaining power of the parties.

If the buyer considers the risk too high, he should withdraw from the transaction.

For a more detailed consideration of environmental issues, see Graham *Contaminated Land* (Jordans, 1995).

Chapter 7

MATTERS OF CONTRACT

Chapter 7 contents

7.1 THE CONTRACT OF SALE

As in residential conveyancing, it is the seller's solicitor who will draft the contract of sale, in duplicate, for submission to the buyer's solicitor for approval. The seller's solicitor may use the *Standard Conditions of Sale* (3rd edn) form of contract and will draft the contract adopting the same drafting principles applicable in residential conveyancing. Further, on the sale of a green field site, where the seller's main interest is in the receipt of money, and the buyer's in obtaining vacant possession, he will include clauses similar to those used in residential conveyancing. It is only where matters are complicated (eg by the need to obtain planning permission before completion) that drafting techniques will differ from residential conveyancing. Many solicitors will use their own word-processed form of contract which will incorporate the *Standard Conditions of Sale* (or some other comparable conditions of sale).

The following points may be noted in connection with a contract to sell a commercial site:

(1) The seller will insist upon the payment of a full 10 per cent deposit on exchange of contracts and is very unlikely to agree to accept a reduced deposit. The buyer, being in business, should be able to meet the demand of the usual contractual deposit. However, he is likely to insist that, notwithstanding the wording of Standard Condition 2.2.3, the deposit is to be held by the seller's solicitor as stakeholder and he may insist that the interest on the deposit (which may itself amount to a sizeable sum) is to be paid to the buyer at completion. Some larger organisations may try to dispense with the payment of a deposit when buying a commercial site on the basis that the size and reputation of the organisation is a sufficient guarantee that completion will take place.

(2) It will be very important to the commercial buyer to ensure that the contract provides for vacant possession of the whole of the site at completion so that the buyer's development plans are not frustrated. In most cases there is an implied term for vacant possession, but for the avoidance of doubt an express term should be included.

(3) VAT must be clearly dealt with in the agreement. The danger for the buyer is that if the contract is silent as to VAT, and after exchange of contracts, the seller (being a person registered for VAT) elects to charge VAT on the purchase price, the buyer will have to add 17.5 per cent VAT to the purchase price. The buyer may want to ensure that the contract contains an express warranty by the seller that he has not, before exchange, elected to charge VAT on the purchase price, and that he will not do so thereafter, or that the purchase price is paid inclusive of VAT. In any case, the buyer will want to make enquiries of the seller to ascertain his intentions regarding VAT on the purchase price. VAT on property is dealt with more fully at **12.1**.

(4) The seller, having entered into a bargain with a chosen buyer, will usually want to deal with the chosen buyer alone and will, therefore, often insert a clause in the contract which prevents the buyer from assigning the benefit of the contract to a third party. Further, the seller will often attempt to prevent the buyer from

entering into a sub-sale of the property by stipulating that the seller cannot be required by the buyer to execute a conveyance or transfer of the property to anyone other than the buyer. (This latter clause does not prevent a sub-sale but makes it less attractive to the buyers since stamp duty will be payable both on the conveyance to the buyer, and on the buyer's conveyance to the sub-buyer.)

(5) Frequently, the seller will deal with the possibility of the buyer becoming bankrupt, or going into liquidation, or becoming subject to other insolvency proceedings before completion of the sale by giving himself the right to rescind the contract upon the happening of any such event. This frees the seller to arrange a sale to another buyer without the delay of having to await completion, and the expiry of a notice to complete.

(6) If the buyer has agreed to pay all or part of the seller's legal and other expenses in connection with the sale, the contract should so provide.

(7) Express provision should be made, where appropriate, for the grant and reservation of easements and the imposition of covenants. If the seller is retaining some adjoining or neighbouring land, he will be anxious to retain some control over the future development of the property.

(8) Where the property already has the benefit of planning permission obtained by the seller, the benefit of that permission will automatically pass to the buyer, since planning permission enures for the benefit of the land concerned (unless it states otherwise). The buyer will no doubt want to develop in accordance with the plans and specifications upon which the application for permission was based, but copyright in those plans and specifications will be retained by the architect who drew them up in the first place. The buyer should, therefore, ensure that the contract provides for the seller to assign to him, or procure the grant to him, of a valid licence to use the plans and specifications.

(9) The seller may wish to exclude Standard Condition 5 to pass to the buyer the risk of damage to the property as from exchange of contracts.

7.2 DIFFERENT TYPES OF CONTRACT

Sometimes the sale will be by simple private treaty; sometimes it will be by way of auction or tender; and sometimes the nature of the transaction may justify a departure altogether from the straightforward kind of sale and purchase contract. There are many types of commercial contracts which can be entered into by a seller and buyer of a commercial site, catering for widely differing circumstances, and the agreement between the seller and buyer will need to reflect the bargain they have struck. This part of the book considers two alternative forms of agreement, although in practice, the reader will meet many other forms drafted for use in the particular circumstances of the case at hand.

7.2.1 Conditional agreements

There will be occasions when one of the parties to the contract will be either unable, or unwilling immediately to enter into an unconditional agreement for the sale or purchase of the property, and so arrangements may be made to effect a conditional exchange of contracts. The seller is usually reluctant to agree to a conditional exchange, since what the seller ordinarily seeks is the security of knowing that his buyer is firmly committed to paying over money on a specified date for completion. A conditional contract rarely serves a useful purpose for the seller. It is normally the buyer who suggests a conditional exchange of contracts, in a situation where the buyer is anxious to avoid losing the property to another buyer, but is not yet in a position to commit himself irrevocably to the purchase.

Types of conditional agreements

A conditional agreement may be contemplated in the following situations:

(1) where planning permission in respect of the development of the site has not yet been obtained;
(2) where the results of the buyer's local search and enquiries of the local authority have not yet been received;
(3) where vacant possession of the site is not yet available owing to the existence of a tenancy agreement in respect of all or part of the site, which the buyer requires to be terminated;
(4) where the property is leasehold, and the consent of the landlord is required (and has not yet been obtained) in respect of the proposed assignment to the buyer (see also Standard Condition 8.3), or in respect of alterations to the property, or a change in the use of the property proposed by the buyer.

Great care must be taken to distinguish between a contract which contains a condition precedent to the formation of the contract itself (in which case no contract exists unless and until the condition is performed), and a contract which contains a condition precedent to performance (in which case a binding contract is immediately created, but if the condition is not fulfilled, the contract becomes unenforceable). In drafting the contract, the seller's solicitor should make it expressly clear which type of agreement is intended.

If the former type of contract is used, then, despite the fact that the parties have entered into a written agreement, effectively they will still be in the same position as if negotiations were continuing since, until the condition has been satisfied, no binding contract exists, and either party is free to back out. The condition must be fulfilled if the contract is to come into effect. If the latter type of contract is used (and in order to obtain a degree of certainty and commitment, both of the parties are likely to favour this type), a binding contract immediately comes into effect so that neither party can back out without the other's consent whilst the condition still remains to be performed. If the condition is not fulfilled, the contract becomes unenforceable, unless the party for whose sole benefit the condition was inserted, waives the benefit of the condition and elects to proceed.

The condition

Certainty is required with conditional agreements. If the court cannot judge with certainty whether the conditionality of the contract has been removed, the court will reluctantly declare the entire contract void. Hence, in *Lee-Parker v Izzet (No 2)* [1972] 2 All ER 800, a contract which was stated to be conditional upon the buyer obtaining a satisfactory mortgage was held to be void since the concept of a satisfactory mortgage was too vague and indefinite. By way of contrast, in *Janmohamed v Hassam* (1976) 241 EG 609, a contract which was conditional upon the receipt of a mortgage offer satisfactory to the buyer was held to be valid, since the court was prepared to imply an obligation upon the buyer to act reasonably in deciding whether the mortgage offer was satisfactory to him.

In drafting the conditional clause, the seller's solicitor should clearly set out what is required to be done, by whom, and by when, in order for the contract to become unconditional. Consider the following situations by way of example:

Examples →

(1) If the buyer has not yet received the results of his local search and replies to enquiries of the local authority, the contract can be made conditional upon the buyer receiving what he considers to be satisfactory results and replies, by a stipulated date. The contract should contain an obligation upon the buyer to submit the correct forms to the local authority and to pay the fees (in case he has not already done so). Upon receipt of the search certificate and replies, the buyer should be obliged to notify the seller of receipt, indicating one of three things:

   (a) that the buyer considers the results and replies to be satisfactory, in which case the contract proceeds to completion; or
   (b) that the buyer considers them to be unsatisfactory, in which case the contract becomes unenforceable, and the contract should provide for the return of the deposit to the buyer, and of the evidence of title to the seller; or
   (c) that the buyer is prepared to waive the benefit of the condition.

   Such a contract is heavily weighted in favour of the buyer, since it is up to him to determine whether or not the condition has been satisfied. A more neutral and objectively-based conditional clause could make the contract conditional upon the receipt by the buyer of a set of results and replies to the local search and enquiries which disclose no adverse matters of a kind which would materially affect the value or beneficial use or occupation of the property by the buyer. This type of clause may not be favoured by the buyer since it leaves some scope for argument.

(2) If the buyer is not prepared to complete without the benefit of planning permission for the type of development he proposes to carry out on the property, the contract could be made conditional upon the receipt of an 'acceptable' planning permission by a stipulated date. Again, the buyer should be obliged by the contract to submit a valid planning application without delay, to serve the correct statutory notices, and to pay the fees for the application. Consideration ought to be given as to whether provision should be made so that, upon refusal of permission (which ordinarily would render the contract unenforceable), the buyer may be allowed or, perhaps, obliged to pursue an appeal. Particular consideration must be given to the definition of an 'acceptable' planning permission. It ought to be one which is granted pursuant to an application, precise details of which are set out in the contract, and which is subject only to the usual planning conditions imposed by statute (eg conditions imposing time-limits for the commencement of development), or which relate simply to the materials to be used or the provision of works of landscaping, or which are conditions which the buyer should reasonably accept. If this clause appears to be too objectively based for a developer's liking, he can be given control over the conditionality of the contract (in the same way as above) by having a clause which allows him to accept or reject the suitability of the permission, or to waive the benefit of the clause.

Time for performance

The condition must be satisfied either by a stipulated date, or if none is stated, by the contractual completion date, or if neither, within a reasonable time. It is good practice to stipulate in the contract a long-stop date by which the condition must be satisfied. The contract can then provide that if the condition is fulfilled by that date, completion is to take place within 14 or 21 days of the contract becoming unconditional. The contract should be drafted to oblige one party to notify the other that the contract has become unconditional (eg if the buyer receives the outstanding local search, then unless the seller is notified, the seller will not know that the contract has become unconditional, and that a completion date has been triggered).

If fulfilment of the condition depends upon action by one of the parties (eg the submission of a local search, or the making of an application for planning permission by the buyer) that party will not be able to rely upon his own inaction to argue that the contract has become unenforceable due to the non-fulfilment of the condition. To avoid this situation arising, the contract should place a contractual obligation upon the party of whom action is required to act with all reasonable speed and endeavour, and to pay the costs of the action required (eg search fees, planning application fees).

7.2.2 Option agreements

Whilst a conditional agreement is useful to a developer who is trying to commit a landowner to a sale of land at a time when the developer is not able unconditionally to commit himself, option agreements have many more varying uses for the developer, and are particularly useful in his attempts to piece together a development site. The usual form of option agreement entered into with a landowner gives the grantee of the option the right, within a specified time, to serve notice upon the grantor requiring the latter to convey the property either at an agreed price, or at the market value of the property at the time the option notice is served. Under a conditional contract, unless the contract is drafted in a manner which favours the developer, the developer is usually obliged to complete the purchase at the contract price once the condition has been fulfilled, even though in the meantime market conditions have caused him to rethink the development. With option agreements, the buyer can exercise the option if he wants to, or he can let it lapse if market conditions are no longer in his favour.

Nature of an option

At one time, there was considerable academic debate (for good practical reasons) as to whether an option agreement was in the nature of a conditional contract, containing a condition precedent to performance which needed to be satisfied by the grantee by his serving a notice to exercise the option, or whether the agreement was simply an irrevocable offer (ie one not capable of being withdrawn), which the grantee could accept by service of an option notice, but until such time, no binding contract for the sale of the property had been entered into. The importance of the debate was that if the latter view prevailed, the contract created by the service of the option notice would fall foul of the strict requirements of s 2 of the Law of Property (Miscellaneous Provisions) Act 1989, since although the option notice might well incorporate, by reference to the option agreement, all of the agreed terms, it would not be signed by or on behalf of both parties.

These problems appear to have been resolved by the case of *Spiro v Glencrown Properties Ltd* [1991] 02 EG 167 where Hoffmann J conveniently described an option contract as a relationship 'sui generis . . . not strictly speaking either an offer or a conditional contract' which had some of the characteristics of each, but not all of either. Whilst not declaring an option to be a conditional contract for every purpose, he was content to view an option for the purposes of s 2 in the light of its characteristics as a conditional contract, which therefore meant that the provisions of s 2 were satisfied.

Once the option agreement has been entered into, the grantee acquires an immediate equitable interest in the land which the grantee must protect by registration of a C(iv) land charge, or notice or caution.

Uses of options

An option agreement may be contemplated in the following situations:

(1) Where planning permission for development proposed by the developer has not yet been applied for, the developer may consider securing an option over the land before investing resources into making an application for permission. Once the application succeeds, the option can be exercised by the developer. This is very similar to a conditional agreement, but with an option, the developer may be able to delay the exercise of the option until he is prepared to part with his money and commence development, whereas under a conditional agreement, as soon as the condition has been satisfied, the developer will have to complete.

(2) Where the land proposed as the site for development is sub-divided amongst landowners, and there is no guarantee that all of them will sell. The developer can assemble the development site gradually, by acquiring options over each parcel of land. Once the entire site is under option, the developer can then apply for planning permission (it would not make financial sense to do so beforehand), and then once permission has been obtained, he could exercise each option.

(3) Where a developer developing a site feels that there is some prospect of his being able to expand the development at some future date, he may attempt to acquire an option over adjacent land which can be exercised when the prospect becomes a reality.

(4) Where a speculator attempts to acquire options over land where there is little immediate prospect of obtaining planning permission (eg because the land forms part of the green belt, or is land not allocated for any particular purpose in the local planning authority development plan). The developer may either adopt a wait-and-see approach in the hope that planning policy in the area changes, or (as is more likely to be the case) he may invest time and resources in seeking to influence planning policy to get the land released for development purposes when the next draft development plan is being prepared. In this way, developers build up considerable land banks to be drawn upon when conditions are right.

Terms of an option

The option will grant the developer the right to acquire the property by serving a written notice on the grantor within a specified period. In an option agreement, time-limits are construed by the courts to be of the essence of the agreement. The option agreement should set out the correct method of serving the option notice, or alternatively incorporate the provisions of s 196 of the Law of Property Act 1925 into the agreement. In specifying a time for the service of the notice, care should be taken to ensure that the rule against perpetuities is not infringed, and that the grantor has sufficient powers vested in him to grant an option capable of being exercised within the time period proposed.

The option will be granted in consideration of an option fee, which can be nominal, but is more likely to be a considerable sum, depending upon the development potential of the land. A landowner, realising the intentions of the grantee, is not likely to grant a valuable interest to him except for adequate consideration. When the option is exercised, the agreement will usually require the land to be conveyed to the grantee for a further consideration (credit usually being given for the option fee already paid) which may be fixed by the agreement at the outset, or may be determined at the time of the exercise of the option either by reference to the market value of the land at that time or by reference to the development value of the land as ascertained by a valuation formula set out in the agreement. It should be noted that both the option agreement, and the subsequent conveyance of the land are subject to ad valorem stamp duty (at the normal rate, with appropriate certificates of value). Further, because of the VAT implications of the transaction, the developer should ensure that the agreement clearly states that the option fee and purchase price is inclusive of VAT. There are also CGT implications for the landowner, since an option is treated as an asset for CGT purposes, separate from the land itself, which is disposed of in consideration of the option fee.

Provision should be made in the agreement for the deduction of title and the raising of requisitions on title after the option notice is served, and for the other usual conveyancing steps which need to be taken before completion. It is usual for the option agreement to incorporate a set of conditions of sale (eg the Standard Conditions of Sale current at the time of the option agreement).

In many cases, the developer will want title to be deduced before the option agreement is entered into (requisitions on title then being barred), and he will require the seller to enter into a condition in the agreement not to incumber the land any further without the developer's consent.

7.3 SEARCHES AND ENQUIRIES

A buyer of development land (or other commercial property) will make the same pre-contract searches, and raise broadly similar pre-contract enquiries as a buyer of residential property. This part of the book does not intend to repeat sections of the LPC Resource Book *Conveyancing* (Jordans), rather it focuses upon the particular concerns of a buyer of a development site at the pre-contract stage.

7.3.1 Local search and enquiries

The usual form of application for a search and enquiries should be submitted to the local authority in duplicate together with the fee. A plan should be attached so that the local authority can identify the land concerned.

In commercial transactions, consideration ought to be given to the possibility of raising the optional enquiries which are set out in Part II of the local authority enquiry form, in addition to the usual Part I enquiries. To make an optional enquiry, the buyer's solicitor should place a tick in the appropriate box at section G on the front page of the enquiry form. An additional fee is payable in respect of each optional enquiry. These enquiries are designed to cover matters which are only relevant in particular kinds of transactions. By way of example, on the acquisition of a development site, the buyer's solicitor ought to consider raising the optional enquiry relating to the location of public footpaths or bridleways which may cross the development site (since consent of the local authority would be required in order to divert them), and the optional enquiry relating to the location of gas pipelines, to see if any run under or near the property (since this may affect development of the land). Prudent purchasers will opt for safety by paying for replies to all of the optional enquiries.

In perusing replies to Part I enquiries, particular attention should be given to information relating to planning matters affecting the property, the location of foul and surface water main drains, and access to the site over adopted highways.

Planning matters

The developer will want to know whether planning permission currently exists in respect of all or part of the site, or whether there have been any past applications for permission which have been unsuccessful. (The fact that an application for development was recently refused will be an important consideration for a developer.) He will also need to know what type of land use is currently indicated by the local planning authority in the development plans for the area in which the site is situated. Any existing or proposed tree preservation orders must be clearly pointed out to the developer.

Drainage

It will be important for the developer to establish how foul and surface water currently drains away from the property to the public sewers (ie through main drains, private drains, or watercourses) so that he can estimate whether the current drainage system will be able to cope with foul and surface drainage from the developed site, or whether new drains will have to be constructed. If the site is vacant land, there are unlikely to be any drains serving it and, therefore, he will need to know the location of the nearest public sewer where connection of newly constructed drains may be made.

Highways

The developer will need to know that immediate access to the site can be obtained from a public highway, and that there are no new highways proposed in the vicinity of the site which would adversely affect his development.

Some of the information to be gleaned from the enquiries may simply confirm matters already known to the developer through site inspections, surveys, and through discussions between the developer and the local authority regarding the possibility of obtaining planning permission to develop the site.

7.3.2 Enquiries of the seller

Pre-contract enquiries of the seller will be raised on one of the standard printed forms of enquiry or on the buyer's solicitors' own word-processed form of enquiry. Additional enquiries may be raised as the buyer's solicitor considers appropriate. These may focus upon discovering further information about the planning status of the site, the location of public drains and highways, and the suitability of the land for building purposes, and possible past contamination of the land. Again, information regarding these matters is often discoverable from other sources, but that alone should not be a sufficient reason for the seller to refuse to provide answers.

7.3.3 Survey and inspection

Even though the land may be vacant, the developer–client should be advised to commission a survey of the land. Primarily, his surveyor will be checking on the suitability of the land for building purposes, both in terms of land stability, and means of access and drainage. However, regard must also be had to the provisions of the EA 1995, and a thorough environmental survey of the land should be conducted to ensure that the developer does not acquire land which could have a potential clean-up liability under that Act.

For a number of reasons, an inspection of the property must always be conducted before exchange of contracts in order to:

(1) assist in establishing ownership of, or responsibility for boundary walls, hedges and fences;
(2) discover the existence of public or private rights of way which may be evidenced by worn footpaths, stiles, or breaks in the hedgerows;
(3) spot the presence of overhead electricity power lines which would prevent or impede development. If there are power lines, the land is likely to be subject to a written wayleave agreement between the landowner and the electricity company giving the company the right to maintain its supply across the land. A copy of the agreement should be requested from the seller;
(4) discover the rights of persons in occupation of the land. Solicitors are accustomed to thinking only in terms of a contributing spouse as the type of person who has occupiers' rights. However, with a development site, it is not unknown for a solicitor to overlook the presence of several cows in the corner of a field, which is unremarkable if the seller is a farmer, but could be serious if the cows are grazing by virtue of rights of common, or under an agricultural or farm business tenancy;
(5) ensure that adjoining landowners do not enjoy the benefit of easements of light or air which would impede the buyer's proposed development.

7.3.4 Special searches

The need to make a search of the commons register maintained by the county council will depend upon the type and location of the land being acquired, but the case of *G & K Ladenbau (UK) Ltd v Crawley and de Reya* [1978] 1 All ER 682 serves as a warning to all solicitors of the dangers of overlooking the necessity for conducting such a search in appropriate cases. In that case, solicitors were held to be negligent for not having carried out a search in respect of a site being acquired for a new factory development. If a rural site is being acquired, a search of the commons register should always be made. If an inner city industrial site is being acquired for redevelopment, such a search would appear to be inappropriate. However, between these two extremes there will be other cases where the buyer's solicitor is unsure as to whether or not such a search is necessary, and in those cases it would, therefore, be prudent to conduct a search.

Other special searches may be appropriate depending on the circumstances of the acquisition.

7.3.5 Investigation of title

Title is almost invariably deduced and investigated at pre-contract stage of the transaction.

A thorough investigation of title is required in the same way as in the case of residential property. The developer–client will be particularly concerned to ensure that the property enjoys the benefit of all necessary easements and rights of access (both for the purpose of developing, and for future occupiers of the completed development) and drainage (for foul and surface water). He will also need to be satisfied that there are no covenants restricting the proposed development or use of the land, or if there are, that they will be released, removed or modified, or that appropriate insurance will be available, and that any easements which burden the property will not prevent or restrict the proposed development or use.

7.4 REPORTING TO THE CLIENT

Before signing the contract, most commercial buyers will expect their solicitor to prepare and deliver a comprehensive written report, covering all aspects of the proposed purchase. The report can serve several useful purposes:

(1) It aids the client in formulating his decision as to whether or not to proceed with the purchase, by identifying all relevant legal considerations upon which his decision will be based, including the drawbacks and risks involved.
(2) It helps the buyer's solicitor to ensure that all necessary steps in the transaction have been taken by serving as a procedural checklist, and it provides written evidence of the advice and information given to the client in connection with the purchase.
(3) It acts as a useful reference aid for both buyer and solicitor in future dealings with the site.
(4) It adds to the quality of service provided by the buyer's solicitor.

The report should be addressed to the client, and should deal with the following matters:

(1) the identity of the property which is the subject matter of the report (described by way of plans where possible);
(2) the name of the seller;
(3) the purchase price stated in the contract;
(4) the title to the property, stating whether it is freehold or leasehold, and registered or unregistered;
(5) any incumbrances affecting the property, including whether the incumbrances are considered to be onerous, and whether indemnity insurance should be considered;
(6) any rights which benefit the property;
(7) the terms of the contract for sale;
(8) matters relevant to planning, and the development of the site;
(9) information obtained from the local search. If there are no onerous entries, the report should say so;
(10) information obtained from the enquiries of the local authority;
(11) information obtained from enquiries of the seller;
(12) the results of other searches.

The report should be signed by the solicitor who prepared the report, dated, and a copy should be kept for the file.

The preparation of a report is an important part of any commercial transaction and it should not be undertaken lightly. Consideration should be given to the recipient of the report (eg trustees of a pension fund with little legal knowledge, or directors of a property company with extensive experience) and drafting techniques should be adapted accordingly. Most commercial firms have their own word-processed form of report which can be used, but it must always be borne in mind that the report will form the basis of an expensive development decision.

Chapter 8

CONSTRUCTION PROJECTS

8.1 INTRODUCTION

Having completed the acquisition of a site which is physically capable of being developed, and which is not incumbered in a way which would impede development, and having obtained satisfactory planning permission and sufficient funds, the client will now want to obtain a building which will be completed within a satisfactory time scale, within budget, and in accordance with his specified requirements.

8.2 WHO WILL BE INVOLVED?

8.2.1 The employer

The employer is the owner of the site who will employ various professionals to design and construct a building upon his land. For the purposes of this book, the employer is a client who has acquired a site with the aim of developing it, and who will grant leases of the completed development. This part of the book assumes that the client, whilst involved in commercial property, is not a member of the construction industry, and will, therefore, need to employ other persons in connection with design and construction.

8.2.2 The building contractor

In a traditional building contract the building contractor is engaged by the employer to construct a building in accordance with plans and specifications prepared by the employer's architect. The contractor (sometimes called the 'main contractor') will enter into a building contract with the employer, although he may not necessarily carry out all, or indeed any, of the building works. Instead, the contractor may enter into sub-contracts with other builders who will carry out the work. The sub-contractors are likely to be specialists in particular areas of the construction industry, so that, in a large project, there may be several different sub-contractors who execute works on different parts of the development. In some building contracts, the employer chooses who will be the sub-contractors, in which case they are called 'nominated sub-contractors'. In other building contracts, it will be the main contractor's responsibility to select the sub-contractors, in which case they are termed 'domestic sub-contractors'. Most traditional forms of building contract only permit sub-contracting with the prior written consent of the employer (to be given through the agency of his architect).

There are many different standard forms of building contract used in the construction industry and this book does not intend a detailed analysis of the obligations of employer and main contractor. The basic obligations of the employer under most traditional forms of contract are to give up possession of the site to the contractor (to enable uninterrupted building to commence), not to interfere with the execution of building works, to appoint an architect for the purposes of the contract (ie to supervise the execution of the works, and to certify when the building has reached the stage of 'practical completion'), to nominate sub-contractors to carry out the works (unless the contractor is to select his own), and to pay the price payable to the contractor as and when the contract requires.

In return, the contractor agrees to complete the work set out in the contract in the form of the architect's plans and specifications. Whether the works have been satisfactorily completed is a matter to be judged by the architect who, if satisfied, will issue a certificate of practical completion which will entitle the contractor to receive full payment of the contract price, and the employer to resume possession of the site for the purpose of granting leases to his tenants. Obligations as to quality and fitness of the building materials are implied under s 4 of the Supply of Goods and Services Act 1982, and s 13 of that Act implies a term that the contractor will exercise reasonable care and skill in the performance of building services. However, notwithstanding his implied obligations, the contractor is likely to have entered into a building contract which contains an express obligation to execute the works in accordance with a standard prescribed by the contract.

It should be noted that there is no privity of contract between the employer and the sub-contractors (whether they are nominated or domestic) since it is the main contractor who engages their services. However, it may be possible to establish an implied collateral contract between them, as in *Shanklin Pier Co Ltd v Detel Products* [1951] 2 KB 854, and further the main contractor may also be liable under the terms of the main contract in respect of the acts or omissions of the sub-contractors.

Some more modern forms of building contract operate quite differently from the traditional form. Design-and-build contracts are increasingly being used in new developments. In simple terms, all of the design work is carried out by the main contractor's architect and, therefore, the employer does not engage an architect. The employer will enter into a single contract with the main contractor under which the contractor agrees both to design (or cause to be designed), and to build. This means that having indicated his requirements to the main contractor, all the employer has to do is wait for the building to be finished, whereupon he can grant a lease of the completed building to a tenant.

8.2.3 The architect

In a traditional form of contract the architect is engaged by the employer to carry out various tasks in relation to the design of the building. Broadly speaking, the architect prepares plans and specifications of the works required by the employer from which the builders will take their instructions, and he will supervise the execution of those works by the building contractor (or sub-contractors) in accordance with the plans and specifications. When the architect is satisfied that the works required by the building contract have been completed, he will issue a certificate of practical completion.

8.2.4 The quantity surveyor

The quantity surveyor is engaged by the employer (or by the architect on behalf of the employer) to estimate the quantities of the materials to be used, and to set them into bills of quantities. What the quantity surveyor does is to measure the amount of work and materials which will be necessary to complete construction in accordance with the architect's plans and specifications. On the basis of his bills of quantities, building contractors will be able to work out the amount of their tenders.

8.2.5 The engineers

In large construction projects, there may be a team of consulting engineers, including a structural engineer, engaged by the employer to give advice on structural design, and mechanical, electrical, heating and ventilating engineers, who give advice to the employer on matters within their areas of competence.

The architect, quantity surveyor and consulting engineers, as professional people, owe the employer a duty by contract to carry out the work required of them with proper care. The standard of care expected is the standard of the ordinary skilled man exercising and professing to have that special skill. If any one of them falls below that standard, or below any higher standard of care set by the contract of engagement under which he is engaged, he will be liable in damages for breach of contract.

8.3 WHAT DUTIES ARE OWED IN TORT?

If the project results in the employer obtaining a completed building which turns out to be defective by reason of its design, or the materials used, or by reason of the manner in which it was constructed, the employer is likely to have an action for breach of contract against those members of the design and construction team who caused the defect. Contractual damages are assessed under the rule in *Hadley v Baxendale* (1854) 9 Exch 341 and are likely to enable the employer to recover any costs incurred in carrying out remedial repairs, subject to the normal limitation rules under the Limitation Act 1980.

However, consider the position of a buyer from the employer who discovers a defect after completion of his purchase of the freehold; or that of a mortgagee of the freehold who discovers that the value of his security is seriously impaired because of a hidden design or construction defect; or that of a tenant of the building who enters into a lease on the basis of a full repairing covenant, which therefore obliges him to repair damage caused by such inherent defects. In the absence of collateral warranties (see **8.4.1**), such persons do not have any contractual relationship with the employer's development team, which means that any remedies they may wish to pursue must be established in tort. However, the problem that the buyer, lender or tenant will encounter is that any loss they sustain as a result of faulty design, materials or workmanship is likely to be classified as pure economic loss and, therefore, generally irrecoverable in tort. For example, in the case of the freehold buyer, if he discovers after completion of his purchase that the foundations of the building have been laid in a negligent fashion, so that the building cannot be used without remedial works first being carried out, he can either execute the repairs himself (thereby incurring repair costs), or dispose of the defective building to someone else (probably at less than the purchase price), or simply abandon the property (thereby wasting the money paid for the building in the first place); but whichever course of action the buyer takes, the loss he incurs is purely economic, and only in limited circumstances will the courts allow the plaintiff to recover such loss in tort.

To establish a claim in negligence the plaintiff will have to show that the defendant owed him a duty of care, that the defendant breached that duty, and that the plaintiff suffered an actionable form of damage as a result. Following a series of House of Lords' decisions in the late 1980s and early 1990s, it is safe to say that liability in the tort of negligence will only arise if there is a breach of one of two categories of duty. The first duty is based upon the decision in *Donoghue v Stevenson* [1932] AC

562 where liability will arise out of a lack of care which results in reasonably foreseeable damage to persons or to property (other than to the property which causes the damage). The second duty is founded upon the case of *Hedley Byrne & Co Ltd v Heller & Partners Ltd* [1964] AC 465 and is concerned with a lack of care which causes non-physical economic loss.

8.3.1 Liability for physical damage

The duty of care under *Donoghue v Stevenson* is a duty to avoid physical injury to person or property. It imposes a duty upon the manufacturer of a product (eg a builder constructing a building) to take reasonable care to avoid damage to person or property through defects in the product. However, it does not impose a duty upon the manufacturer to ensure that the product itself is free from defects. Simply because the design or construction of the building is defective does not necessarily render the person who was responsible for the defect liable in damages, even if a duty was owed, and the damage was foreseeable. The case would turn upon whether the plaintiff suffered a type of loss recognised by the courts as legally recoverable. Pure economic loss (eg the cost of repairing the defect, and the loss of profits while repairs are carried out) is not recoverable under *Donoghue v Stevenson* principles.

In *D & F Estates Ltd v Church Commissioners for England* [1989] AC 177, the House of Lords held that liability in tort only arises where there is some physical damage to person, or to some other property, and that damage to the building itself which merely reduced its value, is pure economic loss, and thus irrecoverable in tort, (except under *Hedley Byrne v Heller* principles). In *Murphy v Brentwood District Council* [1990] 2 All ER 908, the House of Lords reaffirmed its earlier decision, and stated that the idea that component parts of the same building could amount to separate species of property, (the 'complex structure' theory) so that, for example, negligently laid foundations could be said to have damaged 'other' property when they led to cracks appearing in the walls, was not correct.

To give an example of what may be recoverable, consider the position where, after completion of his purchase of the freehold, a defectively constructed roof collapses and causes personal injury to a buyer. The buyer may be able to recover damages in respect of his personal injuries, and any economic loss arising out of those injuries (eg loss of earnings), but he will not be able to recover the cost of repairing the roof itself since that loss is pure economic loss.

8.3.2 Liability for economic loss

Economic loss is a term which can be used to describe any monetary loss. Pure economic loss is monetary loss which is not connected to physical injury to person or property. With one or two isolated and doubtful exceptions (see eg *Junior Books v Veitchi* [1983] 1 AC 520), pure economic loss is only recoverable in tort where, in a special relationship of close proximity, a duty of care is owed to avoid loss arising from a negligent misstatement. In *Hedley Byrne & Co Ltd v Heller & Partners Ltd* [1964] AC 465, the House of Lords decided that, in a relationship of close proximity, where a person was seeking information from one who was possessed of certain skills, a duty was owed by the latter to exercise reasonable care if he knew, or ought to have known that reliance was being placed upon his skill and judgment. Put simply, the duty amounts to a duty to prevent pure economic loss arising from the making of a statement, or the giving of advice. In the context of a building project, many statements are made, and much advice is given, but proximity of the parties, and reliance are the fundamental factors.

The extent of this duty has recently been restated and redefined by the House of Lords in *Caparo Industries plc v Dickman* [1990] 2 AC 605. It is now the case that, in order for there to be the requisite degree of proximity between the parties for the duty to arise, the defendant (ie the person who made the statement, or gave the advice) must have known (both in the preparation of what was said, and in the delivery) that the statement would be communicated to an identified person or group of persons in connection with a transaction of a particular type, and that the recipient would be very likely to rely upon it.

Whilst the employer, by reason of his contractual relationship with his professional advisers (eg the architect, or structural engineer) might easily establish the requisite degree of proximity, and show reliance upon the advice given, his tenant, buyer, or the buyer's lender are unlikely to be able to show the requisite proximity. In other words, the pure economic loss that a successor in title to the employer suffers remains irrecoverable.

As a result of this inability to recover the cost of repairing damage to the building outside a contractual relationship, various devices have been utilised by buyers, their lenders, tenants, and the employer's own financiers.

8.4 PROTECTING OTHER PARTIES

8.4.1 Collateral warranties

A collateral warranty is an agreement (under hand or by deed) entered into by someone engaged in the construction or design of a building by virtue of which that person assumes a contractual duty of care for the benefit of someone who has an interest in seeing that the building is free from defects, but who does not otherwise have a contractual relationship with the warrantor. Collateral warranties are commonly required to be given by the consultants, the main contractor and the sub-contractors to the freehold buyer, his lender, the developer's financiers, and possibly (if negotiated) the tenant. With one exception, the employer does not need warranties, as he is in a contractual relationship with his design and construction team. However, he will require warranties from the sub-contractors with whom the employer has no direct contractual relationship.

The advantages of warranties are twofold. First, they create the certainty of a contractual relationship, as opposed to the uncertainty that exists in tort. All the plaintiff would need to show in order to establish a claim is that the contractual duty contained in the warranty had been breached, and that damage had ensued. Secondly, the beneficiary of the warranty is likely to be able to recover in contract loss that can be described as purely economic. All the plaintiff has to show in this regard is that the loss suffered as a result of the breach of warranty could reasonably be said to have been in the contemplation of the parties at the time the warranty was entered into.

The main disadvantage of collateral warranties appears to be that the Latent Damage Act 1986 which, in certain situations, extends the limitation period for bringing civil actions, does not apply to claims for breach of contract and, therefore, if defects do not manifest themselves until more than 6 years after the warranty was entered into (or 12 years if by deed), no action can then be brought.

Many firms of solicitors have their own preferred form of collateral warranty and, although attempts have been made to standardise the type of warranty to be used in the construction industry, those attempts have not always been enthusiastically received. In practice, the terms of collateral warranties are being dictated increasingly by the warrantor's professional indemnity insurers, who are concerned to limit their potential liability. Most warranties will contain a basic warranty by the warrantor that he has exercised and will continue to exercise reasonable skill and care in the performance of his duties under the contract of engagement with the employer, and that the warrantor will maintain professional indemnity insurance with cover up to a stated amount. There is usually a clause preventing or restricting the assignment of the benefit of the warranty. It is extremely unlikely that warranties will be given after the professional has been engaged. It is therefore essential that the professional is contractually committed to give warranties by the contract of engagement.

It seems that an action in contract arising out of a breach of a collateral warranty will not exclude an alternative action in tort (if a cause of action exists). In *Henderson v Merrett Syndicates Ltd* [1994] 3 All ER 506, Lord Goff said that 'an assumption of responsibility, coupled with the concomitant reliance, may give rise to a tortious duty of care irrespective of whether there is a contractual relationship between the parties, and in consequence, unless the contract precludes him from doing so, the plaintiff, who has available to him concurrent remedies in contract and tort, may choose that remedy which appears to him to be the most advantageous'.

8.4.2 Other methods

Assignment of rights

The employer may consider attempting to satisfy the demands of his financier, buyer or tenant for protection against latent defects by assigning whatever rights the employer may have (primarily under contract law) against the contractor and the consultants. An assignment is probably only appropriate if made in favour of a financier, a buyer or a tenant of the whole of the development site. However, even where a tenant takes a lease of the whole of a development site, a landlord will be reluctant to part with his contractual rights in case the tenant's lease is forfeited or disclaimed.

Building contracts and contracts for the engagement of consultants may contain prohibitions on the assignment of the benefit of the contract without consent and it now seems that, following the House of Lords' decision in *Linden Garden Trust Ltd v Lenesta Sludge Disposals Ltd*, and *St Martin's Property Corporation Ltd v Sir Robert McAlpine Ltd* [1993] 3 WLR 408, most prohibitions will be effective, although each clause will have to be interpreted to discover its exact meaning.

Declaring a trust of rights

Declaring a trust of rights may be considered as an alternative to an outright assignment where the employer is retaining an interest in the property and, therefore, does not wish to part with valuable contractual rights. In this way the employer can retain the benefit of the rights he has against the contractor and consultants, but declares that he holds them upon trust for the benefit of himself and his tenants.

Latent defects insurances

With residential properties, buyers are anxious to ensure that a newly constructed property is covered by the NHBC scheme, or other equivalent insurance. In the commercial field, there are no such standard schemes. However, following the BUILD report (Building Users Insurance against Latent Defects) published in 1988 by the National Economic Development Office, several of the leading insurance companies in the UK have introduced latent defects insurance in respect of commercial properties.

Policies will vary from company to company (and, indeed, from development to development), but the essential elements are likely to be similar across the board. Latent defect insurance commonly provides cover against damage caused by defective design or construction works for a period of 10 years after practical completion of the development (or such longer period as may be agreed with the insurer). The beneficiary of the policy is covered against the cost of making good most (but not necessarily all) damage caused by a design or construction defect (although not other risks), and the policy may cover other items of economic loss such as loss of rent, or loss of use of the building whilst repairs are being carried out. The policy can be taken out to cover the employer (as initial owner of the building) and his financiers. Most policies will also automatically insure subsequent owners and occupiers, which will obviously be the desired aim from the employer's point of view. The premium is likely to be substantial (perhaps 1.5 per cent of development costs).

The advantages of such a policy is that there is no need for the claimant under the policy to establish legal liability for the damage incurred, and there ought to be easy access to funds to finance repairing costs and, possibly, to cover other economic loss. The disadvantages are that, as with other policies, the insurance may be subject to excesses (meaning that the claimant might have to fund, say, the first £50,000 of a claim), and that the insurer will invariably require some element of supervision over the execution of the works, since the risk he is taking on will be considerable. Such insurance is not something which can be obtained economically after the construction process is complete.

Proposals have been put to the European Commission regarding compulsory insurance of all new residential, commercial and civil engineering construction projects (see the Mathurin Report 1990) and legislation in this area may eventually materialise.

Limiting repair covenants

In a landlord and tenant relationship, the tenant should consider limiting the scope of his repairing covenant. The main problem for a tenant is that the landlord is likely to insist upon the tenant entering into a lease which contains a covenant by the tenant to repair the demised premises. Provided the damage amounts to disrepair (see **19.2.6**), the usual repair covenant imposed by the landlord will oblige the tenant to repair damage which is caused by a defect in the design or construction of the building. Whilst the tenant can commission a full structural survey of the premises prior to the grant of the lease in an effort to discover defects, the very nature of a design or construction defect makes it unlikely that it will exhibit itself until some time after the building has been completed and the lease granted.

It is, therefore, suggested that, on the grant of a lease of a relatively new building, the tenant should attempt to limit the scope of his repairing covenant by excluding (either totally, or for a limited period of, say, 3 or 6 years after the grant of the lease) liability to repair damage caused by an inherent, or latent, design or construction defect. Not only should the tenant seek to exclude such liability from his own covenant, but he should make sure that no vacuum is left in the repairing

obligations under the lease by insisting that the landlord assumes this liability. If this is not done, there is a risk that the property may remain in disrepair. The landlord will be anxious to avoid having to bear any repair costs in respect of the building, and so the limitation of the tenant's repairing obligations is a matter to be negotiated and will depend upon the relative bargaining strengths of the parties. It is most unlikely that the tenant would succeed in his negotiations if, in the agreement for lease, the tenant had insisted upon a degree of control and supervision over the execution of the landlord's works (see **29.3.4**). The landlord would probably argue that the tenant had had every opportunity before the lease was granted to discover defects, and that he should, therefore, consider taking action against his professional advisers.

On the grant of a lease of part of a building, where the tenant would not ordinarily undertake repairing responsibilities in respect of the structure and external parts, but would instead be expected to contribute by way of service charge to the landlord's costs incurred in maintaining those parts, the tenant would seek to ensure that he was not obliged to contribute to the landlord's costs of repairing damage caused by design or construction defects (either throughout the term, or for a limited period). Again, whilst the tenant could commission a full structural survey, design defects may not be apparent at the time of the survey, or may be hidden in some other part of the building to which the surveyor was unable to gain access.

Defect liability periods

In a landlord and tenant relationship, the tenant may seek the benefit of a defect liability period. If the landlord will not agree to exclude the tenant's liability for inherent defects in the lease, the tenant ought to press for the inclusion of a clause in the agreement for lease obliging the landlord to remedy any defects which appear within a short period of time following practical completion of the building. If the landlord agrees to the inclusion of a defects liability period, it is likely to mirror a similar clause in the building contract entered into with the contractor. Quite often building contracts provide for the contractor to remedy any defects which manifest themselves within, say, the first 6 or 12 months after practical completion. By including a similar clause in the agreement for lease, the landlord is indirectly passing on the benefit of the clause to the tenant.

Forced enforcement of remedies

A tenant may seek a side letter, or supplemental deed from his landlord whereby the landlord agrees to enforce any rights he may have against the contractor or the consultants, by way of civil proceedings, in respect of defects which would otherwise render the tenant liable to repair under the repairing covenant. However, whether the landlord suffers any loss upon which an action could be based is doubtful where the tenant has entered into a full repairing lease.

A buyer, financier or tenant may seek the inclusion of a provision whereby the employer agrees to enforce his rights as original contracting party against the contractor or the consultants in respect of defects where loss or liability to repair would otherwise fall upon the former. Difficulties have arisen in this area in that, if the employer has received full market value on a sale of the property to a buyer, or has secured the inclusion of a full repairing covenant on the grant of a lease of the property to a tenant, he cannot be said to have suffered any loss upon which an action could be maintained.

However, the House of Lords' decision in the *Linden Garden* case has shown that in a commercial contract where it was in the contemplation of the contracting parties that title to the property which formed the subject matter of the contract might be transferred to a third party before a breach had occurred, the original contracting party is taken to have entered into the contract for the benefit of himself and all persons who may acquire an interest in the property before the breach occurs. What this means is that, in certain circumstances, the employer may be able to recover damages for breach of contract in respect of loss incurred by his buyer, financier or tenant. This area is not without its complications, and the full ramifications of recent developments in this area have not yet been explored.

Obtaining collateral warranties has been, in the past and is likely to be in the future, the preferred method of obtaining protection against construction and design defects.

Chapter 9

FUNDING THE DEVELOPMENT

Chapter 9 contents
Introduction
Who gets involved?
Two principal forms of finance
Various methods of providing finance

9.1 INTRODUCTION

The funding of commercial property transactions is in itself a complex and specialised area of practice, and this chapter is intended only as an introduction to some of the elementary features. Generalisations cannot easily be made, since different funding arrangements are devised by institutions in relation to the particular circumstances of the development concerned. In all cases, there will be accounting and taxation implications behind the chosen method of finance, and issues of corporate share structuring may be involved. However, these issues are beyond the scope of this book.

9.2 WHO GETS INVOLVED?

In any new commercial property development project, there are three essential ingredients: land, development expertise, and finance. Occasionally, all three ingredients are present within one organisation, where, for example, a major construction company, with a sufficient land bank, is able to invest its own resources in the construction of a new building. The organisation may then either retain the completed (and fully let) development as an income-producing investment, or sell the reversion to realise capital.

However, in most cases, the ingredients are provided by separate persons or institutions. For instance, the landowner may be a construction company with the necessary development expertise, but insufficient finance. A funding institution may have identified a site for development, but needs expertise to execute its plans. A property-owning institution may need both finance and development expertise. For ease of explanation this chapter assumes that the person who owns the land, has development expertise, but is in need of finance. Whilst private individuals are sometimes involved in commercial development projects, in most cases the persons involved are private or public limited companies.

Finance frequently comes from leading insurance companies, who are able to invest money comprised in life assurance funds, and the pension funds of large organisations. These are traditional long-term owners of commercial investment properties, having control over substantial sums of long-term investment money, and being interested in long-term capital growth. Other providers of finance include the clearing banks, merchant banks (both domestic and overseas) and some of the larger building societies, who are often more concerned with shorter-term returns on development finance.

9.3 TWO PRINCIPAL FORMS OF FINANCE

Debt financing and equity financing are the two principal forms of development finance.

Debt finance is simply borrowed money. The developer can raise debt finance by borrowing against the strength of the development (in which case, it is called project finance), or against the strength of the company as a whole (in which case it is called corporate finance). Project finance will be secured in some way against the development, either by taking a charge over the development site, or by entering into a funding agreement with the developer, which will result in a transfer of the freehold to the funding institution. Corporate finance, on the other hand, may be secured against all or any of the assets of the company, by way of fixed and/or floating charges. In practice, corporate financing is only available to large established property companies who have sufficient assets to offer as security for the loan to the company. Smaller developers may have little more than the development itself to offer as security.

Equity finance is money which is put up on the basis of an entitlement to share in the profits of the development, or the development company. The simplest example of equity finance is money put up in return for part of the ordinary share capital of the development company. Instead of receiving a return of capital injection with interest, the investor shares fully in the profits of the development, but also in the risks. The benefit of this form of finance from the developer's point of view is that, unlike debt finance, equity finance does not have to be repaid (unless the shares are redeemable). The investor recovers his outlay by way of a dividend on his shares. Usually, the funding institution is given preference shares in the company which carry a preferential right to a dividend. The precise characteristics of preference shares will differ from company to company depending upon the articles of association, but it is common to find that preference shares pay a fixed dividend, in preference to ordinary shareholders, and that they rank ahead of ordinary shares in a liquidation.

Equity finance carries a greater risk than debt finance. If the debt finance is secured, the funder can resort to its security in the event of business failure. However, if equity finance has been given in return for share capital (whether ordinary or preference) the investor will rank behind secured lenders, preferential creditors and unsecured creditors in a liquidation. To compensate for the added risk involved, equity finance usually gives a greater return to the investor than debt finance.

A form of finance which falls mid-way between the above two is mezzanine finance, which is high-risk finance provided over and above normal financing levels. For instance, if a funding institution is ordinarily only prepared to provide finance up to a limit of 80 per cent of total project development costs, but agrees to exceed that level, the institution will expect extra returns in respect of the additional layer of finance, by way of higher interest rates or, more commonly, a share in the profits of the development.

9.4 VARIOUS METHODS OF PROVIDING FINANCE

9.4.1 Loan finance

Loan finance is the simplest form of debt finance. Capital sums are made available to the developer in return for security and interest repayments. Depending on the size of the company and amount of finance, security may be taken over all the assets of the company in the form of a fixed and floating charge, or just over the development site itself. If corporate finance is being provided, the provider will be concerned with the strength of the company (its assets, liabilities, cash flow and profits), whereas with project finance, the provider has to be satisfied with the development itself (its viability, the estimated costs, target rents, time estimates, capital value at completion, pedigree of the builder).

The formalities required for creating fixed and floating security, including the passing of appropriate resolutions, and the requirement for registration, and the powers and remedies of a chargee or debenture-holder are dealt with in the LPC Resource Book *Business Law and Practice* (Jordans).

9.4.2 Joint ventures

The joint venture vehicle is a common method of combining the resources of land, development expertise and finance to execute a particular project, and then share in the profits. It involves a form of equity financing.

The usual vehicle is a joint venture company. The advantages of adopting a limited company as the vehicle is that the company will be a separate legal entity, able to own land and enter into contracts in its own name. Constituent members of the venture can join or leave without the need for a transfer of title. Finance can be provided to the company either in the form of borrowings (secured by fixed and/or floating charges), or in return for shares which can be issued to the funder as preference shares giving the funder a priority return on his shareholding without necessarily giving him a controlling interest. The corporate vehicle will have the benefit of limited liability.

Alternative methods of establishing a joint venture include joint venture partnerships and purely contractual joint venture relationships. Partnership is defined in s 1 of the Partnership Act 1890 as a relationship 'which subsists between persons who carry on a business in common with a view to profit'. Hence the sharing of profits and losses from a property development will generally give rise to a partnership. The benefits of a non-corporate joint venture include the fact that there are no requirements to file annual returns (thereby reducing administrative expenses) and no requirement to disclose accounts. However, in partnerships, ownership of property is not as straightforward, the injection of finance may not be as easy (the constitutions of many pension funds prevent entry by the trustees of the fund into a partnership), and there is unlimited and several liability. Contractual joint ventures cover a wide variety of development and financing agreements where there is an arrangement for the sharing of resources and profits on terms stopping short of a partnership. Taxation considerations, which are not considered here, will also influence the choice of joint venture vehicle.

9.4.3 Funding agreements

Project finance is money provided to a company in respect of a single project, and which is secured in some way against that project. Typically, project finance is given by a funding institution to a development company under the terms of a funding agreement between the two. The developer acquires the land and develops it; the funding institution provides the finance.

In the funding agreement (which is, in essence, a contractual joint venture) the developer agrees to construct (or cause to be constructed), a specified type of building in return for finance which may cover the initial site acquisition cost (if the land is not already owned by the developer), construction costs and professional fees. The finance is likely to be provided in several stages (eg the first at the acquisition of the site, the last at practical completion, and others at various agreed stages of development).

As well as being obliged to construct, the developer will be obliged to secure one letting of the entire development, or separate lettings of identified parts, at a rent level specified in the agreement. The agreement is likely to state that the leases are to be granted in the funding institution's standard form of commercial lease, for a term of 25 years with upward-only rent reviews at every 5th year of the term. The funding institution may want the ability to vet potential tenants procured by the developer.

Once the development has been completed and the building is fully let, the agreement is likely to provide that the developer is to transfer the reversion to the funding institution in return for a capital payment based on the capital value of the development, less development finance (and possibly a development finance fee).

Funding institutions may be reluctant to step in to complete a development where the developer goes into liquidation, or walks away from the development, and frequently the institution will insist that the obligations of the developer are backed up by a parent company guarantee.

9.4.4 Sale and leaseback

Sale and leaseback involves the conversion of a capital asset into development finance at the expense of regular income repayments. In the context of commercial property developments, it involves transfer of the freehold interest in the development site by the developer to the funding institution, in return for a capital sum to finance development, and a long lease of the site (eg 99 or 125 years) at an annual rent which represents repayment of the finance. To make a profit, the developer secures sub-lettings of the completed development on 25-year leases at open market rents. The head-lease rent is likely to provide the funding institution with a guaranteed annual repayment of the development finance, together with a share of the sub-lease rents.

PART II

COMMERCIAL LEASES

Chapter 10

LANDLORD AND TENANT LAW AND COMMERCIAL LEASES

Chapter 10 contents

10.1 INTRODUCTION

A thorough knowledge and understanding of landlord and tenant law is essential for all commercial conveyancers; without such an understanding it would be impossible to properly advise clients on their rights and liabilities under the lease. Consequently, this part of the book starts with a consideration of the more important principles governing the relationship between landlords and tenants of business premises.

10.2 LIABILITY OF THE PARTIES ON THE COVENANTS IN THE LEASE

The detailed rules relating to the enforceability of covenants are considered in Chapter 14. The following is intended only as an outline of the main issues involved.

10.2.1 Leases granted before 1 January 1996

Position of the original parties

Unless the lease provides to the contrary, the original parties will remain liable on their express covenants in the lease by privity of contract throughout the whole term, despite any disposition of their interests. Thus, the original tenant must appreciate that he will be liable not just for breaches committed whilst he is the tenant but also for any breach of covenant committed by his successors. This continuing liability may have serious consequences for the original tenant and means, for example, that he will be liable for any arrears of rent occurring throughout the whole term.

In the same way, through privity of contract, the original landlord will remain liable on his covenants to the original tenant for the whole term, despite any assignment by him of the reversion, ie he will be liable to the original tenant if a buyer of the reversion breaks a covenant.

Position of landlord and tenant for the time being

The relationship between an assignee of the lease and the landlord for the time being and between a buyer of the reversion and the tenant for the time being rests on the doctrine of privity of estate. Liability under this doctrine only extends to those covenants which touch and concern the land.

Further, a party is only liable for breaches committed during his period of ownership of the lease or reversion, as the case may be. Thus, for example, an assignee of the lease, for the period while he has the lease, has the benefit of the landlord's covenants and is liable on the tenant's covenants provided, in both cases, the covenants touch and concern the land.

10.2.2 Leases granted on or after 1 January 1996

The Landlord and Tenant (Covenants) Act 1995 (LTCA 1995) abolished the concept of privity of contract for leases entered into on or after 1 January 1996. Thus once the original tenant has assigned the lease he is not liable for any future breaches (although he may be required to guarantee his immediate assignee: see **20.2.8**). On a sale of the reversion, the landlord may apply to the tenant for release from the landlord's covenants in the lease (see **14.2.2** and Chapter 35).

10.3 SECURITY OF TENURE

The majority of business tenants will enjoy security of tenure under Part II of the Landlord and Tenant Act 1954 (LTA 1954) and the importance of this Act in its effect on termination of the lease cannot be overstated. The protection given to tenants covered by the Act is twofold. First, a business tenancy will not come to an end at the expiration of a fixed term, nor can a periodic tenancy be terminated by the landlord serving an ordinary notice to quit. Instead, notwithstanding the ending of the contractual term, the tenancy will be automatically continued under s 24 until such time as it is terminated in one of the ways specified in the Act. Secondly, upon the expiration of a business tenancy in accordance with the Act, business tenants normally have a statutory right to apply to court for a new tenancy and the landlord may only oppose that application on certain statutory grounds (some of which involve the payment of compensation by the landlord if the tenant has to leave). Any new tenancy granted will also enjoy the protection of the Act.

It is possible, in certain circumstances, for the landlord and tenant to apply to court to contract out of the Act, but certain formalities must be observed.

Further consideration of this Act is dealt with in Chapter 34.

10.4 LEASE/LICENCE DISTINCTION

The security of tenure provisions in the LTA 1954 and other statutory provisions dealt with later do not apply to licences. It therefore becomes necessary to examine the distinction between a lease and a licence. A lease is an interest in land. A licence on the other hand confers no interest in land; it merely authorises that which would otherwise be a trespass. One of the leading cases in this area is *Street v Mountford* [1985] 2 All ER 289. Whilst this case concerned a residential tenancy, similar principles have subsequently been applied to business tenancies. Subject to certain exceptions, for example, lack of intention to create legal relations or occupation pending the grant of a lease, the House of Lords held that as a general rule:

(1) the grant of exclusive possession,
(2) for a term,
(3) at a rent,

will create a tenancy rather than a licence; and the court will ignore any shams or pretences aimed at misleading the court.

In the context of business premises, some arrangements will clearly not confer exclusive possession and will thus remain licences, for example, the 'shop within a shop' sometimes found in department stores, or the kiosks often found in theatres or hotel foyers. Moreover, there seems to be a greater readiness by the courts to find that exclusive possession was not granted than is the case with residential premises (see, eg, *Dresden Estates v Collinson* [1987] 1EGLR 45, and *Esso Petroleum Co Ltd v Fumegrange Ltd* [1994] 46 EG 199).

To avoid the risk inadvertently of creating a lease, the use of licences needs very careful consideration. As an alternative, the parties should consider the 'contracting out' provisions in the LTA 1954.

Chapter 11

THE ROLE OF THE SOLICITOR

Chapter 11 contents

11.1 TAKING INSTRUCTIONS FROM THE LANDLORD

Lease drafting is not just a question of finding the right precedent and filling in the blanks. Each case produces its own problems and these need to be identified as early as possible by taking full and proper instructions from the client upon the terms of the proposed lease. The parties will, no doubt, already have agreed some of the more important matters and terms, such as the extent of the premises, initial rent, the length of the term, and responsibility for repairs, before consulting solicitors. If surveyors have been engaged in the negotiations, they are likely to have reached a much more advanced stage of agreement as to terms. To the extent that the terms were professionally negotiated, there should not be too much need to depart from them. If they were not, care should be taken to assess the terms which the parties have agreed in principle, and decide whether they can safely be proceeded with, or whether the client needs to rethink his proposals.

In any event the landlord's solicitor will need full instructions on the following matters (all of which are dealt with in more detail later). It will also be appreciated that the tenant's solicitor will be equally concerned with these matters but looked at from a different perspective.

11.1.1 Full names and addresses of all the parties and their respective agents

Often, the only parties to the lease will be the landlord and tenant but this is not always the case. From the landlord's point of view, he will be concerned to ensure that the tenant is in a position to pay the rent and perform all the other obligations in the lease, especially where the tenant is a company whose financial standing is unknown. The landlord will no doubt take up bank and other references and ask to see audited accounts (for the last, say, 3 years) and a full company search can also be made. If the landlord is still not satisfied, he may wish to consider whether there should be a guarantor of the tenant's obligations under the lease. If so, the guarantor must be made a party to the lease.

11.1.2 A full description of the premises to be let

On a lease of the whole of a building the postal address may suffice at this stage. On a lease of part of a building the lease will have to define with precision the vertical and horizontal boundaries of the demised premises and thus a professionally prepared plan will be essential. Again, on a lease of part, consideration must be given to the rights to be granted to the tenant and reserved to the landlord. These should be set out in detail in the lease.

If any fixtures are included in the demise a full inventory should be supplied.

11.1.3 Duration

The lease may be periodic or for a fixed term. To give both parties the certainty they need for their respective businesses most business leases are granted for a fixed term (and this will no doubt already have been agreed between the parties). However, there are some other matters upon which instructions may need to be sought and advice given. Is the commencement of the term to be the same date as the date of completion? Is either party to be given the benefit of a break clause? This is a right to bring the lease to an end prematurely at specified intervals or on the happening of specified events. For example, the tenant may be embarking upon a new business venture and may want the right to break the term after, say, 2 years if the venture is making a loss. On the other hand, the landlord may want the right to break the term if at some future date he acquires planning permission to redevelop the premises.

The parties will need to be advised of the effect on the duration of the lease of Part II of the LTA 1954. If the lease is protected by the Act, it will be continued beyond the contractual expiry date on the same terms and at the same rent as before and can only be terminated in certain specified ways. It is possible to contract out of the LTA 1954 but the court's approval must be obtained before the lease commences, and thus it is something which must be considered now.

11.1.4 Rent and premium

Like the length of the term, the rent is already likely to have been agreed by the parties. Other matters to consider include whether the rent is to be paid in advance or arrears and the frequency and method of payment. It is unusual for a premium to be paid by the tenant on the grant of a business lease; instead the tenant will pay a full market rent.

11.1.5 Rent review

The object of a rent review clause is to enable the landlord to ensure that the rent payable throughout the term keeps pace with any general rise in rental values, whether caused by inflation or otherwise. Thus, the clause will usually provide for the rent to be reviewed (usually upwards only) at specified intervals during the term, say, at the end of every 3rd or 5th year. At the review date an open market rent will be substituted for the rent previously payable. There are other methods of assessing the reviewed rent, for example, by reference to the turnover of the tenant's business or by linking it to the rise in the retail prices index (see **18.3**).

11.1.6 Rent-free periods and inducements

Is the tenant being offered a rent-free period? It is not uncommon for a tenant to be given a rent-free period, for example, during fitting out of the premises. It is sometimes thought preferable to allow tenants to fit out premises to their own individual requirements, during which period no rent will be charged as the premises are not yet capable of beneficial use. Further, in difficult times, rent-free periods may also be offered by landlords as an inducement to tenants to take the lease. In a similar way the landlord may offer what is known as a 'reverse premium', this being a sum of money paid by the landlord to the tenant on the grant of the lease as an inducement to the tenant to enter into the lease.

All these are matters upon which specialist valuation advice must be sought.

11.1.7 VAT

Unlike residential conveyancing, VAT may be payable on the sums which the tenant pays to the landlord under the lease. If the landlord has incurred VAT in the course of acquiring, developing, or redeveloping the property, he may decide to elect to charge VAT to the tenant on the rent and other sums payable under the lease, so that the landlord can recover from HM Customs & Excise VAT incurred. However, landlords should be aware of the effect this election may have on potential tenants. If the tenants make mainly standard-rated or zero-rated supplies in the course of their business, they will not be adversely affected by the election because they will be able to recover the VAT on the rent by deducting it from their output tax (actual or deemed). If, however, tenants make only exempt supplies (eg, banks and insurance companies) they will not be able to do this and the VAT they pay will be irrecoverable, and will have to be borne as an overhead of the business. These tenants may seek a covenant from the landlord not to make the election at any time during the lease.

Before electing to charge VAT, specialist tax advice will be required by the landlord.

Detailed consideration of this issue and the implications for both landlord and tenant are dealt with at **12.1**.

11.1.8 Responsibility for repairs

Unless the lease makes it clear which party is responsible for repairing the premises, neither party may be responsible. If the lease is of the whole of a building, it would be usual for the tenant to be made responsible for all repairs. If, however, the lease is of only part of a building, the responsibility for repairs will usually be divided between the parties. For example, the tenant may be made liable for internal non-structural repairs whilst the landlord covenants to repair the remainder of the building. Any expense incurred by the landlord in complying with his obligation is usually recovered from the tenant under the service charge provisions so that the landlord is not out of pocket.

The standard of repair will be determined by reference to the age, character and condition of the premises at the time the lease was granted and thus the tenant need only keep them in the same condition as they were when let to him. If, however, the premises are in disrepair at the date of the lease, a covenant to 'keep in repair' will require the tenant to first put the premises into repair (according to their age, character and locality), and then to keep them in repair. Consideration should also be given to the responsibility for the repair and maintenance of any fixtures included in the demise.

The landlord will usually also require the tenant to decorate the premises at specified intervals during the term, in a manner and with materials to be approved by the landlord.

11.1.9 Alienation

Unless the lease contains some restriction, the tenant will be free to deal with his interest in any way he wishes. He will be able to assign the lease, grant sub-leases of the whole or part, charge the lease and part with possession of the premises, without obtaining his landlord's consent. Complete freedom like this is unlikely to prove acceptable to the landlord because the tenant may, for example, assign the lease to someone who turns out to be unable to pay the rent or perform the other obligations in the lease. For this reason the landlord will wish to exercise some control over dealings with the tenant's interest. The landlord could impose an absolute covenant against any dealing with the lease but this would be unacceptable to the tenant because he would, for example, be unable to dispose of the premises if they became surplus to his requirements. Whilst the landlord might be prepared to allow an assignment in a particular case, there is no obligation on him to do so and no requirement that he give reasons for his refusal to do so. Instead, it is much more likely that the lease will contain a qualified covenant against dealings, ie not to assign, underlet etc without the landlord's consent. In this situation, s 19(1)(a) of the Landlord and Tenant Act 1927 (LTA 1927) provides that, notwithstanding any contrary provision, a covenant not to assign, underlet, charge or part with possession of the demised premises or any part thereof without the landlord's licence or consent, is subject to a proviso that such licence or consent is not to be unreasonably withheld. As an alternative to the provisions contained in s 19(1)(a) of the LTA 1927, the parties may set out in advance the conditions which must be satisfied before the landlord will consent to an assignment (LTCA 1995, and see Chapter 15). If they do not, the provisions of s 19(1)(a) of the LTA 1927 will apply in the usual way.

As a general rule the landlord will probably wish to insert an absolute covenant against dealing with part of the premises, and a qualified covenant against assigning or sub-letting the whole of the premises. In respect of a qualified covenant, the parties should consider whether to modify the provisions of s 19(1)(a) of the LTA 1927 by specifying in advance the conditions which must be satisfied before the landlord will consent to an assignment (see Chapter 20).

11.1.10 User

As between the landlord and tenant, the tenant is entitled to make what legal use he likes of premises let to him unless the lease restricts him in some way. A landlord will, therefore, require his tenant to enter into covenants which restrict the user of the premises to prevent them from being used in a way which reduces their value, or to protect the landlord's interest in other property. For example, in a shopping centre the landlord will want to obtain a balanced mix of retail trades and stop the shops from competing with each other; this makes them more attractive to potential tenants.

Although the lease may impose a positive obligation on the tenant to use the premises for a particular purpose, it is more common to impose a negative form of covenant such as not to use the premises for any purposes other than those specified. It may not always be necessary to insist upon such strict control and merely prohibiting certain trades, perhaps to avoid unwanted competition, or all offensive trades, may suffice in particular circumstances. Covenants restricting use frequently provide for variation with the landlord's consent and this provision may or may not be qualified by the additional requirement that such consent shall not be unreasonably withheld. From the tenant's point of view, expressly including this additional requirement will be essential, since there is no statutory implied proviso that the landlord's consent shall not be unreasonably withheld. Section 19(3) of the LTA 1927 merely prohibits the charging of a fine or increased rent as the price of giving consent under a qualified covenant restricting user (unless structural alterations are involved) and in the absence of express provision the landlord may be as unreasonable as he likes in refusing consent.

The landlord should take care not to draft the user clause too tightly as this may affect the rent payable on the grant of the lease and at review.

Finally, the landlord will need to take account of covenants affecting the freehold and planning requirements. As a general rule there is no implied warranty on the landlord's part that the permitted use of the premises is allowed under the Planning Acts or that it is not in breach of a covenant contained in a superior title. Further, the lease will usually contain an express provision that the landlord does not warrant that the tenant's use is a permitted use and it will, therefore, be for the tenant to satisfy himself that the intended use is permitted (see *Hill v Harris* [1965] 2 QB 601).

11.1.11 Alterations and improvements

To the extent that the lease is silent, the tenant's freedom to make alterations or improvements is governed largely by the law of waste. As this is unlikely to provide the landlord with the degree of control he requires, invariably there will be a covenant in the lease against alterations by the tenant to prevent any undesirable changes from being made. Such a covenant may be absolute, preventing any alterations, or qualified by the addition of the words 'not without the landlord's consent'. If there is a qualified covenant against making improvements, s 19(2) of the LTA 1927 implies a proviso that such consent is not to be unreasonably withheld. The distinction between alterations and improvements is dealt with at **22.3.2**.

Commonly, a landlord will want a fully qualified covenant against making internal alterations, and an absolute bar on external and structural alterations.

11.1.12 Insurance

There is no implied obligation on either party to insure the demised premises. However, it is very important to both parties that their respective interests are fully protected and it is, therefore, essential for the lease to make express provision for insurance. In a lease of business premises, it is common practice for the landlord to effect the insurance cover. On a lease of part of a building, for example, one unit in a shopping centre or a suite of offices in a block, it is more appropriate for the landlord to arrange the insurance for the whole building including all the common parts. On the grant of a lease of a single building to a single tenant, either party could be made to insure but the landlord will usually wish to assume the responsibility rather than run the risk of the tenant failing to comply with his covenant to insure. If the landlord effects the insurance, the tenant, before completion of the lease, will ask to see a copy of the policy so that he can satisfy himself as to the amount and terms of cover. Further, as the tenant has a continuing interest in the insurance of the demised premises, he should require the landlord to produce evidence of the terms of the policy and of payment of the premiums, at any time during the term of the lease.

Where, as usual, the landlord insures, there should be a covenant in the lease requiring the tenant to reimburse to the landlord the cost of the premium. Consideration should also be given to liability for repair of the property in the event of damage by a risk against which the landlord was obliged to insure, the position of the parties if reinstatement after damage is impossible and the liability to pay rent in the meantime.

11.1.13 Leases of part and underleases

The matters of additional concern on the grant of a lease of part of a building are dealt with in Chapter 27.

The matters of additional concern on the grant of an underlease are dealt with in Chapter 28.

11.1.14 Costs

Costs are largely a question of negotiation between the parties and much will depend on the state of the market at the time when the lease is granted but it is not uncommon to see the tenant being asked to pay the landlord's legal costs on the grant of the lease. The tenant should be wary about this and only agree to pay the landlord's reasonable costs or a fixed contribution towards them. The Costs of Leases Act 1958 provides that each party will bear his own legal costs unless there is a written agreement to the contrary. Such agreement is often contained in the lease itself.

Sometimes a landlord will ask for an undertaking from the tenant's solicitor to pay the landlord's legal costs regardless of whether the lease is completed.

11.1.15 The surveyor

In taking instructions, it may also be necessary to liaise with the client's surveyor, especially where the surveyor negotiated the terms of the lease on behalf of the client or where instructions were received through the surveyor. Once prepared, a copy of the draft lease should be sent to the surveyor for his comments; he can assess whether a particular clause is workable, and his advice may be fundamental to the success of the lease in the case of rent reviews, user, alterations, etc.

11.2 ACTING FOR LANDLORD AND TENANT

Rule 6 of the Solicitors' Practice Rules 1990, which is explained in the LPC Resource Book *Conveyancing* (Jordans), applies equally as between landlord and tenant, as between the seller and buyer of freeholds; and thus a solicitor should not act for both landlord and tenant except in the limited circumstances permitted by that rule.

11.3 THE LANDLORD'S TITLE

The landlord's solicitor should obtain and investigate evidence of the landlord's title to check matters such as ownership, the precise location of boundaries, and incumbrances affecting the property.

If there is a mortgage affecting the superior title, a copy must be obtained to see whether it restricts the landlord's powers of leasing; it may be necessary to obtain the lender's consent to the proposed letting. Similarly, if the landlord is himself a tenant, a copy of the lease must be obtained to see whether the superior landlord's consent is needed to the grant of the sub-lease and whether the head-lease dictates any of the terms of the sub-lease.

11.3.1 Tenant's right to see superior title

Under the general law, the tenant is not entitled to call for deduction of the freehold title on the grant of a lease. From the tenant's point of view, this is unsatisfactory because not only will the tenant have no proof of the landlord's right to grant the lease but there may be restrictive covenants affecting the freehold which could be binding on the tenant. If, however, the landlord's title is registered at HM Land Registry, the proposed tenant will be able to obtain his own copy of the register under the 'open register' rules.

On the grant of a sub-lease out of an unregistered lease, the sub-tenant is entitled to call for the head-lease out of which his sub-lease is being created, and all subsequent assignments under which the lease has been held for the last 15 years. But again, under the general law, the sub-tenant is not entitled to call for the freehold title. If the sub-lease is to be granted out of a registered head-lease, it seems that the proposed sub-tenant is not entitled to call for a copy of the leasehold register (Land Registration Act 1925, s 110(1)), although the sub-tenant will be able to obtain his own copy.

In view of the above, the proposed tenant (or sub-tenant) should ask for deduction of all superior titles to satisfy himself that there are no adverse restrictive covenants affecting the user of the premises. This is particularly important because there is usually no implied warranty on the landlord's part that the permitted use is not in breach of a covenant contained in a superior title. However, notwithstanding the tenant's concerns, it is quite common for the superior title not to be deduced in the case of relatively short-term leases where no premium is to be paid.

Despite the availability of title guarantees under the Law of Property (Miscellaneous Provisions) Act 1994, it is highly likely that a commercial landlord will resist a request for any form of guarantee (see LPC Resource Book *Conveyancing* (Jordans)).

11.4 AN OUTLINE OF THE CONVEYANCING PROCEDURE

Grant of lease: basic procedural steps

Landlord	***Tenant***
1 Take instructions (see above)	1 Take instructions (see above)
2 Obtain title deeds/office copy entries – incumbrances? – lender's consent? – is title to be deduced? (see above)	
3 Inspection	
4 Draft lease in duplicate. Send to T's solicitor for approval. If title to be deduced, send abstract or office copies with draft lease	
	2 Upon receipt: – make inspection/arrange survey

	Landlord		*Tenant*
			– make local search and enquiries of local authority – make index map search, if appropriate – if the lease imposes substantial obligations on the landlord, consider a company search against corporate landlord whose financial strength is unknown – other relevant searches – send preliminary enquiries (including leasehold enquiries) to landlord's solicitor – raise requisitions, if title deduced (see above)
5	Reply to tenant's preliminary enquiries and requisitions (if title deduced)		
		3	Consider replies to all searches and enquiries. Check lease terms (including insurance arrangements). Amend if necessary. 'Travelling draft'
6	Consider amendments		
7	Engross agreed draft in two parts		
8	Send counterpart lease to tenant's solicitor together with completion statement setting out details of amount payable on completion. Execute lease in escrow		
		4	Make appropriate pre-completion searches
9	If appropriate, place landlord's Land Certificate on deposit at HM Land Registry	5	Report to client. Send completion statement together with counterpart lease for execution to client

Completion

1	Stamping of counterpart lease	1	Stamping. Ad valorem and PD, within 30 days of completion
2	Account to client for first payment of rent (and premium, if any)	2	If appropriate, apply for registration of title to lease Notice of lease in freehold charges register?
3	Place counterpart lease with deeds	3	Custody of lease (and land certificate if lease registrable)

Note

This outline assumes that:

(1) the tenant does not require a mortgage to acquire the lease;

(2) there is to be no agreement for lease. If there is, the landlord's solicitor will prepare a draft contract and attach to it the draft lease. This will be sent to the tenant's solicitor for approval. In this case the tenant's solicitor will make the usual searches and enquiries, and the terms of the lease will be settled between the parties before exchange. The matter will then proceed to a formal exchange of contracts. The agreement for lease will need to be protected by registration;

(3) it is the grant of a head-lease. If a sub-lease was to be granted, the head-lease should be obtained. Under the terms of this, the superior landlord's licence may be necessary and references may have to be supplied. Consent must be obtained before completion (or exchange if there is to be an agreement for lease). Further, the terms of the head-lease may dictate some of the terms of the sub-lease. The sub-tenant would be entitled to a copy of the head-lease. Following completion of the sub-lease it may be necessary to give notice of it to the superior landlord.

Chapter 12

AN OUTLINE OF TAXATION OF COMMERCIAL PROPERTIES

Chapter 12 contents

12.1 VALUE ADDED TAX

At the outset of any property transaction, it is essential to consider the impact of VAT legislation, and to advise the client accordingly. One of the aims of the Finance Act 1989 was to bring UK law into line with EC Law by bringing many property transactions and the provision of construction and other services within the scope of VAT. The reader will already be aware of the basic principles of VAT, which dictate that VAT may be payable in respect of a supply of goods or services made in the course of a business. Whether VAT is payable depends upon a number of things including whether the supplies in question are exempt, zero-rated or standard-rated. The reader will also be aware of the effects of such supplies, the payment and receipt of input and output tax, and the recovery of VAT incurred.

Supplies of goods and services made in relation to a property transaction can be grouped as follows:

(1) Residential properties:

- (a) sale of a green field site: exempt (but subject to the option to tax, as to which, see **12.1.3**);
- (b) construction services: zero-rated;
- (c) civil engineering works: zero-rated;
- (d) professional services (eg legal and other professional fees): standard-rated;
- (e) sale of a new house: zero-rated;
- (f) grant of a lease of a new house (for a term exceeding 21 years): zero-rated.

(2) Commercial properties:

- (a) sale of a green field site: exempt (but subject to the option to tax);
- (b) construction services: standard-rated;
- (c) civil engineering works: standard-rated;
- (d) professional services: standard-rated;
- (e) sale of a new freehold building or the grant of an option to purchase such a building: standard-rated;
- (f) sale of an old freehold building: exempt (but subject to the option to tax);
- (g) the grant of a lease (for any length of term): exempt (but subject to the option to tax);
- (h) the assignment of a lease: exempt (but subject to the option to tax);
- (i) the surrender of a lease: exempt (but subject to the option to tax by the person who receives the consideration);
- (j) repair, alteration and demolition works: standard-rated.

Rules relating to work carried out on listed buildings are not considered in this book, and the particular problems associated with premises of mixed use are also outside the scope of this book.

Some of the supplies listed above are exempt supplies, but are subject to what is called the 'option to tax' (also known as the 'option to waive exemption'). This is dealt with more comprehensively at **12.1.3**. What the option means is that the person who makes the supply can voluntarily convert the supply from one which is exempt and, therefore, gives rise to no VAT liability into a standard-rated supply.

The VAT consequences arising in residential and commercial developments are now considered.

12.1.1 Residential developments

In a typical new residential development, the VAT consequences will not be too complicated. If, for example, a property company, ABC Limited, buys a green field site, the seller is making an exempt supply to ABC Limited which will not be subject to VAT unless the seller, being a taxable person, has elected to waive the exemption. In any event if, as is often the case, the seller is a private individual, he is not likely to be selling the land in the course of a business, and the supply will, therefore, be outside the scope of VAT. Any construction services (such as work provided by builders and the provision of materials) and civil engineering works (such as the construction of the roads and sewers serving the development) supplied to ABC Limited will be supplied at a zero-rate of VAT. It is, therefore, probable that the only significant VAT incurred by the property company in constructing the residential development will be in respect of professional fees paid to surveyors, solicitors, architects and selling agents for services supplied.

On completion of construction, ABC Limited will dispose of the houses. The purchase price payable on the freehold sale of a newly built house, or the premium (or rent) payable in respect of a lease of the house granted for a term exceeding 21 years does not attract VAT. These supplies are zero-rated. However, when zero-rated supplies are made, whilst no VAT is paid for the supply, tax is deemed to be charged at a nil rate on the output (so that they are still technically regarded as taxable supplies) and therefore related input tax incurred can be recovered. What this means is that ABC Limited will account to HM Customs & Excise for output tax on supplies made (which will be nil), less input tax on related supplies received (ie the VAT paid on professional fees). This clearly leads to a deficit which means that a refund of VAT will be due from HM Customs & Excise.

A subsequent sale of a dwelling (either freehold or leasehold) will be made by a private individual and will not, therefore, be made in the course of a business. In the event that the sale is made in the course of a business (eg by a relocation company), the supply would be exempt.

12.1.2 Commercial developments

In a typical new commercial development, the same process can be followed, with different VAT consequences. The sale of a greenfield site to a developer is again an exempt supply, subject to the option to tax. However, the provision of construction services and civil engineering works to a commercial developer are standard-rated supplies, which means that considerable VAT will be incurred in addition to VAT on the standard-rated supply of professional services.

Once the building has been completed, the developer may either sell the freehold, or grant a lease of it to a tenant. The sale of a 'new' or partially completed building is a standard-rated supply. VAT must be charged in respect of the purchase price. In this context, a 'new' building is one which was completed within the 3 years preceding the sale, and 'completion' of a building takes place on the earlier of either the day upon which the certificate of practical completion was issued by the architect or, the day upon which the building was completely occupied. The grant of a lease of all or part of commercial premises (whether new or old) is an exempt supply, subject to the right of the landlord to opt to tax the rents, premium and other sums payable under the lease. In both cases, whether the freehold sale or the grant of a commercial lease, the developer is able to charge VAT, either because it is a standard-rated supply, or because the exemption has been waived. This means that output tax will be received to facilitate recovery of related input tax incurred.

Take by way of example a commercial development where the construction costs paid by the developer amount to £2 million (with VAT on a standard-rated supply of £350,000), the cost of roads and sewers amounts to £500,000 (with £87,500 VAT) and professional fees total £100,000 (with £17,500 VAT). The total input tax paid by the developer adds up to £455,000.

If the developer, being a taxable person, is able to sell the 'new' freehold building for £4 million, he will have to charge VAT amounting to £700,000. This output tax can be set against related input tax incurred, resulting in only the difference (£245,000) having to be accounted for to HM Customs & Excise. The developer suffers from cash flow difficulties in that he is likely to incur the input tax some time in advance of receiving the output tax, but he is not left out of pocket. The same result will be achieved if, instead of selling the freehold, the developer chooses to grant a lease of the building and elects to charge VAT on the sums payable under the lease. The making of the election facilitates immediate recovery of related input tax.

12.1.3 The option to charge VAT

The election to waive exemption or, as it is more commonly called, the option to tax was introduced on 1 August 1989 in order to lessen the impact of the VAT changes on commercial developers. The purpose of the option to tax is to enable the commercial owner to convert what would otherwise be exempt supplies in respect of a particular property into supplies chargeable to VAT at the standard rate, so that the developer will be able to recover the input tax which he incurred when acquiring or developing the property.

The consequence of making the election is that all future grants in the property by the person who makes the election will be subject to VAT at the standard rate.

How is the election made?

As a preliminary to waiving the exemption, the owner must check that he is registered for VAT, or else the election will be meaningless. There is no prescribed form or procedure for electing, nor is there any requirement to consult with or notify anyone who might be affected by the election. However, from a practical point of view, it is advisable that a landlord notifies his tenants, since it is the tenants who will bear the VAT. The one procedural requirement that must be followed when making the election is that written notice of the election must be given to HM Customs & Excise within 30 days of the election.

If an exempt supply (eg the grant of a lease) has been made by the elector in respect of the relevant property since 1 August 1989, consent of HM Customs & Excise will be required before the election can be made, and consent will only be granted if HM Customs & Excise are satisfied that the input tax which the elector will be able to recover as a consequence of his making the election is fair and reasonable. It is therefore advisable for a landlord intending to make an election to do so before he grants a lease of his property.

In all other cases, consent of HM Customs & Excise is not required.

Since the purpose of making the election is to charge VAT, the elector should ensure that he is registered for VAT.

Who or what is affected?

The election is personal, done on a property-by-property basis and, once made, it may only be revoked within 3 months of the election, or after 20 years (see the Value Added Tax (Buildings and Land) Order 1995). The fact that the election is personal means that whilst a landlord who elects to waive the exemption would have to charge VAT on the rents payable by its tenants, its tenants would not, unless they too elected, have to charge VAT to their sub-tenants, and the same applies to a buyer of the landlord's interest. As an exception to the general rule, an election made by a company in respect of a property will bind other companies (in respect of that property) if they are in the same VAT group of companies at the time of the election, or joined the group later, when the property affected was still owned by a group company.

The fact that the election is made on a property-by-property basis means that a commercial owner can pick and choose which of its properties should be voluntarily standard-rated. Once made, the election affects the whole of the property or, if the elector owns an interest in only part of the property, it will affect the entirety of that part. Hence, the elector cannot choose to waive the exemption in respect of the ground floor and not the upper two floors if he owns the entire building. What may appear to be separate buildings, but which are linked together internally or by covered walkways are to be treated as one building. Therefore, if a shopping precinct is owned by one landlord (as is usually the case) an election by that landlord will affect all of the shops in the precinct.

Should the election be made?

The reason for making the election is to facilitate the recovery of related input tax incurred on the acquisition or development of the property. If no related input tax has been or is likely to be incurred, there is no reason why the election should be made. If considerable input tax has been or will be incurred, consideration must be given to whether or not the election should be made, but the elector must have regard to the effect that the election will have on the persons to whom supplies are being made.

If a developer-landlord, having incurred VAT on acquisition or development costs, wants to waive the exemption and charge VAT on the rents it will receive from its tenants, and those tenants make mainly standard-rated or zero-rated supplies in the course of their businesses (eg tenants of retail foodstores, solicitors or surveyors offices), the tenants would not be adversely affected by a charge to VAT on rent, since there will be output tax (actual or deemed) to offset against the input tax. The tenants will not end up out of pocket.

Tenants who make only exempt supplies in the course of their businesses (eg banks, building societies, insurance companies) will be hard hit by the election. The VAT that these tenants have to pay on the rent will be irrecoverable, and will have to be borne as an overhead of the business. This could have the effect of frightening off a class of tenants whom the developer might have been hoping to attract to the development or lead to their reducing the amount of rent that they would be prepared to pay.

The Finance Act 1997 makes provision for a limited disapplication of the election where the ultimate end-user of the property occupies wholly or mainly for exempt purposes and was involved in some way in the acquisition, construction or financing of the property. The provision is an anti-avoidance device and the circumstances in which the disapplication will apply will be few and far between.

12.1.4 Drafting points

Is the election on its own sufficient to render VAT payable by the person who receives the supply? It is necessary to look at two principal relationships: seller and buyer, and landlord and tenant.

Seller and buyer

If a seller sells a 'new' commercial building (whether it is the first sale or a subsequent sale of the still 'new' building) the seller is making a standard-rated supply, and so there will be mandatory VAT on the purchase price. The basic rule is that, unless the contrary appears, the purchase price stated in the contract is deemed to include VAT. It is, therefore, important that the seller includes a clause in the contract obliging the buyer to pay VAT in addition to the purchase price. Failure to do so will result in the seller having to account to HM Customs & Excise for the VAT out of the purchase price received which, at current rates, will mean that the seller will be left with seven forty-sevenths less than he anticipated. This can result in the seller incurring a huge loss, for which his solicitor would no doubt be liable in negligence. Consider a sale at a price of £1 million. If an express provision is included in the contract, the buyer will have to pay £1.175 million to complete, HM Customs & Excise will get the VAT on the purchase price, and the seller will be left with £1 million. If the express clause is left out, the buyer need only pay £1,000,000 to complete, out of which HM Customs & Excise will get £148,936 leaving the seller with only £851,064.

If the seller sells an old commercial building (ie one which is now more than 3 years old) then the supply which is being made is an exempt supply and the position is different. If the seller waives the exemption before exchange then he converts the supply into a standard-rated supply and the above paragraph would then be applicable. The seller would have to make an express provision in the contract. If the exemption is waived after exchanging contracts then, under s 89 of the Value Added Tax Act 1994 (VATA 1994), the option to tax would operate as a change in the rate of tax from 0 per cent to 17.5 per cent (ie from an exempt to a standard-rated supply) and accordingly the seller could add VAT to the purchase price, without the need for an express clause in the contract enabling him to do so. In this case, it is important that the buyer's solicitor ensures that the contract makes it clear that the purchase price is inclusive of VAT so that no hardship is felt by the buyer if the seller chooses to elect after exchange. Only if the contract expressly excludes s 89, or the purchase price is expressly stated to be payable inclusive of VAT will the seller be unable to add VAT to the purchase price.

Landlord and tenant

The grant of a commercial lease (of either an old or new building) is an exempt supply, unless the landlord has opted to tax. In respect of existing leases, s 89 of the VATA 1994 again operates so that an election by the landlord after the grant of the lease effects a change in the rate of VAT from 0 per cent to 17.5 per cent. The landlord does not need the benefit of an express clause in the lease, and can simply add VAT to the rent (and other sums payable under the lease) unless there is a clause in the lease (which would not usually be the case) expressly exonerating the tenant from liability to VAT on such payments, or excluding s 89.

If the election is made before the grant of the lease, so that the supply is converted to a standard-rated supply from the outset, s 89 will not operate, and the rent will be deemed to be payable inclusive of VAT. It is, therefore, essential that the landlord's solicitor ensures that the lease contains a covenant by the tenant to pay VAT on the rent (and the other sums payable under the lease). Whenever a lease is drafted, irrespective of whether advantage can be taken of s 89, there ought to be a covenant by the tenant to pay VAT in addition to the sums payable under the lease. This avoids problems for the landlord.

12.1.5 Other areas of concern

VAT is a far-reaching tax in the property world which can impact on other aspects of property transactions.

Reverse premiums and rent-free periods

A reverse premium is a payment made by the landlord to a prospective tenant as an inducement to him to enter the lease. Money is passing from landlord to tenant, and is the consideration for a supply being made by the tenant. Such a premium has always been subject to VAT at the standard rate. The tenant should ensure that the agreement for lease stipulates that the premium is paid to him exclusive of VAT.

Rent-free periods give rise to difficult VAT problems. It appears that if the rent-free period is being given because the tenant is carrying out work to the premises which will benefit the landlord, or simply because the landlord is trying to induce the tenant to enter into the lease (as an alternative to a reverse premium), then VAT at the standard rate will be payable on the amount of rent forgone. The tenant is making a supply to the landlord (ie is positively doing something) in consideration of a rent-free period. However, if the rent-free period is given simply because the state of the market means that it is part of the bargain negotiated between landlord and tenant (eg where it is given to allow the tenant some time in which to fit out the premises for his own benefit, or arrange sub-lettings), there will be no VAT on the rent-free period, since nothing is being done in return for it.

Surrenders

When a tenant surrenders his lease to the landlord, consideration may move in either direction, either because the tenant is desperate to rid himself of the liability to pay rent and perform the covenants, or because the landlord is anxious to obtain vacant possession. By virtue of the Value Added Tax (Land) Order 1995, the supply made in either case is an exempt supply, subject to the option to tax by the person who receives the consideration.

Where a surrender is effected by operation of law, it is unclear whether any VAT can be claimed by HM Customs & Excise. Indeed, it may be difficult to establish the value of the supply being made. If such a surrender is to arise, it may be advisable to ensure that liability for VAT is clearly documented by the parties before surrender occurs.

Transfers of going concerns

There are complicated rules regarding the transfer of a going concern, which can include the sale of a tenanted building. However, these rules are outside the scope of this book.

VAT on costs

Sometimes, a lease will oblige the tenant to pay the landord's legal costs incurred on the grant of the lease. Often, a lease will oblige the tenant to pay the landlord's legal costs on an application for licence to assign, or alter, or change use. The position as regards VAT on those costs is complicated by the approach of HM Customs & Excise, who treat the payment of the landlord's legal costs, in either case, as part of the overall consideration for the grant of the lease. Hence, the VAT position depends upon whether the landlord has opted to waive the exemption.

If the landlord's solicitor charges his client £1,000 plus VAT for legal services provided on the grant of the lease, he will issue his client with a VAT invoice requiring payment of £1,000 plus VAT of £175. The landlord, having waived the exemption in respect of this property, and making use of his VAT invoice, will be able to recover the input tax (£175) from the output tax which he will receive on the rents. If the lease contains a clause obliging the tenant to pay those legal costs, the landlord will look to the tenant for a reimbursement of the outstanding £1,000. However, since HM Customs & Excise treat such a payment as part of the consideration for the grant of the lease, and since the landlord has waived the exemption, the tenant must pay £1,000 plus VAT, the landlord must issue the tenant with a VAT invoice, and the landlord must account to HM Customs & Excise for the VAT element received. The tenant may be able to recover the VAT which he has paid, depending on the nature of his business.

If the landlord has not waived the exemption, the position is different. First, he will not be able to recover the VAT charged by his solicitor, since that VAT was incurred in relation to an exempt supply. Secondly, therefore, he will require the tenant to reimburse the full amount of costs and VAT (ie £1,175), but because this reimbursement is treated as part of the consideration for the grant of the lease, and because the supply made by the landlord is an exempt supply, no VAT invoice can be issued to the tenant (as, in fact, there is no charge to VAT being made to the tenant), and the tenant will be unable to recover any part of the reimbursement.

The same principles are adopted where, during the term, the tenant exercises a right given to him under the lease and pays the landlord's legal costs (eg on an application for licence to assign pursuant to a qualified covenant (see **20.2.2**)).

12.2 CAPITAL AND INCOME TAXES

12.2.1 Tax implications on the grant of the lease

In principle, the creation of a lease out of an existing freehold or head-lease constitutes a part disposal for CGT purposes. The landlord's gain would be calculated by deducting a proportion of the acquisition price he paid for the land from any premium he receives on the grant of the lease. However, if, as is likely, no premium is charged, then there is no possibility of a capital gain arising.

For income or corporation tax purposes the landlord's annual profit under a lease will be assessable on a current year basis under Schedule A. Essentially, the profit element will be the rents receivable less the landlord's expenditure on interest charges, maintenance and repair costs, insurance premiums and other management expenses. However, the landlord's expenditure is usually recovered from the tenants by way of a service charge, leaving the landlord with a clear rental income.

As a premium is regarded as a capital receipt, rather than as income, it should not, in principle, attract income tax. However, anti-avoidance provisions exist so that if a premium is taken on the grant of a lease for 50 years or less, part of the premium will nevertheless be taxed as rent under Schedule A. Correspondingly, that element is excluded from the computation of chargeable gains. Although it is unusual for a premium to be paid on the grant of a lease of business premises, similar anti-avoidance provisions will apply if the lease imposes an obligation on the tenant to carry out improvements. In such cases, the attendant increase in value of the landlord's reversion will be treated as a premium for these purposes.

12.2.2 Tax implications on the sale of a lease

The assignment of an existing lease is a disposal for CGT purposes. A lease of land with less than 50 years to run is classed as a wasting asset and special rules apply to calculate the gain arising on its disposal. Instead of the acquisition cost of the lease being written down on a 'straight line' basis over its term, a formula provides for its value to decline slowly to begin with, but with increasing rapidity towards the end of the term.

12.2.3 Tax implications on the sale of the reversion

The sale of the landlord's reversion will constitute a disposal for CGT purposes. If a premium had been charged on the grant of the lease so that a part disposal had occurred then the gain on the sale of the reversion is calculated by reference to the reduced acquisition cost outstanding after some of it had been apportioned to the part disposal on the original grant.

12.3 STAMP DUTY ON LEASES

Ad valorem stamp duty will be assessed on the premium at the rate of one pound per £100 or part thereof, and on the rent depending on the average annual rent and the length of term. Certificates of value are largely irrelevant in commercial conveyancing, since the amounts payable under a commercial lease usually exceed stamp duty thresholds. Fixed duty of 50 pence is payable on the counterpart lease. Stamp duty must be paid within 30 days of the execution of the instrument.

The amount of duty payable on the rent depends upon the length of the lease and the amount of rent. If the term does not exceed 7 years, and the rent exceeds £500 per annum, duty is payable at 50 pence per £50 or part thereof. Where the lease term exceeds 7 years, but does not exceed 35, and the rent exceeds £500 per anum, duty is payable at £1 per £50 or part thereof. Rates of duty rise more steeply where the lease term exceeds 35 years, but in such cases a premium will probably be paid and, consequently, the annual rent is likely to be lower. If no single rent is payable under the lease (eg because of fixed increases), duty is payable on the average rent throughout the term. Where rent is wholly or partly unascertainable, duty will be assessed on the basis of the market rent at the time the lease is executed.

An agreement for lease is required to be stamped as if it were the lease itself, although when the tenant eventually attends to the stamping of the lease, credit will be given for any duty paid on the agreement. However, by virtue of s 240(1) of the Finance Act 1994, if the agreement for lease and the lease are presented for stamping at the same time (ie after completion of the lease), no penalty will be charged for what is likely to be a late presentation of the agreement. This provision is particularly useful with regard to conditional agreements for lease. Duty might otherwise be paid on an agreement which, because the condition is not satisfied, does not complete.

The lease itself must, by virtue of s 240(2), contain either a certificate that there is no agreement for lease to which the lease gives effect, or a denoting stamp which denotes that the agreement was not chargeable with any duty, or denotes the amount of duty paid on the agreement.

Where VAT is or may, at the election of the landlord, become payable on the rent under the lease, the Inland Revenue will assess stamp duty on the VAT element in addition to the rent, whether or not the landlord has actually elected to charge VAT. It seems that the only occasion when the Inland Revenue will not assess stamp duty upon actual or potential VAT payable by the tenant is when the lease makes it clear that no VAT will be payable in addition to the rent. This is done either by stating that the rent payable is inclusive of any VAT that may become chargeable, or by including a covenant by the landlord not to elect to charge VAT at any time during the term (although whether this covenant will bind the landlord's successor as a covenant which has reference to the subject matter of the lease is uncertain). It is usual for the lease to reserve VAT as rent under the lease to avoid any argument that VAT on rent is a consideration payable periodically under the lease, which could, by virtue of s 56 of the Stamp Act 1891, lead to an alternative (and higher) assessment of stamp duty.

Particulars delivered

A tenant under a lease which is granted for a term of 7 years or more must deliver particulars of the transaction to the Inland Revenue and obtain a 'Particulars Delivered' stamp within 30 days of the execution of the instrument.

Chapter 13

LEASE DRAFTING

13.1 PRINCIPLES OF DRAFTING

A commercial property lawyer will encounter many different types of commercial lease, since every firm of solicitors engaged in property matters is likely to have its own commercial lease precedent which it will adapt for use in each commercial letting in respect of which the firm is instructed. Most firms restrict their office precedent to a document of manageable length. However, it is not uncommon when acting for a tenant to receive a draft lease which runs to 60 or more pages of relatively small print, all of which has to be carefully examined by the tenant's solicitor. Brevity and concise language must always be encouraged in the drafting (and the amending) of a lease. If the draft lease is kept short, less time will be taken in the subsequent negotiation of the terms and, therefore, in the transaction generally. It will also be easier to read for both clients and solicitors, and will result in legal fees being kept to a minimum. However, the draftsman cannot always restrict the length of the document where complex and extensive legal obligations are being entered into. Clauses cannot be left out of the lease simply to reduce its length, and even though the possibility of a clause being relied upon during the term might appear slight, if a reason exists for the inclusion of the clause, it should be retained. There are many matters to be contemplated in a landlord and tenant relationship, all of which require regulation in the lease.

When instructed to draft a lease, the usual starting point is to obtain a copy of the firm's office precedent. The draftsman should make a point of constantly reviewing the office precedent to ensure that it is kept up to date with changes in the law and current practice. The draftsman should read through the precedent to check that it is suitable for use in the transaction proposed. The precedent will be in blank form, and basic details, such as the names and addresses of the parties, a description of the premises, length of term, and the amount of rent will need to be inserted. However, the draftsman would be doing his client (and the tenant's solicitor) a disservice if he allowed the draft lease to be submitted for approval without further attention. Each provision of the lease must be scrutinised to see if any amendment or addition is required, or whether any of the clauses can be omitted. There are few things more frustrating for a tenant's solicitor than having to wade through pages of irrelevant material such as covenants which are clearly inapplicable to the transaction proposed. By having to strike out irrelevant provisions, the tenant's solicitor may feel that he is doing the landlord's solicitor's job for him. Further, in the context of the solicitor-client relationship, it does not create a good impression if a document has been prepared without much apparent thought for the transaction at hand.

If the office precedent cannot be used, the draftsman may turn to standard precedent books (eg *The Encyclopaedia of Forms and Precedents*) which contain a wide variety of lease precedents, together with additional clauses for use in particular circumstances. Again, care must be taken to ensure that the precedent used is up to date and is adapted to fit the present circumstances.

If, following the grant of the lease, the reversion is to be sold to an investment fund (which is the case with many commercial developments, both new and old), the draftsman should always have regard to the requirements of institutional investors who will require the form of lease to be as close to their standard 'institutional' form as possible. If an institutionally preferred form of lease has not been granted, the landlord will have greater difficulty in disposing of the freehold. All leading commercial practices ensure that their office precedent is in an institutional form. An 'institutional' lease is one which places all the costs of repairing and insuring upon the tenant, thereby ensuring that the income derived by the landlord from the rent is subject to as little fluctuation (in terms of outgoings) as possible. It is often granted for a term of 25 years with a 5-yearly rent review pattern although in recessionary times, shorter leases are common.

The techniques to be adopted in the drafting of the lease are outlined in the drafting section of the LPC Resource Book *Skills for Lawyers* (Jordans) and are not repeated here.

13.2 RULES OF CONSTRUCTION

The purpose of interpreting any legal contract is to discover the real intention of the parties, but that intention can only be ascertained from the wording of the contract itself, and not from extrinsic evidence. Negotiations which were conducted prior to the grant of the lease are irrelevant, and cannot be taken into account in construing the lease. The classic statement in relation to the construction of legal contracts was given by Lord Simon of Glaisdale in *Wickman Tools Ltd v Schuler AG* [1974] AC 235, who said: 'The question to be answered always is "What is the meaning of what the parties have said?" not "What did the parties mean to say?", it being a presumption (of law), to rebut which no evidence is allowed, that the parties intended to say what they have said'. In ascertaining the intention of the parties from the wording used in the lease, the court will look objectively at what reasonable persons would have had in mind given the circumstances faced by the parties to the lease at the time the lease was entered into. The parties cannot give evidence themselves as to what they intended.

In construing a lease, the court is always reluctant to hold a clause void for uncertainty and thus, if the court can find a way to interpret the clause, some sense will be given to it. Equally, however, the court is generally unwilling to imply terms into a document which has been entered into after extensive negotiations between legally represented parties (although see the approach of the Court of Appeal in *Royal Bank of Scotland plc v Jennings* [1997] 19 EG 152). Faced with an ambiguity, the court will usually adopt the literal approach to interpretation, unless this would lead to a result so absurd that, in the commercial reality of the situation the parties find themselves in, they could not reasonably have intended it (see *Broadgate Square plc v Lehman Brothers Ltd* [1995] 01 EG 111). The court will not examine the offending clause in isolation, but will construe the lease as a whole, to see if some assistance can be gained from other parts of the deed, where similar words and phrases may have been used in other contexts. Ordinary and technical words of the English language will be given the meanings usually attributed to them by the lay person unless the lease clearly directs some other meaning (eg by use of a definitions or interpretation clause).

If, owing to a common mistake between the parties, the lease, as executed, does not embody the common intentions of the parties, the remedy of rectification may be available. This is, however, an equitable and discretionary remedy, and there is a heavy burden upon the plaintiff in an action for rectification to show the existence of a common mistake. Rectification will not be awarded so as to prejudice a bona fide purchaser of the interest of either landlord or tenant who did not have notice of the right to rectify.

If there is a discrepancy between the executed original lease and counterpart, the former prevails over the latter, unless the original is clearly ambiguous.

13.3 THE STRUCTURE OF THE LEASE

13.3.1 Commencement, date and parties

It is customary to commence the drafting of a document by describing the document according to the nature of the transaction to be effected; for example, a lease will commence with the words 'This Lease'. The date of the lease will be left blank until it is manually filled on completion with the date of actual completion. The draft lease should then set out the names and addresses of each party to the lease (eg landlord, tenant and any guarantors).

13.3.2 Definitions

Every well-drafted document should contain a definitions section. If a word is to bear a specific meaning in a document, that meaning ought to be clearly defined at the start of the document. If certain phrases or words are likely to recur in the document, those phrases or words ought to be given a defined meaning at the start of the document. The use of a definitions clause in a legal document avoids needless repetition of recurring words and phrases, and permits a more concise style of drafting. If a word or phrase is to be defined in the definitions clause, the first letter of the defined term should be given a capital letter, and every use of that word or phrase thereafter should appear in the same form.

The following words and phrases are commonly used as defined terms in commercial leases.

'Development'
The lease is likely to regulate the carrying on of building, mining, engineering or other operations at the premises, and the making of a material change in the use of the premises. Rather than having to repeat the statutory definition of development at each reference, it is simpler just to refer to 'Development', which can be defined in the definitions clause as having the meaning given to it by s 55 of the TCPA 1990.

'Exceptions'
Exceptions are certain rights over the premises to be reserved for the benefit of the landlord. They will usually be set out in one of the schedules to the lease.

'Insured Risks'
There are many risks against which the lease will require the premises to be insured, and there will be several references to those risks in the insurance and repairing provisions of the lease (see Chapter 25). A full list of risks can be set out in the definitions clause, and then referred to elsewhere as the 'Insured Risks'.

'Interest'

If the tenant delays paying rent or any other sums due to the landlord under the lease, the landlord will want to charge the tenant interest on the unpaid sums. The rate of interest can be set out in the definitions clause. It is usually agreed to be a rate which is between 3 and 5 per cent above the base lending rate of a nominated bank. The landlord usually stipulates that if the base rate of that bank should cease to exist, the interest rate under the lease will be a reasonably equivalent rate of interest.

'Pipes' or 'Conduits'

The tenant may be granted rights to use pipes in other parts of the landlord's building in order to run services to and from the premises. The landlord may reserve the right to use pipes passing through the tenant's premises. The lease should make it clear that 'Pipes' includes all pipes, sewers, drains, watercourses, wires, cables and other conducting media. In this sense the defined term is not so much a definition, as an expansion of the meaning of the word.

'Planning Acts'

The lease will contain several references to the Town and Country Planning Act 1990, the Environment Act 1995, the Planning and Compensation Act 1991, and other statutes relating to planning and environmental law, and the tenant will have obligations to comply with them. Those statutes can be grouped together and called 'the Planning Acts'.

'Premises'

There will be many references in the lease to the premises demised to the tenant. The draftsman will not want to repeat anything other than 'the Premises' at each reference. Hence, the definitions clause should define the premises demised by the lease, and a full verbal and legal description should be set out either here, or in the parcels clause, or in one of the schedules to the lease.

'Surveyor'

At times, the landlord will want disputes between himself and the tenant (other than ones arising in relation to rent review or service charge provisions) to be settled by a surveyor appointed by the landlord. There may also be disputes between adjoining tenants in the landlord's building that the landlord prefers to be settled by his surveyor. The surveyor can either be named in the lease or (since he cannot be guaranteed to outlive the lease) he can be defined as any person or firm from time to time appointed by the landlord.

'Term'

The term of the lease is one of the phrases most commonly referred to in the lease. Thought should be given to whether the definition should relate just to the contractual term, or whether it should include any extension, holding over or continuation of the term (see **14.3.1**).

'VAT'

In defining value added tax, it should be made clear that 'VAT' also includes any tax replacing VAT, or becoming payable in addition to it, in case the fundamental principles of the tax are changed.

'Rent'

Rent will also be a commonly recurring word. Careful thought should be given as to what 'Rent' is to mean, and in the light of its definition, whether it is appropriate to use the term at every reference to rent in the lease. If the landlord wants to reserve service charge payments, insurance premiums and VAT as rent, so that he enjoys the same remedies for recovery of those sums as he enjoys in respect of rent (eg distress, and forfeiture without the need to serve a s 146 notice), 'Rent' should be defined to include those items. It should also be made clear that 'Rent' means not only the original contractual rent, but also any revised rent which becomes payable by virtue of the rent review clause, and any interim rent which becomes payable under s 24A of the LTA 1954 during a statutory continuation tenancy. In this manner, it is made clear that, in a case where a tenant's liability continues after assignment, the liability relates to the payment of a rent which may be increased after the date he assigns his interest in the premises. The term 'Rent' is not an appropriate term in every case under the lease. For instance, in the rent review clause, it is the annual rent which is to be reviewed from time to time during the term, not necessarily the 'Rent' as defined. Also, the landlord might be prepared to allow payment of the annual rent to be suspended for a period of time if there is damage to the premises by an insured risk, but he may not wish to have suspended the payment of other sums (eg service charge) which have been reserved as 'Rent'.

'Rights'

Rights to be granted to the tenant will be set out in a separate schedule.

'Building'

If the lease is of part only of the landlord's building, the building itself should be identified, as the landlord will probably be entering into covenants in the lease to repair the structure and exterior of the building. There may be other references to the 'Building' with regard to the provision of services and the grant and reservation of easements.

'Common Parts'

Where a lease of part of a building is intended, the tenant will be granted rights to use the 'Common Parts' of the 'Building'. The extent of the 'Common Parts' should be clearly expressed.

13.3.3 The interpretation clause

Certain words or phrases do not require a fixed definition for the purposes of the lease, rather their meaning needs to be expanded or clarified to assist the reader in his interpretation and construction of the lease. Common examples of matters of interpretation are the following.

Joint and several liability

The lease should make it clear that, if the landlord or tenant is more than one person, the obligations placed upon those persons by the lease will be enforceable against either or both of them.

One gender to mean all genders

Section 61 of the Law of Property Act 1925 (LPA 1925) applies in respect of all deeds executed after the 1925 Act came into force so that any reference in a deed to the masculine will include the feminine, and vice versa. However, s 61 does not deal with the neuter (ie 'it'), and it is therefore common to state, for the avoidance of doubt, that a reference to one gender includes all others.

References to statutes

Leases usually provide that, unless a particular clause expressly provides to the contrary (see **21.2.1**), a reference in the lease to a statute or to a statutory instrument is to be taken as a reference to the Act or instrument as amended, re-enacted or modified from time to time, and not restricted to the legislation as it was in force at the date of the lease.

Expanding the meaning of words or phrases

If one of the tenant's covenants states that the tenant is prohibited from doing a certain act, the tenant will not be in breach of covenant if the act is done by a third party. It is, therefore, usual to state that if the tenant is required by the lease not to do a certain act, neither may he permit or suffer the act to be done by someone else. If one of the tenant's covenants prohibits the carrying out of a certain act without the landlord's prior consent, and it is stipulated that the landlord's consent cannot be unreasonably withheld, it is usual to stipulate that his consent may not also be unreasonably delayed. Rather than dealing with these matters of drafting as and when the need arises in the lease, both of these points can be concisely dealt with by using an appropriate form of wording in the interpretation clause at the beginning of the lease.

Clause headings

The draftsman frequently gives each clause a heading for ease of reference. It is usual to state that headings are not to be taken into account when interpreting the lease itself.

13.3.4 The letting

The letting is the operative part of the lease which will create the tenant's interest, define the size of that interest, reserve rent, impose covenants, and deal with the grant and reservation of rights and easements. The clauses will be set out in the following logical sequence.

The operative words

Sufficient words of grant should be used to show the intention of the landlord to grant an interest in favour of the tenant. The landlord usually either 'demises' or 'lets' the premises to the tenant.

The parcels clause

A full description of the premises, including the rights to be granted to the tenant should be contained in the parcels clause. Often, the description is removed to one of the schedules (see below) so that the parcels clause simply refers to 'the Premises' (which will be a defined term).

Exceptions and reservations

Usually, the rights to be reserved for the benefit of the landlord are only briefly referred to in this part of the lease, and are set out extensively in one of the schedules.

The habendum

The habendum deals with the length of term to be vested in the tenant, and its commencement date.

The reddendum

The reddendum deals with the reservation of rent (which may be varied from time to time by a rent review clause), the dates for payment, and the manner of payment (ie whether in advance or in arrear).

The covenants

Although the covenants on the part of landlord, tenant and surety are often set out in separate schedules, the parties expressly enter into them in the operative part of the lease.

13.3.5 The provisos

Grouped together under the heading of provisos is a wide variety of clauses which cannot easily be dealt with elsewhere in the lease, being clauses which are neither in the nature of covenants nor easements, and do not impose obligations upon one or other of the parties to the lease. They are clauses which have no common thread except that most of them are inserted into the lease for the landlord's benefit alone.

The provisos usually include the following clauses:

(1) The proviso for re-entry, (ie the forfeiture clause). This is dealt with in greater detail in Chapter 26.

(2) A provision that all of the tenant's covenants are to remain in full force notwithstanding any waiver of the right to forfeit by the landlord. This clause aims to prevent the landlord from inadvertently waiving his right to forfeit the lease (which could happen by his demanding or accepting rent at a time when he had knowledge of a breach of covenant by the tenant) by stating that any such waiver is to be ineffective. However, even though it is now common to include such a provision in a commercial lease, the validity of such a clause is not clear. The better view may be that the draftsman cannot prevent a waiver in this manner. As to waiver generally, see **33.5.1**.

(3) An option to determine the lease where the premises are damaged by an insured risk so that they are no longer fit for use or occupation, and the landlord either cannot or, after a period of time, has not reinstated the premises (see **25.7**).

(4) A rent abatement clause, which provides that the rent (and, possibly, other sums payable by the tenant under the lease) should cease to be payable if the premises are rendered unusable by damage caused by an insured risk (see **25.7.2**).

(5) A provision which states that the landlord does not, by reason of anything contained in the lease, imply or represent that the tenant's proposed use of the premises is a permitted use under planning legislation. In *Laurence v Lexcourt Holdings Ltd* [1978] 2 All ER 810 (a case at first instance), the landlord had let premises to the tenant as 'offices'. After completion of the lease, the tenant discovered that only part of the premises enjoyed the benefit of planning permission for office use, and that the local planning authority was only prepared to grant planning permission in respect of all of the premises on a temporary basis. The court held that the tenant was entitled to rescind on account of the landlord's misrepresentation, since it was implicit in what was

said in the lease that the premises could lawfully be used by the tenant for the intended purpose throughout the term. The landlord should therefore make it clear in the lease that, simply because the lease (or any licence granted subsequently) permits a certain type of business activity at the premises, the landlord does not warrant that permission is available for that use.

(6) A provision whereby the tenant acknowledges that he has not entered into the lease in reliance upon any statement made by or on behalf of the landlord. This provision seeks to prevent the tenant from pursuing a remedy against the landlord in respect of a misrepresentation, but it will be subject to s 3 of the Misrepresentation Act 1967 (as amended by s 8 of the Unfair Contract Terms Act 1977) and will have to satisfy the test of reasonableness set out in the 1977 Act.

(7) An arbitration clause. The landlord will usually insert a clause in the lease which provides that any disputes which arise between the tenant and the occupiers of any adjoining property belonging to the landlord are to be settled conclusively by the landlord's surveyor (as defined by the lease).

(8) A provision dealing with the removal of the tenant's goods after the termination of the lease. Landlords have a slight concern that the tenant may leave the premises when his lease ends without removing all of his goods or belongings. In such a situation the landlord would want to be able to dispose of the tenant's goods or belongings (by sale or otherwise), but would be concerned about incurring liability in tort for interfering with them. Under s 12 of the Torts (Interference With Goods) Act 1977 a bailee of goods (such as the landlord of premises vacated by a tenant) is entitled, by notice in writing, to impose an obligation on the bailor to take delivery of his goods, and is further entitled to give written notice to the bailor of his intention to sell the goods if delivery is not taken within a reasonable time. If the goods are sold, the bailee is obliged to account to the bailor for the proceeds of sale, less any costs of sale. The provisions of s 12 take effect subject to any express terms of bailment (save that reasonable notice of a sale must always be given to the bailor). The proviso in the lease seeks to deal expressly with the terms of bailment.

(9) A provision regulating the method of service of notices under the lease. On occasions during the lease, one party will want or need to serve a notice on the other under one of the provisions in the lease (eg to implement a rent review clause, or to give notice of an assignment of the lease, or as a preliminary step to the exercise of a right of re-entry). Whether or not a notice has been validly served will be an important issue and should, therefore, be a matter which is capable of conclusive determination. Accordingly, the lease should specify the method of service of notices, either by incorporating the provisions of s 196 of the LPA 1925 (as amended by the Recorded Delivery Service Act 1962) into the lease, or by expressly setting out the methods of service to be permitted by the lease.

(10) Excluding compensation under the LTA 1954. If the parties agree that the tenant should not be entitled to compensation under s 37 of the LTA 1954 at the end of his lease (see **34.6**), this part of the lease should include a clause whereby the tenant's right to compensation is excluded.

(11) Fixing a perpetuity period. The landlord commonly reserves rights in the lease to use service pipes which currently pass through the tenant's premises, or which may at some future date be laid through them. The grant of a future right may be void if it infringes the rule against perpetuities. To avoid any possibility of this, the lease may specify a perpetuity period not exceeding 80 years (Perpetuities and Accumulations Act 1964, s 1(1)).

(12) Limiting the implied grant rules. Frequently, the landlord wants to make it clear that the only easements to which the tenant will be entitled are those expressly set out in the lease, and a proviso to that effect may, therefore, be included.

(13) Excluding the tenant's security of tenure. Occasionally, the parties agree that the security of tenure provisions contained in the LTA 1954, Part II should not apply to the lease (see **34.1.5**). If this is to be the case, the contracting-out provision should appear in this part of the lease. Consent of the court would be required in respect of such an agreement.

(14) Options to break. If either party is to enjoy the right to terminate the lease early by the exercise of an option to break (see **16.2**), the option is usually contained in this part of the lease.

13.3.6 Schedules

Most of the detail of the lease can be omitted from the main body of the document and placed in separate schedules. This will make the lease easier to read, and from the client's point of view, it makes it easier for him to refer to the various provisions of the lease.

Most leases contain schedules dealing with the following matters.

The premises

The first schedule to the lease often contains a description of the premises, which should be complete and accurate, and where appropriate, refer to plans to be incorporated in the lease.

Rights

If rights are to be granted to the tenant (eg on a lease of part), they are usually referred to briefly in the body of the lease and set out in detail in a schedule.

Exceptions

Where the landlord is reserving rights (which will usually be the case) those matters will briefly be referred to in the body of the lease, and set out in detail in a schedule.

Rent review

Provisions relating to revisions of the annual rent during the term will either be contained in a separate clause in the body of the lease, or removed to a schedule.

Covenants

There will be separate schedules detailing the tenant's covenants, the landlord's covenants and the covenants to be entered into by the tenant's guarantor on the grant of the lease, the assignee's guarantor on the assignment of the lease, and an outgoing tenant as an authorised guarantor (as to which, see **20.2.8**).

Service charge provisions

If there is to be a service charge, it is usual to group all the service charge provisions in one schedule to the lease.

13.3.7 Execution

The lease and its counterpart are deeds and, therefore, the usual rules relating to the execution of deeds are applicable. A testimonium clause is not an essential part of a lease but, if one is included, it ought to appear immediately before the first schedule. Attestation clauses will, of course, be essential.

Chapter 14

THE PARTIES TO THE LEASE

Chapter 14 contents

14.1 INTRODUCTION

Following the date and commencement, the lease will set out details of the parties to the lease, namely the landlord, the tenant and any guarantor (who is also often referred to as a surety).

In respect of a corporate party, the lease should give the company's full name and either its registered office or its main administrative office, and the company's registration number. In respect of an individual party, the full name and postal address of the individual will suffice.

The purpose of this chapter is to examine the extent and duration of liability of the parties to a lease, The Landlord and Tenant (Covenants) Act 1995 (LTCA 1995) (which came into force on 1 January 1996) brought about considerable changes in this area. In particular, it abolished the concept of privity of contract in relation to leases which are defined as new leases for the purposes of the Act (see **14.2.2**). Accordingly, this chapter examines the law and practice both in relation to leases already in existence at the date when the Act came into force (the old regime), and those which are new leases (the new regime).

14.2 THE LANDLORD

The landlord's primary purpose as a party to the lease is to grant to the tenant the leasehold interest that both parties intend, upon the terms agreed between them. These terms may require the landlord to enter into covenants with the tenant in order to ensure that the tenant peaceably enjoys occupation of the premises, and a certain quality of accommodation (see, more specifically, Chapter 24).

14.2.1 The old regime

The original landlord

By virtue of the principle of privity of contract, the original landlord, as an original contracting party, remains liable in respect of any covenants entered into in the lease, even after he has sold the reversion. The landlord protects himself against the possibility of being sued for a breach of covenant committed by his successor by obtaining from him an express indemnity covenant in the transfer of the reversion. Such a covenant is not implied at law.

If the landlord has granted a lease of an entire building, it is unlikely that he entered into many covenants with the tenant. If the landlord has granted a lease of part of a building, or of premises forming part of a larger commercial site, the landlord may have entered into covenants to provide services to the tenants (see **27.5.2**). If this is the case, the landlord may have limited expressly the duration of his liability under the covenants to the time the reversion is vested in him, rather than relied upon obtaining an indemnity covenant.

A successor to the reversion

The landlord's successor in title is bound during his period of ownership by all covenants imposed upon the landlord which have reference to the subject matter of the lease (see s 142(1) of the LPA 1925). At the same time, he takes the benefit of the tenant's covenants which have reference to the subject matter of the lease under s 141(1) of the LPA 1925. There was some doubt as to whether the benefit of surety covenants contained in the lease would pass to a buyer of the reversion without an express assignment, but it now appears in the light of *P & A Swift Investments v Combined English Stores Group plc* [1988] 3 WLR 313 that it will, provided the lease made it clear that a reference in the lease to the landlord includes his successors in title.

14.2.2 The new regime

The original landlord

Under a lease affected by the LTCA 1995 (as a general rule, those granted on or after 1 January 1996), on an assignment of the reversion by the original landlord, while there is no automatic release from his obligations under the lease, ss 6 and 8 of the Act provide a procedure whereby the assigning landlord can apply to the tenant to be released from his obligations under the lease. The outgoing landlord may serve a notice (in a prescribed form) on the tenant (either before or within 4 weeks after the assignment) requesting his release. If, within 4 weeks of service, the tenant objects by serving a written notice on the landlord, the landlord may apply to the county court for a declaration that it is reasonable for the covenant to be released. If the tenant does not object within that time-limit, the release becomes automatic. Any release from a covenant under these provisions is regarded as occurring at the time when the assignment in question takes place.

Once a landlord is released under these provisions, he ceases to be entitled to the benefit of the tenant covenants in the lease as from the date of the assignment of the reversion.

A successor to the reversion

The landlord's successor becomes bound, as from the date of the assignment, by all of the landlord covenants in the lease, except to the extent that immediately before the assignment they did not bind the assignor (eg covenants expressed to be personal). Similarly, the new landlord becomes entitled to the benefit of the tenant covenants in the lease. Sections 141 and 142 of the LPA 1925 do not apply in relation to new leases, so there is no need to enquire whether the relevant covenant is one which 'has reference to the subject matter of the lease'. The benefit of surety covenants (not being tenant covenants for the purposes of the Act) will pass to an assignee of the reversion in accordance with *P & A Swift Investments* on the basis that the assignee has acquired the legal estate, and the surety covenants touch and concern that estate. In the same manner, the benefit of a former tenant's authorised guarantee agreement (see **20.2.8**) will pass to the assignee.

A successor can apply to be released from his obligations under the lease when, at some future time, he assigns the reversion. If at that time a former landlord is still liable on the lease covenants (because he did not obtain a release from the tenant when he assigned the reversion), he can make another application to the tenant to be released.

14.3 THE TENANT

The person to whom the lease is granted is known as the original tenant. The person to whom the tenant later assigns his lease is known as the assignee. The original tenant will be required to enter into many covenants in the lease regulating what can be done in, on or at the premises.

14.3.1 The old regime

The original tenant – privity of contract

Prior to the LTCA 1995, basic principles of privity of contract dictated that the original tenant, as an original contracting party, remained liable in respect of all of the covenants in the lease for the entire duration of the term, even after he assigned the lease. The original tenant under the existing regime is in the undesirable position of being liable for a breach of covenant committed after he has parted with his interest in the premises. If, for example, the tenant was granted a 25-year term which he assigned at the end of the 5th year to an assignee who then failed to pay rent and allowed the premises to fall into disrepair, the landlord could choose to sue, not the assignee, but the original tenant for non-payment of rent and breach of the repairing covenant. It does not matter that since the assignment the rent has been increased under the rent review clause (unless the increase is referrable to a variation of the lease terms agreed between the landlord and assignee – see s 18 of the LTCA 1995 and the case of *Friends' Provident Life Office v BRB* [1995] 48 EG 106).

The effect of privity of contract becomes increasingly significant in recessionary times. If the reason why the assignee has defaulted in his obligations under the lease is that the assignee has become insolvent, instead of pursuing a worthless action against the assignee, the landlord would look to the original tenant for payment of rent.

For how long is the original tenant liable?

The original tenant's liability lasts for the entire duration of the contractual term. Once he has assigned his interest in the lease, his liability will not extend into any continuation of that term that may arise under s 24 of the LTA 1954, unless there is an express provision in the lease to the contrary. As will be seen later (at **34.1.6**), a tenancy which is protected by Part II of that Act will not come to an end on the expiration of the contractual term. Instead, s 24 continues the tenancy on exactly the same terms, and at the same rent, until the tenancy is terminated in one of the methods prescribed by the Act. Hence, the contractual rent remains payable beyond the expiry date of the lease, but the effect of the House of Lords' decision in *City of London Corporation v Fell* [1993] 49 EG 113 is that, where the original tenant has already assigned his lease before the contractual expiry date of the lease, his liability will cease at that date, and will not be continued.

However, even before *City of London Corporation v Fell*, landlords were drafting leases to include a provision to ensure that the original tenant (and any assignees who entered into a direct covenant with the landlord) would remain liable to perform the covenants during a statutory continuation. This would be done by defining 'the Term' in the lease to include 'the period of any holding over or any extension or continuance whether by agreement or operation of law'. The tenant is then required to pay the rent and perform his covenants during 'the Term'. The one consolation for a tenant who has assigned the lease but remains liable because of the definition of 'the Term' is provided by *Herbert Duncan Limited v Cluttons* [1993] 04 EG 115, which held that the continuing liability to pay rent relates only to the contractual rent under the lease, and not to any interim rent fixed by the court under s 24A of the LTA 1954 unless the lease states otherwise.

The need for an indemnity

As a result of the continuing nature of the original tenant's liability under the old regime, it is essential that, on an assignment, the original tenant obtains an indemnity from the assignee against all future breaches of covenant (whether committed by the assignee or a successor in title). An express indemnity may be taken, but this is not strictly necessary since s 77 of the LPA 1925 automatically implies into every assignment for value a covenant to indemnify the assignor against all future breaches of covenant. If the lease is registered at HM Land Registry, s 24(1)(a) of the Land Registration Act 1925 implies a similar covenant for indemnity into a transfer of the lease, whether or not value is given.

From a practical point of view, it should be noted that an indemnity from an assignee (whether express or implied) is worthless if the assignee is insolvent, and this may be the very reason why the landlord is pursuing the original tenant in the first place.

Where there has been a succession of assignments, and the original tenant finds that he is unable to obtain a full indemnity against his immediate assignee, the assignee in possession may be liable at common law to indemnify the original tenant who has been sued for breach of covenant (see *Moule v Garrett* (1872) LR 7 Exch 101), but again the indemnity may be worthless owing to the insolvency of the defaulting assignee.

The assignee – privity of estate

By virtue of the doctrine of privity of estate, an assignee under the old regime is liable in respect of all of the covenants in the lease which 'touch and concern' the demised premises, for as long as the lease remains vested in him.

An assignee cannot be sued for a breach of covenant committed prior to the lease being vested in him, save to the extent that the breach in question is a continuing breach (eg breach of a covenant to repair) which effectively becomes the assignee's breach from the date of the assignment. If, at the time of the assignment there are arrears of rent, the landlord's action to recover the arrears would be against the assignor, not the assignee. However, from a practical point of view, the landlord is unlikely to give his consent to an assignment (assuming the lease requires his consent) unless the arrears are cleared. Further, the assignee is unlikely to take the assignment while rent is in arrear because of the risk of forfeiture of the lease on account of the outstanding breach.

An assignee is not liable for breaches of covenant committed after he has parted with his interest in the premises, (although he may still be sued in respect of breaches committed while he was the tenant) and he is not liable in respect of covenants which do not touch and concern the premises (but see below).

Covenants which touch and concern

Under the old regime, an assignee is only liable in respect of those covenants which touch and concern the demised premises. These are covenants which are not in the nature of personal covenants, but have direct reference to the premises in question by laying down something which is to be done or not to be done at the premises, and which affect the landlord in his normal capacity as landlord, or the tenant in his normal capacity as tenant. If the purpose of the covenant is to achieve something which is collateral to the relationship of landlord and tenant, then the covenant does not touch and concern.

Nearly all of the covenants in a typical commercial lease touch and concern the demised premises. For example, the covenants:

(1) to pay rent;
(2) to repair;
(3) to use the premises for a particular purpose;
(4) not to make alterations without consent;
(5) not to assign or sublet without consent;

are all covenants which relate to the premises and have reference to the landlord and tenant relationship in respect of those premises.

By contrast, the following covenants do not touch and concern:

(1) to pay a periodic sum to a third party;
(2) to build premises for the landlord upon some other land;
(3) to repair or renew chattels (as distinct from fixtures, which would form part of the premises).

These covenants do not have any reference to the relationship of landlord and tenant in respect of the land in question and, therefore, would not bind an assignee.

Direct covenants

Landlords have never liked the limited duration of an assignee's liability under the doctrine of privity of estate. In practice, therefore, it is common for the landlord to try to extend the liability of an assignee under the old regime by requiring him, as a condition of the landlord's licence to assign, to enter into a direct covenant to observe the covenants in the lease for the entire duration of the term, thereby creating privity of contract between landlord and assignee. This covenant is usually contained in the formal licence to assign (see **30.2**). The landlord will always then have a choice between original tenant and present assignee as to whom to sue for a breach of covenant committed by the latter. Where intermediate assignees have entered into direct covenants in this manner, the landlord's options are increased.

If an assignee has given a direct covenant to the landlord, the extent of his continuing liability is governed by the *Fell* case, and the definition of 'the Term' in the lease in the same way as applies to the original tenant.

The need for an indemnity

The assignee from the original tenant will have covenanted, either expressly or impliedly, with the original tenant to indemnify him against liability for loss arising out of any future breach of covenant (whether committed by the assignee or a successor in title). Irrespective of whether the assignee is affected by privity of estate or contract, because he gave an indemnity covenant to his assignor, he needs to obtain one from his assignee. An express indemnity may be taken, but s 77 of the LPA 1925 and s 24(1)(a) of the Land Registration Act 1925 will operate in the same way as before.

14.3.2 The new regime

As stated above, the main purpose of the LTCA 1995 was to abolish privity of contract in leases, and it is therefore in the area of tenant liability that the Act has the most significant impact.

The original tenant – privity of contract release

The basic rule is that a tenant under a lease which is a new lease for the purposes of the LTCA 1995 is only liable for breaches of covenant committed while the lease is vested in him. Thus, on assignment of the lease, the assignor is automatically released from all the tenant covenants of the tenancy (and he ceases to be entitled to the benefit of the landlord covenants). This means that while the outgoing tenant can be sued for breaches of covenant committed at a time when the lease was vested in him, he cannot be sued for any subsequent breaches.

The assignee – liability on covenants

The basic rule applies equally to assignees. As from the date of assignment, an assignee becomes bound by the tenant covenants in the lease except to the extent that immediately before the assignment they did not bind the assignor (eg they were expressed to be personal to the original tenant), but when he assigns the lease, he is automatically released from all of the tenant covenants. One slight change for leases under the new regime is that an assignee will be liable on all the tenant covenants in the lease whether or not they 'touch and concern' the land. The combination of this slight change, and the statutorily imposed limitation on the duration of an assignee's liability, makes the practice under the old regime of obtaining direct covenants from assignees inapplicable to leases granted under the new regime.

In the same way that the assignee becomes bound by the tenant covenants, so too does the assignee become entitled, as from the date of the assignment, to the benefit of the landlord covenants in the lease.

Excluded assignments

Assignments in breach of covenant (eg where the tenant has not complied with a requirement in the lease to obtain his landlord's consent before assigning) or by operation of law (eg on the death or bankruptcy of a tenant) are excluded assignments for the purposes of the LTCA 1995. On an excluded assignment, the assignor will not be released from the tenant covenants of the lease, and will remain liable to the landlord, jointly and severally with the assignee, until the next assignment, which is not an excluded assignment, takes place.

Authorised guarantee agreements

To counterbalance the loss to the landlord of the benefits of the old privity regime, the LTCA allows the landlord to require an outgoing tenant, who will be released from liability under the Act, to enter into a form of guarantee whereby the outgoing tenant guarantees the performance of the tenant covenants by the incoming tenant (see **20.2.8**).

Indemnity covenants?

As an assigning tenant is not liable for the breaches of covenant committed by his successor, the LTCA 1995 has repealed s 77 and s 24(1)(a) in relation to leases granted under the new regime. However, it should be noted that an outgoing tenant may remain liable to the landlord for an assignee's breaches of covenant under the terms of an authorised guarantee agreement and, in such circumstances, an express indemnity from the assignee should be obtained.

14.4 THE GUARANTOR

Much attention in practice is given to the financial status of the proposed tenant, and a consideration of what is called 'the strength of the tenant's covenant'. A tenant is said to give 'a good covenant' if it can be expected that the tenant will pay the rent on time throughout the term, and diligently perform his other obligations under the lease. An established, high performing and renowned public limited company (such as one of the large retail food companies) will be regarded as a good covenant in the commercial letting market, whereas newly formed public limited companies and many private companies, whose reputation, reliability and financial standing are unknown in the property market, will not be perceived as giving a good covenant. If the covenant is so bad that the landlord has reservations about the proposed tenant's ability to maintain rental payments throughout the term without financial difficulties, the landlord will consider not granting a lease to that tenant in the first place. However, in situations which fall between these two extremes, the landlord often requires a third party, known as a guarantor, to join in the lease to guarantee the tenant's obligations.

14.4.1 Practical points

The landlord's aim is to ensure that he receives the rent due under the lease on time throughout the term, either from the tenant, or if the tenant defaults, from the guarantor. Therefore, just as the landlord ought to investigate the financial status of his proposed tenant, so too should he investigate the status of the guarantor nominated by the tenant.

With private limited companies or newly formed public limited companies (who, even with plc status, may be just as likely to be in breach as any other tenant) many landlords will ask for one or more of the company's directors to guarantee the tenant's performance of its obligations. However, the landlord should not necessarily be so blinkered in his approach, since other options may prove to be more fruitful. Does a subsidiary company have a parent or sister company which can stand as guarantor? If the directors are not of sufficient financial standing, are the shareholders of the company in any better position to give the landlord the element of reliability he requires? Will the tenant's bank guarantee the obligation of its client?

The guarantor should be advised to seek independent advice, since there is a clear conflict of interests between tenant and guarantor. The conflict arises in that, on the one hand the advice to be given to the tenant is that, without a guarantor, the tenant will not get a lease, whilst on the other hand, the advice to give to the guarantor would be to avoid giving the guarantee. Further, in seeking to make amendments to the surety covenants in the lease on behalf of the guarantor, the solicitor may be prejudicing the negotiation of the lease terms between the landlord and his tenant–client, causing delay or disruption.

14.4.2 The extent of the guarantee

The old regime
The purpose of the guarantee is to ensure that the guarantor will pay the rent if the tenant does not, and will remedy or indemnify the landlord against any breaches of covenant committed by the tenant. Two points should be noted. First, it is usual for the landlord in drafting the lease to define 'the Tenant' to include the tenant's

successors in title. This means that in guaranteeing the obligations of 'the Tenant', the guarantor has guaranteed the performance of future (and as yet unknown) assignees of the lease. His liability would, therefore, extend throughout the duration of the lease (even after the original tenant had assigned the lease). Secondly, even if the guarantee was limited to a guarantee of the original tenant's obligations, an original tenant remains liable by virtue of privity of contract under the existing regime to perform the covenants in the lease for its entire duration. Should, therefore, the landlord choose to sue, not the assignee in possession, but the original tenant, the guarantee would remain active.

Ideally, the guarantor should seek to limit the extent of his liability so that the guarantee applies only for so long as the lease remains vested in the tenant in respect of whom the guarantee was originally sought. This is a matter for negotiation with the landlord.

The new regime

Abolition of the concept of privity of contract in leases applies equally to guarantors. Section 24(2) of the LTCA 1995 provides that where a tenant is released under the LTCA 1995 from the tenant covenants of the lease, any person (ie the guarantor) who was bound, before the release, by a covenant imposing liability upon that person in the event of default by the tenant, is released to the same extent as the tenant. Any attempt to extend the liability of a guarantor beyond the duration of the liability of the tenant whose performance was guaranteed is likely to fall foul of the anti-avoidance provisions of s 25 of the LTCA 1995. However, it is arguable that a guarantor can be required to undertake a separate obligation to guarantee the tenant's performance under any authorised guarantee agreement he may enter into.

There is some comfort for the guarantor in either regime in that, unless there is an express provision in the lease to the contrary, the liability of the guarantor will cease upon the contractual term date and will not continue during a statutory continuation tenancy under s 24 of the LTA 1954 (see *Junction Estates Ltd v Cope* (1974) 27 P & CR 482). However, it is common practice to define the lease term to include 'the period of any holding over or any extension or continuance whether by agreement or operation of law,' and to prolong the guarantor's liability by requiring him to covenant with the landlord throughout 'the term' as so defined.

14.4.3 Discharge or release

The guarantor cannot unilaterally revoke his guarantee, but in certain cases, usually where the landlord acts to the prejudice of the guarantor, the conduct of the landlord might operate as a release.

Variations

If the landlord, without obtaining the consent of the guarantor, agrees with the tenant to vary the terms of the lease (eg by substituting more onerous repairing obligations), the variation of the lease will operate to discharge the guarantor. A guarantor cannot stand as surety and be made liable for the tenant's default in the performance of terms different to those guaranteed to be performed, unless the guarantor has agreed to the variation. However, an immaterial variation of the lease which would not prejudice the guarantor (eg by substituting less onerous repairing obligations) is not likely to discharge the guarantor, although authority appears to suggest that it is for the guarantor to decide whether or not he would be prejudiced by the proposed variation. In *Holme v Brunskill* (1877) 3 QBD 495, a surrender of part of the premises comprised in the lease (which might not appear in any way to prejudice the guarantor, particularly if the rent is reduced as a result), which was agreed without the consent of the guarantor, operated to discharge the guarantee. However, a variation which does not affect the terms of the (tenant's) principal contract will not affect the guarantor's secondary contract (see *Metropolitan Properties Co (Regis) Ltd v Bartholomew* [1995] 14 EG 143).

A surrender of the whole of the premises comprised in the lease will operate to end the liability of the guarantor as from the date of surrender, but not in respect of any breaches of covenant outstanding at that time.

Increasing the rent by exercising a rent review clause does not amount to a variation and so will not release the guarantor. This means that a guarantor may be guaranteeing the payment in future of an unknown level of rent (although see the protection given to guarantors of former tenants by s 18 of the LTCA 1995 and the *Friends' Provident* case).

'Giving time'

'Giving time' to the tenant may operate to discharge the guarantee. A landlord 'gives time' to a tenant if, in a binding way, he agrees to allow the tenant to pay rent late, or not at all. It does not seem that a mere omission to press for payment (eg due to an oversight, or perhaps to avoid a waiver of the right to forfeit the lease) will amount to the giving of time.

Release of co-guarantor

According to general principles of suretyship, if there is more than one guarantor, the release by the landlord of one of them operates as a release of all of them.

Death

The death of the tenant is not likely to bring an end to the guarantee, since the lease will vest in the tenant's personal representatives who, as the tenant's successors in title, will become 'the Tenant' under the lease, whose obligations are guaranteed by the guarantor. Under the new regime, such a vesting would be an excluded assignment, and so the guarantor would not be released. Further, the death of the guarantor will not necessarily bring an end to the guarantee since the guarantor's own personal representatives will remain liable under the guarantee to the extent of the deceased's assets passing through their hands. However, it is more common for the landlord to make provision for the possible death of the guarantor by obtaining a covenant from the tenant obliging him to find a suitable replacement.

Bankruptcy or liquidation

The bankruptcy or liquidation of the tenant will not operate to release the guarantor. On the bankruptcy of an individual tenant, the lease will vest in the trustee-in-bankruptcy who will become 'the Tenant' for the purposes of the lease (and such a vesting is an excluded assignment under the new regime), whilst on the liquidation of a corporate tenant the lease will remain vested in the company (unless the liquidator obtains an order under s 145 of the Insolvency Act 1986).

Even if the trustee or liquidator chooses to disclaim the lease, the disclaimer will not operate to end the guarantor's liability (see **32.1.2**).

14.4.4 Drafting points for the landlord

The landlord should ensure that the guarantor joins in the lease to give the covenants the landlord requires.

The two basic obligations of a guarantor are to pay the rent (and any other sums payable by the tenant under the lease) if the tenant does not pay, and to remedy, or to indemnify the landlord against loss caused by, any breaches of covenant committed by the tenant. The landlord will ensure that the guarantor is liable for the period in respect of which the tenant is liable under the lease (and, possibly, under any authorised guarantee agreement that the tenant may enter into).

Several other provisions are usually required by the landlord:

(1) A covenant from the tenant to provide a replacement guarantor should one of several unfortunate or undesirable events happen. For instance, if the guarantor is an individual who dies, or becomes mentally incapable (ie a receiver is appointed under s 99 of the Mental Health Act 1983) or has a petition in bankruptcy presented against him (or is affected by other proceedings under the Insolvency Act 1986 which the landlord considers serious enough to warrant substitution) the landlord will require the tenant to find a replacement of equivalent financial standing. If the guarantor is a company and a winding-up commences (or, as above, it is affected by other adverse insolvency proceedings), again the tenant will be required to find a reasonably acceptable replacement.

(2) A provision protecting the landlord against the tenant's trustee-in-bankruptcy or liquidator disclaiming the lease to bring the tenant's liability to an end. The effect of a disclaimer is dealt with at **32.1.3**. For present purposes it can be said that, whilst disclaimer does not end the liability of a guarantor, most landlords will nevertheless want the ability to require the guarantor to take a lease from the landlord in the event of disclaimer, for the full unexpired residue of the term then remaining.

(3) A provision to deal with situations which might otherwise operate to release the guarantor. As part of the guarantor's covenants, the landlord will include a declaration that a release will not be effected by the giving of time to the tenant, or by a variation in the terms of the lease, (although as a concession, the landlord might accept that a variation prejudicial to the guarantor will still operate as a release unless the guarantor has consented to it). The effect of stating in the lease that the guarantor will not be released 'by any other event which, but for this provision, would operate to release the Surety' is doubtful.

14.4.5 Drafting points for the guarantor

If the guarantor has accepted the principle of giving a guarantee, he should make all efforts to minimise his liability. There are several provisions a guarantor can seek to negotiate:

(1) A limit on the length of his liability; whilst the LTCA 1995 releases a guarantor to the same extent as it releases the tenant, the guarantor should try to ensure that he is not contractually bound to guarantee the tenant under any authorised guarantee agreement (as to which, see **20.2.8**).

(2) An obligation on the landlord's part to notify the guarantor of any default by the tenant; one would expect the tenant to tell his guarantor if the tenant was experiencing difficulties in meeting his obligations under the lease. However,

this might not always be the case, and in order to alert the guarantor to possible claims under the guarantee and, perhaps, to enable him to put pressure on the tenant, he could seek to include a covenant by the landlord to notify him in writing whenever the tenant falls into arrears with the rent, or otherwise breaches a covenant in the lease.

(3) Participation in rent reviews; as the guarantor guarantees payment of future unascertained rents he may try to persuade the landlord to allow him to play a part in the rent review process. This would necessitate amendments to the usual rent review clause, and would not be attractive to the landlord. Further, the tenant would not be keen either to hand over the review negotiations to the guarantor or to have him involved as a third party in the review process, and an assignee of the lease would certainly see it as an unattractive proposition.

(4) An ability to demand an assignment of the lease from the tenant where the tenant is in default under the lease. This would enable the guarantor to minimise his liability by being able to call for an assignment and then assign the lease to a more stable assignee.

14.4.6 An assignee's guarantor

The above paragraphs have concentrated on the guarantee to be provided by the original tenant on the grant of the lease. However, as a condition of granting licence to assign the lease, the landlord may require the assignee to provide a suitable guarantor in respect of his obligations (see **20.2.3**). Under the old regime, it will be the landlord's intention to fix the new guarantor with liability for the duration of the contractual term and beyond, in the same way that he tries to fix the liability of the original tenant's guarantor. Under the new regime, liability should not exceed the liability of the assignee.

14.5 RENT DEPOSITS

As an alternative (or in addition) to a guarantee, the landlord may require the tenant to enter into a rent deposit deed whereby the tenant is required to deposit with the landlord, on the grant of the lease, a sum of money equivalent to, say, 12 months' rent, which the landlord is allowed to call upon in the event of tenant default. At the end of the lease (or, perhaps, on lawful assignment), the deposit should be returned to the tenant.

Careful thought must be given to the setting up of this arrangement and to the drafting of the rent deposit deed. The following factors should be kept in mind:

(1) The deed should specify what default by the tenant will trigger access to the deposit (eg non-payment of rent, VAT or interest, or other breaches of covenant).

(2) If the deposited money is to be viewed as belonging to the landlord, it will be at risk if the landlord becomes insolvent. For instance, it would fall under the control of the landlord company's liquidator if the company went into liquidation. Equally, if the money is to be viewed as belonging to the tenant, it will be at risk at the precise moment when the tenant is likely to be in default in the performance of the lease terms (ie the occasion of his insolvency). It is, therefore, usual to place the money in a separate deposit account (managed in such a way that only the landlord and his nominees may draw money out of the account) which is then charged to the landlord in order that the landlord has

first call on the money in a liquidation or bankruptcy. If the tenant is a company, the charge it creates will have to be registered at Companies House pursuant to s 395 of the Companies Act 1985.

(3) Under the old regime, the obligations under the rent deposit deed are personal obligations between the original landlord and the original tenant, and the obligation to repay the deposit at the end of the term will not bind an assignee of the reversion: see *Hua Chiao Commercial Bank Ltd v Chiaphua Industries Ltd* [1987] 1 AC 99. Further, the benefit of the obligation to repay does not pass to an assignee of the lease and thus, if the landlord inadvertently repaid the deposit to an assignee, the obligation to pay to the original tenant would still exist. The deed should deal with the personal nature of the obligations by providing that the landlord should not assign his interest in the reversion other than to a buyer who, by supplemental deed executed in favour of the tenant, expressly takes over the obligations of the landlord contained in the rent deposit deed. It should further provide that, on assignment of the lease, the deposit should be repaid to the tenant if the landlord has consented to the assignment in the usual manner under the alienation covenant. The assignee will be required to enter into a fresh rent deposit agreement.

    Under the new regime, unless expressed to be personal, the obligation to repay the deposit will pass to an assignee of the reversion as one of the landlord covenants of the tenancy. Similarly, the benefit of repayment will pass to an assignee of the lease. The original tenant should, therefore, ensure either that the benefit of repayment is expressed to be personal to him, or that the assignee pays to him a sum equivalent to the deposit at the time of the assignment. An assignee of the reversion should ensure that, as he will have the burden of the covenant to repay the deposit, he has control of the deposit itself. An original landlord may be reluctant to part with the deposit unless he is able to secure a release from the covenant to repay the deposit under the LTCA 1995. If he is unable to secure a release, he may prefer to retain the deposit and act as the assignee's attorney in relation to accessing the deposit on occasions of tenant default.

(4) The parties should consider to whom the interest earned on the money belongs (usually the tenant), whether the interest can be drawn out of the account, and at what stage the tenant will be required to make up any shortfall in the deposit (if, eg, the level of the account drops below an agreed figure due to the tenant's default). The deed will also have to make clear the situations in which the landlord will be entitled to draw upon the deposit.

One overriding factor that remains is that the tenant may not have sufficient money to put up a deposit in the first place.

Chapter 15

THE PARCELS CLAUSE

Chapter 15 contents

15.1 PURPOSE

The purpose of the parcels clause is to accurately and unambiguously describe the property being let to the tenant so that it is clear what is included and what is excluded. Where the whole of a building is being let, the parcels clause will contain the same sort of description as in the case of the sale of freehold land. Moreover, provided the boundaries are clearly identifiable it may be possible to adequately describe the premises in words alone. However, where a lease of part only of a building is intended, the parcels clause needs more care and attention and a plan will be essential (see **27.2**).

15.2 AIRSPACE AND UNDERGROUND

A lease of land includes the buildings on it and everything above and below the land. Thus, a lease of a building includes the airspace above it to such a height as is necessary for the ordinary use and enjoyment of the land and buildings. However, the parties may limit the extent of the parcels clause by excluding the airspace above the roof. If there is such a limitation, this will prevent the tenant from adding extra floors by extending upwards since to do so would be a trespass. The tenant should also appreciate that problems may be caused if he had to erect scaffolding above roof height to comply with his obligation to repair the roof; that would also amount to a trespass. The tenant should, therefore, ensure that he has any necessary right to enter the airspace above his building to the extent necessary to comply with his obligations under the lease. Without any limitation on the airspace the tenant will be free to extend upwards subject only to obtaining any necessary planning permission and consent under the alterations covenant.

15.3 FIXTURES

The point about a fixture is that it is part of the demised premises and prima facie belongs to the landlord. If an article is not a fixture, it will be a chattel. Yet, despite the apparent simplicity of the matter, it is not always easy to distinguish between the two, and over the years the courts have developed a test based on the degree of annexation of the item to the land and the purpose of annexation (see, eg, *Holland v Hodgson* (1872) LR 7 CP 328). However, the application of this test to a given set of facts is notoriously difficult and the reader is referred to one of the standard works on land law for further consideration of this issue (and in particular the House of Lords judgment in *Elitestone v Morris* [1997] 2 All ER 513).

For the avoidance of doubt, a prospective tenant should always compile a full inventory of the fixtures which are present at the commencement of the lease.

15.3.1 Repair of fixtures

If an article is a fixture, it is treated as part of the demised premises and the tenant will become responsible for its repair under his obligation to repair 'the demised premises'. This can have a significant impact on the tenant bearing in mind that many business premises include expensive fixtures such as central heating and air conditioning plant. For this reason the tenant should always inspect the condition of the fixtures before completion of the lease and if any defects are discovered, the tenant must make sure that he does not become liable to remedy those defects under his repairing obligation. This can be achieved by getting the landlord to do any necessary repairs before the lease commences or by agreeing the state and condition with the landlord and ensuring that the covenant to repair does not require any higher standard than that existing at the date of commencement.

15.3.2 Removal of fixtures

The tenant may have the right to remove fixtures at the end of the lease depending upon whether they are 'landlord's fixtures', which cannot be removed, or 'tenant's fixtures', which the tenant is entitled to remove unless the lease provides to the contrary. Tenant's fixtures are those articles:

(1) affixed by the tenant;
(2) for the purpose of his trade; and
(3) which are capable of removal without substantially damaging the building and without destroying the usefulness of the article.

The terms of the lease may require the tenant to yield up the premises at the end of the term together with all fixtures. Whether this excludes the tenant's right to remove tenant's fixtures depends on the form of wording used; very clear words will be required before the right is excluded. However, it has been held that an obligation to yield up the premises 'with all and singular the fixtures and articles belonging thereto', is sufficient to exclude the right but the tenant should resist such a clause. Where the tenant is entitled to remove fixtures, he must make good any damage he causes by their removal and, as a general rule, the right only exists during the term.

15.4 RIGHTS TO BE GRANTED AND RESERVED

The tenant may need to be granted rights to enable him to use the demised premises to their full extent. For example, he may need the right to enter upon the landlord's adjoining property to comply with his obligation to repair; this can be particularly important where the walls of the demised premises are flush against the boundary. The tenant may also need the right to connect into services on the landlord's adjoining property.

From the landlord's point of view, he may need to reserve rights such as a right to enter the demised premises to view the state and condition or to repair. The service pipes and cables for the landlord's adjoining property may pass under or through the demised premises and the landlord will thus need to reserve rights in respect of them. These rights will be set out after the parcels clause and because these issues most frequently arise on a lease of part of a building they are considered further at **27.3**.

Chapter 16

TERM

16.1 INTRODUCTION

Chapter 16 contents
Introduction
Break clauses
Options to renew

The duration of a lease for a term of years must be fixed and certain before the lease takes effect. Thus, for example, a tenancy 'until the landlord requires the land for road widening', is void for uncertainty (*Prudential Assurance Co Ltd v London Residuary Body* [1992] 3 All ER 504). This principle applies to all leases, including periodic tenancies. A provision that one party is unable to determine a periodic tenancy, or for it only to be determined in certain circumstances, is inconsistent with the concept of a periodic tenancy. If termination on the happening of an uncertain event is required by either party, this can be achieved by granting a long fixed term with a break clause exercisable only on the happening of the event in question (see **16.2**).

Most business tenancies will be for a fixed term in which case the lease must specify the date of commencement of the term and its duration (eg 'for a term of ten years from and including the 29 September 1994'). There is no need for the commencement of the term to be the same date as the date of completion of the lease. It may be more convenient for the landlord, particularly when he is granting several leases in the same block, to choose one specific date from which the term of each will run. If this is an earlier date than completion then, unless the lease provides to the contrary, the tenant's rights and obligations will only arise on completion, not the earlier date. However, for the avoidance of doubt, the lease should expressly state the precise date from which the rent is to be payable.

In specifying the date of commencement, it is important to avoid any ambiguity so that it is clear beyond doubt when the term expires (but note the effect of the lease being protected under Part II of the LTA 1954). The presumption is that if the term is stated to run 'from' a particular date, the term begins on the next day. If, however, the term is expressed to begin 'on' a particular date, that day is the first day of the term. To avoid any possible argument, it is always best to use clear words such as 'beginning on', 'beginning with' or 'from and including' (see *Meadfield Properties Ltd v Secretary of State for the Environment* [1995] 03 EG 128).

16.2 BREAK CLAUSES

The possibility of the lease containing a break clause has been mentioned above, see **11.1.3**.

16.2.1 Who may operate them and when?

Either or both parties may be given an option to determine the lease at specified times during the term, or on the happening of certain specified events. For example, the tenant may be given the option to determine a 21-year lease at the end of the 7th and 14th years, or if he is prevented from trading due to the withdrawal of any necessary statutory licences. The landlord may be given an option to determine if he, at some future date, wishes to redevelop the premises or to occupy them for his own business purposes. The tenant should try to stipulate that the landlord cannot exercise the option until after a specified number of years as otherwise from the tenant's point of view the venture will be too uncertain in its duration.

Some options to break are expressed to be personal to the original tenant in order to prevent them being exercised by successors in title following an assignment. However, in *Brown & Root Technology v Sun Alliance* [1997] 18 EG 123, the court held that following the assignment of a registered lease to the tenant's parent company, the option was still exercisable by the original tenant until the assignment was completed by registration. It was only on registration of title that the legal estate vested in the assignee; until then the assignor remained the tenant and thus retained the ability to exercise the option. The case concerned the assignment of a lease granted before the Landlord and Tenant (Covenants) Act 1995 came into force (1 January 1996), and the position may well be different for leases granted on or after that date.

16.2.2 How are they exercised?

The break clause must be exercised in accordance with its terms. Thus, it must be exercised at the correct time and in the correct manner. If there are any pre-conditions for the exercise of the option, they must be strictly complied with. Consequently, the tenant should be wary of any provision in the lease making compliance of tenant covenants a pre-condition for the exercise of the option. In such a case even a trivial, immaterial breach of covenant on the part of the tenant may prevent him from validly exercising the option. The tenant should modify such a pre-condition so that it requires 'substantial' or 'material' compliance (see, eg, *Bairstow Eves (Securities) Ltd v Ripley* [1992] 2 EGLR 47). Similarly, any notice requirements for the exercise of the option must be strictly complied with because, unless the lease states to the contrary, time is of the essence of a break clause (*United Scientific Holdings v Burnley Borough Council* [1978] AC 904). If an incorrect date is specified in the break notice, the court may be prepared to correct it if the mistake would not have misled a reasonable recipient (*Mannai Investment Co Ltd v Eagle Star Life Assurance Co Ltd* [1997] 24 EG 122).

16.2.3 Effect of exercise on sub-tenants

The effect of the exercise of an option in a head-lease may be to terminate any sub-lease granted. This is dealt with further at **33.4**.

16.2.4 Relationship with the LTA 1954, Part II

The landlord must be aware of the inter-relationship with Part II of the LTA 1954 and may wish to give thought to drafting the circumstances giving rise to the exercise of the option in line with the requirements of s 30(1)(f) or (g) of that Act (see **34.5**). This is desirable because the exercise of the option may not necessarily entitle the landlord to recover possession as he must also, where necessary, comply with the provisions of the 1954 Act (see **34.2**). Further, where necessary, regard should be had to the relationship between the notice required under the break clause and the notice provisions of the 1954 Act.

16.3 OPTIONS TO RENEW

Options to renew are not often found in business leases because most tenants are protected under Part II of the LTA 1954 and will, therefore, have a statutory right to a new tenancy which the landlord may only oppose on certain grounds (see Chapter 34).

Chapter 17

RENT

Chapter 17 contents

17.1 INTRODUCTION

One of the primary purposes in granting the lease is to enable the landlord to receive income in the form of rent. However, the payment of rent by the tenant is not essential to the landlord and tenant relationship and it is not uncommon, when property is difficult to let, for landlords to grant rent-free periods to tenants as an inducement for them to take the lease or to allow the tenant to fit out the premises.

The lease must contain a covenant by the tenant to pay the rent. In certain rare situations the tenant may have the right to deduct sums from the rent payable. For example, the tenant has the right to deduct those sums allowed by statute and, where the landlord is in breach of his repairing obligation, the tenant seemingly has an ancient right to undertake the repairs himself and deduct the expense from future payments of rent (see **31.2**). In addition, the tenant may be able to exercise a right of set-off and deduct an unliquidated sum for damages where the landlord is in breach of covenant and the tenant has thereby suffered a loss. Landlords often seek to counter the tenant's right to make deductions by stating in the covenant to pay rent that rent is to be paid 'without deduction'. However, this will not prevent a tenant from making a deduction authorised by statute, nor from exercising his right of set-off (see *Connaught Restaurants Ltd v Indoor Leisure Ltd* [1993] 46 EG 184). To exclude the tenant's right of set-off, very clear words must be used.

The covenant to pay rent is usually followed by a covenant by the tenant to pay all taxes, rates, assessments and outgoings imposed on the demised premises; this will include rates and water rates. For the avoidance of doubt, the tenant should make it clear that this obligation does not extend to any taxes payable by the landlord arising out of the receipt of the rent or due to any dealing by the landlord with the reversion.

In the definitions clause of the lease the landlord should seek to define 'Rent' as also including any 'interim rent' which may become payable under s 24A of the LTA 1954 (see **34.4**). If this were not done and the original tenant's continuing liability was stated by the lease to extend into the statutory continuation (under s 24), he would only remain liable for the contractual rent during that period and not for any interim rent which an assignee may be ordered to pay as part of any future renewal proceedings under the 1954 Act (*Herbert Duncan Ltd v Cluttons* [1993] 04 EG 115).

17.2 AMOUNT

The amount of rent must be certain. However, the actual amount need not be stated as long as some means is provided by which the exact amount can be ascertained. For example, the rent may be fixed at £25,000 per annum for the first 5 years of a 10-year lease and then at 'such revised rent as may be ascertained'. Provided the means of ascertaining the new rent are clearly stated, this is a valid method of dealing with the rent. Such clauses are dealt with in Chapter 18 where consideration is also given to the different methods of assessing the revised rent.

17.3 TIME FOR PAYMENT

The lease should set out:

(1) the date from which the rent is payable and the date of the first payment. It is usual to state that the first payment, or an apportioned part of it, is payable on the date of the lease unless a rent-free period is to be given;
(2) the payment dates, otherwise, in the case of a tenancy for a fixed term of years, there is authority for the proposition that the rent will be payable yearly. It is common practice in business leases to make the rent payable on the usual quarter days, ie 25 March, 24 June, 29 September and 25 December;
(3) whether rent is to be payable in advance or arrear. Unless the lease provides to the contrary, as is usual, the general law provides that rent is payable in arrears.

In modern commercial leases, provision is often made for the payment of rent by way of direct debit or standing order to minimise the risk of delay.

17.4 OTHER PAYMENTS RESERVED AS RENT

It is common for leases to provide for the tenant to make other payments to the landlord such as a service charge, or reimbursement of insurance premiums paid by the landlord. Landlords will often require the lease to state that such sums are payable as additional rent. The advantage to the landlord is that if the tenant defaults, the remedy of distress will be available; a remedy which can only be used for non-payment of rent and not for breaches of other covenants. Further, the landlord will be able to forfeit the lease for non-payment of sums defined as rent without the need to serve a notice under s 146 of the LPA 1925, see **33.5**.

It would also be possible for any VAT payable on the rent to be reserved as additional rent.

17.5 SUSPENSION OF RENT

In the absence of any contrary provision in the lease, the rent will continue to be payable even if the premises are damaged or destroyed and so cannot be used by the tenant. The contractual doctrine of frustration will only apply to leases in exceptional circumstances (see *National Carriers Ltd v Panalpina (Northern) Ltd* [1981] AC 675). From the tenant's point of view, therefore, he should insist on a proviso that the rent is suspended if the premises become unfit for use. If the lease contains a service charge, provision should also be made for this to be suspended as otherwise it too would continue to be payable. This issue is considered further at **25.7**.

17.6 INTEREST

Unless there is provision to the contrary, interest cannot be charged by the landlord on any late payment by the tenant of rent or other sums due under the lease (unless judgment is obtained against the tenant for such amounts). It is, therefore, usual for a lease to provide that interest is payable by the tenant on any late payment of money due under the lease (from the due date to the date of actual payment). If, as usual, the rate of interest is geared to the base rate of a named bank (eg 4 per cent above), a problem may arise if that bank no longer fixes a base rate. It is, therefore, sensible to provide for an alternative rate should this situation arise. For the tenant's protection, this should be stated to be 'some other reasonable rate as the landlord may specify'. Without the addition of the word 'reasonable' the tenant would have no right to dispute any new rate he thought excessive.

From the landlord's point of view, it is preferable for the lease to state that the interest rate is to apply 'both before and after any judgment'.

17.7 VAT

The implications of VAT on business leases has been discussed in Chapter 12. The landlord should include an appropriate clause entitling him to add VAT to the rent and other payments due from the tenant by providing that the rent and other sums are payable exclusive of VAT.

Chapter 18

THE RENT REVIEW CLAUSE

Chapter 18 contents

18.1 THE NEED FOR REVIEW

If the lease is granted for a term longer than about 5 years, the parties will have to address their minds to the question of whether provision should be made in the lease for varying the annual rent at intervals during the term. Traditionally, rent review clauses are included in commercial leases in order to give the landlord the ability to increase the rent, and this chapter generally proceeds on the basis that only upward revisions of rent are contemplated by the parties. However, thought may be given by the tenant, particularly in recessionary times, to the possibility of negotiating a flexible rent review clause which allows both upward and downward revisions in the annual rent.

Numerous factors motivate the landlord to include a rent review clause in the lease. If the tenant requires the security of a medium or long-term letting (eg 10 to 25 years), the landlord will not want the rent to be fixed throughout the term. The landlord will require protection against increases in the value of property interests and falls in the value of money that will inevitably occur during the term. What may be a fair market rent at the commencement of the term will nearly always become a wholly uneconomic rent after a few years because of inflation. If the landlord wants a realistic commercial return from his capital investment, he must have the opportunity to increase the rent. Moreover, should he intend to sell his reversion, it is a common requirement of an institutional investor that the rent is capable of upward-only revisions at regular intervals.

18.2 REGULARITY

Reviews are commonly programmed to occur at 3, 5 or 7-year intervals during the term. In a modern 25-year 'institutional' letting (so called because a 25-year lease, where the tenant is obliged to repair and pay for the insurance of the premises has always been the type of letting favoured by those institutions which frequently invest in the commercial property market), reviews will be programmed to occur at every 5th anniversary of the term. In recent recessionary times, a 15-year term, with reviews at 5-year intervals, has become common.

It is suggested that computation of the review dates in the lease is best achieved by reference to anniversaries of the term commencement date. However, if this method is adopted, the tenant should check that the term commencement date has not been significantly backdated by the landlord, as this would have the effect of advancing the first review date (eg if the term runs from 29 September 1996, but the lease is only completed on 1 November 1997, the 5th anniversary of the term is now less than 4 years away). Instead of calculating the dates as anniversaries of the start of the term, some leases set out the exact review dates in the lease. This, however, ought to be avoided since it can create valuation problems at review if the rent review clause in the lease (with its specific review dates) is incorporated as a term of the hypothetical letting (as to which, see **18.5**).

Landlords may attempt to insert a rent review date on the penultimate day of the term. At first sight, this might seem illogical since the term is about to end, but of course the tenant is likely to enjoy a statutory continuation of his tenancy under s 24(1) of the LTA 1954 whereby his tenancy will continue beyond the expiry date at the rent then payable. Where the tenant enjoys the benefit of a statutory continuation, the landlord may be able to apply to the court under s 24A of the LTA 1954 for an interim rent to be fixed (see **34.4**) in order to increase the rent payable by the tenant during the continuation. However, some landlords are not content to rely on the provisions of s 24A, preferring instead to achieve a rental uplift by implementing a contractual rent review clause on the penultimate day of the contractual term (ie just before the statutory continuation is due to begin). In practice, because the contractual method of assessment in the rent review clause is likely to differ from the statutory basis of assessment adopted by the court, a penultimate day rent review usually secures a greater increase in rent and, therefore, ensures that the rent payable during the statutory continuation is greater than would be the case under the interim rent provisions. An interim rent is often assessed at some 10–15 per cent below a full market rent (see **34.4.2**).

The tenant ought to resist a penultimate day rent review for the obvious reason that s 24A is likely to give him a better deal, and that a penultimate day review takes away the 'cushion effect' of s 24A (see **34.4.3**).

18.3 TYPES OF RENT REVIEW CLAUSES

There are various ways in which rent can be varied during the term.

18.3.1 Fixed increases

The lease could provide, for example, that in a lease for a 10-year term, the rent is set at £10,000 for the first 3 years of the term, £15,000 for the next 3 years, and £20,000 for the remainder of the term. This sort of clause is very rare since the parties to the lease are placing their faith in the fixed increases proving to be realistic.

18.3.2 Index-linked clauses

Some of the early forms of rent review clauses required the rent to be periodically reassessed by linking the rent to an index recording supposed changes in the value of money. Indexes such as the General Index of Retail Prices and the Producer Price Index can be used in order to revise the rent either at the review dates, or at every rent payment date. Reference should be made to one of the standard works on landlord and tenant law for information as to how such clauses work in practice.

There are problems with index-linked clauses. First, the index to which the rent is to be linked has to be agreed upon by the parties. Secondly, the parties must consider the possibility of the index ceasing to exist, or the method of compiling the index being altered, or the index from time to time being rebased to take account of excessive inflation. Finally, whilst the index may bear some relation to the current rate of inflation, it is likely to bear very little relation at all to changes occurring in the property market. Most importantly, an index-linked clause ignores factors which regularly have an impact on rental values, such as the state of the property market in the locality, and the type and quality of the accommodation.

Property values may rise faster than the chosen index, or may even fall during a time of inflation. For this reason, such clauses are not widely used.

18.3.3 Turnover and sub-lease rents

A turnover rent is one which is geared to the turnover of the tenant's business, and can only, therefore, be considered by the landlord where turnover is generated at the premises. A turnover rent would be impractical in the case of office or warehouse premises. The tenant's rent is worked out as a percentage of his turnover. If a turnover rent clause is to be used, thought will have to be given in the lease to the definition of the turnover of the business (eg whether credit sales are to be included with cash sales as part of the turnover), how the turnover is to be ascertained (eg whether a qualified accountant will be required in order to certify the amount of turnover, and whether access will be given to the landlord to inspect the tenant's books), how turnover is to be apportioned if it is generated at the demised premises and other premises, and whether the tenant is to be obliged in the lease to continue trading from the premises in order to generate turnover. Reference should be made to one of the standard works on landlord and tenant law for further details of the operation of turnover rent clauses.

The main problem from the tenant's point of view in gearing the rent to the tenant's turnover is that his turnover can increase, because the price at which the tenant buys in his product increases, but his gross profit may stay the same; (eg the tenant buys wholesale at 60p and sells retail at 100p with a profit of 40p per sale. If the wholesale price rises to 70p and the tenant, therefore, increases the retail price to 110p, his turnover will have increased, but his gross profit will have remained constant). If the tenant is paying as rent a percentage of his pure turnover, the amount of rent might increase, but his overall net profit may be reduced.

The tenant would, therefore, prefer the rent to be geared to actual profit rather than the turnover of the business, although this may concern the landlord in that the level of rent would then become dependent upon the profitability of the tenant's business, and ultimately upon the tenant's efficiency.

A compromise approach is for the lease to reserve a basic annual rent with an additional rent to be assessed as a percentage of the tenant's gross profit, or turnover as the case may be.

A similar form of rent clause is one which gears the annual rent to actual rents receivable, or the market rental value in respect of sub-lettings of the premises. The complex workings of sub-lease rents are beyond the scope of this book.

18.3.4 Open market revaluation

An open market revaluation review clause requires the rent to be revised in accordance with changes in the property market.

The most common form of rent review clause will provide that at every rent review date (eg every 5th anniversary of the term) the parties should seek to agree upon a figure that equates to what is then the current open market rent for a letting of the tenant's premises. The aim of the exercise is to find out how much a tenant in the open market would be prepared to pay, in terms of rent per annum, if the tenant's premises were available to let in the open market on the relevant review date. This agreement is achieved either by some form of informal negotiated process between the landlord and the tenant, or by the service of notices and counter-notices which

How much a T in OM would be prepared to pay if T premises were available to let in the open market.

specify proposals and counter-proposals as to the revised rent. If agreement cannot be reached, the clause usually provides for the appointment of an independent valuer who will determine the revised rent. The valuer will be directed by the review clause to take certain matters into account in conducting his valuation, and to disregard others, and he will call for evidence of rental valuations of other comparable leasehold interests in the locality.

A clause which provides for an open market revaluation is the type of review clause most frequently encountered in practice, and is the one upon which the rest of this chapter will concentrate.

18.4 OPEN MARKET REVALUATIONS

To understand the concept of an open market assessment of rental value, and before seeing how it works in relation to rent review, it is necessary to explore some basic principles of the valuation of leasehold interests which are adopted by valuers in the assessment of rent during the negotiations for the lease. Those principles will have to be borne in mind when drafting the rent review clause, and also at the stage(s) during the term when the review is implemented.

18.4.1 Principles of valuation

First and foremost, it should be understood that a valuer of commercial leasehold premises cannot find the rental value of 'the premises' since 'the premises' as such are not capable of rental valuation. It is a leasehold interest in the premises, a lease granted for a particular length of time, for a particular purpose, and upon certain terms and conditions, which is capable of rental valuation and which must fall to be valued.

The following is a list of factors (not necessarily exhaustive) which will need to be considered by the valuer in assessing the open market rental value (the OMRV) of a leasehold interest.

The length of the term

Whether the lease is for a short term or a long term will affect how much rent a tenant is prepared to pay. Whilst a landlord often needs to guarantee rental income by granting a long-term lease, in recessionary times tenants often prefer short-term lettings in order to retain a degree of flexibility, and to avoid long-term liability in the event of business failure. If a short-term letting is more attractive to tenants in the current market, it follows that a tenant would be prepared to bid more in terms of rent per annum for such a letting than if a longer-term was proposed. On the other hand, other tenants with long-term business plans and a desire for stability and security would be prepared to increase their rental bid in return for a longer letting.

The condition of the premises

A tenant is likely to pay more in terms of annual rent (and therefore the OMRV increases) if the premises are in good condition, especially if they have been fully fitted out and are ready for occupation by an incoming tenant, because in that case the tenant will not have to go to the expense of fitting out the premises to his requirements. If the premises are improved during the term, the OMRV increases, because the quality of accommodation increases. If the tenant, in breach of covenant, allows the premises to fall into disrepair, the OMRV decreases because the quality of accommodation decreases.

The type of premises

Office premises command a certain level of rent per square foot, as do shop premises, factories and warehouses. However, much depends on the location of the premises (compare an Oxford Street shop with a provincial high street shop, or city centre office space with offices outside the central business district), accessibility and the suitability of the premises for their intended purpose.

The consideration for the grant

Any consideration moving between the parties at the time of the grant is likely to have a bearing on the amount of rent to be paid by the tenant. The landlord may induce the tenant to enter into the lease at a certain level of rent by offering him a reverse premium without which the tenant might only be prepared to pay rent at a lower level. A rent-free period may be offered by the landlord, either as a straightforward inducement as above, or to compensate the tenant for the costs that he will incur in fitting out the premises at the start of the term. Without the rent-free period, the tenant might only be prepared to pay a lower rent. If the tenant pays a premium to the landlord at the outset, this may be reflected in the tenant paying a rent lower than he would otherwise pay.

The terms of the lease

The valuer, in ascertaining the OMRV of a leasehold interest, must look at all of the proposed terms of the lease. The more onerous the lease terms, the less attractive the lease becomes from a tenant's point of view and, therefore, the lower the OMRV of the interest. A tenant in the open market is likely to reduce his rental bid for a letting of premises on account of the following.

ONEROUS REPAIRING OBLIGATIONS

If the tenant is obliged by the lease to repair damage caused by an inherent design or construction defect present in a new building, or if the covenant obliges the tenant, in addition to repairing the premises, to renew and rebuild them, the tenant may feel that in taking on such a heavy responsibility he ought to pay a lower rent. If the premises at the time of grant are in a state of disrepair, a simple covenant to keep in repair will be onerous since it will ordinarily involve the tenant in expense in order to put the premises into repair.

RESTRICTIONS ON ALIENATION

An inalienable lease would lead to a heavy reduction in the amount of rent a tenant would be prepared to pay, since the tenant would be obliged to keep the premises for the entire duration of the term, and would not be able to dispose of the premises should his business fail. If the landlord requires what the tenant considers to be an excessively restrictive alienation covenant (eg by imposing over-stringent conditions on assignment, or by prohibiting subletting), the tenant may again feel inclined to lower his rental bid for a lease of the premises.

RESTRICTIONS ON CARRYING OUT IMPROVEMENTS

Particularly with respect to longer-term lettings, an inability to execute improvements to the premises with relative freedom is likely to dissuade a tenant from taking a lease of the premises (thereby reducing its OMRV) since the tenant would be unable to adapt the premises to progress his business as he sees fit.

A RESTRICTIVE PERMITTED USE

If the lease narrowly defines the use to be permitted at the premises and allows little or no scope for the tenant to alter that use, a tenant bidding for the lease in the open market is likely to reduce his rental bid to reflect the fact that he would be severely hindered should he wish to dispose of the premises during the term, or change the nature of his business.

THE PRESENCE OF A BREAK CLAUSE

If the lease gives the landlord an option to break the term, this may have a detrimental effect on the OMRV since the break clause creates the possibility of the tenant's business being disrupted. If the market for these particular premises favours a longer term, the presence of a break clause will certainly damage the OMRV. A tenant's break clause is likely to increase the OMRV since it gives the tenant a benefit for which he would be prepared to pay more in terms of rent per annum. The benefit derives from the knowledge that if his business is unsuccessful, the tenant is able to walk away from his obligations under the lease.

PAYMENT OF VAT

If the landlord has waived the VAT exemption in respect of a particular property so that VAT is payable in addition to the rent, this will badly affect a tenant who has an adverse VAT status. Organisations such as banks, building societies and insurance companies make exempt supplies in the course of their business and, therefore, do not receive any output tax and are, therefore, unable to recover the input tax to be paid on the rent. These organisations have to bear the VAT on the rent as an overhead of the business. If the premises available for letting are likely, because of location or style of building, to attract mainly VAT-adverse organisations as tenants, and the landlord has waived the VAT exemption, the OMRV of the letting may suffer, since the tenants in the market might reduce their bids in order to compensate for the VAT overhead that they will have to absorb. In respect of the same premises, the opposite may be true if the landlord has not waived the exemption and includes a covenant in the lease not to waive it. If that were the case, tenants might be prepared to increase their bid to reflect the fact that in respect of these premises (as opposed to other premises available on the market), there is no possibility of their having to absorb VAT as an overhead.

THE PRESENCE OF A RENT REVIEW CLAUSE

In any commercial letting for more than just a short term it is normal for the lease to contain provisions for rent review without adversely affecting the OMRV of the letting. However, the absence of rent review provisions in a medium or long-term letting is almost certain to increase the OMRV of that letting for the simple reason that a tenant would be prepared to pay a higher rent in the knowledge that the rent will be fixed at that level for the entire duration of the term.

Goodwill

A letting of premises will be more attractive in the open market if there is existing goodwill at the premises, in the shape of a regular flow of clients or customers, or the benefit of a good reputation. The letting would command a higher rent than could otherwise be expected, as tenants will be eager to obtain possession of the premises in order to take advantage of the goodwill. For a number of reasons, goodwill being one of them, rent per square foot on a letting of the premises forming the site of Harrods (unlikely though this may be) would inevitably be higher than at most other similar stores.

The state of the market

The overriding factor for the valuer to bear in mind is the state of the commercial letting market for premises of this particular kind in this particular locality, which is why a valuer will always have regard to rents currently being paid by tenants occupying other similar premises, subject to comparable lease terms. It is obviously the case that if there is an abundance of properties available to let, rental values will fall, whilst if there is a glut of tenants desperate to secure a letting of premises, rental values will rise. Much depends upon the current economic climate.

18.4.2 The interest to be valued at review?

Having established that it is not the premises, but an interest in the premises which has to be valued at each review date, it must be clearly understood that it is not the tenant's own interest as it exists at review that will be valued, but a hypothetical interest in the premises (based on the terms of the tenant's interest). The reason for this is that valuing the tenant's interest gives rise to many problems, uncertainties and injustices. The following list reveals just some that can arise:

(1) At each successive review date, assuming a 5-yearly review pattern, the length of the tenant's interest is progressively reduced by 5 years. The landlord would want to maximise the OMRV of the tenant's interest but he knows that different lengths of term produce different rental values. If at present the most commercially desirable letting from a tenant's point of view and, therefore, the highest yielding length of term in the market is, for example, a 25-year term, then the landlord will not be happy that at year 5, a 20-year term is valued, and at year 10, a 15-year term is valued, and so on. (In fact, in recent times, tenants have tended to favour shorter-term lettings, for example 5 years, but the same principle applies in reverse.)

(2) Consider the position of the tenant who, in the 4th year of the term, at his own expense, voluntarily made improvements to the premises which had the effect of increasing the OMRV of his interest in the premises. Is it fair that the tenant should suffer at rent review by having to pay an increased rent which reflects in part the rental value attributable to his improvements?

(3) On the other hand, consider the position of the tenant who, in breach of his obligations under the lease, has allowed the premises to fall into disrepair, which has had the effect of reducing the OMRV of the premises. Is it fair that the landlord should suffer at rent review by having the rent depressed on account of the tenant's breach of covenant?

(4) Consider the tenant's position if the landlord had recently elected to waive the VAT exemption and was now charging VAT on the rent. Many tenants would not be adversely affected by this as they are able to recover VAT that they pay on rent by making standard or zero-rated supplies during the course of their business. However, if a tenant, by the nature of its business, is making VAT exempt supplies (eg an insurance company, where no VAT is charged by the company on insurance premiums because the supply of insurance services is an exempt supply), the tenant will not be receiving any VAT to facilitate recovery of the VAT the landlord is charging on the rent. The VAT on the rent has to be absorbed by the tenant as a business overhead. The point to bear in mind is that, because the landlord has opted to charge VAT, the tenant's interest has become less valuable to the tenant, but should the OMRV suffer as a result?

(5) If the lease has been drafted to include a user covenant which is very restrictive in its terms, so that there are very few tenants (other than the actual tenant) who could comply with the covenant, the OMRV of the tenant's interest would

be depressed; the simple reason being that hardly anyone would want to take on the tenant's lease. This works to the detriment of the landlord.

These are just some of the problems inherent in a valuation of the tenant's interest. As a result of the difficulties and injustices connected with such a valuation, it is accepted that the valuer should be instructed by the rent review clause to ascertain the OMRV of a hypothetical interest in the premises. He should be directed by the clause to calculate how much rent per annum a hypothetical willing tenant would be prepared to pay for a letting of the premises, with vacant possession, for a hypothetical term. He is directed by the lease to make certain assumptions about the terms of the letting and to disregard certain matters which might otherwise distort the OMRV, in order to overcome the difficulties and eradicate the injustices referred to above.

18.5 THE HYPOTHETICAL LETTING

It is important that the parties ensure that the terms and circumstances of the hypothetical letting (which will form the basis of valuation at review) are clearly stated in the lease, and achieve a fair balance between the parties without departing too far from the reality of the tenant's existing letting.

The lease should make it clear that the date of valuation, when the OMRV is assessed, is the review date itself. A negotiated agreement as to the revised rent between the landlord and the tenant, or a determination by an independent valuer, may occur several months before or after the relevant review date, although the new rent is usually stated to be payable from the review date itself. Irrespective of the date of assessment, the tenant should not allow the valuation date to be capable of variation; it should be fixed at the relevant review date. Any clause which purports to allow the valuation date to be fixed by the service of a notice by the landlord is to be resisted for the simple reason that, in a falling market, the landlord would serve his notice early to secure a higher rent, whilst in a rising market he would serve his notice late at a time when the market was at its peak, safe in the knowledge that the revised rent would be backdated and payable from the review date. In a similar way, any clause which defines the valuation date as the day upon which agreement is reached, or the third party determination is to be made is to be resisted, as it might encourage the landlord to protract the review process to get the benefit of a later valuation date.

18.5.1 The aim of the exercise

The valuer will be directed by the lease to ascertain the open market rental value of a hypothetical letting of the premises at each review date. Different phrases are used by different clauses to define the rent to be ascertained. Some leases will require the valuer to find a 'reasonable rent' for a letting of the premises, or a 'fair rent', or a 'market rent', or a 'rack rent' or 'the open market rent'. The latter clause is the preferred phrase to adopt, as it is the one most commonly used in practice and is, therefore, a phrase with which professional valuers are familiar. Other phrases are less common, and are open to adverse interpretations by valuers and the court.

Most tenants would want to avoid the use of the expression 'the best rent at which the premises might be let' since this might allow the valuer to consider the possibility of what is known as a 'special purchaser's bid'. If, by chance, the market for a hypothetical letting of the premises contains a potential bidder who would be prepared to bid in excess of what would ordinarily be considered to be the market rent, the 'best' rent would be the rent which the special bidder would be prepared to pay. For example, if the premises which are the subject matter of the hypothetical letting are situated next to premises occupied by a business which is desperate to expand, the 'best' rent might be the rent which that business would be willing to pay.

18.5.2 The circumstances of the letting

To enable the valuer to do his job, the rent review clause must clearly indicate the circumstances in which a hypothetical letting of the premises is to be contemplated. For example, he must be able to establish which premises are to be the subject matter of the letting, whether there is a market for such a letting, whether the premises would be available with or without vacant possession, and what the terms of the letting would be. It is common for the clause to require the valuer to find the open market rent of a letting of the tenant's vacant premises, for a specified duration, on the assumption that there is a market for the letting which will be granted without the payment or receipt of a premium, and subject only to the terms of the actual lease (except as to the amount of the annual rent).

The premises

Usually, the valuer is required to ascertain the rental value of a hypothetical letting of the premises actually demised by the tenant's lease. The draftsman should, therefore, ensure that the demised premises are clearly defined by the parcels clause in the lease, and that they enjoy the benefit of all necessary rights and easements to enable them to be used for their permitted purpose.

A valuer uses comparables as evidence in his valuation of a letting of the premises. He draws upon evidence of rents currently being paid by tenants of comparable buildings, let in comparable circumstances, on comparable terms. If the actual premises demised to the tenant are unique or exceptional (eg an oversized warehouse) there may be no comparables in the area for the valuer to use. In that case, the lease ought to require the valuer to adopt a different approach to his valuation, perhaps by directing him to take account of rental values of other premises which would not ordinarily count as comparables. This in itself may lead to valuation problems as, for example, in *Dukeminster (Ebbgate House One) Ltd v Somerfield Properties Co Ltd* [1997] 40 EG 157, where the precise location of hypothetical premises was in dispute.

The market

As the hypothetical letting is an artificial creation, and since leasehold valuations cannot be carried out in the abstract, an artificial market has to be created. If the rent review clause does not create a well-balanced hypothetical market in which the letting can be contemplated, it would be open for the tenant (in appropriate cases) to argue at review that no market exists for a letting of the tenant's premises and that, therefore, an 'open market' rent for the premises would be merely nominal, or a peppercorn. An example of this could occur if the tenant was occupying premises which were now outdated to such an extent that they were impractical for modern use, or that the premises were so exceptional that only the tenant himself would contemplate occupying them. Only the actual tenant would be in the hypothetical market for such premises, and even he might not be in the market if he can show that he has actively been trying to dispose of his lease. The market might truly be dead.

To create a market, the rent review clause usually requires the valuer to assume that the hypothetical letting is taking place in the open market and being granted by a 'willing landlord' to a 'willing tenant'. In *FR Evans (Leeds) Ltd v English Electric Co Ltd* (1977) 245 EG 657, it was held that where such phrases are used, the valuer must assume that there are two hypothetical people who are prepared to enter into the arrangement, neither of whom is being forced to do so, and neither of whom is affected by any personal difficulties (eg a landlord with cash-flow problems, or a tenant who has just lost his old premises) which would prejudice their position in open market negotiations. A willing landlord is an abstract person, but is someone who has the right to grant a lease of the premises, and a willing tenant, again an abstraction, is someone who is actively seeking premises to fulfil a need that these premises would fulfil. It is implicit in the use of these phrases that there is at least one willing tenant in the market, and that there is a rent upon which they will agree.

Even if the lease is silent as to whether there is assumed to be a willing tenant, the Court of Appeal has held in *Dennis & Robinson Ltd v Kiossos Establishment* [1987] 1 EGLR 133 that such a creature is in any case to be assumed, since a rent review clause which asks for an open market valuation by its nature requires there to be at least one willing tenant in the market. This means that for rent review purposes, where an open market valuation is required, there will always be someone in the hypothetical market who would be prepared to take a letting of the premises and, therefore, the tenant cannot argue that the market is completely dead. However, quite how much a willing tenant would be willing to pay is for the valuer to decide.

If the market is well and truly dead, the landlord's only protection is an upwards-only rent review clause.

The consideration

It is common for the rent review clause to assume that no consideration (in the form of a premium) will be moving between the parties on the grant of the hypothetical letting. A premium (reverse or otherwise) can distort the amount of initial rent payable by a tenant (see **18.4.1**). Therefore, to get the clearest indication of what the market rent for the letting would be, it ought to be assumed that no premium is to be paid on the grant of the hypothetical letting.

Furthermore, the landlord may seek to include a provision which states that no inducement in the form of a rent-free period will be given to the tenant on the grant of the hypothetical lease. One of the products of the late 1980s property boom was that landlords were able to extract highly advantageous rent review terms from tenants. At that time, many leases were granted on the basis that the revised rent at review would be ascertained by reference to rental levels existing after the expiry of a notional rent-free period, of the kind a tenant in the open market might expect to receive by way of an inducement.

In the open market, if a rent-free period is offered to a tenant to persuade him to take a lease, the effect on rent is to reduce the overall level of rent. For example, if the tenant agrees to take a lease at £100,000 per annum for a term of 5 years, but is to receive a 12-month rent-free period, whilst the headline rent (ie the rent stated to be payable under the terms of the lease) remains at £100,000 per annum, the annual rent effectively payable (hence the term 'effective rent') is only £80,000. At review, therefore, the landlord would argue that the effect of a provision that the level of rent is to be fixed after the expiry of the hypothetical tenant's notional rent-free period (ie one that might otherwise be available in the open market), is that the new rent payable from review should be a headline rent, not an effective rent. The tenant would argue that, since the hypothetical tenant is not getting the benefit of a rent-free period (as might a real tenant on a letting in the real world), therefore the revised rent should be discounted to compensate the hypothetical tenant for a benefit he has not received.

Late 1980s leases, with 5-yearly review patterns, have recently come up for review, and there have been several cases reported at first instance on the effect of these types of provisions. However, the Court of Appeal, in *Broadgate Square plc v Lehman Brothers Ltd* [1995] 01 EG 111, applying the purposive approach to the construction of various rent review clauses put before the court, said that '... the court will lean against a construction which would require payment of rent upon an assumption that the tenant has received the benefit of a rent-free period, which he has not in fact received ...' (per Leggatt LJ). Nevertheless, such an approach cannot be adopted in the face of clear, unambiguous language. According to Hoffmann LJ, '... if upon its true construction the clause deems the market rent to be whatever is the headline rent after a rent-free period granted ... the tenant cannot complain because in changed market conditions it is more onerous than anyone would have foreseen'. The presence of such a clause in the hypothetical letting may itself be an onerous provision which justifies a reduction in the OMRV (possibly to the extent that it negates the effect of the landlord's clever drafting).

Possession

As the valuer is assessing the rental value of a letting of the tenant's existing premises, is he to assume that the tenant is still there (in which case rent to be paid by a hypothetical bidder would be very low), or is he to assume that the tenant has vacated? Naturally, he must assume that the tenant has moved out and, therefore, most rent review clauses of this type include an assumption that vacant possession is available for the hypothetical letting.

Care must be taken in making this assumption, because in certain cases it can give rise to problems.

(1) If the tenant has sub-let all or part of the premises, an assumption that vacant possession is to be available will mean that the effect on rent of the presence of the sub-tenant will have to be disregarded. If the sub-tenant occupies for valuable business purposes (eg the premises in question are High Street offices where the ground floor has been sub-let as a high class shop), the presence of the sub-tenancy would ordinarily increase the rental value of the head leasehold interest since the head tenant would expect to receive lucrative sub-lease rents. The assumption of vacant possession would deny the landlord the opportunity to bring a valuable sub-letting into account at review. If the sub-tenancy was for residential purposes yielding little in terms of sub-lease rents, the assumption of vacant possession would allow the landlord to have the sub-letting disregarded and, depending on the other terms of the hypothetical letting, enable the premises to be valued as a whole for the permitted business purpose.

(2) The assumption of vacant possession means that the tenant is deemed to have moved out of the premises and, as all vacating tenants would do, he is deemed to have removed and taken his fixtures with him. In respect of shop premises, this might mean that all the shop fittings must be assumed to have been removed, leaving nothing remaining but a shell. (Of course, in reality, the premises are still fully fitted out, but for hypothetical valuation purposes, the tenant's fixtures are assumed to have gone). If a hypothetical tenant were to bid

in the open market for these premises then, depending upon market forces prevalent at the time, he might demand a rent-free period in order to compensate him for the time it will take for him to carry out a notional fitting out of the premises (ie to restore the fittings that have notionally been removed). Since the revised rent has to be a constant figure payable throughout the period until the next review date, this notional rent-free period would have to be spread out during the review period, or possibly over the rest of the term, thereby reducing the general level of rent (eg the valuer finds that the rent for the next 5 years should be £10,000 per annum, but that an incoming tenant would obtain a rent-free period of 12 months. By spreading the notional rent-free period over the 5-year review period the rent would be £8,000 per annum). The landlord can counter this problem by including an assumption that, notwithstanding vacant possession, the premises are fully fitted out for occupation and use (see **18.5.3**).

The terms

If the rent review clause is silent, the hypothetical letting will be assumed to be granted upon the terms of the tenant's existing lease, since the court does not like to stray too far away from reality, and there is a general preference by the court to construe rent review clauses in such a way as to ensure that the tenant does not end up paying in terms of rent for something that he is not actually getting. Usually, however, the clause directs the valuer to assume that the letting is to be made upon the terms of the tenant's actual letting, as varied from time to time. (The fact that the valuer must take account of variations means that it is imperative that, when conducting the review, the valuer checks the terms of all deeds of variation entered into, and all licences granted since the date of the lease to see if the terms of the actual lease have been changed.)

Each of the terms of the lease will be analysed by the valuer at review to see if they will have any effect on the rental value. If either party, with sufficient foresight, feels that a particular term will have a detrimental effect on the rental value (because the term is too wide, or too narrow) that party may seek to have the term excluded from the hypothetical letting, by use of an assumption or a disregard (see, eg, **18.5.3** and **18.5.4**).

The valuer will look closely at all of the terms of the lease, but in particular at the following.

THE ALIENATION COVENANT

If the alienation covenant is too restrictive, its incorporation as a term of the hypothetical letting may lead to a decrease in the OMRV of that interest. If the actual lease imposes over-stringent conditions on assignment or allows only the named tenant to occupy the premises (or only companies within the same group of companies as the tenant), it will be advisable for the landlord to seek to exclude the alienation covenant from the terms of the hypothetical letting. The tenant might consider this to be unfair and, perhaps, a compromise would be to widen the alienation covenant.

THE USER COVENANT

If the user covenant permits a narrowly defined use, and is absolute in its terms, its incorporation as a term of the hypothetical letting will also decrease the OMRV. It became clear in *Plinth Property Investments Ltd v Mott, Hay & Anderson* [1979] 1

EGLR 17 (a Court of Appeal decision) that the possibility of the landlord agreeing to waive a breach of covenant (eg by allowing a wider use of the premises than the covenant already permits) has to be ignored. This principle is not just applicable to user covenants (although the *Plinth* case specifically concerned a user covenant) but to all covenants where the landlord is freely able to withhold his consent to a change. It is not open to the landlord at review to disregard the detrimental effect on rent of a restrictive clause which has been incorporated into the hypothetical letting by saying that he is or might be prepared to waive the restriction. Further, a landlord cannot unilaterally vary the terms of the lease (see *C & A Pensions Trustees Ltd v British Vita Investments Ltd* [1984] 2 EGLR 75). If the landlord is intent on tightly restricting the tenant in the user clause in the actual lease, but wants to maximise the rental value of the hypothetical letting at review and is concerned that the incorporation of the restrictive clause into the hypothetical letting will harm the OMRV, he should draft the review clause so that the actual user covenant is to be disregarded, and an alternative permitted use is to be assumed. Obviously, the tenant should resist such an approach, since he would find himself paying a rent from review assessed on the basis of a freedom that he does not in fact possess. Again, a compromise might be to widen the user covenant.

If the lease allows only the named tenant to use the premises for a named business (ie a very restrictive user covenant), the landlord should try to have the user covenant disregarded at review. If he fails to do so, the court might be prepared to step in to assist the landlord as in *Sterling Land Office Developments Ltd v Lloyds Bank plc* (1984) 271 EG 894 where a covenant not to use the premises other than as a branch of Lloyds Bank Limited was incorporated into the hypothetical letting, but with the name and business left blank, to be completed when the name and business of the hypothetical tenant were known.

IMPROVEMENTS

If the covenant relating to improvements is too restrictive, the landlord may suffer at rent review, and the possibility of a variation or waiver must be ignored.

If the lease gives relative freedom to the tenant to alter, then the potential for unrestricted improvements in years to come may be rentalised. See *Lewisham Investment Partnership Ltd v Morgan* [1997] 51 EG 75.

RENT

The review clause will state that the hypothetical letting is to be granted upon the same terms as the actual lease save as to the amount of rent. As the aim of the review exercise is to vary the amount of rent, it is clear that the rent initially reserved by the lease must not be incorporated into the hypothetical letting. However, the tenant must guard against any form of wording which has the effect of excluding from the hypothetical letting not only the amount of rent reserved, but also the rent review clause itself. It is a commonly held view that a tenant bidding for a medium or long-term letting of premises in the open market, where the annual rent cannot be increased during the term, is likely to pay more than if the letting contained a rent review clause. The tenant would pay a rent in excess of the current market rent in return for a guarantee that the rent will not rise. A long series of cases followed the decision in *National Westminster Bank plc v Arthur Young McClelland Moores & Co* [1985] 1 WLR 1123 where the provisions of a rent review clause were interpreted in such a way as to exclude from the hypothetical letting the rent review provisions. This alone led to the annual rent being increased from £800,000 to £1.209m, instead of £1.003m if the rent review clause had been incorporated. Courts today tend to shy away from interpreting a rent review clause in such a way as to exclude a provision for review from the hypothetical letting. In the absence of clear words directing the rent review clause to be disregarded, the court will give effect to the underlying purpose of the clause and will assume that the hypothetical letting contains provisions for the review of rent. However, the tenant must always check carefully that the review clause is not expressly excluded from the hypothetical letting, since the court would be bound to give effect to such clear words. Ideally, the hypothetical letting should be 'upon the terms of this lease, excluding the amount of rent but including the provision for review of rent'.

THE LENGTH OF TERM

The rent review clause must define the length of the hypothetical letting. The length of term will clearly have an impact on the rental value of the letting. The landlord will want to maximise the rental value of the hypothetical letting by specifying as the hypothetical term a length which is currently preferred in the market by prospective tenants of premises of the type in question. The landlord will have to ask his surveyor for advice in this regard, since the term to be adopted is purely a matter of valuation, which will differ from lease to lease.

When the valuer makes his valuation, he is allowed to take into account the prospect of the term being renewed under the LTA 1954 (see *Secretary of State for Employment v Pivot Properties Limited* (1980) 256 EG 1176). Obviously, the rent will turn out to be higher if there is a strong possibility of renewal. In the *Pivot* case, that possibility led to an uplift in the rent of £850,000 per annum.

18.5.3 Assumptions to be made

Several assumptions have already been made in respect of the circumstances of the hypothetical letting. Certain other assumptions are commonly made as follows:

(1) An assumption that the premises are fully fitted out and ready for immediate occupation and use by the incoming tenant. An assumption of vacant possession necessarily leads to an assumption that the tenant has moved out and taken all of his fixtures with him. The assumption that the premises are fully fitted out attempts to counter the deemed removal of fixtures by assuming that the hypothetical incoming tenant would be able to move straight into the premises without asking for a rent-free period in which to carry out his notional fitting out works. Hence, the assumption removes any discount the tenant would claim at review in respect of the rent-free period that the hypothetical tenant might have claimed. The phrase 'fit for occupation' does not appear to go as far as 'fully fitted out' since the former assumption anticipates a stage where the premises are simply ready to be occupied for fitting out purposes, in which case the hypothetical tenant might still demand a rent-free period (see *Pontsarn Investments Ltd v Kansallis-Osake-Pankki* [1992] 22 EG 103). Some solicitors prefer to deal with this problem in a different way by including an assumption that '... no reduction is to be made to take account of any rental consession which on a new letting with vacant possession might be granted to the incoming tenant for a period within which its fitting out works would take place'.

(2) An assumption that the covenants have been performed. Most rent review clauses include an assumption that the tenant has complied with his covenants under the lease. In the absence of such a provision, a court is willing to imply one in any case, since it is a general principle that a party to a transaction

should not be allowed to profit from its own wrongdoing (see *Family Management v Grey* (1979) 253 EG 369). A tenant cannot argue in reduction of the rent at review that the premises are in a poor condition, if it is through his own default that the disrepair has come about.

The landlord may try to include an assumption in respect of his own covenants (ie that the landlord has performed his covenants). The tenant ought to resist this, especially where the landlord will be taking on significant obligations in the actual lease. For example, in a lease of part of the landlord's premises, the landlord may be entering into covenants to perform services, and to repair and maintain the structure, exterior and common parts of the building. If the landlord fails to perform his covenants, the likely result is that the rental value of an interest in the building will decrease, since the building will be less attractive to tenants in the market. Accordingly, the rent at review would be adjusted to reflect this. However, an assumption that the landlord has performed his covenants enables the landlord to have the review conducted on the basis that the building is fully in repair (without regard to his own default), which means that the tenant would be paying for something at review (ie a lease of premises in a building which is in first-rate condition) that he does not in fact have. Such an assumption should be resisted by the tenant.

The landlord will not concede the tenant's argument easily. Landlords will argue that, without it, the valuer will assess the new rent at a lower level, even though immediately afterwards the tenant might bring proceedings against the landlord in respect of the landlord's breach of covenant, forcing the landlord to put the building into repair. They argue that it is unfair that the rent will be set at a low level for the entire review period on the basis of a temporary breach of covenant, which the landlord might soon be required to remedy. The tenant's counter-argument is that an action for breach of covenant is no substitute for a dilapidated building.

(3) An assumption that the incoming tenant can recover any VAT that may be payable under the lease. The landlord might be concerned that the hypothetical market for a letting of the premises, because of the nature and location of them, will consist mainly of organisations whose operations involve only or mainly the making of VAT exempt supplies. A hypothetical incoming tenant in such a market might lower his bid to reflect the fact that any VAT charged by the landlord will have to be absorbed by him as an overhead of his business. This may lead to a reduction of the OMRV of the hypothetical letting. Some landlords counter this by including an assumption that the incoming tenant will be able to recover its VAT in full (removing the need for the hypothetical tenant to ask for a discount on rent to cover his VAT overhead) or by ensuring that the hypothetical letting includes a covenant by the landlord not to waive the exemption for VAT purposes. Tenants ought to try to resist such a provision where they have an adverse VAT status, leaving the valuer to value the lease on the basis of the reality of the actual letting.

18.5.4 Matters to be disregarded

In order to be fair to the tenant, the landlord usually drafts the clause so that certain matters which would otherwise increase the OMRV of a letting of the premises are disregarded.

Goodwill

If the tenant, his predecessors, or his sub-tenants have generated goodwill at the premises, it is only fair that any effect on rent of the goodwill ought to be disregarded at review.

Occupation

The fact that the tenant, his predecessors or his sub-tenants have been in occupation of the premises is usually disregarded. It is accepted that, if the tenant was bidding for a letting of his own premises, he would bid more than most others in the market in order to avoid the expense of having to move to other premises. The rental effect of occupation should, therefore, be disregarded. In appropriate cases, where the tenant also occupies adjoining premises, his occupation of those premises should also be disregarded, to avoid the argument that the tenant would increase his bid for the demised premises to secure a letting of premises which are adjacent to his other premises.

If the rent review clause requires occupation by the tenant to be disregarded, but makes no similar requirement as regards his goodwill, the valuer should nevertheless disregard the rental effect of the tenant's goodwill, since goodwill must necessarily be the product of the tenant's occupation (see *Prudential Assurance Co Ltd v Grand Metropolitan Estate Ltd* [1993] 32 EG 74).

Improvements

If the tenant improves the premises, then he usually does so at his own expense, but the result will inevitably be that the rental value of an interest in the premises will increase. It is unfair for the landlord to ask for the rent to be increased at review to reflect the increase in rental value brought about by the tenant's improvements. If improvements were to be taken into account, the tenant would be paying for his improvements twice over (once on making them, and once again when the revised rent becomes payable). The landlord usually drafts the rent review clause so that the effect on rent of most of the tenant's improvements are disregarded.

Which improvements are to be disregarded? The tenant will want to make sure that the effect on rent of all improvements that have been carried out either by him or his sub-tenants or his predecessors in title are disregarded, whether they were carried out during the term, during some earlier lease or during a period of occupation before the grant of the lease (eg during a pre-letting fitting out period). He will also want to have disregarded the effect on rent of improvements executed by the landlord, but which were carried out at the tenant's expense. The landlord will want to make sure that any improvements that the tenant was obliged to make are taken into account. These will include improvements made under a lease granted in consideration of the tenant carrying out works to the premises, or improvements the tenant was obliged to carry out under some other document, such as an agreement for lease, or by virtue of a statutory provision requiring the tenant to carry out work (eg the installation of a fire escape and doors). An obligation in a licence to alter to execute permitted works in accordance with agreed drawings, or by a stipulated time, is not an obligation in itself to do the works, but merely permission to do the works in a particular way (see *Historic Houses Hotels Ltd v Cadogan Estates* [1993] 30 EG 94).

User, alienation and improvements

It is possible that for his own benefit the landlord might try to have disregarded some of the more restrictive covenants contained in the actual lease such as user, alienation and improvements. This is unfair to the tenant who should be advised to resist such a disregard.

18.6 THE MECHANICS OF THE REVIEW

There are two principal ways in which the review process can be conducted:

(1) by negotiations between the parties, but in default of agreement, by reference to an independent third party for determination (see **18.6.2**);
(2) by the service of trigger notices and counter-notices in an attempt to agree the revised rent, but in default, by reference to a third party (see **18.6.3**).

Whichever method is to be adopted, the first consideration to be dealt with is whether time is to be of the essence in respect of any time-limits contained in the clause, or in respect of the rent review dates.

18.6.1 Is time of the essence?

As a general rule, if time is of the essence of a particular clause, a party who fails to act by the time-limit specified loses the right given by that clause. If time is of the essence of the whole rent review clause, the slightest delay will mean that the landlord will be denied the opportunity to increase the rent until the next review date, (or, indeed, the tenant will be denied the opportunity to decrease the rent until the next review date if the clause permits downward reviews).

The House of Lords in *United Scientific Holdings Ltd v Burnley Borough Council* [1977] 2 All ER 62 held that, in the absence of any contrary indications in the express wording of the clause, or in the interrelation of the rent review clause with other clauses in the lease, there is a presumption that time is not of the essence of the clause and that the review can still be implemented and pursued, even though specific dates have passed. It follows from this decision that there are three situations where time will be of the essence, either of the whole clause, or in respect of certain steps in the review procedure.

An express stipulation
Time will be of the essence in respect of all or any of the time-limits in the review clause if the lease expressly says so.

Any other contrary indication
The phrase 'time of the essence' might not have been used in the lease, but there are cases where other forms of wording used by the draftsman have been sufficient to indicate an intention to rebut the usual presumption (see *Lewis v Barnett* [1982] 2 EGLR 127 and *Henry Smith's Charity Trustees v AWADA Trading & Promotion Services Ltd* [1984] 1 EGLR 116 and, by way of contrast, *Taylor Woodrow Property Co Ltd v Lonrho Textiles Ltd* [1985] 2 EGLR 120, and the attempts to reconcile those cases in *Bickenhall Engineering Co Ltd v Grandmet Restaurants Ltd* [1995] 10 EG 123).

The interrelation of the review clause with other clauses in the lease
The usual way in which a clause might interrelate with the review clause in such a way as to make time of the essence is if the tenant is given an option to break the term on or shortly after each review date. The inference in such an interrelation is that, if the tenant cannot afford to pay the revised rent or, where the level of rent is

not yet known, he does not envy the prospect of an increase, he is given an opportunity to terminate the lease by exercising the break clause. Since time is usually of the essence in respect of the exercise of a break clause, time may also be construed to be of the essence of the rent review clause. It does not matter that the review clause and the option are separate clauses in the lease; the court simply has to be able to infer a sufficient interrelation. Nor, apparently, does it matter that the option to break is mutual and linked to only one of several rent review dates (*Central Estates Ltd v Secretary of State for the Environment* [1997] 1 EGLR 239).

Unless a rigid timetable for conducting the review is required by either party, it is not often that time will be made of the essence, because of the fatal consequences arising from a delay. It might be advisable to state expressly that time is not of the essence. However, in most leases the timetable is so flexibly drafted that the parties do not feel the need to make express declaration that time is not of the essence, preferring instead to rely upon the usual presumption. If any time clauses are intended to be mandatory, the lease should clearly say so.

18.6.2 The negotiated revision

The informal approach to arriving at a revised rent usually provides for the new rent to be agreed between the parties at any time (whether before or after the relevant review date), but if agreement has not been reached by the review date, either or both of the parties will be allowed by the clause to refer the matter to an independent third party for him to make a determination as to the new rent. If such an approach is adopted, the tenant should ensure that the rent review clause does not reserve the right to make the reference to the third party exclusively to the landlord. The tenant must ensure that he also has the ability to make the reference. Even though the rent review clause may permit only upward revisions, it may be in the tenant's interests to have a quick resolution of the review, particularly if he is anxious to assign his lease or sell his business. In exceptional cases (eg *Royal Bank of Scotland plc v Jennings* [1997] 19 EG 152), the court might be prepared to imply an obligation upon the landlord to refer a review to the third party to give business efficacy to the clause.

18.6.3 Trigger notices

The service of a trigger notice is the more formal approach, which usually requires the parties to follow a rigid timetable for the service of notices. One party sets the review in motion by the service of a trigger notice, specifying his proposal for the revised rent, and the other party responds by the service of a counter-notice. A typical clause might provide for the landlord to implement the review by the service on the tenant of a trigger notice, between 12 and 6 months before the relevant review date, in which the landlord specifies a rent that he considers to be the current market rent for the premises. The tenant should be given the right to dispute the landlord's proposal by serving a counter-notice within, say, 3 months of the service of the trigger notice. The parties would then be required to negotiate, but in default of agreement within, say, 3 months of the service of the counter-notice, either or both parties may be given the right to make a reference to a third party for a determination. Time may be stated to be of the essence in respect of all or part of the timetable.

Great care must be taken with this more rigid style of approach, particularly if time is of the essence. Problems can easily arise as follows:

(1) There is no requirement for the landlord to be reasonable when he specifies his proposal for the revised rent in his trigger notice (see *Amalgamated Estates Ltd v Joystretch Manufacturing Ltd* (1980) 257 EG 489). This is very dangerous for the tenant where time is of the essence in respect of the service of the tenant's counter-notice. If the tenant fails to respond within the time-limit required by the lease, he will be bound by the rent specified in the landlord's notice. A well-advised tenant should avoid such a clause.

(2) There has been much litigation surrounding the question of whether a particular form of communication, often in the form of a letter between the parties' advisers, suffices as a notice for the purposes of the review clause. If a communication is to take effect as a notice it ought to be clear and unequivocal, and must be worded in such a way as to make it clear to the recipient that the sender is purporting to take a formal step, or exercise some right under the review clause. Phrases such as 'subject to contract' and 'without prejudice', although not necessarily fatal to the notice, are to be avoided.

(3) For the same reasons stated in connection with informally negotiated reviews, the tenant must ensure that the review timetable allows him to implement the review and to refer the rent revision for determination by the third party. These rights must not be left exclusively with the landlord.

Unless there is some compelling reason to the contrary, the informal approach is to be preferred.

18.6.4 The third party

A surveyor usually acts as the independent third party. The lease will provide for the parties to agree upon a surveyor, failing which one or both of the parties will be allowed to make an application to the President of the Royal Institution of Chartered Surveyors (RICS) for the appointment of a surveyor to determine the revised rent. The RICS operates a procedure to deal efficiently with such applications, and will appoint a surveyor with knowledge and experience of similar lettings in the area. It is important that the lease makes it clear in which capacity the surveyor is to act; as an arbitrator between the parties, or as an expert. There are considerable differences between the two:

(1) An arbitrator seeks to resolve a dispute by some quasi-judicial process, whereas an expert imposes his own expert valuation on the parties.

(2) The arbitrator is bound by the procedure under the Arbitration Act 1996, which deals with hearings, submission of evidence and the calling of witnesses. An expert is not subject to such external controls, and is not bound to hear the evidence of the parties. Whilst an arbitrator decides on the basis of the evidence put before him, an expert simply uses his own skill and judgement.

(3) There is a limited right of appeal to the High Court on a point of law against an arbitrator's award, whereas an expert's decision is final and binding unless he gave a reasoned award (ie in his decision, he set out the reasons upon which his decision was based), and it appears that his reasons were wrong.

(4) An arbitrator is immune from suit in negligence, whereas an expert is not.

Using an expert tends to be quicker and cheaper and is, therefore, recommended in lettings of conventional properties at modest rents. Where there is something unorthodox about the property, which might make it difficult to value, or where there is a good deal of money at stake in the outcome of the review, an arbitrator is to be preferred so that a fully argued case can be put. Alternatively, the review clause could leave the capacity of the third party open, to be determined by the party who makes the reference at the time the reference is made.

18.7 ANCILLARY PROVISIONS

The landlord invariably includes several additional provisions to deal with:

(1) payment of the revised rent where the review is implemented after the review date;
(2) recording a note of the revised rent;
(3) the possibility of the lease being affected by rent control legislation.

18.7.1 The late review

If time has not been made of the essence of the rent review date, the landlord can attempt to increase the rent by implementing the clause after the date for review has passed. To deal with this possibility, the review clause is usually drafted to include the following types of provisions:

(1) that the existing rent (the old rent) continues to be payable on account of the new rent until the new rent has been ascertained;
(2) that the new rent, once ascertained, becomes payable from, and is backdated to the rent review date;
(3) that as soon as the new rent has been ascertained, the tenant is to pay to the landlord the amount by which the old rent paid on account of the new rent since the review date actually falls short of the new rent, and because the landlord has been denied the benefit of this shortfall pending the outcome of the review, the tenant is to pay it with interest calculated from the rent review date until the date of payment.

The tenant should check the operation of these provisions. If the rent review clause permits both upward and downward reviews, he should ensure that there is some equivalent provision for the landlord to pay any shortfall (with interest) to the tenant if the new rent turns out to be lower than the old rent (although in *Royal Bank of Scotland v Jennings* (above) the court was prepared to imply such a term in any case). He should also check that the rate of interest at which the shortfall is to be paid is not set at the usual interest rate under the lease (4 or 5 per cent above base rate, see **17.6**). The usual rate is intended to operate on the occasion of tenant default, whereas in the case of a late rent review, the fault may lie with a delaying landlord as much as a delaying tenant. The interest rate should be set at base rate itself or, perhaps, 1 or 2 per cent above base rate. Finally, the tenant should check that the review clause allows the tenant to instigate the review process, and to force negotiations or the third party reference, since the tenant might prefer a speedy settlement of the review as an alternative to facing a future lump sum payment of a shortfall with interest.

18.7.2 Recording the review

It is good practice to attach memoranda of the revised rent to the lease and counterpart as evidence for all persons concerned with the lease of the agreement or determination. The rent review clause usually obliges both parties to sign and attach identical memoranda to their respective parts of the lease. It is usual for both parties to bear their own costs in this regard.

18.7.3 Rent control legislation

Landlords often try to cover all eventualities. It is common to find the inclusion of a clause to the effect that if the government introduces rent control or counter-inflation legislation at some stage during the term (as it did in 1973) which prevents the landlord from exercising one or more of the reviews, the landlord is to be allowed to implement the reviews which have been denied him within a short time after a relaxation of the legislation. Tenants need not be too concerned about such a clause since the risk of this type of legislation being introduced is slight.

Chapter 19

REPAIRING COVENANTS

Chapter 19 contents

19.1 INTRODUCTION

Responsibility for repairs is one of the most common sources of dispute between landlord and tenant and unless the matter is dealt with expressly in the lease there is a danger that neither party will be liable to repair. Whilst it is true that certain obligations will be implied, these are of relatively little practical importance; they include the following:

(1) the tenant is under a duty to use the premises in a tenant-like manner;
(2) the landlord may be liable if he fails to take care of the common parts of the building, for example, the neglect of a lift or staircase in a high rise block, but much will depend on the surrounding circumstances (see *Liverpool City Council v Irwin* [1971] AC 239, a case concerning a block of residential flats);
(3) in rare situations the landlord may be under an implied obligation to repair so as to give business efficacy to the agreement between the parties (see *Barrett v Lounova (1982) Ltd* [1990] QB 348).

Thus, in the absence of a comprehensive code of implied obligations, it is imperative that the responsibility for repairs is dealt with expressly in the lease. The landlord's objective on granting anything more than a short-term letting will be to obtain a 'clear' lease, under which the rent always represents the landlord's clear income so that the tenant ends up paying the cost of any repairs, regardless of who carries them out. If the lease is of the whole of a building, the landlord will usually impose a full repairing covenant on the tenant. If, however, the lease is of only part of a building, the responsibility for repairs will usually be divided between the parties. For example, the tenant may be made liable for internal non-structural repairs whilst the landlord covenants to repair the remainder of the building. However, any expense incurred by the landlord in complying with his obligation will be recovered from the tenant under the service charge provisions. The special problems associated with a lease of part of a building and service charges are dealt with in Chapter 27.

19.2 TENANT'S COVENANT TO REPAIR

19.2.1 Subject matter of the covenant

In the lease the tenant will invariably covenant to repair the demised premises and, therefore, it must be made clear what the subject-matter of the covenant is, ie what is the covenantor liable to repair? Thus, it will be necessary to read the repairing covenant in conjunction with the definition of the 'demised premises' in the parcels clause. On the grant of a lease of the whole of a building there should not be any difficulty as the responsibility for repairs will doubtless extend to the whole of the demised premises. On the grant of a lease of part of a building where the responsibility for repairs is to be divided between the parties it must be made clear who is to be responsible for repairing each part of the building. This will require very careful drafting of both the parcels clause and the repairing covenant (see **27.4** where this matter is dealt with in more detail).

As general rule, a covenant to repair the demised premises will also extend to:

(1) any landlord's fixtures attached to them;
(2) any buildings erected after the date of the lease. If, however, the covenant is to repair 'the buildings demised', it will only extend to the buildings existing at the date of the lease.

One further issue which requires clarification is the question of responsibility for site contamination. If the site is subsequently discovered to be contaminated, can the tenant be required to remove the contamination under a simple repairing covenant? As yet there is a lack of judicial authority but it is submitted that there may be a problem for the landlord in persuading the court that a simple repairing covenant can be extended to the soil as well as the buildings. In the absence of judicial guidance the matter should be dealt with expressly in the lease; perhaps by defining the term 'repair' to include the remediation of site contamination.

19.2.2 Extent of liability

In examining the extent of the tenant's liability, a number of important matters need to be considered. For example, are the premises in disrepair? What is the standard of repair? Does the covenant require the tenant to renew or improve the premises? Is the tenant liable for inherent defects? Each of these is considered in turn.

19.2.3 Are the premises in disrepair?

If the tenant is under an obligation to repair the premises, he will only be liable if it can be shown that there is damage or disrepair to them. In other words, before the tenant incurs any liability, the landlord will need to show that the premises have deteriorated from their previous physical condition so that they are in a worse condition now, than when they were let. This requirement led to the downfall of the landlord in *Post Office v Aquaris Properties Ltd* [1987] 1 All ER 1055, where the basement of a building flooded due to a defect in the structure. The landlord's problem in fixing the tenant with responsibility for repair was the fact that the defect had caused no damage to the building itself. This being so, the court held that the tenant was not liable to remedy the defect under his covenant to repair.

19.2.4 The standard of repair

Sometimes the word 'repair' is qualified by the addition of the word(s), 'good', 'tenantable', or 'sufficient', but it would appear that these additions add little to the word 'repair' itself (*Anstruther-Gough-Calthorpe v McOscar* [1924] 1 KB 716). The standard of repair required is 'such repair as having regard to the age, character and locality would make it reasonably fit for the occupation of a reasonably minded tenant of the class likely to take it' (per Lopes LJ in *Proudfoot v Hart* (1890) 25 QBD 42). Further, the standard will be determined by reference to the age, character and condition of the premises at the time the lease was granted. It makes no difference that the neighbourhood now attracts a superior or inferior class of tenant; the tenant need only keep them in the same condition as they were when let to him. If, however, the premises are in disrepair at the date of the lease, a covenant to keep in repair will require the tenant to first put the premises into repair (according to their age, character and locality), and then to keep them in repair.

19.2.5 Is the tenant liable to renew or improve the premises?

If the tenant is just under an obligation to 'repair', difficult questions can arise as to the meaning of that word. Do the works contemplated fall within the obligation, or are they more properly classified as works of renewal or improvement, for which the tenant is not responsible under a simple covenant to repair. It was said in *Lurcott v Wakeley* [1911] 1 KB 905, that 'Repair is restoration by renewal or replacement of subsidiary parts of a whole. Renewal, as distinguished from repair, is the reconstruction of the entirety, meaning by the entirety not necessarily the whole but substantially the whole...'. Thus, the fundamental question is whether the work done can properly be described as repair, involving no more than renewal or replacement of defective parts, or whether it amounts to renewal or replacement of substantially the whole. This will be a question of degree in each case. In *Lurcott v Wakeley*, the rebuilding of a defective wall of a building was held to be within the tenant's covenant because it was the replacement of a defective part rather than the replacement of the whole. However, the tenant may be required to replace part after part until the whole is replaced. On the other hand, in *Lister v Lane* [1893] 2 QB 212, the tenant was held not to be liable for the cost of rebuilding a house which had become unsafe due to poor foundations: 'a covenant to repair . . . is not a covenant to give a different thing from that which the tenant took when he entered into the covenant. He has to repair that thing which he took; he is not obliged to make a new and different thing . . .', per Lord Esher MR. In deciding whether the tenant is being asked to give back to the landlord a wholly different thing from that demised, guidance may sometimes be found by considering the proportion which the cost of the disputed work bears to the value or cost of the whole premises (see also *Elite Investments Ltd v TI Bainbridge Silencers Ltd* [1986] 2 EGLR 43). It must be stressed, however, that decided cases can do no more than lay down general guidelines and each case will turn on its own facts.

In the same way that the tenant need not renew the premises, a covenant to repair does not impose any obligation on the tenant to improve them. A tenant may sometimes be concerned that his landlord is trying to get him to upgrade or improve the premises under the guise of carrying out repairs. The distinction is not always easy to make but Lord Denning stated in *Morcom v Campbell-Johnson* [1955] 3 All ER 264 that 'if the work which is done is the provision of something new for the benefit of the occupier, that is, properly speaking, an improvement; but if it is only the replacement of something already there, which has become dilapidated or worn out, then, albeit that is a replacement by its modern equivalent, it comes within the category of repairs and not improvements' (see also *New England Properties plc v Portsmouth News Shops Ltd* [1993] 23 EG 130).

19.2.6 Inherent defects

At one time it was thought that a covenant to repair did not require the tenant to repair damage caused by 'inherent defects' (ie defects in design or construction of the building). However, it now seems that this approach was wrong and that there are no special rules relating to damage caused by inherent defects. As with all kinds of disrepair it will, therefore, be a question of degree as to whether what the tenant is being asked to do can properly be described as repair or whether it would involve giving back to the landlord something wholly different from that which he demised (*Ravenseft Properties Ltd v Davstone (Holdings) Ltd* [1980] QB 12). Even the possibility of the tenant being liable for damage caused by such defects will alarm the tenant as it may require, not only repair of the damage, but also eradication of the defect itself if this is the only realistic way of carrying out the repairs (see **19.2.7**).

If the inherent defect has not caused any damage to the premises, they are not in disrepair and thus the tenant is not liable on his covenant.

19.2.7 Varying the obligation

In drafting the repairing obligation, it is possible to restrict or widen its scope from that imposed by a simple covenant to repair (the case of *Credit Suisse v Beegas Nominees Ltd* [1994] 11 EG 151, is a good illustration of this). Looked at from the landlord's point of view, it is possible to extend the liability of the tenant by the use of clear words which make the tenant liable to renew or improve the demised premises. Whilst this is possible, the landlord should bear in mind the impact of such onerous obligations on the rent payable.

From the tenant's point of view, there are a number of ways in which he may seek to reduce his liability:

(1) The tenant may be alarmed at the prospect of having to repair inherent defects. For that reason, tenants of new buildings will often seek to limit their liability by excluding from their obligation liability for defects caused by design or construction faults, at least for a specified period of time. From the tenant's point of view, the landlord should covenant to repair damage caused by these defects (see **8.4.2**).

(2) In most leases the landlord will insure the premises against a number of stated risks. The tenant should always insist that his repairing covenant does not render him liable to repair damage caused by a risk against which the landlord has or should have insured. The landlord should not object since he will be able to claim on the insurance policy. However, the landlord will insist that the tenant remains liable if the insurance is avoided because of an act or omission of the tenant or someone at the premises with the tenant's consent (see **25.7.1**).

(3) If the premises are in disrepair at the commencement of the lease but it has been agreed between the parties that the tenant need not repair the premises to a higher standard, this should be expressly stated in the covenant. Further, for the avoidance of future disputes, a detailed schedule of condition, with appropriate photographic evidence, should be prepared by a surveyor, agreed by the parties and annexed to the lease.

(4) The covenant to repair may be qualified by a proviso 'fair wear and tear excepted'. This will exclude from the obligation to repair damage attributable to the normal effects of time and weather and of normal and reasonable use of the premises but it will not exclude liability for consequential damage.

19.2.8 Access by landlord to execute works in default

A covenant to repair given by the tenant is often followed by a covenant to permit the landlord to enter the demised premises, upon reasonable notice, to ascertain their state and condition. This covenant should make two further provisions. First, a provision for the landlord to serve a notice of disrepair on the tenant if he is found to be in breach of his repairing obligation. Secondly, a covenant to repair by the tenant upon receipt of the notice followed by a right for the landlord to enter upon the premises to carry out the repairs, at the tenant's expense, if the tenant fails to do so within a specified time. The expense incurred by the landlord acting under such a power should be expressed to be recoverable 'as a debt'. This is an attempt to avoid the restrictions imposed by the LTA 1927 and the Leasehold Property (Repairs) Act 1938 on the recovery of damages, as opposed to a debt, for disrepair (see **31.1.2**).

The landlord should be aware, however, that if he reserves the right to enter the demised premises to carry out repairs in default, he will, in certain circumstances, become liable under the Defective Premises Act 1972 (see **19.3**).

19.3 LANDLORD'S COVENANT TO REPAIR

The only common situation in which a landlord will covenant to repair is on the grant of a lease of part of a building, where the landlord will be able to recover his expenditure under the service charge provisions. A landlord's covenant to repair will be subject to the same rules of construction as a tenant's covenant and thus, for example, the landlord need not carry out works so as provide the tenant with something wholly different from that originally demised.

Where the covenant is to repair the demised premises it is implied that the landlord is not liable until he has had notice of the disrepair (see, eg, *O'Brien v Robinson* [1973] AC 912). This requirement of notice is not affected by the fact that the landlord has a right of entry onto the premises. Once the landlord has notice, he must take steps to carry out the necessary repairs. If immediate permanent repairs are not possible, the landlord must take immediate steps to render the premises temporarily safe. If, on the other hand, the landlord's obligation is to keep in repair some part of the building not comprised in the demise (eg the common parts), the landlord's liability runs from the moment the disrepair occurs, regardless of the question of notice (*British Telecommunications plc v Sun Life Assurance Society plc* [1995] 45 EG 133).

Where the landlord is under an obligation to repair, there is an implied right for him to enter upon the demised premises to carry out those repairs (but this should always be dealt with expressly).

Under the Defective Premises Act 1972, a landlord who is under an express or implied obligation for the repair of the demised premises owes to all persons who might reasonably be expected to be affected by defects in the state of the premises a duty to take such care as is reasonable in all the circumstances to see that they are reasonably safe from personal injury or damage to their property. This duty arises as soon as the landlord knows or ought to have known of the defect. Further, even where the landlord is under no obligation to repair but merely has a right to do so, he is made subject to the same duty, although he will not be liable to the tenant if the defect arose from the tenant's failure to comply with an express covenant to repair.

19.4 COVENANT TO YIELD UP IN REPAIR

The tenant will often enter into a covenant to yield up the premises in repair at the end of the term. This covenant, which requires the tenant to leave the premises in repair, is entirely independent of the covenant to repair by the tenant. Thus, if the landlord had previously obtained judgment against the tenant for breach of the repairing covenant, yet the premises remain in disrepair, he will still be able to bring an action at the end of the term on the covenant to yield up in repair (but obviously the amount of damages will be affected).

19.5 DECORATING

Because some doubt exists as to the amount of decoration required by a covenant to repair, the matter is best dealt with expressly in the lease. The usual form of covenant requires the tenant to decorate the exterior and interior of the demised premises at specified intervals during the term, and during the last year of the term. The obligation to decorate in the last year could require the tenant to decorate in two consecutive years depending on when the lease is terminated (eg in a 10-year lease with a decorating obligation every 3 years). The tenant may, therefore, wish to provide that the obligation to decorate in the last year shall not apply if he has decorated in the previous, say, 18 months. The landlord may wish to retain some control by requiring the tenant to obtain consent (not to be unreasonably withheld) before any change in the colour scheme is made.

Some covenants specify the materials to be used, for example 'with two coats of good quality oil paint'. Care should be taken to ensure that the materials specified are appropriate to the type of building concerned as it is not uncommon to find that the specified materials are wholly inappropriate to the nature of the building and its method of construction. More modern covenants simply require the tenant to carry out his obligation 'in a good and workmanlike manner with good quality materials'.

On the grant of a lease of part of a building the exterior decoration would normally be undertaken by the landlord who would recover his expenses under the service charge.

19.6 STATUTORY CURTAILMENT

Oppressive enforcement of a tenant's repairing obligations may be curtailed as follows:

(1) A landlord's right to bring an action for damages in respect of the tenant's breach of a repairing covenant may be limited by the operation of the Leasehold Property (Repairs) Act 1938 (see **31.1.2**).
(2) Under s 147 of the LPA 1925, the court may, in certain circumstances, relieve a tenant of his obligations in respect of a covenant relating to internal decorative repairs (see **33.5.3**).

Chapter 20

ALIENATION

Chapter 20 contents

20.1 INTRODUCTION

Unless the lease contains some restriction, the tenant will be free to deal with his interest in any way he wishes. He will be able to assign the lease, grant sub-leases of the whole or part, charge the lease and part with possession of the premises, without obtaining his landlord's consent. Complete freedom like this is unlikely to prove acceptable to the landlord for a number of reasons and thus a fair balance between the competing concerns and aims of both parties will have to be reached. These are summarised below together with a consideration of more wide-ranging matters.

20.1.1 Assignment

From the tenant's point of view, the lease may become a burden if he is unable to dispose of it freely when he no longer has any use for the premises. This situation may arise, for example, where the premises have become surplus to his requirements or because they are no longer suitable for his needs. The tenant would also be in difficulty if his business venture failed and he could no longer afford the rent. However, from the landlord's point of view, close control over assignment is essential, because without it the landlord may find his premises occupied by an unsatisfactory tenant, and the value of his reversionary interest may be reduced. The assignee will become responsible for the rent and the performance of the other covenants in the lease, and the landlord will want to ensure that he is of good financial standing. The identity and status of any potential assignee is, therefore, important to the landlord for financial reasons. Further, there may be estate management reasons why the landlord will wish to exercise some control over assignees, for example, where the landlord owns the adjoining premises.

A covenant against assignment is not broken by an involuntary assignment such as occurs on the death or bankruptcy of the tenant. Nor is a restriction on assignment broken by a sub-letting of the premises.

20.1.2 Sub-letting

In some situations the tenant may wish to grant a sub-lease of the demised premises (see **28.2**). The landlord will want the ability to control sub-letting because in certain circumstances the head tenancy may cease to exist and the sub-tenant will become the immediate tenant of the landlord. This could happen, for example, on the surrender of the head-lease or on the forfeiture of the head-lease followed by the sub-tenant's successful application for relief. A similar situation could arise at the end of the contractual term if the head tenant does not apply (or is unable to apply) for a new tenancy under Part II of the LTA 1954 but the sub-tenant does; the sub-tenant may be granted a new tenancy of his part against the head landlord. In all these situations the landlord would want to be sure that the sub-tenant was able to pay the rent and perform the covenants and will, therefore, wish to have some control over the identity and status of any proposed sub-tenant. Where a tenant mortgages his lease by way of sub-lease, this has been held to be a breach of the covenant; and possibly also where the mortgage is by way of legal charge (but see

Re Good's Lease [1954] 1 All ER 275). However, a covenant against sub-letting will not prevent the tenant from granting licences. Similarly, a covenant against sub-letting 'the demised premises' will not be broken by a sub-lease of part only (*Cook v Shoesmith* [1951] 1 KB 752). If such a restriction is intended, it must be dealt with expressly.

20.1.3 Parting with/sharing possession

A covenant preventing the tenant from parting with possession of the premises is wider in its effect than the two provisions mentioned above but it will not prevent the tenant from allowing another person to use the premises provided the tenant retains legal possession. It will not, therefore, prohibit a tenant from granting a licence of the premises to another unless the licence confers exclusive possession on the licensee (see *Street v Mountford* [1985] AC 809).

Arrangements under which a business tenant shares his premises with someone else are not uncommon with 'shops within shops' being frequently encountered. However, such an arrangement would not be possible if there was a covenant against sharing possession in the lease, forbidding, as it does, the granting of licences by the tenant. The tenant should try to resist the imposition of such a wide restriction, particularly where the tenant is a member of a group of companies and intends to share the premises with other members of the group.

20.1.4 The landlord's concerns on a dealing of part of the demised premises

Landlords often impose much stricter control on a dealing with part only of the demised premises because of the estate management problems which dealings of part can create. A sub-tenant can in certain circumstances become the immediate tenant of the head landlord. If a number of sub-leases have been granted, a landlord who had let a building as a whole to a single tenant could, at some future date, be faced with the estate management problems associated with having a number of different tenants each with a lease of a different part of the building.

Further, if the tenant was allowed to grant a sub-lease of part only of the premises, this could lead to the division of the demised premises into commercially unattractive units. If, in the future, the head-lease was forfeited and the sub-tenant successfully applied for relief in respect of his part, the head landlord might have difficulty in re-letting the vacant part if that part is no longer attractive to the market because of the way in which the premises have been sub-divided.

20.2 RESTRICTIONS ON ALIENATION

For the reasons mentioned above, it is common for the landlord to impose restrictions on dealing, such restrictions being either absolute in effect, ie an unqualified (absolute) covenant by the tenant not to assign, underlet, part with possession, etc or alternatively, in the form of a qualified covenant: not to deal with the premises without the landlord's consent.

20.2.1 Absolute covenants against dealings

If the covenant is absolute, the tenant cannot assign or underlet without being in breach of covenant. Whilst the landlord may be prepared to waive the covenant in a given case, the tenant will be entirely at the mercy of his landlord who may refuse consent quite unreasonably subject only to the restrictions imposed by the Sex Discrimination Act 1975 and Race Relations Act 1976. Also, if the covenant is absolute, the landlord is not obliged to give any reason for his refusal. An absolute covenant against dealings is unusual in business leases, except in very short-term leases, or to the extent that it prohibits dealings with part of the premises (see **20.2.3**). Any wider form of absolute restriction should be resisted by the tenant and if, exceptionally, there is such a restriction, the tenant should make sure its presence is reflected in the rent he has to pay.

20.2.2 Qualified covenants against dealings

A qualified covenant prohibits alienation by the tenant without the landlord's consent. Sometimes, the covenant will state that the landlord's consent is not to be unreasonably withheld; this is known as a fully qualified covenant.

20.2.3 A common form of covenant

The form of covenant encountered in practice will contain elements of both the absolute and qualified restrictions by prohibiting absolutely dealings in relation to part only of the premises, and dealings which stop short of an assignment or sub-letting of the whole (eg parting with possession or sharing occupation of the premises), and then prohibiting without the landlord's prior written consent assignments or sub-lettings of the whole.

Such a clause attempts to strike a fair balance between both landlord and tenant as it will allow the tenant to assign or sub-let the whole of the premises subject to obtaining the landlord's prior consent (and, as will be seen at **20.2.4**, the landlord will not be able to unreasonably withhold his consent). This should meet the tenant's main concern of being unable to divest himself of the lease should his circumstances change. At the same time, it will allay the landlord's fears by imposing an absolute prohibition on dealings with part only of the premises.

Other provisions will be found in a common form of alienation covenant. For example:

(1) Assignments. In relation to leases granted before 1 January 1996, the lease will invariably require the assignee to enter into a direct covenant with the landlord to perform the covenants in the lease. This will make the assignee liable on the covenants in the lease during the whole term, rather than just during the currency of his ownership. Further, on an assignment to a limited company, the alienation clause may require the assignee company to provide sureties.

(2) Sub-leases. If the landlord is prepared to permit sub-letting, the terms of the sub-lease will often be dictated by the alienation clause (see, for example, *Blockbuster Entertainment Ltd v Leakcliff Properties Ltd* [1997] 08 EG 139). In particular, the landlord will wish to ensure that any sub-lease is at a rent no less than that in the head-lease and with similar review provisions; that the sub-tenants enter into direct covenants with the head landlord; and that no further sub-letting is allowed. Sometimes, the prohibition against sub-letting part will be absolute only insofar as it applies to sub-leases of less than a certain area; for example, in an office block to sub-leases of less than one floor.

(3) Conditions on assignment. In relation to commercial leases granted on or after 1 January 1996, the lease will usually stipulate conditions which must be satisfied, or circumstances which must exist before the landlord will give his consent to the assignment (see below).

20.2.4 Consent not to be unreasonably withheld

Section 19(1)(a) of the LTA 1927 provides that, notwithstanding any contrary provision, a covenant not to assign, underlet, charge or part with possession of the demised premises or any part thereof without the landlord's licence or consent, is subject to a proviso that such licence or consent is not to be unreasonably withheld. In other words, a qualified covenant can be converted into a fully qualified covenant by the operation of s 19(1). The section has no application to the operation of an absolute covenant, where the landlord remains free to refuse his consent to an assignment quite unreasonably. Furthermore, the section has to be read in the light of s 19(1A) of the LTA 1927 (introduced by s 22 of LTCA 1995) as regards covenants against assigning.

The Landlord and Tenant Act 1988 (LTA 1988) further strengthens the position of a tenant seeking consent to assign or sub-let. The Act applies where the lease contains a fully qualified covenant against alienation (whether or not the proviso that the landlord's consent is not to be unreasonably withheld is express or implied by statute). When the tenant has made written application for consent, the landlord owes a duty, within a reasonable time:

(1) to give consent, unless it is reasonable not to do so (see below). Giving consent subject to an unreasonable condition will be a breach of this duty; and
(2) to serve on the tenant written notice of his decision whether or not to give consent (see LTA 1988, s 1(3)(b), and *Footwear Corporation Ltd v Amplight Properties Ltd* [1988] EGCS 52), specifying in addition:
    (a) if the consent is given subject to conditions, the conditions; or
    (b) if the consent is withheld, the reasons for withholding it.

The burden of proving the reasonableness of any refusal or any conditions imposed is on the landlord. The sanction for breach of this statutory duty is liability in tort for damages. The LTA 1988 does not specify what is to be regarded as a reasonable time nor when refusal of consent is to be deemed reasonable. Again, this Act has to be read in the light of s 19(1A) of the LTA 1927. Nevertheless, landlords will have to give careful consideration to the financial consequences of having delayed or refused consent unreasonably. The operation of the LTA 1988 is further considered in Chapter 30.

20.2.5 Can the landlord refuse consent?

Whether the landlord can refuse consent will depend upon whether the landlord has made use of s 19(1A) of the LTA 1927 or, if not, his reasonableness in the circumstances of the case.

Making use of s 19(1A)

Section 19(1A) of the 1927 Act (which operates only in relation to qualified covenants against assigning) allows the landlord, in commercial leases granted on or after 1 January 1996, to stipulate in the lease (or in a written agreement entered into with the tenant at any time before he applies for licence to assign) conditions which need to be satisfied, or circumstances which must exist, before the landlord will give his consent to the assignment. It is provided by s 19(1A) that if the landlord withholds his consent on the grounds that the specified circumstances do not exist, or that the specified conditions have not been satisfied, then the landlord will not be unreasonably withholding his consent. If the landlord withholds his consent on grounds other than those specified, s 19(1)(a) of the LTA 1927 will apply in the usual way (see **20.2.4** and below). However, it can be seen that the effect of s 19(1A) is to reduce the protection afforded to tenants by s 19(1)(a).

The nature and type of condition to be satisfied (or circumstances which must exist) is left to the parties to decide, but s 19(1C) of the LTA 1927 envisages their falling in two categories: those which can be factually or objectively verified; and those where the landlord has a discretion.

Factual conditions or circumstances might include a requirement that the proposed assignee is a publicly quoted company on the London Stock Exchange, or has pre-tax net profits equal to three times the rent, or a requirement that the assignor enter into an authorised guarantee agreement (see **20.2.8**), or that the assignee procure guarantors.

Discretionary circumstances or conditions are those which cannot be verified objectively, and a judgment or determination will have to be made as to whether they have been satisfied. This type of condition will only be valid if either it provides for an independent third party reference (in the event of the tenant disagreeing with the landlord's determination), or the landlord commits himself to making a reasonable determination. Typical examples of discretionary circumstances or conditions may include a provision that the proposed assignee must, in the opinion of the landlord, be of equivalent financial standing to the assignor, and should the tenant not agree, the matter is to be referred to an independent third party; or a provision that the assignee must not, in the reasonable opinion of the landlord, be in competition with other tenants in the same development.

Where s 19(1A) does not apply

Section 19(1A) has no application to covenants against sub-letting, charging or mortgaging, and does not apply in relation to leases granted before 1 January 1996. In such cases, s 19(1)(a) of the LTA 1927 applies in the usual way, meaning that, notwithstanding any express provision to the contrary, the landlord cannot unreasonably withhold his consent where the covenant is a qualified one. Whether the landlord is acting reasonably in such cases has to be judged from the circumstances existing at the time of the landlord's decision. Here, the parties to the lease cannot lay down in advance that refusal of consent for a particular reason shall be deemed to be reasonable since that is for the court to decide. However, it is open to the landlord to agree that he will not refuse his consent to an assignment or sub-letting in favour of, for example 'a respectable and responsible person'. If the proposed assignee or sub-tenant is respectable and responsible, the landlord will be unable to refuse his consent, even on other reasonable grounds (*Moat v Martin* [1950] 1 KB 175). Further, it has been held that a lease may validly provide that, before applying for consent to assign or sub-let, the tenant shall first offer to surrender the lease. Such a requirement does not contravene s 19(1)(a), since if the landlord accepts the offer to surrender, no question of consent to assign arises. However, if the lease is protected under Part II of the LTA 1954, the landlord's acceptance of the tenant's offer may be void. Even so, the tenant may still have to make his offer if he is not to be found in breach of covenant (see *Allnatt London Properties Ltd v Newton* [1984] 1 All ER 423, and **34.1.5**).

The Court of Appeal laid down a number of guidelines on the issue of the landlord's reasonableness under s 19(1)(a) in *International Drilling Fluids Ltd v Louisville Investments (Uxbridge) Ltd* [1986] 1 All ER 321:

(1) the purpose of a fully qualified covenant against assignment is to protect the landlord from having his premises used or occupied in an undesirable way, or by an undesirable tenant or assignee;
(2) a landlord is not entitled to refuse his consent to an assignment on grounds which have nothing whatever to do with the relationship of landlord and tenant in regard to the subject matter of the lease;
(3) it is unnecessary for the landlord to prove that the conclusions which led him to refuse to consent were justified, if they were conclusions which might be reached by a reasonable man in the circumstances;
(4) it may be reasonable for the landlord to refuse his consent to an assignment on the ground of the purpose for which the proposed assignee intends to use the premises, even though that purpose is not forbidden by the lease;
(5) while a landlord need usually only consider his own relevant interests, there may be cases where there is such a disproportion between the benefit to the landlord and the detriment to the tenant if the landlord withholds his consent to an assignment, that it is unreasonable for the landlord to refuse consent;
(6) subject to the above propositions, it is, in each case, a question of fact, depending on all the circumstances, whether the landlord's consent to an assignment is being unreasonably withheld.

In deciding whether to give his consent to an assignment, the landlord may reasonably be influenced by considerations of proper estate management, but he is bound in this regard by the purpose of the covenant at the time the lease was granted, having regard to the circumstances existing at that date: 'If the refusal of the landlord was designed to achieve that purpose then it may not be unreasonable, . . . but if the refusal is designed to achieve some collateral purpose wholly unconnected with the terms of the lease . . . then that would be unreasonable, even though the purpose was in accordance with good estate management', per Dunn LJ in *Bromley Garden Park Estates Ltd v Moss* [1982] 2 All ER 890. The more recent case of *Crown Estate Commissioners v Signet Group plc* [1996] 2 EGLR 200 confirms that principles of good estate management can be grounds for reasonably withholding consent to assign (although, of course, each case will turn on its own facts).

The following are examples of situations where consent has been held to have been reasonably withheld:

(1) where the proposed assignee's references were unsatisfactory (*Shanley v Ward* (1913) 29 TLR 714). A landlord is rightly concerned that any assignee should be in a position to pay the rent and perform the covenants in the lease. Can the landlord, therefore, require the provision of a surety by the assignee as a condition of consent? If the lease does not require the provision of sureties, the reasonableness of the landlord's request for one will depend to a large extent on the financial strength of the assignee. The landlord will wish to see a bank reference and, usually, 3 years' audited accounts, but if he still entertains reasonable doubts, it may not be unreasonable for him to require a surety in which case the landlord will wish to be satisfied that their combined strength is sufficient to secure compliance with the lease terms. However, it has been held that the provision of a surety is not always a substitute for a satisfactory and responsible tenant in possession (*Warren v Marketing Exchange for Africa* [1988] 2 EGLR 247). In cases where s 19(1A) of the LTA 1927 has not been

used, if the alienation covenant in the lease expressly required the production of sureties, the question arises as to whether the landlord can insist on a surety, however unreasonable that may be. There are conflicting views on the issue but the case of *Vaux Group plc v Lilley* [1991] 1 EGLR 60, contains obiter remarks suggesting that this may be possible, at least if the requirement was appropriately drafted;

(2) where there was a long-standing and extensive breach of the repairing covenant by the assignor and the landlord could not be reasonably satisfied that the assignee would be in a position to remedy the breach (*Orlando Investments v Grosvenor Estate Belgravia* [1989] 2 EGLR 74);

(3) where the assignee would be in a position to compete with the landlord's business;

(4) where the assignment would reduce the value of the landlord's reversion (but see *International Drilling Fluids Ltd v Louisville Investments (Uxbridge) Ltd* above);

(5) where the proposed assignee intends to carry on a use detrimental to the premises;

(6) where the assignee would, unlike the assignor, acquire protection under Part II of the LTA 1954.

The following are examples of situations where consent has been held to have been unreasonably withheld:

(1) where the landlord has refused consent in an attempt to obtain some advantage for himself, for example, the surrender of the lease by the tenant;

(2) where the landlord anticipated a breach of the user covenant by the assignee. This was held to be unreasonable because it was not a necessary consequence that the covenant would be broken and, in any event, the landlord would have had the same right to enforce the covenant against the assignee as he would have had if the assignor had been in breach (see *Killick v Second Covent Garden Property Co Ltd* [1973] 2 All ER 337). However, the position is not entirely clear and this case has been distinguished where (inter alia) there was already a breach of covenant committed by the assignor and the assignment would have involved a continuation of that breach (*FW Woolworth plc v Charlwood Alliance Properties Ltd* [1987] 1 EGLR 53). The landlord's refusal of consent to a sub-lease has been upheld in similar circumstances because he would have been unable to directly enforce the user covenant against the subtenant;

(3) where there are minor breaches of the repairing covenant;

(4) where, on an application to sub-let the premises, the landlord refused consent because the underlease rent was to be less than the market value (something which was not prohibited by the terms of the lease). The landlord argued that a sub-letting below market value, whilst not affecting the value of the reversion of the demised premises, would adversely affect the reversionary value of neighbouring properties it owned. The court held this to be a case of the landlord seeking a collateral advantage unconnected with the demised premises (*Norwich Union Life Insurance Society v Shopmoor Ltd* (1997) *Current Law Digest* 97/3250).

Under the provisions of the Race Relations Act 1976 and the Sex Discrimination Act 1975, any discrimination in withholding consent for the disposal of the demised premises on grounds of race or sex is generally unlawful.

What if consent is refused?

If, having applied for consent to assign or sub-let, the tenant thinks his landlord is being unreasonable in his refusal to give such consent, the tenant has a number of options open to him. These are dealt with at **30.1**.

20.2.6 No consent required in the case of certain building leases

Section 19(1)(b) of the LTA 1927 provides that in the case of a building lease (ie one made in consideration wholly or partially of the erection or substantial improvement, addition or alteration of buildings) of more than 40 years, there is an implied proviso to any qualified covenant against assigning or sub-letting that no consent shall be required if the dealing takes place more than 7 years before the end of the term, provided written notice is given to the landlord within 6 months. This proviso applies notwithstanding anything to the contrary in the lease; but does not apply if the landlord is a government department, a local or public authority. Section 19(1)(b) does not apply to a building lease granted on or after 1 January 1996, to which the rules in **20.2.5** apply.

20.2.7 Restrictions on charging for consent to assign or sub-let

In the case of a qualified covenant against dealings, s 144 of the LPA 1925 implies a proviso that no fine or like sum of money shall be charged for giving such consent to assignment or sub-letting, unless the lease expressly provides for this. However, this does not prevent a landlord from requiring his tenant to pay a reasonable sum for legal and other expenses incurred in connection with the grant of consent.

20.2.8 Authorised guarantee agreements

Although the LTCA 1995 has abolished privity of contract in relation to leases caught by the Act, an outgoing tenant may sometimes be required to guarantee his immediate assignee's performance of the obligations contained in the lease. This is achieved by the outgoing tenant entering into an authorised guarantee agreement (AGA) with the landlord. The landlord may require an AGA from an outgoing tenant in the following circumstances, where:

(1) the lease provides that the consent of the landlord (or some other person) is required to the assignment;
(2) such consent is given subject to a condition (lawfully imposed) that the tenant is to enter into the AGA. For example, the requirement of an AGA may be one of the conditions which the parties had previously agreed had to be satisfied before the landlord was prepared to give his consent to an assignment (see **20.2.5**);
(3) the assignment is entered into by the tenant pursuant to that condition.

The terms of the guarantee are left to the parties (provided that the purpose of the LTCA 1995 is not frustrated) but the Act specifically permits the guarantee to require the outgoing tenant to enter into a new lease should the current lease be disclaimed following the assignee's insolvency (as to which, see **32.1.2**).

20.3 NOTICE OF ASSIGNMENT OR SUB-LETTING

There is no common law obligation for a tenant to give his landlord notice of any dealing with the lease, but a well-drafted lease will provide for this so that the landlord knows at any given time in whom the lease is vested and whether any sub-lease has been granted. The clause should specify the occasions on which the covenant is to operate (eg assignment, sub-letting, mortgage). The tenant is usually required to pay a registration fee to the landlord with each notice served.

In the case of assignment, it will fall to the assignee to give notice (and pay any registration fee prescribed by the lease), since it will be his interest which will be jeopardised by the breach of covenant involved in failing to give notice.

Chapter 21

USER COVENANTS

Chapter 21 contents

21.1 THE NEED FOR A USER COVENANT

There are several ways outside the terms of the lease in which the tenant's use of the premises may be restricted:

(1) Planning legislation. The tenant may not be able to carry out any building or other operations at the premises, and he will not be able to make a material change in the use of the premises without obtaining planning permission from the local planning authority. Generally, there is no implied warranty by the landlord that the tenant's use of the property is an authorised use under the planning legislation. It is, therefore, for the tenant to satisfy himself that planning permission is available for the use intended.
(2) Covenants affecting a superior title. There may be restrictive covenants affecting the landlord's reversionary title (or if the landlord is himself a tenant, affecting a superior title) which bind the tenant and prevent him from carrying out certain activities at the premises. Despite being restricted by statute as to the evidence of title he can call for, the tenant should always press the landlord for evidence of all superior titles.
(3) Common law restraints. The law of nuisance may prevent the tenant from using the premises in a such a way as to cause disturbance to a neighbour.

Whilst these restraints operate to exert some degree of control over the tenant, they do not provide the landlord with any remedy should the tenant act in breach. A user covenant (together with several ancillary clauses) will, therefore, be required to give the landlord the desired level of control.

21.1.1 The landlord's concerns

There are various financial and estate management reasons why a landlord will wish to control use of the premises by the tenant:

(1) to maintain the value of the landlord's interest in the premises;
(2) to maintain the rental value of the premises;
(3) to avoid damaging the reputation of the premises by immoral or undesirable uses;
(4) to maintain the value of adjoining premises owned by the landlord;
(5) to avoid the tenant competing with other premises of the landlord in the vicinity;
(6) to maintain a good mix of different retail uses in a shopping precinct owned by the landlord.

The landlord has to be careful when drafting the user covenant to ensure that he does not restrain the tenant's use of the premises any more than is strictly necessary for the landlord's purposes, since a tight user covenant may have an adverse impact from the landlord's point of view on rental values both initially and at rent review. The wider the scope of the user covenant, the more attractive would be a letting of the premises on the open market and, therefore, the higher the rental value may be, both initially and at review. The tighter the covenant, the less attractive would be a letting of the premises on the open market (since the number of potential bidders for this letting would be restricted by the narrowness of the user covenant) and, therefore, the lower the rental value would be. The landlord is not able to argue at rent review that the valuer should assess the revised rent on the basis that the landlord might be prepared to waive a breach of the user covenant in order to permit a more profitable use (thereby increasing the rental value of the tenant's interest), nor is he allowed to vary the lease unilaterally in order to gain a benefit at review (see *Plinth Properties Ltd v Mott, Hay & Anderson* [1979] 1 EGLR 17 and *C & A Pension Trustees Ltd v British Vita Investments Ltd* [1984] 2 EGLR 75 and the comments made at **18.5.2**).

The landlord will, therefore, need to perform a balancing act between control of the tenant and good estate management on the one hand, and maximisation of rental values on the other. Valuation advice may be necessary here.

21.1.2 Tenant's concerns

From the tenant's point of view, a narrow user covenant ought to be avoided since, although the clause would work favourably for the tenant on rent review, his ability to dispose of the premises at some stage in the future will be hampered in that he will only be able to assign or sub-let to someone who is capable of complying with the covenant and who does not require any greater flexibility.

Additionally, the tenant must have regard to his own future use of the premises. There is a risk that the nature of the tenant's business may change to such a degree that he is taken outside the scope of the user covenant and, therefore, finds himself in breach. The tenant must ensure that sufficient flexibility is built into the covenant to permit future diversification of the tenant's business. However, he should not allow the landlord to insert a covenant that is wider than is strictly necessary for his purposes, since this may penalise the tenant at rent review by increasing the rental value of the tenant's interest. Once again a balancing act is required.

The user clause usually contains a principal covenant by the tenant governing the permitted use of the premises, followed by a range of ancillary clauses prohibiting or controlling a range of other activities.

21.2 THE PERMITTED USE

There are several ways in which the permitted use can be defined in the lease. First, the landlord may be prepared to permit a wide range of uses by broadly stipulating the type of use to be permitted on the premises, for example, use as offices, or as a retail shop, or for light industrial purposes. This would give the tenant a large degree of flexibility and enable him to diversify his business operations within the broad range permitted.

Alternatively, the landlord may choose to restrict the tenant to a very narrow range of uses by defining the permitted use by reference to the nature of the business to be carried on at the premises, for example, use as offices for the business of an estate agency, or as a retail shop for the sale of children's footwear, or as a factory for the manufacture of computer software. This would give the tenant no flexibility to diversify and would hamper the tenant in any efforts to assign his lease, or sub-let the premises to someone who was not in the same line of business.

As a third possibility, the landlord may adopt an approach which is mid-way between the first two by restricting the tenant's use of the premises to a class of similar uses by, for example, defining the permitted use as offices for the business of a solicitor, accountant, architect or other professional person. If the landlord intends permitting the tenant to use the premises for one of a number of similar uses, he may consider defining the use by reference to the Town and Country Planning (Use Classes) Order 1987 (as amended).

21.2.1 Making use of the Use Classes Order

It is often considered desirable that the permitted user is linked to available planning permission. For example, if planning permission is available for any office use within class B1 of the Use Classes Order 1987, then the landlord, being quite happy for the premises to be used for any such office purposes, may choose simply to prohibit any use other than B1 office use. However, if this approach is to be adopted, the landlord should check carefully to ensure that there are no uses which could conceivably fall within the definition of B1 office use which the landlord would consider to be unattractive. The same principle is more clearly demonstrated if the lease prohibits any use other than as a retail shop within class A1. This is a very wide-ranging class of uses and there are likely to be several types of shop uses within that class which the landlord would not be prepared to tolerate at the premises.

If the landlord is to make use of the Use Classes Order in the user covenant, he should ensure that the lease clearly states that any reference to the Use Classes Order 1987 is intended to refer to the Order as enacted at the time the lease was granted. The danger is that at some stage during the term the Use Classes Order could be amended to bring within the class of use permitted by the lease a use which the landlord considered to be undesirable, thereby converting that use into a permitted use under the lease.

21.2.2 A covenant that names the tenant

It is sometimes difficult to define the type of business to be carried on by the tenant at the premises because of its peculiar nature, and so the landlord feels inclined to restrict use of the premises to the tenant's particular business. This is a dangerous approach to adopt, and it can lead to problems for the tenant (in terms of his ability to dispose of the premises) and can give rise to complicated valuation problems at rent review (*Sterling Land Office Developments Ltd v Lloyds Bank plc* (1984) 271 EG 894 and *Post Office Counters Ltd v Harlow District Council* [1991] 2 EGLR 121).

If the user covenant restricts the use of the premises to, for example, the offices of a particular company which is named in the lease, this would effectively prevent an assignment or sub-letting by the original tenant, even if the lease otherwise anticipated alienation (*Law Land Co Ltd v Consumers Association Ltd* (1980) 255 EG 617).

If the user covenant, without specifically naming the tenant, restricts use of the premises to 'the tenant's business', problems of interpretation will arise. Does the clause refer to the original tenant, or the current tenant? Does it refer to the business being conducted at the outset or the business being conducted from time to time? The danger from the landlord's point of view is that if, as is usually the case, the lease defines 'the Tenant' to include his successors in title, such a clause is likely to be construed by the court as permitting whatever business is currently being carried on by whoever is then the tenant. In other words, the landlord will have lost control. If reference is made to 'the tenant's business as a solicitor', does that mean that only the original tenant can comply with the covenant, or can an assignee? Would sub-letting be impossible since a sub-tenant, not being a tenant under the lease, would inevitably be in breach?

In view of these complications, it is advisable to avoid the use of covenants which either name the tenant, or refer to the tenant's business without sufficient clarity.

21.2.3 A positive or negative covenant?

If the covenant is positive, it will require the tenant 'to use the premises for the purposes of [the named permitted use]'. The benefit from the landlord's point of is that non-user (eg because of a temporary shut-down during a recession) will amount to a breach of covenant entitling the landlord to damages should the landlord suffer loss. Loss can arise if the premises form part of a shopping precinct which is dependent upon the continued presence of the tenant's shop in order to generate a flow of shoppers into the precinct. If the tenant's shop is a large food store, its closure will reduce the number of shoppers in the precinct, thereby affecting the profitability of other shops in the precinct and resulting eventually in an adverse effect on the value of the landlord's reversion. The tenant ought to resist a positive covenant (see **31.1.3**).

Most user covenants are negative obliging the tenant 'not to use the premises other than for the purposes of ... [permitted purpose]' in which case a breach is only committed by the tenant if he uses the premises for a purpose not authorised by the landlord. A negative user covenant is not breached by non-user.

Neither form of covenant will be breached if the tenant uses the premises for a purpose ancillary to the permitted use. For example, use of some rooms in a shop for storage purposes where the user covenant permits the retail sale of books, magazines and periodicals would not amount to a breach.

21.3 THE EXTENT OF THE LANDLORD'S CONTROL

The principal covenant may be absolute, qualified or fully qualified.

21.3.1 Absolute covenants

An absolute covenant gives the landlord absolute control over any change in the use of the premises in that it permits the tenant to use the premises for the purpose of the permitted use and no other. The tenant will not be able to use the premises for a use falling outside the scope of the covenant without obtaining from the landlord a waiver of the tenant's breach, or getting the landlord to agree to a variation of the lease. If the permitted use is narrowly defined, the tenant should be advised to resist an absolute covenant, unless he is sure that he will not want to assign or sub-let the premises, or diversify his business. If the permitted use is sufficiently widely defined (eg use as offices only), then an absolute covenant should not unduly concern the tenant.

21.3.2 Qualified covenants

A qualified covenant allows the tenant to alter the use of the premises from a permitted use to some other use with the landlord's prior consent, which is usually required to be given in writing. However, such a covenant gives the tenant little extra comfort than is afforded by an absolute covenant since, unlike qualified covenants relating to alienation and improvements, there is no statutorily implied proviso that the landlord's consent is not to be unreasonably withheld. This means that, despite the additional wording added to the covenant, the tenant is still at the mercy of the landlord who may decline the request for a change of use for whatever reason he chooses. The only benefit from the tenant's point of view of a qualified covenant is derived from s 19(3) of the LTA 1927 which states that, provided the change of use will not entail any structural alterations to the premises (which would not often be the case), the landlord is not allowed to demand as a condition of his giving consent the payment of a lump sum or an increased rent (as to which, see *Barclays Bank Plc v Daejan Investments (Grove Hall) Ltd* [1995] 18 EG 170). However, s 19(3) does allow the landlord, as a condition of his consent, to insist upon the payment of reasonable compensation in respect of damage to or diminution in the value of the premises or any neighbouring premises belonging to the landlord (which might occur if a valuable use of the premises is abandoned), and the payment of expenses incurred in the giving of consent, such as legal and surveyor's fees.

Section 19(3) does not apply to agricultural or mining leases.

21.3.3 Fully qualified covenants

A fully qualified covenant allows the tenant to change the use of the premises from a permitted use to some other use with the prior consent (in writing) of the landlord, whose consent is not to be unreasonably withheld. Most covenants of this kind will also stipulate (either in the wording of the covenant, or in the interpretation section of the lease) that the landlord cannot unreasonably delay giving consent. Should the landlord, in the tenant's opinion, be guilty of an unreasonable refusal of consent, the tenant may, if he is certain of his ground, change the use of the premises without the landlord's consent. However, this course of action carries a risk and, therefore, most tenants would prefer to follow the safer course of action which is to apply to the court for a declaration that the landlord is acting unreasonably, and then proceed without the landlord's consent. The question of the landlord's reasonableness is ultimately left in the hands of the court. The only potential drawbacks of such a clause for the tenant are that, without an express provision in the lease, there is no obligation on the landlord to provide the tenant with reasons for refusing consent (making it difficult for the tenant to assess whether he has a good chance of success in his application for a declaration) and there is no positive duty upon the landlord to give consent along the lines of the statutory duty imposed by the LTA 1988 in respect of alienation covenants, which means that the tenant does not have a remedy in damages if he suffers loss as a result of an unreasonable refusal.

Section 19(3) of the LTA 1927 applies equally to fully qualified covenants.

21.4 ANCILLARY CLAUSES

It is usual for the landlord to impose many other covenants upon the tenant which also impact upon user, obliging the tenant:

(1) to comply in all respects with the Planning Acts (as defined in the definitions section of the lease). It is important for the landlord to have the benefit of this

covenant since enforcement action for a breach of planning control committed by the tenant could be taken against the landlord, resulting in a possible fine.

(2) not to apply for planning permission, or to carry out acts of development at the premises. This covenant may be absolute, qualified or fully qualified. The landlord will not want the tenant to have freedom to change the authorised use of the premises as this may result in an existing profitable use being lost, thereby reducing the value of the premises. Although, as owner of the reversion, the landlord may be able to raise objections at the application stage, he would prefer to be able to veto the application under the terms of the lease in the first place. It should be noted that such a covenant may restrict the tenant's ability to alter or change the use of the premises even if elsewhere in the lease such action is more freely permitted;

(3) where the landlord has consented to an application for planning permission, and development has commenced, to fully implement all permissions obtained before the end of the term in accordance with any conditions attached to the permission;

(4) not to cause a nuisance, annoyance or inconvenience to the landlord or its tenants of adjoining premises. Whether an activity amounts to a nuisance is to be determined on the basis of ordinary tortious principles. An annoyance is anything which disturbs the reasonable peace of mind of the landlord or an adjoining occupier, and is a wider concept than nuisance. The concept of inconvenience is probably wider still;

(5) not to use the premises for any immoral or illegal use (since such uses may tarnish the reputation of the building and reduce its value);

(6) not to carry out any dangerous activities, or bring any noxious or inflammable substances onto the premises. The landlord's primary purpose behind this covenant is to preserve the premises. One consequence of a breach by the tenant might be an increase in the insurance premium for the premises, and although the tenant is likely to be obliged to pay the increased premium by virtue of the insurance covenant, the landlord would not want the level of insurance premiums to rise;

(7) not to overload the premises in any way. The landlord is simply trying to preserve the premises with this covenant;

(8) not to allow anyone to sleep or reside at the premises;

(9) not to allow any licence which benefits the premises to lapse (eg gaming licences, liquor licences). If the premises consist of a betting shop, the value of those premises will depend to a large extent on the continued existence of a betting office licence. The tenant will, therefore, be obliged by the landlord to maintain and where necessary renew the licence.

Chapter 22

ALTERATIONS

22.1 EXISTING RESTRICTIONS

As with user covenants, there are external restraints, outside the scope of the lease, which may prevent the tenant from altering the premises, or may at least regulate the way in which they are carried out, for example:

(1) Planning legislation. If the alterations proposed by the tenant amount to development within the meaning of s 55 of the TCPA 1990 then planning permission will be required.
(2) The Building Regulations. Any works to be carried out by the tenant will have to comply with the Building Regulations.
(3) Covenants affecting a superior title. The tenant's proposed works may be prohibited by the terms of a covenant affecting the landlord's reversion (which may either be the freehold title, or a leasehold title if the landlord is himself a tenant), or may require the consent of the person currently benefited by the covenant.
(4) The common law. The tenant will have to ensure that any works he carries out at the premises do not give rise to a cause of action in the tort of nuisance. He will also have to ensure that he will not, in executing his works, infringe an easement benefiting an adjoining property (eg a right to light or air over the tenant's premises).
(5) Other legislation. The tenant, in altering the premises, will have to bear in mind any requirements of the fire authority in regard to fire safety, and if his works are more than just minor works, the tenant must have regard to environmental legislation regarding noise and other kinds of pollution.

22.2 THE NEED FOR AN ALTERATIONS COVENANT

22.2.1 The landlord's concerns

There are various reasons why the landlord will want to control the ability of the tenant to make alterations to the premises:

(1) to ensure that the tenant does not breach the external restraints set out at **22.1**, which may well lead to action being taken against the landlord;
(2) to ensure that at the end of the lease the tenant would not be giving back to the landlord premises differing substantially from those demised;
(3) to maintain the character, appearance and reputation of the building and, therefore, the value of the landlord's interest in the building and any adjoining premises;
(4) to maintain the rental value of the premises;
(5) to preserve the physical state of the premises.

In a short-term letting the landlord will probably want to exercise tight control over the tenant's ability to make alterations to the premises. However, in a longer-term letting, where the tenant may need to adapt the premises during the term to suit his changing business needs, the landlord will be prepared to allow the tenant a greater degree of freedom. In the commercial letting market, a lease for a term of 25 years will not be an attractive prospect for a tenant if there are severe restrictions in the lease on his ability to make alterations. Such restrictions would give the landlord problems at the outset in securing a letting of the premises, and later on at rent review where the restrictive alterations covenant may be taken into account in reduction of the rental value of the premises.

22.2.2 The tenant's concerns

The tenant will be anxious to ensure that the lease gives him the right degree of flexibility. In considering the alterations covenant, the tenant must bear in mind four things:

(1) Will the tenant need to make any immediate alterations to the premises, before occupying them for the purposes of his business? For example, if the premises form the shell of a large shop, and the tenant has not been allowed access to the premises before completion of the lease, the tenant will need to fit out the premises before being able to trade. If the premises are open-plan offices, the tenant may need to install internal partition walls. If the premises in their present state are unsuited to the tenant's needs, the tenant may need to convert them. The tenant should ensure that the alterations covenant does not prohibit these works, or if the covenant permits them with the consent of the landlord, the tenant should ensure that such consent will be forthcoming.

(2) Does the tenant anticipate that his business needs may change during the term in such a way that he will need to alter the premises to accommodate these changes?

(3) Will the tenant's assignee be content with the restrictions on alterations in the lease? Even if the tenant does not anticipate the need to make any changes during the term, an assignee might need to make changes, and if the alterations covenant is too restrictive, an assignee might be dissuaded from taking an assignment of the lease.

(4) Will the tenant suffer at rent review? If the tenant secures a covenant that is too flexible, in that it gives the tenant extensive freedom to alter and improve the premises as he sees fit, the rental value of the letting may be increased at review as a result.

The tenant should ensure that, in the light of the above points, he has sufficient flexibility, but he should not let the landlord give him any more freedom than is strictly required, or else the tenant might suffer at review.

The covenant against alterations is usually drafted by the landlord to prohibit all alterations and additions to the premises save those expressly permitted by the terms of the lease, or those in respect of which written consent of the landlord has been obtained.

22.3 THE EXTENT OF THE LANDLORD'S CONTROL

As with other covenants, the covenant against alterations may be absolute, qualified or fully qualified.

In all cases, the landlord must first consider the type of premises involved, and the length of term proposed. In a short-term letting of, say, 3 years or less, an absolute prohibition against all alterations may be appropriate. In a letting of a large warehouse or factory or other industrial premises, the landlord may only require absolute control over alterations affecting the structure and exterior of the premises, leaving the tenant free to do more or less as he pleases on the inside. In a shopping parade, in order to maintain the general appearance of the parade and the quality of the development, the landlord may feel that he wants to have a very tight control over all alterations, inside and out.

On occasions, the landlord may allow the tenant unrestricted freedom to carry out certain types of alterations or additions. In office leases, where the initial design of the building is open-plan, the lease often allows the tenant to erect internal partitioning walls without having to obtain the landlord's prior consent. The lease would merely require the tenant to notify the landlord of the additions, and to remove them if required to do so by the landlord at the end of the term.

However flexible the landlord proposes to be, in many cases the landlord will consider imposing an absolute covenant against structural alterations for the simple reason that the structure, being such a fundamental part of the building, should not be tampered with by the tenant.

22.3.1 Absolute covenants

If the lease contains an absolute covenant against the making of any alterations, or against the making of a particular type of alteration, the landlord will have total control over the tenant in that regard. As was the case with user covenants, this does not necessarily mean that the tenant will be unable to carry out prohibited alterations, since, although the tenant is at the mercy of the landlord, at some later date the landlord may be prepared to agree to vary the lease, or grant a specific waiver in respect of the tenant's proposed breach of covenant.

Sometimes, the requirements of a particular statute permit the tenant to obtain a court order varying the terms of an absolute covenant where the tenant has been required to carry out works to the premises by a body acting under statutory authority (eg a fire authority ordering the tenant to install a fire escape, see the Fire Precautions Act 1971). Further, the provisions of the LTA 1927 (see **22.6**) can, in certain circumstances, enable the tenant to alter the premises notwithstanding an absolute covenant.

The tenant should be advised to avoid an absolute covenant except, perhaps, where the covenant only relates to structural or external alterations (in which case the tenant may agree that it is reasonable that he should not be allowed to tamper with the structural parts of the building) or where the letting is for a short term and the tenant is confident that he will not need to alter the premises in the future to accommodate changes in his business, and that he will not need or want to assign the lease during the term. However, the longer the term, the more the tenant should ensure that he has sufficient flexibility to alter the premises.

22.3.2 Qualified covenants

A qualified covenant against alterations prohibits alterations to the premises by the tenant without the landlord's prior consent (which is usually required to be given in writing). A typical lease of office premises might be drafted to contain an absolute covenant against all alterations to the premises 'except those expressly permitted by this clause'. This absolute covenant would then be followed by a qualified covenant obliging the tenant 'not to make any internal non-structural alterations without the prior written consent of the landlord'.

Section 19(2) of the LTA 1927 implies into a qualified covenant against making improvements a proviso that the landlord's consent is not to be unreasonably withheld. The proviso cannot be excluded by the landlord. However, under s 19(2), the landlord can, as a condition of his giving consent, require payment by the tenant of reasonable compensation in respect of damage to or diminution in the value of the premises or any adjoining premises belonging to the landlord, payment of any legal and other expenses (eg legal and surveyor's fees) properly incurred in the giving of consent and, where it is reasonable to do so, an undertaking from the tenant to reinstate the premises at the end of the term to the condition they were in prior to the execution of the improvement.

Section 19(2) leaves the tenant with three questions as set out below.

(1) When does an alteration amount to an improvement?

In deciding whether the tenant's proposed works amount to improvements to the premises, the matter is to be viewed through the eyes of the tenant, not the landlord (see *Lambert v FW Woolworth & Co Ltd* [1938] 2 All ER 664). Provided the alteration has the effect of increasing the value or usefulness of the premises from the tenant's point of view, it is irrelevant that the alterations will inevitably lead to a decrease in the value of the landlord's reversionary interest. The tenant may propose knocking through a party wall to an adjacent building which is also in the occupation of the tenant, but which is not owned by the landlord. If such alterations increase the usefulness of the premises to the tenant (which they surely will), they will amount to improvements, and the landlord will not be able to withhold his consent unreasonably. As a consequence of the judicial interpretation of 'improvements', most disputes arising under s 19(2) revolve around the amount of compensation payable to the landlord rather than the classification of the tenant's works, since the tenant should always to be able to show that his alterations will improve the premises from his point of view.

(2) When will the landlord be acting unreasonably in withholding his consent?

A landlord will only be acting reasonably in refusing consent where his reasons relate to the relationship of landlord and tenant in regard to the premises in question. Withholding consent on the grounds that the premises, if improved, would be more attractive and, therefore, likely to take trade away from the landlord's own premises in the neighbourhood would appear to be unreasonable on the grounds that the landlord is seeking to gain some collateral advantage outside the landlord and tenant relationship.

Since s 19(2) allows the landlord to be compensated for a reduction in the value of the reversion, a landlord would be acting unreasonably if he withheld consent to improvements on the ground of the reduction. The correct approach for the landlord would be to seek reasonable compensation under s 19(2). However, should the tenant refuse to pay a reasonable sum in compensation, or should he refuse to give an undertaking to reinstate the premises at the end of the term where it is reasonable for the landlord to ask for one (eg in the example above, where the tenant is uniting the premises with other premises not owned by the landlord), the landlord would be acting reasonably in withholding consent.

If the landlord gives his consent, but subject to an unreasonable condition (eg that the tenant pays an excessive amount of compensation to the landlord, or that the tenant agrees to surrender his lease one year earlier than the end of the term), the landlord will be unreasonably withholding his consent.

(3) What remedies does the tenant have?

If the landlord, in the tenant's opinion, unreasonably withholds consent to improvements, the tenant may seek a declaration from the court that the landlord is acting unreasonably and that the tenant may, therefore, proceed without the landlord's consent. Alternatively, confident in the belief that the landlord is acting unreasonably the tenant may decide to take a risk by proceeding to execute his proposed works without waiting for the landlord's consent. If subsequently sued for a breach of covenant for altering the premises without the landlord's consent, the tenant can use the landlord's alleged unreasonable withholding of consent as a defence to the action. However, unless there is an express provision in the lease, there is no obligation on the landlord to give any reasons for refusing consent, and so it may be difficult for the tenant to assess his chances of succeeding either in his application for a declaration, or in the defence of the landlord's action for breach if the tenant proceeds without waiting for the landlord's consent.

The tenant does not have an action in damages against the landlord if the refusal of consent results in loss to the tenant (eg where the tenant's well-advanced business plans are thwarted by the landlord's refusal) since, unlike alienation covenants, there is no positive duty on the landlord to give consent.

Section 19(2) does not apply to mining or agricultural leases.

22.3.3 Fully qualified covenants

Section 19(2) converts a qualified covenant against alterations into a fully qualified covenant insofar as improvements are intended by the tenant. However, to avoid the argument that the tenant's works are not improvements, most tenants will insist on converting a qualified covenant into a fully qualified covenant expressly by adding to the qualified covenant drafted by the landlord the words 'such consent not to be unreasonably withheld or delayed'. That having been done, the landlord may not now unreasonably withhold, nor delay giving his consent in respect of an application by the tenant to carry out any alterations of a kind permitted by the clause.

22.4 OTHER LEASE CLAUSES

The landlord is likely to include many other covenants in the lease which have a bearing on what the tenant will be allowed to do to the premises:

(1) If the terms of the lease permit certain alterations (either with or without the landlord's consent), the landlord may include a provision requiring all alterations and additions to be removed and the premises reinstated at the landlord's request at the end of the term. Section 19(2) of the LTA 1927 allows the landlord to impose this requirement as a condition of the licence to alter where it is reasonable to do so. By including the requirement in the lease, the landlord is trying to avoid the argument that he is attaching an unreasonable condition to his consent. Further, by obliging the tenant to reinstate the premises at the end of the term, the landlord may be able to avoid paying compensation to the tenant on account of his improvements (see **22.6**) on the

basis that, if the improvements have been removed, there will be nothing in respect of which compensation can be paid at the end of the term.

(2) In the same way that the licence to alter may impose a requirement to reinstate, the landlord may also impose a condition obliging the tenant to allow the landlord access to the premises to view the tenant's works. To avoid the argument that such a condition is an unreasonable one to impose, many landlords prefer to insert an express right of entry for inspection in the lease itself.

(3) The doctrine of waste may operate to prevent the tenant from altering the premises. Waste is any act which changes the nature of the premises, and can be voluntary, permissive, ameliorating or equitable. Reference should be made to text books on land law for a more detailed consideration of the doctrine of waste. It is common to find a prohibition on waste (save to the extent that it might otherwise be permitted in the lease) in the alterations covenant.

(4) Many landlords impose a covenant on the tenant not to tamper with the electrical supply or installations, especially in a lease of part of a building.

(5) The landlord will want to control the tenant's ability to make applications for planning permission. This covenant may be absolute, qualified or fully qualified. If the tenant is allowed to obtain planning permission, the landlord is likely to require the tenant to fully implement all permissions obtained before the end of the term where development has been commenced by the tenant.

(6) The landlord will usually require a covenant by the tenant not to display any signs or advertisements at the premises without the landlord's prior written consent, since a proliferation of signs or advertising hoardings can give the premises an unsightly appearance, thereby reducing the value of the landlord's interest in the building. In a shopping precinct, some landlords want to prevent tenants emblazoning 'sale' signs in shop front windows, as they feel that a 'sale' can sometimes imply that the business of the shop is suffering, which might be interpreted by some people as an indication that the shop is badly situated in the precinct. This can in turn lead to a reduction in the rental value of the premises, and a possible reduction in the value of the landlord's reversion. The tenant will normally ask, and is usually able to negotiate that the covenant is fully qualified.

(7) The decorating covenant can be said to control the manner in which the tenant may alter the premises since it may dictate that the tenant is not to change the colour of the premises (either inside, outside or both) without the landlord's prior consent.

22.5 TAX CONSEQUENCES

The landlord should be aware of the possible tax consequences under the Income and Corporation Taxes Act 1988 of granting a lease to a tenant in consideration of the tenant carrying out works to the premises. If the lease obliges the tenant to improve the premises, he is deemed to have paid a premium to the landlord at the grant of the lease, which becomes liable to income or corporation tax as the case may be. Standard works on revenue law will contain details of the exact scope of the charge to tax.

22.6 COMPENSATION FOR IMPROVEMENTS

Part I of the LTA 1927 (as amended by Part III of the LTA 1954) makes provision for the tenant to claim compensation from the landlord upon the termination of the lease in respect of improvements which the tenant (or his predecessor) has carried out to the premises. The concept is fair in that the tenant will be returning to the landlord an asset that has increased in value as a result of the tenant's expenditure.

In addition, the Act provides a mechanism whereby the tenant may obtain permission for improvements he would like to carry out to the premises even in the face of an absolute covenant.

The Act provides that a tenant of business premises (defined under the Act as any premises held under a lease and used wholly or partly for the carrying on upon them of a trade or business) is entitled to compensation upon quitting the premises at the end of his lease (no matter how it is terminated) in respect of certain improvements.

22.6.1 Qualifying improvements

To qualify as an improvement for the purposes of the compensation provisions:

(1) it must be one which, at the termination of the lease, adds to the letting value of the premises;
(2) it must not consist of trade or other fixtures which the tenant is entitled to remove at the end of the lease;
(3) it must be reasonable and suitable to the character of the premises;
(4) it must not diminish the value of any adjoining premises belonging to the landlord; and
(5) it must not be made in pursuance of a contract made for valuable consideration (where, eg, the lease obliged the tenant to make the improvement, or the improvement was made under some statutory obligation and the tenant was bound by the lease to perform all statutory obligations affecting the premises, or the landlord paid for the tenant to improve the premises, or reduced his rent).

In order to be entitled to compensation on quitting, the tenant must have obtained prior authorisation for his improvements by using the statutory procedure, and he must claim within the statutory time-limits.

22.6.2 Authorisation

To obtain authorisation, the tenant must serve upon the landlord notice of intention to make improvements. It does not matter that the covenant in the lease is absolute, or is qualified and the landlord has reasonable grounds to withhold consent. There is no prescribed form for the tenant's notice and, therefore, a letter would suffice, but the tenant should submit with his notice plans and specifications of his proposed works. The landlord has 3 months from receipt to serve written notice of objection upon the tenant. If the landlord fails to object, the improvements are treated as automatically authorised and will, therefore, attract compensation under the Act. If the landlord does object in time, the tenant may apply to the court for a certificate that the improvement is a proper one to make. The court will grant the certificate if satisfied that the improvement qualifies as an improvement for the purposes of the Act (see **22.6.1**). The tenant is then authorised to make the improvements in accordance with his plans and specifications. Again, it does not matter that the improvements are prohibited by the lease, since it is provided that if the tenant has received no objection from the landlord, or has obtained the certificate of the court, he can carry out the improvements notwithstanding 'anything in any lease of the premises to the contrary'.

22.6.3 Amount of compensation

The amount which the tenant is to receive must not exceed either the net addition to the value of the premises directly resulting from the improvements or the reasonable cost (as at the date of termination of the tenancy) of carrying out the improvement. It follows, therefore, that if the improvement does not add to the value of the premises, no compensation will be payable.

22.6.4 Time-limits

If the landlord does not voluntarily pay compensation to the tenant, the tenant must apply to the court for compensation within 3 months of the service of the landlord's s 25 notice, or counter-notice to the tenant's s 26 request (see **34.2**) or within 3 months of the forfeiture of the lease (either by re-entry, or court order). If the lease is to expire by effluxion of time, application must be made between 3 and 6 months before the expiry date of the lease.

The parties cannot contract out of the provisions relating to compensation for improvements.

The Law Commission has recommended abolition of compensation for improvements.

Chapter 23

OTHER COMMON COVENANTS

23.1 ENCROACHMENTS

It is usual for the lease to deal with the danger of third party encroachments onto the demised premises and the possibility of others acquiring easements over it. This would obviously affect the landlord's reversion and it is, therefore, usual for the lease to include a covenant by the tenant to immediately notify the landlord of any new easement being acquired or encroachment being attempted. The covenant will usually then go on to require the tenant to take such steps as are reasonably necessary to prevent any encroachments or easements.

23.2 STATUTORY REQUIREMENTS

The lease will require the tenant to comply with the requirements of all existing and future statutory obligations affecting the demised premises. There are a number of reasons for this:

(1) a contravention by the tenant may bring penalties, not only upon the tenant, but upon the landlord as well, and the landlord will thus wish to be able to take action against his tenant;
(2) the breach of statutory requirement may result in an indirect loss such as the inability to obtain the renewal of a licence for the premises;
(3) if a statutory obligation required expensive works to be carried out to the premises, the tenant would have to bear the cost.

There will usually be a separate covenant by the tenant to comply with all the provisions of the Planning Acts (as defined in the lease) and not to make any application for planning permission without first having obtained the landlord's written consent.

23.3 COVENANTS PECULIAR TO THE TYPE OF PROPERTY

Most of the covenants already considered will be applicable to all business leases, regardless of the type of property involved. However, there are some covenants which are more likely to be found in certain types of property.

23.3.1 Shops

On the grant of a lease of one shop in a parade of shops or a shopping centre, the landlord will have a number of concerns which may need to be reflected in the covenants he imposes on the tenant:

(1) Many large retail chains have their own corporate identity and want all their properties to have a similar appearance. This may necessitate fitting out the shop in a particular way or the installation of a new shop front. For existing properties the landlord's consent will be needed under the covenant against

making alterations. With new properties the landlord may simply impose an obligation on each tenant to install a suitable shop front together with the usual shop fixtures and fittings in accordance with plans to be approved by the landlord. From the tenant's point of view, he should seek to have the effect of fitting out works disregarded on rent review.

(2) The landlord will wish to achieve a well-balanced mix of retail uses and to stop tenants from competing with each other. The landlord will thus wish to impose a tight user clause on the tenant but should be aware that this may have an adverse effect on rental values at rent review. To counter this, the rent review provisions may provide that for the purposes of the hypothetical lease, the permitted user is assumed to be any retail user, except one which is likely to reduce the rental value. The tenant will try to resist this and, as always, it will become a matter for negotiation.

(3) A positive obligation might be imposed on the tenant to use the premises and keep them open for the purposes of the permitted user, otherwise the tenant could simply stop trading and leave the premises empty. This may have an adverse effect on the rental value of the other shops in the parade or centre because of the decreased pedestrian flow, and the landlord would then suffer on rent review. Breach of such an obligation by the tenant would entitle the landlord to bring an action for damages (see **31.1.3**). The tenant should try to resist such a clause as it would require him to keep trading even though the business was making a loss. In any event the tenant should make sure that the covenant allows the shop to be closed to allow for the normal business and retail activities such as stocktaking. The question of Sunday trading may also need to be addressed. Any lease entered into before 26 August 1994 requiring a shop to open during, eg, 'normal business hours' will not require the tenant to trade on Sundays; but leases granted on or after that date should expressly deal with the issue of Sunday trading.

(4) The landlord may wish to impose other covenants in the interests of good estate management, for example, controlling advertisements, requiring the windows to be attractively dressed and a covenant not to do anything which may be a nuisance or annoyance to the adjoining owners or occupiers.

(5) From the tenant's point of view, he will be concerned about the possibility of competition from other shops in the parade or centre. The tenant should, therefore, try to negotiate for a covenant from the landlord not to let, or allow to be used, any of the adjoining shops in the centre for a competing business.

23.3.2 Industrial premises

If the landlord is granting a lease of industrial premises, for example, a small factory on an industrial estate, he should give consideration to ensuring that any industrial processes carried out at the premises do not cause a nuisance or annoyance to the adjoining units. Particular attention should be paid to environmental issues such as smoke abatement, pollution and making sure that the land does not become 'contaminated' (see Chapter 6).

Other matters to consider include a prohibition on the tenant bringing any plant or machinery onto the premises which might cause structural damage.

23.4 LANDLORD'S RIGHT OF ENTRY

It is usual for the lease to include a covenant by the tenant to permit the landlord to enter upon the demised premises to view the condition of them, and to carry out an inspection to ascertain whether the tenant is complying with his obligations under the lease. This is particularly important as far as the tenant's repairing covenant is concerned (see **19.2.8** for a more detailed consideration of this issue). The landlord may also need a right of entry to carry out repairs to any adjoining premises, or to the demised premises where the landlord is under an obligation to repair them. The tenant should seek to ensure that any right of entry is exercised only on reasonable notice, for example, 48 hours, and only at reasonable times (except in an emergency).

Chapter 24

THE LANDLORD'S COVENANT FOR QUIET ENJOYMENT

24.1 NATURE OF THE COVENANT

Most leases will contain an express covenant for quiet enjoyment by the landlord (and, even in the absence of an express covenant, one will be implied). The usual form of express covenant provides that if the tenant pays the rent and performs his covenants, he may quietly hold and enjoy the demised premises without interruption by the landlord or anyone lawfully claiming under him. This usual form of covenant is restricted in that it only extends to interruption of or interference with the tenant's enjoyment of the demised premises by the landlord or any person lawfully claiming under him; it does not extend to the acts of anyone with a title superior to that of the landlord. However, the parties are free to negotiate a more extensive covenant for quiet enjoyment which does extend to the acts of those with a superior title, thereby providing the tenant with a greater degree of protection.

The covenant only extends to the lawful acts of those claiming under the landlord since, if they are unlawful (eg, trespass) the tenant will have his own remedies against the person committing the act. This means that there is no breach of the covenant in the event of an interruption by an adjoining tenant which is unauthorised by the landlord.

24.2 ACTS CONSTITUTING A BREACH

The covenant will provide the tenant with a remedy in the case of unlawful eviction or where there is substantial interference with the tenant's use or enjoyment of the demised premises. Whilst this is a question of fact in each case the following situations have given rise to a breach:

(1) where the landlord erected scaffolding on the pavement in front of a shop which blocked the access to the shop (*Owen v Gadd* [1956] 2 QB 99). This illustrates that it is not necessary for there to be any physical intrusion into the demised premises provided (it would seem) that there is physical interference with the enjoyment of the premises;
(2) where the demised premises were flooded due to the landlord's failure to repair a culvert on his adjoining land (*Booth v Thomas* [1926] Ch 397);
(3) where the landlord carried out work to the building in a manner which caused prolonged and substantial interference to the tenant by reason of 'dust, noise, dirt . . . deterioration of common parts . . . general inconvenience . . . and water penetration' (see *Mira v Aylmer Square Investments Ltd* [1990] 1 EGLR 45).

Until recently, it had been understood that noise nuisance emanating from the premises of adjoining tenants would not (of itself) amount to a breach of the covenant. However, the Court of Appeal in *Baxter v Camden LBC* [1997] EGCS 102 held that, where the level of noise affected the tenant's reasonable enjoyment of the demised premises, it could amount to a breach. This judgment amounts to an extension of the scope of the covenant; with the potential for yet further extension. In the words of Lord Justice Sumner:

> 'A landlord is liable for any mischief that arises from the natural and necessary result of what he has authorised and required. ... It is no defence that the premises were being used in a normal way if the premises are not fit to be used in this way without interfering with the reasonable enjoyment of adjoining occupiers. The landlord would equally be held liable for breach of the implied covenant for quiet enjoyment where the contemplated use for which the adjoining premises were let was one which interfered with the reasonable enjoyment of the plaintiff's premises.'

The covenant for quiet enjoyment is closely linked with the landlord's implied obligation not to derogate from his grant; which is dealt with at **31.2.2**.

Chapter 25

INSURANCE

Chapter 25 contents

25.1 INTRODUCTION

There is no implied obligation on either party to insure the demised premises. However, it is very important to both parties, and their lenders, that their respective interests are fully protected and it is, therefore, essential for the lease to make express provision for insurance. There are a number of important issues which will need to be addressed by the draftsman.

25.2 WHO IS TO INSURE?

In a lease of business premises, it is common practice for the landlord to effect the insurance cover. On a lease of part of a building (eg one unit in a shopping centre, or a suite of offices in a block) it is more appropriate for the landlord to arrange insurance for the whole building including any car parks, pedestrian areas etc, as in this way only one policy is needed. Further, all the common parts of the building will be covered under the same policy and there is no danger of any parts of the building being left uninsured. On the grant of a lease of the whole of a building, either party could be made to insure but the landlord will usually wish to assume the responsibility, rather than face the risk of the tenant failing to comply with his covenant to insure. Whilst the landlord would be able to sue the tenant for breach of covenant, the tenant may have insufficient funds to satisfy the judgment.

If the landlord effects the insurance, before completion the tenant should ask to see a copy of the policy so that he can satisfy himself as to the amount and terms of cover. As the tenant has a continuing interest in the insurance of the demised premises he should also require the landlord to produce evidence of the terms of the policy and of payment of the premiums, at any time during the term of the lease.

25.3 WHO IS TO PAY?

Where the landlord has insured the demised premises, there will be a covenant in the lease requiring the tenant to reimburse the cost of insurance to the landlord. This sum is likely to be reserved as rent in order to give the landlord better remedies for recovery. If the demised premises are part of a larger building which the landlord has insured, recovery can either be through the service charge provisions or, alternatively, there may be a separate covenant by the tenant to reimburse an apportioned part of the premium. The tenant must ensure that the apportionment of the premium between the tenants is fair, particularly if the business of some of the tenants involves hazardous activities which lead to an increase in the premium.

It should be noted that a covenant by the tenant to reimburse premiums that the landlord 'shall from time to time properly expend' does not impose an obligation on the landlord to shop around for a reasonable level of premium (see *Havenridge Ltd v Boston Dyers Ltd* [1994] 49 EG 111).

25.4 IN WHOSE NAME?

Where the landlord is to insure, the tenant should press for it to be effected in the joint names of the landlord and tenant. This will be to the tenant's advantage because the insurance company will not allow the policy to lapse unless both parties have been given notice. It will also ensure that the proceeds of the policy will be paid out to both parties jointly, and thus give the tenant some control over how they are laid out.

Another advantage to the tenant is that insurance in joint names will prevent subrogation. This is the right of the insurer to step into the shoes of the insured and pursue any claims that the insured has against third parties to recover the loss. This means that if the landlord had a cause of action against the tenant arising out of some default on the tenant's part which caused the damage, the insurers would be able to pursue that claim. If, however, the insurance is in the joint names of the landlord and tenant, subrogation will not be possible. Even in those cases where the insurance is in the landlord's name alone, the tenant may still be able to prevent subrogation occurring where it can be shown that the insurance has been taken out for the mutual benefit of both parties (eg, see *Mark Rowlands Ltd v Berni Inns Ltd* [1985] 3 All ER 473, where the tenant agreed to reimburse the landlord the premiums paid; see also *Lambert v Keymood Ltd* [1997] 43 EG 131).

If the landlord objects to insurance in joint names, or if it is not a realistic possibility, for example, where the demised premises consist of one shop in a large shopping centre, the tenant should seek to have his interest 'noted' on the landlord's policy so that he will be notified before the policy lapses.

25.5 RISKS COVERED

The lease should contain a comprehensive definition of the insured risks listing, for example, fire, lightning, explosion, impact, storm, tempest, flood, overflowing and bursting of water tanks or pipes, riot, civil commotion, and many other risks commonly included in a buildings insurance policy. To give the landlord flexibility, at the end of the definition there should be a 'sweeping up' provision along the lines 'and such other risks as the landlord may from time to time reasonably consider to be necessary'. To protect the landlord, the definition of 'insured risks' may exclude any risk against which insurance may not, from time to time, be reasonably available, so that the landlord does not remain liable to insure in a situation where insurance is difficult or expensive to obtain (eg in respect of acts of terrorism, and see the Reinsurance (Acts of Terrorism) Act 1993). This can, however, have serious drawbacks for the tenant.

25.6 THE SUM INSURED

Whilst the demised premises could be insured for their market value, the better approach for the tenant is to require cover for the full reinstatement cost. This will allow the landlord to replace the building should it be totally destroyed. Care must be taken to ensure that site-clearance costs, professional fees and fees for any necessary planning applications, and any VAT are also recoverable. As to the actual amount of cover, specialist advice will be needed and the insuring party should consult experienced insurance brokers.

25.7 WHAT IF THE PREMISES ARE DAMAGED?

Although the doctrine of frustration is capable of applying to leases (*National Carriers Ltd v Panalpina (Northern) Ltd* [1981] AC 675), it will only do so in exceptional circumstances. Accordingly, unless the doctrine applies, the lease will continue notwithstanding any accidental damage to the demised premises, and the loss will fall on the party obliged to repair.

25.7.1 Will the tenant have to repair?

Since the tenant will be paying for the insurance taken out by the landlord, he should ensure that he is not obliged to repair the premises if they are damaged by one of the insured risks. It is common practice to exclude from the tenant's repairing covenant liability for damage caused by an insured risk, unless the insurance policy had been invalidated, or the insurance proceeds are not fully paid out by reason of the act or omission of the tenant (or some other person who was at the premises with the tenants' authority).

It is important that the tenant carefully checks the definition of insured risks, since, if there were significant omissions from the definition, the benefit of the limitation of the tenant's repair covenant would be seriously eroded. To take an extreme example, if fire was not an insured risk, the tenant would remain liable to repair damage caused by fire under the basic obligation to repair. The tenant must, therefore, make sure that the definition of insured risks includes all risks normally covered by a comprehensive buildings insurance policy.

If the tenant allows the definition of insured risks to exclude risks against which insurance may not, from time to time be reasonably available, the tenant should beware that liability to repair damage caused by such a risk will fall upon him.

25.7.2 Will the rent be suspended?

Unless the lease is frustrated, rent continues to be payable where the premises are damaged, even if the damage is extensive. It is, therefore, common to include a provision in the lease that if the demised premises are damaged by an insured risk, and become unfit for occupation or use by the tenant, the rent (or a fair proportion of it, depending on the extent of the damage) should cease to be payable.

The landlord will only agree to a rent suspension if the damage results from an insured risk, so that the tenant will remain liable for rent where the demised premises become unusable as a result of damage for which the tenant is ordinarily liable under his repair covenant. Again, it is important that the tenant examines the defined list of insured risks to ensure that the rent abatement clause operates on the occasion of damage by all usual insurable risks. The landlord will want to further qualify the suspension by stipulating that rent continues to be payable where the landlord's insurance policy has been invalidated by the act or omission of the tenant (or someone at the premises with the tenant's consent). If this were not the case, the landlord might lose both the rent, and the insurance proceeds.

The suspension will continue for such period as is specified in the lease. The landlord usually seeks to limit it to a period of 2 (or perhaps 3) years, or, if earlier, until the premises have been reinstated and are again fit for use and occupation, for the purpose permitted by the lease. It should be noted that there is a subtle difference between premises being fit for occupation and use, and the premises being fit for occupation or use.

The tenant should press for a similar suspension in respect of other payments under the lease, such as the service charge, because if the premises are damaged, and the tenant is unable to occupy them, he will not be able to take advantage of the services provided by the landlord. However, the landlord will not give way to the tenant easily. If damage is occasioned to the tenant's premises alone, this is not likely to reduce significantly the level of services provided to the rest of the tenants, and the landlord will, therefore, argue that he is not prepared to suffer any reduction in the amount of service charge income.

If the demised premises are damaged, and the rent abatement clause operates, the landlord will lose rental income. The landlord will, therefore, require insurance against loss of rent during the period of suspension, and since the tenant is getting the benefit of the rent abatement clause, he will require the tenant to pay the premiums. If a rent review is possible during the period of suspension, the review clause will almost certainly require the rent to be revised on the assumption that the demised premises have been fully restored. This being so, the insurance against loss of rent should be for a sum which anticipates an increased rent on review. Valuation advice will be needed in this regard.

25.7.3 Who will reinstate?

If the insurance is in the joint names of landlord and tenant, the proceeds of the policy will be paid to both of the insured who have equal control over the application of the proceeds and, therefore, the reinstatement of the premises. However, where the policy is in the sole name of the landlord, unless the lease provides to the contrary, there is no obligation on the landlord to use the proceeds of the policy to reinstate the demised premises. Whilst the Fires (Prevention) Metropolis Act 1774 (which applies throughout England and Wales) entitles any person interested in a building (whether as landlord or tenant) to require the insurers to apply the proceeds of a fire policy for that building towards its repair or replacement, the Act has no application to damage other than by fire, and the requirement must be made clear before the moneys are paid out. In those cases where the tenant is under an obligation to pay the cost of the insurance, it has been held that the landlord may be presumed to have insured on behalf of the tenant as well as himself, and thus the tenant can require the proceeds to be laid out on reinstatement (*Mumford Hotels Ltd v Wheler* [1964] Ch 117). Notwithstanding this, where the landlord insures in his sole name, the tenant should always insist on an express covenant from the landlord to apply the proceeds of the policy in reinstating the demised premises.

A covenant by the landlord to reinstate often provides that in the event of damage to or destruction of the premises by an insured risk, the landlord will use the insurance proceeds in reinstating the premises. The landlord should make it clear that any insurance money in respect of loss of rent is not to be applied in the reinstatement of the premises. From the tenant's point of view, he should pay particular attention to the wording of the covenant which is often an obligation just to lay out the insurance moneys received in respect of damage to the premises in the reinstatement. This does not deal with the situation where the insurance proceeds are insufficient to cover the entire cost of reinstatement. Although the landlord might be in breach of covenant for underinsuring the premises, the tenant should nevertheless press for a covenant by the landlord to make up the difference, or, more effectively, an unqualified covenant to reinstate. Where this latter form of covenant is chosen, the landlord should qualify the absolute nature of his obligation by providing that he is not liable in the event that the policy is invalidated, or the proceeds irrecoverable by reason of the act or omission of the tenant (or anyone at the premises with the tenant's consent).

In any event, the landlord would not want to be liable to reinstate the premises if circumstances beyond the landlord's control contrive to prevent him from doing so (eg strikes, lock-outs, shortages of materials).

25.7.4 What if reinstatement is impossible?

The tenant should try to specify a reasonable period (eg 2 or 3 years) within which reinstatement must take place. If reinstatement has not been completed within that period, so that the premises are still incapable of use, or if reinstatement simply proves to be impossible, for example, because the landlord is unable to obtain the necessary planning and other consents required for reinstatement, the lease may provide for either party to serve notice to terminate the lease. Indeed, the tenant may consider it appropriate to negotiate a provision allowing him to terminate the lease immediately the premises are rendered unfit for occupation or use by an insured risk, so that he may relocate his business without delay. The landlord should always bear in mind that the tenancy may be protected by Part II of the LTA 1954, and consequently the lease would need to be terminated in accordance with the provisions of that Act (see Chapter 34).

If reinstatement is not possible (or the parties do not desire it), in the absence of an express provision in the lease, it is unclear as to whom the insurance proceeds will belong, and it will be left to the court to ascertain the intention of the parties by looking at the lease as a whole. In *Beacon Carpets Ltd v Kirby* [1984] 2 All ER 726, the courts found an intention that the moneys belonged to the landlord and tenant in proportion to the value of their respective interests in the premises. It may be considered fair that the lease provides likewise, although often, the tenant's interest has little capital value, and it is the landlord who suffers most of the loss.

25.8 ADDITIONAL PROVISIONS

Certain other covenants on the part of the tenant are commonly included in relation to the insurance of the premises:

(1) not to cause the insurance to be invalidated;
(2) to pay any increased or additional premiums that become payable by reason of the tenant's activities at the premises;
(3) to pay the cost of annual valuations for insurance purposes. The tenant should beware the cost of such regular valuations;
(4) not to bring dangerous or explosive items onto the premises;
(5) to comply with the requirements and recommendations of the landlord's insurers and the fire authority;
(6) to insure and reinstate any plate glass at the premises;
(7) to bear the responsibility of any excess liability under the landlord's insurance policy.

25.9 INSURANCE BY THE TENANT

If, exceptionally, the tenant covenants to insure the demised premises, the landlord must make sure his interest as landlord is fully protected. The landlord will have similar concerns to those expressed above on behalf of the tenant and so will wish to ensure:

(1) that insurance be effected in the joint names of the landlord and tenant, with insurers to be approved by the landlord;
(2) that the insurance is effected upon terms to be approved by the landlord (eg as to the basis of cover, the risks insured and amount);
(3) that in the event of damage or destruction the tenant covenants to reinstate the demised premises.

There will not be a rent abatement clause.

Chapter 26

PROVISO FOR RE-ENTRY

The lease should always contain a proviso enabling the landlord to re-enter the demised premises and prematurely end the lease on breach by the tenant of any of his covenants, or upon the happening of certain specified events. The right to forfeit the lease is a valuable remedy for the landlord but the right is not automatic; it only exists where the lease expressly includes such a right (or where, rarely, the lease is made conditional upon the performance by the tenant of his covenants; or where the tenant denies his landlord's title).

The proviso for re-entry should specify the events giving rise to the right. These are commonly:

(1) where the rent reserved by the lease is in arrear for 21 days after becoming payable (whether formally demanded or not);
(2) where there is a breach by the tenant of any of the covenants, agreements and conditions contained in the lease;
(3) where the tenant has execution levied on his goods at the demised premises;
(4) upon the bankruptcy or liquidation of the tenant, or the happening of other insolvency events such as:

   (a) the presentation of a petition in bankruptcy;
   (b) the presentation of a petition for a winding-up order, or the passing of a resolution for a voluntary winding up;
   (c) the presentation of a petition for an administration order, or the making of such an order;
   (d) the creation of a voluntary arrangement; or
   (e) the appointment of a receiver or an administrative receiver.

The landlord's intention is to give himself as many opportunities as possible to forfeit the lease where the tenant is in financial difficulty. In some insolvency proceedings, the landlord will want to give himself two attempts at forfeiting the tenant's lease (eg once on the presentation of the petition in bankruptcy, and once on the making of the bankruptcy order) in case the landlord inadvertently waives his right to forfeit on the first occasion.

A tenant should resist the inclusion of some of the less serious events (eg the mere presentation of the petition) or those insolvency events which are designed to cure insolvency (eg administration proceedings, voluntary arrangements, liquidations for the purpose of restructuring). Further, if the tenant's lease is likely to possess sufficient capital value to provide security for a loan (though this may be unlikely), the tenant should try to restrict the landlord's right to forfeit in these circumstances.

Despite the existence of a right of forfeiture and the happening of one of the above events, the lease does not end automatically; but the landlord will have the right to end the lease. The way in which that right is exercised, and the complex formalities surrounding its exercise, are dealt with at **33.5**.

Chapter 27

LEASE OF PART

27.1 INTRODUCTION

The purpose of this chapter is not to deal with every single issue of relevance on the lease of part of a building; some can only be dealt with in the context of particular clauses. The reader will, therefore, find references to leases of parts elsewhere in this book. However, there are some important issues which can be dealt with separately and by drawing these together in this chapter, particularly the service charge provisions, the reader will become aware of the special considerations which apply whenever a lease of part of a building is contemplated.

27.2 THE PARCELS CLAUSE

The purpose of the parcels clause is to accurately and unambiguously describe the property being let to the tenant so that it is clear what is included and what is excluded. Where there is a lease of part only of a building (eg one floor of an office block), it is essential for the property demised to be clearly identified and the incorporation of a detailed plan will be essential. Furthermore, the Land Registration Rules 1925 make the use of a plan compulsory for any registrable transaction dealing with part of a registered title.

In any case where a plan is to be used, it should be prepared by a surveyor and be of a sufficient scale to show clearly where each boundary runs. There will, of course, also be a verbal description in the parcels clause and a decision will have to be made as to which is to prevail in the event of any conflict; plan or words? If a large-scale plan has been professionally prepared showing the precise line of each boundary so that there is no longer any doubt as to the matter, the plan can be made to prevail. This can be achieved by the use of words such as 'more particularly described on the plan annexed'. If the plan is not to prevail over the verbal description, words such as 'for the purposes of identification only' should be used. In this exceptional case, the parcels clause should contain a very detailed description of the premises. Care should be taken never to use both phrases together.

Another reason for accuracy in the parcels clause is that unless it is carefully drafted, the obligations of the parties regarding such matters as repairs, alterations, insurance and service charges will not be clear, giving rise to inevitable disputes.

27.2.1 Boundaries

In the absence of a proper description, there is little authority as to where the boundaries lie, and the problems will differ according to which part of the building is involved – the basement, the ground floor, middle floor or top floor, and whether the whole or part of a floor is let. Some of these problems are now examined in more detail.

External and internal walls

Any external walls bounding the premises are included in the demise if no contrary provision has been made in the lease (*Sturge v Hackett* [1962] 3 All ER 166); and this remains so even if the landlord is under a duty to repair them. Therefore, in the absence of a contrary provision, or some other restriction in the lease, the tenant may (and the landlord may not) place advertisements on the outside wall.

The position with regard to internal walls (eg those between suites of offices and/or common parts of the building) is less clear. It was said in *Phelps v City of London Corporation* [1916] 2 Ch 255, that some part of an internal wall is included in the demise; but no guidance was given as to which part!

Ceilings and floors

If one storey in an office block has been let, where are the horizontal boundaries between the storeys above and below the demised premises? Case-law is of little help but it has been said that the demise will include the ceiling, at least to the underside of the joists to which it is attached. This, of course, is not precise enough: where exactly is the boundary – the underside, middle or top side of the joists? In *Graystone Property Investments Ltd v Margulies* (1983) 269 EG 538, the judge, without wishing to lay down a rigid rule, expressed the view that tenants would normally expect to acquire all the space between the floor of their property and the underneath of the floor above.

Foundations, basement and roof

As far as a lease of a basement is concerned, does this include any part of the foundations? If so, this could be very expensive for the tenant as he is usually under an obligation to repair 'the demised premises'. In the same way, the tenant of the top floor should consider whether he will become responsible for the roof. This is a question of construction of the lease concerned. If some limitation is placed on the uppermost limit of the demised premises, this may mean that the tenant of the top floor will be prevented from extending upwards (see **15.2**).

Drafting considerations

Case-law is of very little help in deciding the precise location of the vertical and horizontal boundaries. Such cases as do exist often deal with outdated building methods and are not helpful when dealing with modern buildings. What is clear, is that it is not sufficient for the parcels clause to read something like, 'all those premises on the top floor of the building as the same are shown edged red on the plan annexed hereto'. The precise location of the boundaries must be considered, so that those parts of the boundary walls, floors and ceilings intended to be included in the demise are defined with precision. A well-drafted parcels clause should also deal with ownership of:

(1) the paint and other finishes on the inside face of any external walls which have been excluded from the demise;
(2) the doors and windows;
(3) ceiling and floor finishes;
(4) load bearing walls which are located internally, ie within the demised premises; and
(5) the conducting media, ie all the drains, sewers, cables, pipes, wires and other conduits which serve the demised premises and the remainder of the building.

This painstaking approach is essential because the obligation to repair is often co-extensive with ownership, although this is not always the case. As a general rule, those items mentioned in (1), (2) and (3) above will often fall within the demise (and thus be repaired by the tenant) whilst (4) will be excluded and the responsibility for (5) split between the parties.

Often it will be necessary to consult a surveyor or engineer so that all the potential problems can be considered at the outset.

27.3 EASEMENTS

On a letting of part, the tenant will usually need to be granted rights over the parts of the building retained by the landlord or let to other tenants. These rights will be set out after the parcels clause or in a schedule, and will be followed by rights to be excepted and reserved for the rest of the building. As in the case of a sale of freehold land, the precise rights will depend on the circumstances.

Even on the grant of a lease of the whole building various rights may need to be granted and reserved. For ease of reference, these are also referred to below.

27.3.1 Rights to be granted to the tenant

Certain rights over the landlord's retained premises will be impliedly granted to the tenant, for example, under s 62 of the LPA 1925 (see LPC Resource Book *Conveyancing* (Jordans)). Notwithstanding such implied rights, the tenant should insist on the express grant of any right he needs to enjoy the property to its full extent. Even from the landlord's point of view, it is better to deal with these matters expressly and perhaps to exclude the operation of the implied grant rules altogether to prevent the tenant from impliedly acquiring rights which the landlord does not wish to grant. Where the landlord grants to the tenant rights to use roads, service pipes and cables etc which are not yet constructed, care must be taken not to offend the rule against perpetuities.

In considering rights to be granted to the tenant, regard must be had to the needs of the tenant's business. For example, will there be a large number of visitors to his premises; will heavy lorries be making deliveries; will facilities be required for a large number of employees?

Access

Access is an issue which can arise on the grant of any lease, not just a lease of part of a building. The extent of any right needed will depend on the circumstances of each case. For example, the tenant may need to be granted a vehicular right of way over any private road(s) owned by the landlord which serve the demised premises. This could be important, for example, on the lease of a factory on an industrial estate. If the road only serves the demised premises, the landlord may consider including it within the demise, in which case the tenant may become liable for its repair under his general repairing obligation. If, however, the road serves a number of buildings, it is likely that the landlord will not demise it and instead grant a right of way over it to each tenant. The number of other tenants sharing the right should be considered by the tenant as this will have an impact on his share of the cost of repair, which will probably be recoverable under the service charge provisions. In this case the tenant should obtain a covenant from the landlord to repair and maintain the road.

In a lease of part of a building the tenant must be given sufficient rights over the common parts. The common parts of an office block will include, for example, the forecourt, service roads, parking and amenity areas, ground floor entrance area, lifts, corridors, and staircases. In a shopping centre the common parts will also include the pedestrian ways and loading bays. In granting such rights the landlord may consider limiting the hours of access to or opening of the building. This will avoid the need for the landlord to keep the building open outside normal working hours and provide services for the benefit of one tenant only. From the tenant's point of view, he will point out that any increased costs of the landlord will probably be recoverable under the service charge provisions, and thus the landlord will not suffer any increased financial burden.

Parking spaces

Modern city centre office blocks often include a limited number of parking spaces for the occupiers to use and the provision of parking spaces is a feature of many large multi-occupied buildings. The allocation of these spaces should be dealt with in the lease. The lease can either include designated spaces as part of the demised premises or each tenant can be given a general right to park in any available space. Both methods have their disadvantages; the former is inflexible whereas the second does not provide any tenant with guaranteed places. A solution often used in practice is for the landlord to give to the tenant an exclusive right to park in X number of spaces as designated from time to time by the landlord.

Conducting media

If the location of mains services is separated from the demised premises by other property, the tenant will need to be granted rights through the intervening property in order to be able to use these services. This need arises most obviously when considering the position of, for example, the tenant of part of an office block, the tenant of one unit in a shopping centre, or the tenant of a building which is separated from the public highway by a strip of land outside the demise. In all these cases the tenant will require an easement for the free passage of water, gas, electricity, sewage, telecommunications, etc to and from the demised premises through the conducting media passing through the building or the landlord's adjoining land. Care must be taken to ensure that any rights granted are sufficient for the present and future business needs of the tenant.

Other rights

On the lease of part of a building, the tenant may need other rights including:

(1) toilets. The landlord may have a choice of how to proceed. He can either include toilets in each demise or grant all the tenants the right to use communal facilities with access from the common parts;
(2) right of support. The tenant should endeavour to obtain an express right of support for the demised premises from the rest of the building;
(3) nameplates and signs. The tenant may be given the right to display a nameplate in the ground floor entrance area. In return for this the landlord may prohibit the display of signs, advertisements etc on any part of the demised premises;
(4) access. The tenant may need to be granted access to the landlord's adjoining premises (eg to perform his covenants). This could be important where, for example, the tenant is under an obligation to repair which necessitates access on to neighbouring premises;
(5) fire escape. The right to use the fire escape.

27.3.2 Exceptions and reservations for the landlord

Certain rights will be impliedly reserved to the landlord but, as with the grant of easements, these implied rights should not be relied upon. The landlord must expressly set out in the lease all the exceptions and reservations he needs. Again, the rule against perpetuities must not be offended.

Rights of entry

The landlord will wish to reserve a right to enter the demised premises for a number of purposes, for example:

(1) to view the state and condition of the demised premises and to carry out repairs where the tenant is found to be in breach of his repairing obligation;
(2) to inspect and repair the demised premises where the landlord is under an obligation to repair. In this situation the landlord has an implied right to enter but as mentioned above the matter should be dealt with expressly;
(3) to inspect and effect repairs to any adjoining property of the landlord. On a lease of part of a building, this will be a right to inspect and repair those parts of the building which are outside the demised premises but accessible from within it;
(4) to inspect, maintain, repair, remove and replace the conducting media in the demised premises;
(5) to make improvements.

In many cases where the landlord does reserve a right of entry the tenant should press for some restriction on the manner of its exercise so that, for example, it is only exercisable (except in an emergency) on reasonable notice (eg 48 hours) and only during normal working hours. In the same way, where the landlord has reserved a right of entry to repair other parts of the building, it is usual to add a proviso that the landlord will make good any damage caused to the demised premises as a result of the exercise of that right.

Right to use conducting media

The landlord will usually need to reserve rights over the demised premises on behalf of himself and others claiming title under him (eg the tenants of other units in the block) to use the pipes, cables etc serving the other units in the block which pass through the demised premises. Some thought must also be given to extending this right to cover the installation and use of new forms of conducting media rather than just the use and replacement of what is already there.

Right to develop adjoining property

Where the landlord owns property adjoining the demised premises he should give consideration to the future development of that adjoining property. In certain circumstances, this may amount to a derogation from grant if it results in the tenant being unable to use the demised premises for the purpose for which they were let. For that reason the safest course of action for the landlord is to expressly reserve the right to develop any adjoining property.

Right of support

If, on the grant of a lease of part of a building, the tenant has been granted a right of support over and against the remainder of the landlord's building, a reciprocal right will be implied in favour of the landlord. Notwithstanding this, it is usual to deal with such a reservation expressly.

27.4 RESPONSIBILITY FOR REPAIRS

On the grant of a lease of part of a building, for example, one floor in an office block or one unit in a shopping precinct, it would be unusual to impose the responsibility for repairing the demised premises on one party alone. It is more practical for the responsibility to be shared between the parties. Whilst every lease and building is different, a common division of the repairing obligation in a large multi-occupied building is to make the tenant responsible for the internal non-structural parts of the demised premises whilst the landlord covenants to repair the remainder of the building. Any expense incurred by the landlord in complying with this obligation will usually be recoverable under the service charge provisions, see **27.5**.

Great care must be exercised in drafting the appropriate obligations.

27.4.1 Drafting considerations

(1) The whole building must be covered; there must be no doubt over who is responsible for the repair of each part of the building. If the tenant's covenant is limited, as it often is, to repairing the internal non-structural parts of the demise, he must make sure that the landlord assumes responsibility for the structure (including the roof, main loadbearing walls and foundations), the common parts, the conducting media, and the exterior (including any landscaped areas, forecourts, roadways and fences). To guard against the inadvertent omission of a part of the building from the landlord's repairing obligation, many repairing covenants begin by obliging the landlord generally to repair the 'Building and Grounds' (as defined in the lease) and then go on to list the items intended to be covered, adding 'without prejudice to the generality of the foregoing'. The following are some of the matters which will need consideration:

- (a) Walls. It must be made clear who is responsible for each wall in the building. Often the landlord will assume responsibility for the structural walls and possibly the outer half of the internal non-structural walls dividing the demised premises from the other parts of the building. The obligation to repair should be attributed as regards each physical layer of the wallcovering, plaster, brick etc.
- (b) The same meticulous approach is required for floors, ceilings and the joists and girders, etc, which lie between them.
- (c) Windows. There are conflicting authorities on the responsibility for the repair of windows and thus the matter should be dealt with expressly in the lease, usually by making the tenant responsible.
- (d) Roofs and roof spaces. Again, this is a notoriously grey area and the matter must be dealt with expressly in the lease.
- (e) Conducting media. Often the landlord will be made responsible (unless perhaps the conduits exclusively serve the demised premises), but the lease must put the matter beyond doubt.
- (f) The plant, including all heating and cooling systems, generators, boilers etc.
- (g) Decorative repairs. The landlord will usually assume responsibility for the exterior decoration and recover his costs under the service charge (see **27.5**).

(2) The obligation to repair is often co-extensive with ownership, and care must be taken to link together the repairing obligations with the definition of the demised premises in the parcels clause.
(3) The draftsman must also appreciate the precise meaning of certain words and phrases which have been judicially defined in a plethora of case-law. Thus, for example, 'structural repairs', 'main walls', 'external walls' and 'exterior' have all been judicially considered; and reference should be made to one of the standard works on landlord and tenant law for a more detailed analysis of such technicalities.

27.4.2 Other considerations

The lease should attribute responsibility for repair of every part of the building. If, however, the lease is silent on a particular point the question arises as to whether the courts will imply a repairing obligation on behalf of either the landlord or tenant? In this regard there are a number of cases in which the landlord of residential properties have been held impliedly liable to carry out various repairs. For example, in *Barrett v Lounova (1982) Ltd* [1990] QB 348, it was held that a covenant by a periodic tenant of an old house to keep the interior in repair would lack business efficacy unless there were implied a corresponding obligation on the landlord to maintain the structure and exterior. It remains to be seen to what extent cases like this will be applied to business leases. See Chapter 19 for a discussion of repairing covenants in general.

27.5 SERVICE CHARGES

In a letting of the whole of a property the landlord will normally wish to impose all responsibility for the repair and maintenance of the property on the tenant. This will not usually be possible in the case of lettings of part of a building, but the landlord will seek to achieve the same economic effect by the use of a service charge. The landlord will be responsible for repair and maintenance and the provision of services but will require the costs he incurs on these matters to be reimbursed by the tenants. The landlord could charge a higher inclusive rent to cover his anticipated costs, but he then runs the risk of inflation or unexpected outgoings proving his estimate incorrect. The inclusive rent method is unpopular with institutional landlords and lenders who prefer a 'clear lease', where the rent will always represent the landlord's clear income from the property and the landlord is reimbursed for the expenditure on the provision of services by means of a service charge which fluctuates annually according to the actual costs incurred.

From the landlord's point of view, it is necessary to decide whether the service charge should be reserved as additional rent. The advantages of reserving it as rent have already been considered (see **17.4**).

27.5.1 Services to be provided

Tenants need only pay for the provision of those services specified in the lease. If there is no provision for the tenant to pay, the landlord cannot recover his expenditure. Therefore, when drafting the service charge provisions, the landlord's solicitor needs to be careful to include all the expenditure to be laid out on the building (excluding those parts for which the tenant is made responsible). This will require a thorough examination of all the lease terms. The following is not a comprehensive list of items to be included in a service charge as each lease needs individual consideration. However, some common items of expenditure are set out below.

Repairs and decoration

The clause should allow the landlord to recover all his expenses in performing his repairing obligation. Thus it may need to allow him to recover his expenses in inspecting, cleaning, maintaining, repairing and decorating the common parts and any other parts of the building for which he is responsible, for example, the conducting media, roof, structural parts, plant, etc. Whether the landlord can go beyond 'repair', and rebuild or carry out improvements is a question of construction of the relevant clause but the tenant must be aware of the danger of having to contribute to work which would be outside a simple covenant to 'repair', for example, the replacement of defective wooden window frames with modern double glazed units. In such a case the landlord would be unduly profiting at the tenant's expense. Another concern of the tenant is that the clause may require his contribution to expenditure incurred by the landlord in remedying inherent defects in the building, for example, those caused by a design defect or through the use of defective materials. The tenant should resist such an onerous obligation.

The landlord should pay particular attention to the wording of the service charge provision. In *Northways Flats Management Co v Wimpey Pension Trustees* [1992] 31 EG 65, the clause required the landlord, before carrying out the work, to submit details and estimates to the tenants. The court held that this was a pre-condition to the recovery of the service charge and since it had not been complied with, the landlord was unable to recover his expenditure.

Heating, air-conditioning etc

The landlord will wish to recover his costs in supplying heating, air-conditioning and hot and cold water to the common parts of the building and possibly the demised premises as well. Sometimes, the landlord will restrict the provision of heating to the winter months. The tenant may want some minimum temperature to be specified but the landlord may be unwise to agree to this, preferring to provide heating to a temperature which the landlord considers adequate. The landlord should also ensure that he is not liable to the tenant for any temporary interruption in supply due to a breakdown.

Staff

The landlord will wish to recover his costs in employing staff in connection with the management of the building such as receptionist, maintenance staff, caretakers and security personnel. The clause should also extend to any staff employed by the managing agents for the purpose of providing services at the building. From the tenant's point of view he should guard against having to pay the full-time wages of staff who are not wholly engaged in providing the services.

Managing agents

If the landlord employs managing agents to provide the services, he should ensure that the service charge allows him to recover their fees since in the absence of an express provision it is unlikely that the landlord would be able to recover those fees. A company owned by the landlord can be employed as managing agents provided such an arrangement is not a sham (*Skilleter v Charles* [1992] 13 EG 113).

The tenant must make sure that the amount of fees recoverable is reasonable and may want some restriction placed on them in the lease.

If the landlord performs his own management services, the service charge should enable him to recover his reasonable costs for so doing.

Other common items of expenditure

Other common items of expenditure include:

(1) maintaining the lifts, boilers and other plant and machinery;
(2) lighting of the common parts;
(3) refuse removal;
(4) fire prevention equipment;
(5) window cleaning;
(6) legal and other professional fees;
(7) service staff accommodation;
(8) insurance (although sometimes this is dealt with outside the service charge provisions);
(9) interest on the cost of borrowing money to provide the services;
(10) maintenance of landscaped areas;
(11) outgoings payable by the landlord;
(12) advertising and promotion costs, in the case of a shopping centre.

'Sweeping up' clause

No matter how comprehensive the landlord thinks he has been in compiling the list of services to be provided, it is advisable to include a sweeping up clause to cover any omissions and to take account of any new services to be provided over the lifetime of the lease. However, careful drafting of such a clause is required as the courts construe them restrictively (see *Mullaney v Maybourne Grange (Croydon) Ltd* [1986] 1 EGLR 70). From the tenant's point of view he should guard against the clause being drafted too widely and insist on the service being of some benefit to him before having to pay for it.

27.5.2 Landlord's covenant to perform the services

The services to be provided often fall into two categories: essential services which the landlord should be obliged to provide (eg heating and lighting the common parts and repairing and maintaining the structure) and other non-essential services which he has a discretion to provide. From the tenant's point of view, he must make sure that, in return for paying the service charge, the landlord covenants to provide the essential services. Without such an express provision, it is by no means certain that one would be implied, leaving the tenant with no remedy if the services were not provided (see, however, *Barnes v City of London Real Property Co* [1918] 2 Ch 18).

In drafting the covenant the tenant should require the services to be provided in an efficient and economical manner; and to a reasonable standard, rather than a standard the landlord considers adequate. The Supply of Goods and Services Act 1982 provides that where a service is provided in the course of a business there is an implied term that the supplier will carry out the service with reasonable care and skill but it is obviously better for the tenant to deal with the matter expressly. In *Finchbourne v Rodrigues* [1976] 3 All ER 581 the view was expressed that the costs claimed should be fair and reasonable to be recoverable under the service charge. However, this view may no longer reflect current judicial thinking (see *Havenridge*

Ltd v Boston Dyers Ltd [1994] 49 EG 111) and therefore, again, an express provision is preferable. From the landlord's point of view, he may wish to restrict the covenant so that he is only liable to use 'reasonable endeavours' or 'best endeavours' to provide the services, rather than be under an absolute obligation to do so. In any event, the covenant should be limited so that the landlord is not liable to the tenant for failure to provide the services due to circumstances outside his control such as industrial action.

As a general rule, the obligation to provide the services is independent of the obligation to pay for them. Therefore, in the event of non-payment by the tenant, the landlord cannot withdraw services (and in any event it is unlikely that the landlord could withdraw services from one tenant alone).

27.5.3 The tenant's contribution: basis of apportionment

In addition to setting out the items which can be charged to the tenant, the clause must deal with how the total cost is to be apportioned between the tenants in the building. The following are some commonly used methods:

(1) by reference to rateable value. This can be arbitrary since rateable values can vary for reasons which bear no relationship to the amount of services consumed;
(2) according to floor areas. This can be a reasonable method, depending on the nature of the building, but some method of measurement will have to be agreed;
(3) according to anticipated use of services. This can be difficult to assess and depends on the nature of each tenant's business and its location within the building;
(4) as a fixed percentage. This provides certainty for both parties but is inflexible. Further, the landlord must make provision for any future enlargement of the building which would necessitate a recalculation of the percentages.

Each method has its own advantages and disadvantages and reference should be made to one of the standard works on the drafting of business leases for further consideration of the matter. Whatever method is adopted, the tenant will want to ensure that he does not become liable for any unlet units; the landlord should be required to pay the service charge for these.

27.5.4 Payment of the charge

Advance payments

Typical service charge provisions stipulate that the service charge is to be paid by the tenant periodically in advance (usually on rent days). Advance payments are necessary because otherwise the landlord would have to fund the provision of work and services out of his own resources and recoup his expenditure from the tenants later. The amount of the advance payments can give rise to disputes between the parties unless the tenant can be sure such payments are not excessive. There are different ways of calculating the payments, for example, it can be based on the previous year's actual expenditure or on an estimate of the likely expenditure in the current year. If the latter method is adopted, the tenant should insist on the amount payable being certified by, for example, the landlord's surveyor, and that the payment is only to be made upon receipt of such a certificate (see below).

The tenant may wish to consider a requirement that the landlord is to pay the advance payments into a separate account to be held on trust in order to avoid the problems which will arise if the landlord becomes insolvent.

Final payments and adjustments

At the end of the year the service charge provisions will, typically, require the landlord to prepare annual accounts showing his actual expenditure in the year: such accounts to be certified by the landlord's accountant (see below). Where advance payments have been made an adjustment will be necessary to correct any over or underpayment. In the case of underpayment the tenant will be required to pay this amount within a specified time. If there is an overpayment, the lease may provide for its refund to the tenant or, more usually, it will be credited to the following year's payments.

Certification of amounts due

It is common for the service charge provisions to stipulate that the landlord pro vides a certificate given by his surveyor or accountant, acting as an expert, in connection with the amount of both the advance and end of year payments. Unless the lease provides to the contrary, the expert must be independent from the landlord (*Finchbourne v Rodrigues* above), although the tenant may wish this to be expressly stated in the lease. If the certificate is said to be 'final and conclusive as to the facts stated', its finality is likely to be upheld by the courts. If the lease makes the expert's certificate conclusive on matters of law, for example, as to the construction of the lease, there are conflicting views on its validity but it may be that it will be upheld if the expert is given the exclusive right to determine the issue (see *Nikko Hotels (UK) Ltd v MEPC plc* [1991] 2 EGLR 103 and *British Shipbuilders v VSEL Consortium plc* [1997] 1 Lloyds Rep (1) 106).

27.6 SINKING AND RESERVE FUNDS

The object of sinking and reserve funds is to make funds available when needed for major items of irregular expenditure. A sinking fund is a fund established for replacing major items such as boilers and lifts which may only be necessary once or twice during the lifetime of the building. A reserve fund is established to pay for recurring items of expenditure such as external decoration which may need attending to, not annually, but perhaps every 4 or 5 years. The estimated cost of such decoration will be collected over each 5-year period to avoid the tenants from being faced with a large bill every 5 years.

The advantage of such funds is that money is available to carry out these major works when needed without any dramatic fluctuations in the service charge payable from one year to another. However, the creation of such a fund needs careful thought and many difficult questions will need to be addressed at the drafting stage. Who is to own the fund? Is it to be held absolutely or on trust? What is to happen to the fund when the landlord sells the reversion? What will be the position upon termination of the lease? (See *Secretary of State for the Environment v Possfund (North West) Ltd* [1997] 39 EG 179.) Further, there may be considerable tax disadvantages. Such matters are beyond the scope of this book, but the parties will need specialist advice about these matters.

27.7 INSURANCE

On a lease of part of a building in multi-occupation the landlord will usually insure the whole building and recover the premium from the tenants under the service charge provisions or in a separate insurance clause. Insurance is dealt with in Chapter 25.

Chapter 28

UNDERLEASES

Chapter 28 contents

28.1 LIABILITY OF SUB-TENANTS

Ordinarily, there is neither privity of contract nor privity of estate between a head landlord and a sub-tenant and, therefore, the head landlord is unable to sue a sub-tenant in respect of any breaches of the terms of the head-lease. However, it is a common practice for the head landlord to require a sub-tenant as a condition of granting consent to the sub-letting, to enter into a direct covenant with the head landlord to observe and perform the covenants in the head-lease. This will make the sub-tenant liable to the head landlord in contract. Further, a sub-tenant may be bound by those restrictive covenants in the head-lease of which he had notice when he took his sub-lease. As the sub-tenant is entitled to call for production of the head-lease on the grant of his sub-lease (LPA 1925, s 44), he will be deemed to have notice of the contents of the head-lease even if he does not insist on his right to inspect it (see the LPC Resource Book *Conveyancing* (Jordans) for further consideration of this matter).

28.2 REASONS FOR SUB-LETTING

There are many reasons why a tenant may want to grant an underlease of all or part of the premises demised by the head-lease. It may be that the tenant finds that he has surplus accommodation which is not required for the purpose of his business and, therefore, instead of leaving that part vacant (thereby wasting money) the tenant may try and cut his losses by finding a sub-tenant. Indeed, the tenant may well seek to create space for a sub-letting in the knowledge that the current market would lead to the sub-tenant paying a rent per square foot in excess of what the tenant is paying to the head landlord.

On other occasions, the tenant may be sub-letting the premises as an alternative to assigning the lease. Where a tenant has a continuing liability (either under privity of contract or under an authorised guarantee agreement), despite his ability to call for an overriding lease in the event of later default by an assignee (see **31.1.4**), the tenant might prefer to retain control of the premises by sub-letting rather than assigning.

A further reason for sub-letting may be that consent of the landlord to an assignment is not available. An example of this occurred in the case of *Ponderosa International Development Inc v Pengap Securities (Bristol) Ltd* [1986] 1 EGLR 66 where the landlord, having already indicated to the tenant that it would be prepared to consent to an underletting of the premises, successfully opposed the tenant's court application for a declaration that he was unreasonably withholding consent to an assignment. It was important to the landlord that the person responsible for the payment of the head rent was a person of substance, and so, whilst the landlord was prepared to allow the proposed assignee to take a sub-lease from the tenant, he was not prepared to allow him to take the place of the existing tenant under the lease. It might also be the case that the tenant is unable to satisfy conditions for assignment imposed by the landlord under s 19(1A) of the LTA 1927, leaving sub-letting as the only other possibility.

28.3 DRAFTING POINTS

Where the tenant proposes to grant an underlease of all or part of the premises, he must have regard to the terms of his own lease, and in particular to the terms of the alienation covenant which is likely to control or regulate in some way the content of the underlease. The head-lease will usually require the tenant to obtain the consent of the head landlord before granting the sub-lease. Section 19(1)(a) of the LTA 1927 and s 1 of the LTA 1988 apply to qualified covenants against sub-letting.

In drafting the sub-lease, the tenant should bear in mind the following matters.

28.3.1 The term

The tenant should ensure that the term of the sub-lease is at least one day shorter than the unexpired residue of his head-lease term, since a sub-lease for the whole residue of the head-lease term will take effect as an assignment of that term. Not only will this be contrary to the tenant's intention, it will also probably breach the alienation covenant in the head-lease, as the landlord will have given his consent to a sub-letting, but not an assignment.

In taking up possession, the sub-tenant will be in occupation for the purpose of a business and may, therefore, enjoy security of tenure under Part II of the LTA 1954 (see Chapter 34). The tenant may want to consider excluding the sub-letting from the protection of the Act so that he can be sure to resume occupation at the end of the sub-lease. Indeed, it may be a requirement of the alienation covenant in the head-lease that any sub-leases are to be contracted-out of the LTA 1954, so that if the tenant's interest is terminated in circumstances which result in the sub-tenant becoming the immediate tenant of the head landlord, the head landlord will be guaranteed possession at the end of the sub-lease.

28.3.2 The rent

The tenant will want to ensure that the rent to be paid by the sub-tenant is as high as the market will currently allow, and if the sub-lease is to be granted for anything longer than a short term, the tenant will want to review the rent from time to time. Careful attention must again be paid to the alienation covenant in the head-lease which might dictate the terms upon which any sub-lettings are to be granted.

It is common for the head landlord to attempt to include several requirements in the head-lease:

(1) that any sub-letting by the tenant is granted at a rent which is the greater of the rent payable under the head-lease, and the full open market rent for the premises;
(2) that any sub-letting is granted without the payment of a premium; and
(3) that the sub-letting contains provisions for the review of rent (in an upwards direction only) which match the head-lease review provisions in terms of frequency, timing and basis of review.

The reason the landlord seeks to impose such conditions is that at some future date, the interest of the intermediate tenant might determine (eg by reason of surrender) leaving the sub-tenant as the landlord's immediate tenant upon the terms of the sub-lease. However, if the tenant, at the grant of his lease, had agreed to excessively restrictive conditions on sub-letting, he may now find it difficult to arrange a sub-letting, particularly at a time when the market is falling and potential sub-tenants are only prepared to pay a rent below the current rent payable under the head-lease. This could cause financial problems for the tenant.

The sub-tenant should be wary of an obligation in the sub-lease which simply requires him to pay the rents payable from time to time under the head-lease, since such a provision would give him no input into any negotiations for the review of rent during the term, and is likely to give little incentive to the tenant to argue with any vigour against the landlord at review, since he knows that whatever figure is agreed, it will be paid by the sub-tenant.

If the head landlord has elected to waive the exemption for VAT purposes, so that VAT is payable by the tenant, the election in no way affects the sub-lease rents. It would, therefore, be wise for the tenant to waive the exemption in respect of these premises so that VAT can be charged to the sub-tenant, although careful consideration must always be given to the effect of waiving the exemption.

28.3.3 The covenants

In drafting the sub-lease, the tenant will attempt to mirror the provisions of the head-lease. He should be careful not to allow the sub-tenant scope to do anything at the premises which is forbidden under the provisions of the head-lease.

Particular attention should be paid to:

(1) Alienation. It is unlikely that the head-lease will allow any further sub-letting of the premises. Care should, therefore, be taken to impose appropriate restrictions in the sub-lease. There ought to be an absolute covenant against sub-letting (or sharing or parting with possession of the premises), with a qualified covenant against assigning the sub-lease.

(2) Repair. The same repairing obligation as affects the tenant (or an even tighter one) ought to be imposed upon the sub-tenant. In interpreting a repair covenant, regard is to be had to the age, character and locality of the premises at the time the lease was granted. If there has been a considerable lapse of time between the grant of the head-lease, and the grant of the sub-lease, different standards of repair might be required by the respective repair covenants, leading to a possible residual repair liability on the part of the tenant. The sub-tenant's obligation will be to repair 'the premises'. The tenant must make sure that 'the premises' are defined in the sub-lease to include all of the premises demised by the head-lease, or if a sub-letting of part is contemplated, that the division of responsibility is clearly stated.

(3) Insurance. In all probability, the head landlord will be insuring the premises, with the tenant reimbursing the premium. The sub-lease should, therefore, provide that the sub-tenant reimburses the premiums paid by the tenant (or a proportionate part if a sub-lease of part is contemplated).

(4) Decoration. The tenant should ensure that the sub-lease obliges the sub-tenant to decorate the premises as frequently as, and at the times, and in the manner required by the head-lease.

28.3.4 Rights of access

The tenant is unlikely to extend the usual covenant in the sub-lease for quiet enjoyment to cover liability for the acts and omissions of someone with a title paramount (eg the head landlord). If he did so, he would be in breach of the covenant if the head landlord disturbed the sub-tenant's occupation by exercising a right of entry contained in the head-lease. However, in any case, to avoid a possible dispute, the tenant should ensure that in reserving rights of entry onto and access over the sub-let premises, those rights are reserved for the benefit of the tenant and any superior landlord.

28.3.5 An indemnity

Despite imposing broadly similar covenants in the sub-lease to those contained in the head-lease, the tenant will also want to include a sweeping-up provision obliging the sub-tenant to perform all of the covenants in the head-lease in so far as they affect the sub-let premises, and to indemnify the tenant against liability for breach. The sub-tenant might prefer, however, to enter into a negative obligation not to cause a breach of the head-lease covenants. Care must be taken on a sub-lease of part to ensure that a correct division of liability is made between tenant and sub-tenant in respect of the head-lease covenants.

28.4 THE SUB-TENANT'S CONCERNS

Before the sub-lease is granted, the sub-tenant must ensure that the consent of the head landlord (if required) has been obtained. The usual condition of granting consent is that the sub-tenant is to enter into a direct covenant with the head landlord to perform the covenants in the head-lease (at least insofar as they relate to the sub-let premises). Ordinarily, there is no privity of contract or estate between a head landlord and a sub-tenant, but the direct covenant creates a contractual relationship.

As he is likely to be giving a direct covenant, and as he is also likely to covenant with the tenant in the sub-lease to perform the head-lease covenants, it is essential that the sub-tenant inspects the head-lease (including all licences and supplemental deeds which may have effected a variation of its terms). The sub-tenant's liability under the direct covenant with the head landlord should not extend beyond his liability on the tenant covenants in the sub-lease.

With regard to the drafting of the sub-lease, the following points may be borne in mind:

(1) The direct covenant entered into in the licence to sub-let will not work both ways, and so the sub-tenant does not have any means of enforcing a breach of covenant by the head landlord. The sub-tenant should consider insisting upon a covenant by the tenant in the sub-lease obliging the tenant to enforce a breach of covenant by the head landlord as and when required by the sub-tenant. The sub-tenant is likely to concede that he should bear the cost of any action.
(2) The usual covenant for quiet enjoyment exempts an intermediate landlord from liability in respect of the acts or omissions of a superior landlord. The sub-tenant may consider extending the usual covenant.
(3) The sub-tenant should ask the tenant to covenant with him to pass on to him any notices received from the head landlord (eg s 146 notices).
(4) The sub-tenant should explore the possibility of having his interest noted on the head-landlord's insurance policy. He should ask for details of the policy and ensure that provision is made to enable the policy to be produced to him from time to time. The provision referred to at (1) above should enable the sub-tenant to force the tenant to force the landlord to reinstate the premises if they are damaged by an insured risk.

28.5 A SUB-LEASE OF PART

Particular care should be taken with regard to the following where a sub-lease of part is contemplated:

(1) Repair. The extent of the sub-let premises should be clearly defined so that the division of responsibility for repair between tenant and sub-tenant can easily be ascertained.

(2) Insurance payments and service charges. Payments made to the head landlord with regard to insurance will have to be apportioned between tenant and sub-tenant, as will any service charge payable under the head-lease.

(3) Direct covenants and indemnities. The sub-tenant should ensure that he does not enter into a covenant to perform the head-lease covenants except and only insofar as those covenants relate to the sub-let premises.

Chapter 29

AGREEMENTS FOR LEASE

29.1 INTRODUCTION

The agreement for lease, if used, will be drafted by the landlord's solicitor in duplicate, and submitted to the tenant's solicitor for approval together with the draft lease in duplicate (attached to each part of the draft agreement). If the landlord requires the tenant to pay the landlord's costs of drafting, negotiating and executing the lease, he is also likely to require the tenant to pay his costs in connection with the agreement for lease. In recessionary times, the tenant is likely to resist such requirements.

If an agreement for lease is used, the agreement is liable to ad valorem stamp duty as if it were the lease itself (Stamp Act 1891, s 75(1), as amended by s 111 of the Finance Act 1984). When the lease is completed and is presented to the Inland Revenue for stamping, the amount of duty payable on the lease will be reduced by the amount of duty already paid on the agreement (which will, in most cases, reduce the amount of duty payable on the lease to nil).

The agreement for lease is an estate contract and can be protected by way of a C(iv) land charge against the landlord's name, or notice or caution against the landlord's registered title. The circumstances in which an agreement may be used will necessarily involve a delay between exchange and completion, in which case it might be considered advisable to protect the agreement against the possibility of the landlord selling the reversion and defeating the tenant's interest. In the light of s 240(1) of the Finance Act 1994 (see **12.3**), HM Land Registry will require the agreement to be stamped before entering a notice of it on the register. The tenant may, therefore, prefer to lodge a caution.

29.2 WHEN ARE THEY USED?

In most commercial letting transactions, the parties proceed straight to the completion of the lease without concerning themselves with the formality of entering into an agreement for lease. The reason for this is that the agreement would simply exist as a contractual commitment between the parties to enter into a lease, the form and content of which had already been agreed by negotiation. With the terms of the lease already agreed, why bother to embody them in an agreement for lease, when the parties could proceed immediately to the execution and exchange of the lease and counterpart? There is little risk in either party backing out of the arrangement in the time between the conclusion of negotiations and completion of the lease, especially since both parties will have invested considerable time and resources in the negotiation process.

The circumstances when an agreement for lease is used are usually limited to occasions where one (or both) of the parties is required to do something to the premises prior to the grant of the lease.

Typically, an agreement for lease is used where the landlord has commenced, or is about to commence constructing the premises. The landlord's aim is to secure an agreed letting of the premises to a prospective tenant as soon as possible so that, when construction has been completed, the tenant will be bound to complete the lease, and rent will become payable to the landlord to provide income to offset his building costs. On other occasions, an agreement may be used where the landlord, at the request of the tenant, is carrying out substantial works of repair or refurbishment to the premises prior to the grant of the lease. In this kind of situation the landlord would not want to go to the expense of executing works without a commitment from the tenant to enter into a lease once the works have been carried out. An agreement may also be used where it is proposed that the tenant carries out major works to the premises prior to the grant of the lease, in which case both parties would ideally like the security of a binding commitment to enter into a lease upon completion of the works.

The main aim of the agreement, apart from recording the agreed terms of the lease to be entered into, is to stipulate the nature of the works to be carried out to the premises, the time in which they are to be carried out, and the manner in which they will be executed. There is little point in the landlord agreeing to grant a lease of premises to the tenant upon the completion of the construction of a building if the agreement does not state, amongst other things, who will construct the building, and by when, and to what specifications.

29.3 A TYPICAL AGREEMENT

In order to consider the type of clauses commonly found in an agreement for lease where works are required to be carried out, this part of the book concentrates on an agreement in which the landlord will be obliged to construct a building prior to the grant of the lease. Many of the points raised will be equally applicable, or can be adapted to a situation where it will be the tenant who is carrying out works to the premises before completion.

The basic thrust of the agreement will be that the landlord, as the owner of the site, will construct (or, by engaging building contractors, cause to be constructed) premises for occupation by the tenant. Once the premises reach a stage of 'practical completion' (see **29.3.5**) the tenant will be obliged to enter into the form of lease attached to the agreement. Rent will then become payable under the terms of the lease, giving the developer/landlord a return on his investment. Naturally, the terms of the agreement are open for negotiation. In particular, negotiations will revolve around the extent of control, input or supervision the tenant will be allowed to have in respect of the execution of the works, and how much protection he will have if, after completion of the lease, the works turn out to be defective.

The following is a list of some of the problems to be addressed in the drafting and negotiation of the agreement.

29.3.1 What works will be carried out by the landlord?

In the type of agreement under consideration, the works will involve the construction of the entire building which will house the premises to be demised by the lease. The extent of works proposed by the landlord must be clearly indicated in the agreement. It will, therefore, be necessary for detailed plans and specifications, recording exactly what is to be constructed, to be attached to the agreement for lease, and for the agreement to stipulate that the landlord is to develop in accordance with them.

29.3.2 Will the landlord be able to depart from the agreed plans and specifications?

The tenant will not want the agreement to permit the landlord's development to vary from the plans and specifications, since this might result in the tenant being obliged to take a lease of premises radically differing from those originally planned. On the other hand, the landlord would like to build into the agreement a degree of design and construction flexibility, so that if, as the development proceeds, it becomes apparent to the architect that a variation in design or construction is necessary or desirable (either on economic, architectural, or purely aesthetic grounds), the agreement will permit a variation to be made. This is a matter for negotiation between the parties. A possible compromise might be reached if the agreement allows certain 'permitted variations', which could be defined to mean those required by the local planning authority under the terms of any planning permission for the development of the site, or those which are insubstantial and are reasonably required by the landlord.

It should be noted that if a contract is varied in a material manner, outside the scope of existing contractual provisions, a new contract will come into being which will have to satisfy the requirements of s 2 of the Law of Property (Miscellaneous Provisions) Act 1989 (see *McCausland v Duncan Lawrie Ltd* [1996] 4 All ER 995).

29.3.3 What standard of works is required?

It is usual to include an obligation in the agreement on the landlord's part to ensure that the works described in the agreement are carried out with reasonable skill and care, and in accordance with all relevant statutory approvals (eg planning permission, Building Regulations).

29.3.4 Is there to be any degree of supervision?

The landlord will want complete freedom to enable his builders to progress the development of the site without any interference from the tenant, and may be able to insist upon this in his negotiations. However, the tenant may have sufficient bargaining strength to demand a degree of control and supervision over the execution of the landlord's works. He may require the agreement to make provision allowing a surveyor, appointed by the tenant, to inspect the works as they are being carried out, in order to make comments and representations to the landlord (or his architect), and to point out errors in the works, and variations not permitted by the agreement. The issue of whether the tenant is to have any involvement in the development and, if so, the degree of control to be allowed, is a matter which will depend heavily upon the relative bargaining strengths of the parties.

29.3.5 Who decides when the building is ready for occupation?

The determination of the date upon which the building is completed is important since it will trigger the commencement of the lease (and therefore liability for rent). A landlord is interested in achieving completion as soon as possible in order to obtain rent, whereas the tenant may have an interest in delaying completion (unless he is especially keen to gain possession). The tenant will not want the agreement to force him to complete the lease until the premises have been fully completed to his satisfaction, and are ready for immediate occupation and use. However, the landlord will not want to give the tenant any scope for delaying the transaction beyond a date when the premises are sufficiently ready. The landlord will want to be able to force the tenant to complete the lease notwithstanding one or two imperfections. It is, therefore, a representative of the party who is carrying out the works who usually certifies that the building has reached the stage of 'practical completion' for the purposes of the agreement.

Practical completion occurs when the building works have been sufficiently completed to permit use and occupation for the intended purpose, even though there may be some minor matters outstanding.

The certificate of practical completion, in the type of agreement under consideration, will be given by the landlord's architect (as defined by the agreement). Care should be taken where the agreement is drafted 'back-to-back' with a design-and-build building contract, where the landlord will not have engaged the architect (see **8.2.3**). Issues which will concern the tenant are whether the tenant should have any control over who should act as the architect, whether the architect is to be independent (ie whether he may be someone who is in the employ of the landlord), and whether, at the final inspection of the works, the tenant can insist upon the attendance of his own representative to make representations to the landlord's architect, or to carry out a joint inspection for the purpose of issuing the certificate. The tenant's main aim in this regard is to be able to object to and delay the issue of the certificate of practical completion (which triggers completion) if in his opinion the works have not yet been satisfactorily completed. As ever, this is a matter upon which negotiations are required.

29.3.6 Will the agreement specify a completion date?

If the building is being built between exchange and completion, there will not be a fixed date for completion. The agreement will provide for the lease to be completed within a specified number of days after the issue of the certificate of practical completion. The landlord would seek to resist being obliged to complete his building works within a fixed time-scale, since there are any number of reasons why the execution of the works might be delayed. However, on the other hand, the tenant would like the agreement to impose some time restraints upon the landlord, as he will not want to be kept waiting indefinitely for the building to be completed. Presumably the tenant would be anxious to obtain possession of a completed building as soon as possible in order to satisfy his business needs. The tenant may press for the inclusion of a clause which requires the landlord to use his best (or reasonable) endeavours to ensure that the building is completed by a certain date. The landlord may be prepared to accept such a clause provided he is not liable for delays caused by matters outside his control.

29.3.7 Is the person carrying out the works to be liable for any delay?

It is usual for the agreement to include what is called a 'force majeure' clause to ensure that the person executing the works will not be in breach of the requirement to complete the works by a certain date if the delay is caused by matters which are outside his control. A 'force majeure' clause covers delaying factors such as adverse weather conditions, strikes, lock-outs, or other industrial action, civil commotion, shortages of labour or materials and others.

29.3.8 Will there be any penalties for delay?

Usually, the tenant can only delay the transaction by failing to complete the lease within the stipulated number of days after the issue of the certificate of practical completion. To discourage the tenant from delaying completion, and to compensate the landlord, the agreement should stipulate a 'rent commencement date' from which rent will become payable under the lease, regardless of whether the tenant has completed the lease. If the tenant delays completion beyond the rent commencement date, he will still be bound to pay rent to the landlord on completion of the lease calculated from the earlier rent commencement date. In this way the tenant is penalised for his delay by having to pay rent in respect of a period when he was not in occupation of the premises, and the landlord is thus not left without income. The rent commencement date is usually stated to be the day upon which the lease is due to be completed (ie a certain number of days after the issue of the certificate of practical completion) or, if a rent-free period is being given to the tenant, a certain number of months after the day upon which completion is due.

If the landlord fails to complete the building by any long-stop date inserted in the agreement, and is unable to avail himself of the force majeure clause, the tenant could just sit tight and await completion, in the knowledge that rent will not become payable until then. However, most tenants will not want to be kept waiting indefinitely, since premises are usually required for immediate business needs. Therefore, as an incentive to the landlord to build within the timescale specified by the agreement, the tenant should insist upon a clause providing for liquidated damages to be payable by the landlord if he delays beyond the long-stop date. The agreement ought to state a daily rate of damages payable to the tenant in the event of a delay. The landlord should ensure that the building contract entered into with his building contractors runs 'back-to-back' with the agreement for lease so that he may claim liquidated damages from his contractors in the event of a delay. The tenant may want a further provision enabling him to terminate the agreement in the event of a protracted delay.

29.3.9 What if there are any defects in the works or materials?

If, after completion, the tenant discovers that there are defects in the design or construction of the premises, or in the materials used, then insofar as the defects amount to disrepair (see **19.2.6**) the tenant will be bound to remedy them under the repairing covenant in the lease. A well-advised tenant will have instructed a surveyor to look for defects in the works prior to the grant of the lease. However, the nature of a design or construction defect is such that it rarely manifests itself until some time after the lease has been completed. The tenant should, therefore, ask for some protection in the agreement (or in the lease itself) against the prospect of such 'latent' or 'inherent' defects arising. There are several ways in which this can be done:

(1) In negotiating the terms of the repairing covenant, the tenant could seek to exclude liability (either absolutely, or during the first few years of the term) in respect of any disrepair which arises out of a defect in the design or construction of the building, or in the materials used. Liability for repair necessitated by latent defects, if excluded from the tenant's covenant, ought to be transferred to the landlord under the lease.
(2) In the agreement for lease, the tenant could negotiate the inclusion of a clause which creates a 'defects liability period' to oblige the landlord to put right any defects which become apparent within, for example, the first 12 months after practical completion.
(3) In the agreement, the tenant could insist upon a provision obliging the landlord to enforce a clause in the building contract entered into by the landlord with his building contractor whereby the contractor had undertaken to remedy any

defects becoming apparent within an initial defects liability period. Similarly, the agreement could oblige the landlord to pursue, for the tenant's benefit, any other contractual remedies the landlord may have against the other members of his design and construction team (eg architects, engineers, surveyors) under their contracts of engagement.

(4) The tenant could either take out, or require the landlord to take out insurance for the benefit of the tenant and his successors in title against damage caused by design of construction defects.

(5) In the agreement the tenant could insist that the landlord procures collateral warranties for the tenant from the landlord's design and construction team (eg builders, architects, engineers and surveyors) whereby those persons who have been involved in developing the site enter into a warranty with the tenant (and successors in title) that they have exercised reasonable skill and care in performing their duties under their respective contracts of engagement. The problem is that the tenant has no contractual relationship with the landlord's builders and designers, and so would be without a remedy in contract if their contractual obligations were not met. Further, it should be remembered that the ability to pursue an action in tort in respect of negligently designed or constructed premises has been substantially restricted by the House of Lords decision in *Murphy v Brentwood District Council* [1990] 2 All ER 908 so that such an action may only be maintained if there is some actual or threatened injury or physical damage to person or property (other than the defective property itself). This means that the tenant would be left with little or no remedy at all against the landlord's development team. To fill the gap, the tenant may seek to create a contractual relationship by requiring the landlord to ensure that the development team enters into collateral warranties with the tenant. If warranties are to be procured for his benefit, the tenant will want an agreed form of warranty to be appended to the agreement, and will need to see the various contracts of engagement to check the scope of responsibility of each team member. He will also require evidence that each warrantor has sufficient professional insurance cover.

29.3.10 Who is to be responsible if the premises are damaged after practical completion, but before completion of the lease?

If the premises are damaged before practical completion, then the certificate will not be issued, for the obvious reason that the premises will not have reached the stage of practical completion. The landlord will have to put right the damage before the certificate can be issued. If the premises are damaged after practical completion, but before actual completion, the agreement ought to stipulate that the premises remain at the landlord's risk since the tenant is not yet entitled to possession. The landlord ought to maintain insurance cover until the premises are handed over, and the agreement may make this a requirement.

29.3.11 What form will the lease take?

Before the agreement is entered into, the final form of the lease which the tenant will be required to enter into must have been agreed between landlord and tenant. Full negotiations must have taken place regarding the terms of the lease. The agreed form of draft should be appended to the agreement, with an obligation in the agreement upon the tenant to take a lease in that form on the date of actual completion. It is unwise to attach the travelling draft lease which, after amendments and counter-amendments, may now be untidy and difficult to interpret. A fair copy of the agreed draft should be prepared and attached to the agreement. There seems little point in the parties entering into an agreement for lease unless all negotiations regarding the lease terms have been concluded.

29.3.12 To which premises will the agreement relate?

The agreement will normally describe the premises by reference to the parcels clause in the draft lease, which in turn will refer to plans attached to the agreement showing the exact extent of the premises. Plans will be essential where a lease of part is intended.

29.3.13 Should any conditions of sale be incorporated?

The terms of the agreement for lease ought to set out extensively the rights and obligations of the landlord and tenant, in which case there may be no need to incorporate a set of conditions of sale. However, safety ought to dictate that they be incorporated in any case, with a provision that they apply except insofar as they are inconsistent with any other terms of the agreement.

29.3.14 Will the agreement require the landlord to deduce title, and will he disclose incumbrances in the agreement?

As to title matters generally, see **11.3**. If title is deduced to the tenant, the agreement will usually prohibit requisitions after exchange.

29.3.15 Will the agreement merge with the lease?

The usual conveyancing doctrine of merger applies to an agreement to grant a lease, but it is common practice to include a clause excluding the doctrine since many of the contractual obligations are intended to continue in operation post-completion.

Insofar as they do continue in operation, they may be construed as landlord or tenant covenants of the tenancy, and therefore binding upon successors in title (see the definition of 'covenant' and 'collateral agreement' in s 28(1) of the LTCA 1995).

29.4 OTHER USES

There are other occasions when an agreement for lease may be used which are not dealt with in this book. For example, an agreement might be required where the grant of the lease is conditional upon the consent of a third party (eg the head landlord on the grant of a sub-lease), or upon the grant of an order of the court under s 38(4) of the LTA 1954 (see **34.1.5**).

Chapter 30

SELLING THE LEASE

30.1 APPLICATIONS FOR CONSENT TO ASSIGN

It will nearly always be the case that the lease will restrict the tenant's right to assign the lease. There may be an absolute covenant against assignment, in which case the tenant is absolutely prohibited from assigning his lease. The landlord may (or may not) agree to waive the breach in a particular case but the tenant will be entirely at the mercy of his landlord. An assignment in breach of an absolute covenant will be effective, but the lease will be liable to forfeiture by the landlord because of the breach of covenant. More commonly, there will be a qualified covenant, ie not to assign without the landlord's prior written consent. In the case of a qualified covenant against assignment, s 19(1)(a) of the LTA 1927 implies a proviso that, notwithstanding any contrary provision, the landlord's licence or consent is not to be unreasonably withheld. The reasonableness of the landlord's refusal of consent has been dealt with earlier in this book (see **20.2.5**), and it will be recalled that if the parties have specified for the purposes of s 19(1A) of the LTA 1927 conditions to be satisfied, or circumstances to exist, before consent is to be given, a refusal of consent on the grounds that they are not satisfied, or they do not exist, is not an unreasonable withholding of consent.

Assuming the alienation covenant is qualified, the first step is for the tenant to make written application to his landlord for consent to assign. If the landlord consents, the tenant can proceed with the assignment. If the landlord unreasonably refuses consent, the tenant can proceed to assign and will not be deemed in breach of covenant. The danger for the tenant is in knowing whether the landlord's refusal is unreasonable or not, because if the landlord's refusal turns out to have been reasonable, the landlord will have the right to forfeit the lease. Further, for the purposes of the LTCA 1995, the assignment will be an excluded assignment, meaning that the assignor will not be released from the tenant covenants in the lease. Alternatively, the tenant may pursue the safer course of action of seeking a court declaration that the landlord is acting unreasonably in withholding consent, but this may prove costly and time-consuming. A further problem, prior to the passing of the LTA 1988, was that the tenant could not, in the absence of an express covenant by the landlord, obtain damages if the landlord withheld consent unreasonably.

Section 1 of the LTA 1988 (which only applies to qualified covenants) provides that where the tenant has made written application to assign, the landlord owes a duty, within a reasonable time:

(1) to give consent, unless it is reasonable not to do so. Giving consent subject to an unreasonable condition will be a breach of this duty; and
(2) to serve on the tenant written notice of his decision whether or not to give consent, specifying in addition:
    (a) if the consent is given subject to conditions, the conditions; or
    (b) if the consent is withheld, the reasons for withholding it.

No doubt the landlord will wish to see a bank reference, audited accounts (eg for the last 3 years) and, if appropriate, trade references for the proposed assignee and these should accompany the tenant's application. If the landlord needs any further information to enable him to process the application, he should request this from the tenant.

The Act does not define what amounts to a reasonable time and each case will turn on its own facts (but see, eg, *Norwich Union Life Insurance Society Ltd v Shopmoor Ltd* (1997) *Current Law Digest* 97/3250).

As to whether the landlord is unreasonably withholding his consent, this is left to the general law. The burden of proving the reasonableness of any refusal or any conditions imposed is on the landlord and the sanction for breach of the statutory duty is liability in tort for damages. As a result of the Act, landlords must give careful consideration to the financial consequences of having delayed or refused consent unreasonably and they should set up efficient procedures to ensure that each application for consent is dealt with expeditiously and in accordance with the Act.

If the landlord is himself a tenant and the applicant for consent is the sub-tenant, then if the head-lease requires the superior landlord's consent to the assignment, the Act imposes a duty on the immediate landlord to pass on a copy of the application to the superior landlord within a reasonable time.

Section 3 of the Act deals with the situation where a head-lease contains a covenant by the tenant not to consent to a disposition by a sub-tenant without the consent of the head landlord, such consent not to be unreasonably withheld. In such circumstances, a similar duty to that contained in s 1 is imposed on the head landlord towards the sub-tenant.

In considering whether or not to give consent, the landlord does not owe earlier tenants a duty of care to ensure that the assignee is of sufficient financial standing. If the assignee turns out to be unsatisfactory, the landlord will still be able to serve a default notice on those former tenants who may still be liable to the landlord (according to whether it is an 'old' or 'new' lease for the purposes of the LTCA 1995) (*Norwich Union Life Insurance Society v Low Profile Fashions Ltd* (1992) 21 EG 104). In such a situation, the earlier tenants may then be able to secure an overriding lease under the provisions of the LTCA 1995 (see **31.1.4**).

The landlord's solicitor, on receiving the tenant's application to assign, will often seek an undertaking from the tenant's solicitor to pay the landlord's legal and other costs of dealing with the application and preparing the licence (plus VAT) (see *Dong Bang Minerva (UK) Ltd v Davina Ltd* [1996] 31 EG 87). This does not infringe s 144 of the LPA 1925. Care should be taken in drafting the undertaking to make it clear whether the obligation to pay the landlord's costs applies in the event of the licence not being granted; this may be a requirement of the lease in any case.

To prevent the court from finding that consent has been given before the licence to assign is entered into, the landlord would be wise to head all correspondence with the tenant's advisers 'subject to contract' until completion of the licence (see *Next plc v National Farmers Union Mutual Insurance Co Ltd* [1997] EGCS 181).

30.2 THE LANDLORD'S LICENCE

If the landlord is prepared to give his consent to the assignment, a licence to assign will usually be prepared by the landlord's solicitor in which the landlord will formally grant his consent. If the tenant and assignee are to enter into covenants in the licence then all three (ie landlord, tenant and assignee) will be parties to the licence, which will be in the form of a deed. The licence will include various covenants and conditions such as:

(1) a direct covenant by the assignee with the landlord, to observe and perform the covenants in the lease for the entire duration of the term. The reason for this is that it makes the assignee liable to the landlord in contract for the full term of the lease and not just for breaches of covenant committed during the assignee's ownership. As the assignor is likely to have given a similar covenant to the landlord when he acquired the property, the assignor must appreciate that he will remain liable for future breaches even after the assignment has taken place. It is thus in the assignor's interest to make sure that the assignee is responsible and financially sound;

(2) a covenant by the tenant:
   (a) to pay the landlord's costs and expenses in dealing with the tenant's application;
   (b) not to allow the assignee to take up possession until the assignment has been completed;

(3) that the licence only extends to the transaction specifically authorised;

(4) that the licence is not to act as a waiver of any breach committed by the tenant prior to the date of the licence;

(5) that the licence shall cease to be valid unless the assignment is completed within, say, 2 months.

30.3 ADDITIONAL RULES FOR LEASES GRANTED ON OR AFTER 1 JANUARY 1996

If the lease was granted on or after 1 January 1996 the provisions of the LTCA 1995 will apply and the above rules may need to be modified to take account of that Act:

(1) the LTCA 1995 allows parties to leases containing a qualified covenant against assignment to agree in the lease, or at a later stage, to modify the controls of s 19(1)(a) of the LTA 1927 so that conditions of the parties' own choosing should instead govern assignment. This enables the landlord and tenant to set out in advance the conditions which must be satisfied before the landlord will consent to an assignment. If the parties do not lay down conditions for assignment in this way, or if the landlord seeks to withhold consent on grounds other than those agreed, then the provisions of s 19(1)(a) of the LTA 1927 will apply in the usual way (see **20.2.5**);

(2) the landlord may require an AGA from the assignor (see **20.2.8**);

(3) any licence to assign should not require the assignee to enter into a direct covenant with the landlord making the assignee liable on the lease covenants for the entire duration of the lease.

The detailed working of the LTCA 1995 in this regard is dealt with in Chapter 20.

30.4 THE CONVEYANCING PROCEDURE

In many respects the conveyancing steps are the same as those dealt with in Chapter 36 of the LPC Resource Book *Conveyancing* (Jordans). The following outline is, therefore, intended to highlight the matters of additional concern on the sale of a business lease whilst, at the same time, serving as a brief reminder of the usual conveyancing steps.

Assignment of lease: basic procedural steps:

	Assignor		***Assignee***
1	Take detailed instructions: – advise on tax implications – is a premium to be paid (eg where lease has acquired a capital value)? – are any fixtures and fittings included?	1	Take detailed instructions: – advise assignee on the VAT position and the effect of Part II of the LTA 1954 – ensure financial arrangements satisfactory
2	Obtain evidence of leasehold title, including the lease itself: – investigate title and check terms of the lease – is the superior title to be deduced?	2	Arrange inspection, survey and a report on the condition of any fixtures
3	If the landlord's consent to assign is needed, ascertain the landlord's requirements and receive draft licence to assign. Check financial standing of assignee. If the sale is to a company, consider making company search to establish its financial strength (assignor may remain liable on lease covenants even after assignment)	3	Provide assignor with information needed to secure landlord's licence
4	Draft the contract for sale and submit to assignee's solicitors in duplicate together with a copy of the lease and draft licence to assign, for approval (title may be deduced at this stage)	4	Peruse the draft contract, accompanying lease and draft licence: – is superior title to be deduced? – are the lease terms satisfactory? – consider making company search against landlord company with extensive obligations in the lease, whose financial standing is unknown
5	Obtain service charge accounts and details of insurance. Obtain last receipt for outgoings, including last payment of rent and service charge (+ VAT invoice) for inspection by assignee on completion. If service charge payable in advance on basis of landlord's estimate, contract should provide for post-completion adjustment (see, eg, Standard Condition 6.3.5)	5	Make the appropriate pre-contract searches and enquiries. Ask for accounts for the last, say, 3 years' service charge to give the assignee an indication of the sums involved. Request details of insurance

6	Reply to assignee's pre-contract enquiries	6	Peruse replies to searches and enquiries. Return one copy of the approved draft contract and licence
7	If the lease has been charged find out the amount needed to redeem it	7	Attend to execution of the contract and licence to assign (if necessary)
8	Attend to execution of the contract and licence to assign (if necessary)		

Exchange

(If the licence to assign has not been completed by exchange, the contract should be made conditional on its execution before completion, see Standard Condition 8.3.)

1	Deduce title, if not previously done	1	If title not investigated pre-exchange, do so now and raise requisitions. Peruse replies
2	Reply to assignee's requisitions and approve draft purchase deed	2	Prepare draft purchase deed and send to assignor's solicitor for approval
3	If necessary, obtain redemption statement from lender	3	Engross approved draft purchase deed. Attend to execution by assignee and send to assignor's solicitor for execution by assignor
4	Apportion outgoings including rent, insurance premium and service charge and send completion statement to assignee's solicitor	4	Make pre-completion searches
5	Attend to execution of engrossment of purchase deed supplied by assignee's solicitor	5	Send completion statement to client
6	Proceed to completion	6	Proceed to completion

Completion

1	If necessary attend to discharge of any outstanding mortgage	1	Give notice of assignment to landlord in accordance with the lease, and pay the registration fee
2	Account to assignor for any proceeds of sale	2	Attend to stamping within 30 days of completion
		3	If necessary, attend to registration of title
		4	Custody of deeds

Chapter 31

REMEDIES FOR BREACH OF COVENANT

Chapter 31 contents

31.1 LANDLORD'S REMEDIES

Before the landlord takes any steps against a defaulting tenant, he should first consider whether any other party is also liable. For example, are there any sureties or guarantors, is the original tenant under a continuing liability, or did any of the previous assignees give the landlord a direct covenant on assignment, upon which they may still be liable? The reader will recall that the ability of the landlord to proceed against some of these other parties is affected by the Landlord and Tenant (Covenants) Act 1995 (LTCA 1995). These issues have been dealt with earlier in the book.

Before proceeding against a former tenant or his guarantor for a 'fixed charge', ie:

- rent; or
- service charge; or
- any liquidated sum payable under the lease; or
- interest on such sums,

the LTCA 1995 requires the landlord to serve a notice of the claim upon the former tenant or his guarantor, as the case may be, within 6 months of the current tenant's default (there is no requirement to also serve a notice on a former tenant before serving a notice on that tenant's guarantor: *Cheverell Estates Ltd v Harris* [1998] 02 EG 127). Failure to serve a valid notice will mean that the landlord is unable to recover that sum from the person concerned. This requirement applies to all leases and not just those granted after the commencement of the LTCA 1995.

Where the landlord does proceed against a former tenant or his guarantor, that person may be able to regain some control over the property by calling for an overriding lease (see **31.1.4**).

31.1.1 For non-payment of rent

Only 6 years' arrears of rent are recoverable, whether by action or distress (Limitation Act 1980).

By action
If the tenant, or one of the parties mentioned above, is liable for the rent, the landlord may pursue his normal remedies for recovery through the High Court or county court. As to the choice of court and type of proceedings, see the LPC Resource Book *Civil Litigation* (Jordans).

Bankruptcy and winding up
If the sum owed exceeds £750, the landlord, as an alternative to action, may wish to consider the possibility of serving a statutory demand on the tenant with a view to commencing bankruptcy or winding up proceedings, in the event of non-compliance with the demand (Insolvency Act 1986). The landlord must bear in mind that the

enforced bankruptcy of the tenant may reduce the chances of payment in full since he will become an ordinary unsecured creditor.

Distress

Distress is the landlord's ancient common law right, when the tenant is in arrears with his rent, to enter upon the demised premises and seize chattels to the value of the debt. The remedy is lost once the landlord has obtained judgment for the outstanding sum and the remedy should, therefore, be regarded as an alternative to proceeding by way of action. The distress can be carried out by the landlord personally, or as is more often the case, by a certificated bailiff acting on the landlord's behalf.

The rules concerning entry onto the demised premises are technical and easily broken, for example, entry can be gained through an open window but a closed window must not be opened. Such rules are beyond the scope of this book. Once on the demised premises, the landlord (or bailiff) may seize goods to satisfy the outstanding debt. The seized goods are then impounded either on or off the premises. If they are impounded on the premises, they may be left there and the tenant will be asked to sign a 'walking possession agreement' to avoid any argument that the landlord has abandoned the distress. This agreement will list the goods against which distress has been levied. If the tenant removes the goods, he commits 'pound-breach' and will become liable for treble damages. After the expiry of 5 days the landlord may remove the goods and sell them to pay off the arrears and the costs of distress. Whilst a public auction is not essential, the landlord must obtain the best price and for that reason most landlords will auction the goods.

Certain goods which are on the premises cannot be distrained against, for example, cash, perishable goods, tools of the tenant's trade up to £150 in value, things in actual use and goods delivered to the tenant pursuant to his trade. In addition, there are provisions to protect the goods of third parties contained in the Law of Distress Amendment Act 1908.

Special rules apply in the event of the bankruptcy or winding up of the tenant.

The Law Commission has recommended the abolition of the remedy and the above is only intended as an outline of the subject. More detailed coverage is contained in the standard works on landlord and tenant law.

Collecting the rent from a sub-tenant

If the premises have been sub-let, the superior landlord can serve notice on the sub-tenant under s 6 of the Law of Distress Amendment Act 1908, requiring the sub-tenant to pay his rent to the superior landlord until the arrears are paid off.

Forfeiture

Forfeiture for non-payment of rent is dealt with at **33.5.2**.

31.1.2 Breach of tenant's repairing covenant

From a practical point of view, and as a first step, the landlord, exercising his right of entry in the lease, should enter onto the demised premises with his surveyor to draw up a schedule of dilapidations. This should be served on the tenant with a demand that the tenant comply with his repairing obligation. If the tenant remains in breach of his obligation to repair the demised premises, the landlord has various remedies available to him.

Action for damages

THE MEASURE OF DAMAGES

The landlord may bring an action for damages against the tenant either during the term or after its expiry. Section 18 of the LTA 1927 limits the maximum amount recoverable in all cases by providing that the damages cannot exceed the amount by which the value of the reversion has been diminished by the breach. It follows that the cost of repairs will be irrecoverable to the extent that they exceed this statutory ceiling.

Where proceedings are commenced during the term of the lease the reduction in the value of the reversion will be influenced by the length of the unexpired residue: the longer the unexpired term, the less the reduction should be.

In proceedings commenced at or after the end of the lease the court may be prepared, at least as a starting point, to accept the cost of repairs as evidence of the measure of damages, subject to the ceiling imposed by s 18, see *Smiley v Townshend* [1950] 2 KB 311.

If a sub-tenant is in breach of a repairing covenant in the sub-lease, the measure of damages is the reduction in value of the intermediate landlord's reversion. If the sub-tenant knows of the terms of the superior tenancy, the intermediate landlord's liability to the superior landlord will be relevant in assessing these damages.

Section 18 further provides that no damages are recoverable for failure to put or leave the premises in repair at the termination of the lease, if the premises are to be pulled down shortly after termination or if intended structural alterations would render the repairs valueless. To benefit from this provision the tenant must show that the landlord had a firm intention (to pull down or alter) at the end of the lease.

It is important to appreciate that s 18 only applies to actions for damages by the landlord and has no application where the sum owed by the tenant is in the nature of a debt. If, therefore, the tenant covenants to spend £X per year on repairs, but fails to do so, the landlord may recover the deficiency as a debt without regard to the statutory ceiling in s 18.

THE NEED FOR LEAVE TO SUE

If the lease was granted for 7 years or more and still has at least 3 years left to run, the Leasehold Property (Repairs) Act 1938 lays down a special procedure which the landlord must follow before being able to sue for damages (or forfeit the lease) for breach of the tenant's repairing covenant. Where the Act applies, it requires the landlord to serve a notice on the tenant under s 146 of the LPA 1925. Apart from the normal requirements of such a notice (see **33.5.3**), it must in addition, contain a statement informing the tenant of his right to serve a counter-notice within 28 days claiming the benefit of the Act. If such a counter-notice is served, the landlord cannot proceed further without leave of the court, which will not be given unless the landlord proves (and not just shows an arguable case):

(1) that the value of the reversion has been substantially diminished; or
(2) that the immediate remedying of the breach is required for preventing substantial diminution, or for complying with any Act or bye-law, or for protecting the interests of occupiers other than the tenant, or for the avoidance of much heavier repair costs in the future; or
(3) that there are special circumstances which render it just and equitable that leave be given.

Even if the landlord makes out one of the grounds, the court still has a discretion to refuse leave but this should only be exercised where the court is clearly convinced that it would be wrong to allow the landlord to continue. The court may, in granting or refusing leave, impose such conditions on the landlord or tenant as it thinks fit.

The Act does not apply to breach of a tenant's covenant to put premises into repair when the tenant takes possession or within a reasonable time thereafter.

Self-help

If the tenant is in breach of his repairing obligations, can the landlord enter the demised premises, carry out the necessary works and recover the cost from the tenant? In the absence of a statutory right or an express provision in the lease, the landlord has no general right to enter the demised premises even where the tenant is in breach of his obligations. Indeed, the tenant may be able to obtain an injunction to restrain the landlord's trespass. For that reason most leases will contain an express right for the landlord to enter the demised premises and carry out any necessary repairs at the tenant's expense, in default of the tenant complying with a notice to repair. In the case of *Jervis v Harris* [1996] 10 EG 159, the court accepted the landlord's argument that his action against the tenant to recover this expenditure was in the nature of a debt action rather than one for damages. Thus, the landlord was able to evade the statutory restrictions in the 1927 and 1938 Acts, mentioned above.

Specific performance

In *Rainbow Estates Ltd v Tokenhold Ltd* [1998] NPC 33, the court held that, in principle, there is no reason why the equitable remedy of specific performance should not be available to enforce compliance by a tenant with his repairing obligation. However, other remedies are likely to be more appropriate and the court stressed that specific performance will only be awarded in exceptional circumstances.

Forfeiture

The landlord may be able to forfeit the lease for breach of the tenant's covenant to repair; forfeiture is dealt with at **33.5**.

31.1.3 Breaches of other covenants by the tenant: an outline

Damages

Damages for breach of covenant are assessed on a contractual basis, the aim being to put the landlord in the same position as if the covenant had been performed. The general principle is that the landlord may recover as damages all loss which may be fairly and reasonably considered as arising in the natural course of things from the breach, or such as may be reasonably supposed to have been in the contemplation of both parties, at the time of entering into the lease as the probable result of that breach (*Hadley v Baxendale* (1854) 9 Ex 341). In the majority of cases the damages will be equal to the diminution in the value of the reversion.

The breach of some particular covenants will now be considered.

COVENANT TO INSURE

The landlord usually assumes responsibility for insurance. If, however, the tenant has covenanted to insure, there will be a breach of covenant if the premises are uninsured or under-insured at any time during the term. If the premises are damaged during the period of default, the measure of damages will be the cost of rebuilding (*Burt v British Transport Commission* (1955) 166 EG 4).

COVENANT AGAINST DEALINGS

There is little authority on the measure of damages obtainable by a landlord where, for example, the tenant has assigned the lease without consent. However, the landlord will probably be entitled to compensation for the fact that his new tenant is less financially sound than the assignor and the value of his reversion is thus reduced.

USER COVENANT

Damages may be awarded for breach by the tenant of a positive covenant to keep the premises open. For example, if the anchor tenant, in breach of covenant, closes its shop premises in a shopping centre, it may have such an adverse effect on the profitability of the other shops in the centre that the landlord may be forced to offer rental consessions to the other tenants. The landlord should be compensated for this loss by an award of damages; but there may be difficult problems in quantifying the amount of the damages. If the landlord can prove that his financial loss arises wholly from the tenant's breach, there should be no difficulty for the landlord. However, it may be the case that the centre was already in decline long before the tenant ceased trading so that the defaulting tenant's breach merely contributed to the already falling profitability of the centre (see, generally, *Transworld Land Co Ltd v J Sainsbury plc* [1990] 2 EGLR 255).

Injunction

In certain circumstances, the landlord may be able to obtain an injunction against the tenant. An injunction is an equitable remedy and thus at the discretion of the court which may award damages instead. In an appropriate case the landlord may be able to obtain an interlocutory injunction pending the full hearing. There are two types of injunction:

(1) Injunctions prohibiting a breach of covenant. The landlord may consider the use of such an injunction to prevent, for example

   (a) an assignment in breach of covenant;
   (b) the carrying out of unauthorised alterations;
   (c) an unauthorised use.

(2) Mandatory injunctions. These injunctions compel the tenant to do something to ensure the performance of a covenant. The court is cautious in its grant of mandatory injunctions.

Other standard works on landlord and tenant law contain a more detailed consideration of the subject of injunctions.

Specific performance

Like the injunction, this is an equitable remedy and is therefore discretionary. The House of Lords has recently confirmed that specific performance is not available against a tenant who is in breach of his 'keep open' covenant (*Co-operative Insurance Society Ltd v Argyll Stores (Holdings) Ltd* [1997] 23 EG 137).

Forfeiture

Often the landlord's most effective remedy will be to commence (or threaten to commence) forfeiture proceedings against the tenant with a view to ending the lease. This remedy is dealt with at **33.5**.

31.1.4 Right of former tenant or his guarantor to an overriding lease

If a former tenant, or guarantor, is served with a notice by the landlord requiring payment of a fixed charge (see **31.1**), the LTCA 1995 allows him to call for an overriding lease within 12 months of payment. For example, L granted a lease to T in 1980. The lease is now owned by A who fell into arrears with his rent. L served notice on T requiring T to pay this sum. T duly made full payment and now claims an overriding lease from L. This will be a headlease 'slotted in' above the lease of the defaulting tenant. The lease of the defaulting tenant moves one step down the reversionary line and becomes a sub-lease. Thus, T will become the immediate landlord of A and in the event of continued default by A can decide what action to take against him, eg forfeiture of the occupational lease (sub-lease). Under the overriding lease, T now has some control over the premises for which he is being held liable. The same situation would arise in leases granted on or after 1 January 1996 where the former tenant had been required under an authorised guarantee agreement to guarantee the performance of his immediate assignee, and that assignee is now in default (see **20.2.8**).

The terms of the overriding lease will be on the terms of the defaulting tenant's lease (with consequential adjustments to add a small reversionary period).

Before deciding to call for an overriding lease, a former tenant (or guarantor) should be made aware that he may become liable for significant landlord's covenants.

31.2 TENANT'S REMEDIES

31.2.1 Breach of an express covenant

In general, a breach by the landlord of one of his covenants in the lease will entitle the tenant to bring an action for damages. The measure of damages will usually be the difference between the value of the tenant's interest in the premises with the covenant performed and the value with the covenant broken. In certain circumstances, the tenant may seek a more appropriate remedy, such as specific performance or an injunction.

Particular attention should be paid to the landlord's repairing covenant.

Breach of landlord's repairing covenant

Unless the lease is of part of a building, it is unusual for the landlord to enter into a covenant to repair. Even where the landlord has assumed the responsibility for repairs, he will generally only be liable if he has notice of disrepair. If the landlord fails to carry out the repairs for which he is liable, the tenant has various remedies available to him. These include the following.

ACTION FOR DAMAGES

The tenant's normal remedy will be to bring an action against his landlord for damages for breach of covenant. Section 18 of the LTA 1927, which restricts a landlord's claim for damages (see **31.1.2**), is not relevant to a tenant's claim. Here, damages will be assessed by comparing the value of the premises to the tenant at the date of assessment with their value if the landlord had complied with his obligation. The tenant will also be entitled to damages for consequential loss such as damage caused to the tenant's goods. If the disrepair was such that the tenant was forced to move into temporary accommodation, the cost of this should also be recoverable, provided the tenant had acted reasonably to mitigate his loss.

SELF-HELP

Subject to notifying the landlord and giving him a reasonable opportunity to perform his covenant, the tenant is entitled to carry out the repair himself and deduct the reasonable cost of so doing from future payments of rent (*Lee-Parker v Izzet* [1971] 1 WLR 1688). If the landlord sues the tenant for non-payment of rent, the tenant will have a defence (see **17.1**).

SPECIFIC PERFORMANCE

The tenant, unlike the landlord, may be able to obtain an order of specific performance. The granting of the order is entirely at the discretion of the court, and being an equitable remedy it will not be granted if damages are an adequate remedy. Further, there must be a clear breach of covenant and must be no doubt over what is required to be done to remedy the breach.

APPOINTMENT OF RECEIVER

In the tenant's action against the landlord for breach of covenant, the tenant may seek the appointment of a receiver to collect the rents and manage the property in accordance with the terms of the lease (including the performance of the landlord's covenants). The court has this power whenever it appears just and convenient to make such an appointment (Supreme Court Act 1981, s 37). The power has been exercised not only where the landlord had abandoned the property but also where he has failed to carry out urgently needed repairs in accordance with his covenant (see *Daiches v Bluelake Investments Ltd* [1985] 2 EGLR 67).

The tenant must nominate a suitably qualified person to act as receiver, for example, a surveyor and before agreeing to act, the potential appointee should ensure that the assets of which he will have control will be sufficient to meet his fees or that he obtains an indemnity in respect of them from the applicant.

A receiver may also be appointed where the landlord collects a service charge from the tenants but fails to provide the services he has promised.

31.2.2 Breach of an implied covenant

Covenant for quiet enjoyment

Most leases will contain an express covenant by the landlord for quiet enjoyment (see Chapter 24). In the absence of an express covenant one will be implied arising out of the relationship of landlord and tenant. The implied covenant only extends to interruption of or interference with the tenant's enjoyment of the demised premises by the landlord or any person lawfully claiming under him; it does not extend to acts done by anyone with a title superior to that of the landlord. Express covenants are often similarly restricted, in which case the only significant difference between the express and the implied covenant is that under an express covenant the landlord will remain liable throughout the term granted, whereas under an implied covenant the landlord's liability operates only during the currency of his ownership of the reversion.

The covenant will provide the tenant with a remedy in the case of unlawful eviction or where there is any substantial interference with the tenant's use and enjoyment of the premises either by the landlord or by the lawful (rightful) acts of anyone claiming under him. The acts likely to amount to a breach of the covenant are discussed at **24.2**. The normal remedy will be damages, assessed on a contractual basis, to compensate the tenant for the loss resulting from the breach.

Derogation from grant

A landlord is under an implied obligation not to derogate from his grant. This covenant complements the covenant for quiet enjoyment and sometimes the two overlap. The landlord will be in breach of his obligation if he does anything which substantially interferes with the use of the demised premises for the purpose for which they were let. Having given something with one hand the landlord cannot take away its enjoyment with the other. The principle is often used to prevent the landlord from using his retained land in a way which frustrates the purpose of the lease. Thus, it has been held to be a derogation from grant for a landlord to grant a lease for the purpose of storing explosives and then to use his retained land in such a way as to render the storage of explosives on the demised premises illegal (*Harmer v Jumbil (Nigeria) Tin Areas Ltd* [1921] 1 Ch 200). Similarly, if the landlord uses machinery on his retained land which by reason of vibration affects the stability of the demised premises there will be a breach of the implied covenant. However, there will be no derogation from grant where the landlord's use of the adjoining land merely makes the user of the demised premises more expensive, for example, by letting the adjoining premises to a business competitor of the tenant (*Port v Griffith* [1938] 1 All ER 295 and *Romulus Trading Co Ltd v Comet Properties Ltd* [1996] 2 EGLR 70).

Until the decision in *Chartered Trust plc v Davies* [1997] 49 EG 135, it was generally believed that it was insufficient to amount to derogation from grant for a landlord to stand back while tenant A, in breach of covenant, committed acts of nuisance against tenant B thus driving tenant B out of business. Just because the landlord failed to take action against tenant A to prevent the nuisance did not, so it was thought, amount to a repudiation of B's lease. However, the Court of Appeal held that inaction by the landlord in these circumstances may amount to derogation from grant. The implications of this decision will be felt most where, as in the instant case, the landlord has retained management control of a shopping centre and is responsible for the common parts. If, in breach of covenant, one of the tenants does something in the common parts which adverely affects another tenant, the landlord will have to consider acting to enforce the lease obligations or else run the risk of being found to have derogated from grant.

Chapter 32

THE EFFECT OF INSOLVENCY

Chapter 32 contents

32.1 BANKRUPTCY OF THE TENANT

32.1.1 The trustee-in-bankruptcy

On the making of a bankruptcy order, the Official Receiver assumes control of the bankrupt tenant's property pending the appointment of a trustee-in-bankruptcy at a meeting of the bankrupt's creditors. As soon as he is appointed, the estate of the bankrupt automatically vests in the trustee to enable the trustee to realise the bankrupt's assets and pay off the creditors. Since he becomes the owner at law of the bankrupt's property, the trustee incurs personal liability in respect of that property until he disposes of it, or unless he exercises his right of disclaimer (see **32.1.2**). The leasehold interest of a bankrupt tenant will vest in the trustee, but not, therefore, without the obligation to pay the rent and the liability to repair the premises and observe the other covenants in the lease. The automatic vesting of the lease in the trustee is an involuntary assignment and does not breach the covenant against assigning without consent.

If the lease has some value attached to it (ie a premium could be demanded on an assignment), the trustee will seek to sell the lease to raise some money for the benefit of the creditors. He will have to comply with the alienation covenant in the lease which will probably involve obtaining the consent of the landlord, and he will be liable to pay rent until the assignment is completed. More often than not the lease does not have any value and amounts to a burden on the bankrupt's estate owing to the continuing obligation to pay rent and perform the covenants. In this case the trustee would prefer to disclaim the lease.

32.1.2 Disclaimer

Section 315 of the Insolvency Act 1986 (IA 1986) gives the trustee power to disclaim onerous property. Onerous property is defined as including any property comprised in the bankrupt's estate which is such that might give rise to a liability to pay money or perform any other onerous act. This clearly covers the typical commercial lease, which by its nature contains onerous continuing obligations. The trustee disclaims the lease by giving to the landlord notice of disclaimer in the prescribed form.

Initially, the landlord will not know whether the trustee intends retaining the lease, with a view to selling it at a premium, or disclaiming it. However, under s 316, the landlord can force the hand of the trustee by requiring him to decide whether or not he is going to disclaim the lease. If the trustee does not give notice of disclaimer within 28 days of receiving a written application from the landlord under s 316, he cannot then disclaim. Section 316 is of no relevance to a landlord who has decided to forfeit the lease (see **33.5**).

32.1.3 The effect of disclaimer

The effect of disclaimer is that it operates to determine the rights, interests and liabilities of the bankrupt and his estate in respect of the disclaimed property, and it discharges the trustee from all personal liability in respect of that property as from the date of his appointment. The lease will no longer form part of the bankrupt's estate; the trustee will no longer be liable to pay the rent or perform the covenants; the bankrupt and his trustee will have washed their hands of the lease. Any claims the landlord may have in respect of unpaid rent up until the date of disclaimer, or other breaches of covenant, or any loss arising out of the disclaimer (including future rent) will have to be proved for in the bankruptcy.

If the bankrupt tenant was the original tenant (with no sub-tenancies having been created, and no guarantor backing up the original tenant's obligations), disclaimer ends the lease itself and the landlord is entitled to recover possession. If the bankrupt tenant was an assignee, whilst disclaimer ends the lease, it does not destroy the liability of any other persons still liable to the landlord (eg the original tenant, his guarantor, any intermediate assignees who have given direct covenants to the landlord and their respective guarantors, and any former tenant under an AGA). To this extent, there is a deemed continuing tenancy for the purpose of preserving the liability of others (see *Hindcastle Ltd v Barbara Attenborough Associates Ltd* [1996] 15 EG 103). This leaves the landlord in the position of being able to pursue those persons for payment of the rent for the remainder of the term, unless and until the landlord takes steps to bring the deemed continuing tenancy to an end.

One option available to a predecessor who finds himself in this invidious position is to make an application to court under s 320 of the IA 1986. Under that section, any person who claims an interest in, or who is under any liability in respect of the disclaimed property (such as the original tenant who is under a liability to pay the rent) may apply to the court for an order vesting the lease in him. Having to pay the rent is bad enough, but not having possession of the leasehold interest out of which that liability arises is unacceptable. Once the lease is vested in him, the predecessor can either resume possession or, as will more often be the case, try to curtail his continuing liability to meet the rent by assigning the lease, with the landlord's consent, to a more reliable assignee. Note that once the lease has been disclaimed, a former tenant cannot claim an overriding lease (see s 19(7) of the LTCA 1995).

Whilst the effect of a disclaimer on the bankrupt tenant's guarantor (including an authorised guarantor under an AGA) is that it does not release the guarantor from the guarantee it is common to include a provision in the lease (or in the AGA) requiring the guarantor to take a lease from the landlord in the event of disclaimer.

The IA 1986 does not deal with the effect of a disclaimer on a sub-lease in an entirely satisfactory manner. Section 315(3) provides that disclaimer 'does not . . . affect the rights or liabilities of any other person'. Arguably, if disclaimer results in the lease ceasing to exist, the sub-lease must also end. However, this is subject to the principle of the deemed continuing lease established by the House of Lords in the *Hindcastle* case. Furthermore, the sub-tenant can apply under s 320 for a vesting order, and indeed the landlord can require the sub-tenant to take a vesting order and if the sub-tenant declines to accept it, his right to remain will cease. The court will grant the order on such terms as it thinks fit and the effect of the order will be to make the sub-tenant the immediate tenant of the landlord.

32.2 LIQUIDATION OF THE TENANT

Unlike bankruptcy, title to the lease does not vest in the liquidator (unless the liquidator takes the unusual step of applying for an order under s 145 of the IA 1986 to vest title in him) and the liquidator does not, therefore, incur any personal liability under the lease. It is the company that remains liable to pay the rent, but it may have stopped doing so, owing to its insolvency. However, if the liquidator is making efforts to assign the lease at a premium, and in the meantime pays rent under the lease, the rent may be considered to be an expense of the liquidation and, therefore, recoverable by the liquidator in priority to other debts.

The liquidator has the same power of disclaimer as the trustee-in-bankruptcy (IA 1986, s 178(2)). There are similar provisions allowing the landlord to force the liquidator to decide whether or not he will disclaim (s 178(5)), providing for notice of disclaimer to be served on any sub-tenants (s 179), and enabling persons having an interest in or being subject to a liability in respect of the premises to apply to the court for a vesting order (s 181).

Disclaimer is a possibility in a compulsory liquidation and a creditors' voluntary liquidation, but is unlikely in a members' voluntary liquidation where it is thought that the directors would either have to assign the lease, or quantify the company's liability under the lease by negotiating a surrender of it before making the declaration of solvency required by such a liquidation. If the liquidator in a members' voluntary liquidation disclaimed the lease, the landlord would be able to claim for his loss arising out of the disclaimer. This unliquidated claim would upset the declaration of solvency.

32.3 THE TENANT IN ADMINISTRATION

Administration is a process available to assist ailing companies. It is a short-term intensive care operation supervised by the court aimed at putting an insolvent company back on its feet. An application for an administration order is made by petition by the company, its directors or its creditors. Once the petition has been presented to the court, a general moratorium is imposed on all proceedings against the company, which means that no actions can be commenced or continued against the company without leave of the court or, once appointed, the administrator. As to when the court might grant leave, see *Re Atlantic Computer Systems plc* [1992] 1 All ER 476.

The administrator is appointed by the court to do all such things as may be necessary for the management of the affairs, business and property of the company with a view to achieving the survival of the company. He has no power to disclaim the company's property, but ordinarily he should not want to, since his purpose is to revive the company, and this would be frustrated by the loss of the company's operating premises. If the company does have surplus leasehold premises which are a drain on the limited resources of the company, the administrator should seek licence to assign the lease, and dispose of the lease in the usual way.

An administrator incurs no personal liability under the lease. The lease does not vest in him; his status is merely as the agent of the company.

32.4 THE TENANT IN RECEIVERSHIP

Receivership is a state of affairs which exists when a person is appointed to enter onto another's property to seize and sell assets charged by a mortgage or debenture deed in order to secure repayment of a debt, interest and costs. Usually, the receiver will be either an administrative receiver or a Law of Property Act receiver. An LPA receiver is appointed to take possession of and receive the income of a specific asset charged by an individual or a company. However, landlords will not often be faced with an LPA receiver since lenders rarely accept rack-rent leases (having precious little capital value) as security for a loan. An administrative receiver is appointed to take possession of the whole (or substantially the whole) of a company's assets which have been charged to the lender under a floating charge. A company tenant's main charge to the bank will contain a floating charge over all the assets of the company, including the lease of the company's premises and, therefore, a landlord is likely to have to deal with this type of receiver.

Both types of receiver act as agent of the borrower-tenant and do not, therefore, incur any personal liability for rent. There is no question of the receiver disclaiming the lease and nor should there be. The principal task of the receiver is to sell the assets charged in order to realise cash and repay the borrowings. Licence to assign will be required in the usual way, provided the landlord has not already forfeited the lease. If the lease is particularly onerous, the receiver will either negotiate a surrender or advise his appointor to release the asset from the charge.

There are no restrictions on a landlord's remedies when his tenant is in receivership.

32.5 INSOLVENCY AND FORFEITURE

Earlier chapters have dealt with the drafting issues relating to forfeiture clauses. The landlord will probably have drafted the clause to enable forfeiture to be effected upon non-payment of rent, breach of covenant, or the happening of one of several insolvency events.

If the tenant is insolvent, all three elements of the clause may be operative in that the tenant may have stopped paying rent, allowed the premises to fall into disrepair and a winding up petition may have been presented to the court. A tenant in financial difficulties in a shopping precinct may close down its premises in breach of a covenant to keep open for trade, withhold rent, and suffer the appointment of a receiver.

With regard to the happening of insolvency events, the landlord will wish to ensure that the forfeiture clause gives him more than one attempt at forfeiting the lease in the event of insolvency proceedings being instigated, in case the landlord inadvertently waives one right to forfeit the lease, when, with knowledge of circumstances giving rise to his right to forfeit, he demands or accepts rent. Hence, the landlord will reserve the right to forfeit both on the occasion of the presentation of the petition (for a winding up, bankruptcy or administration order as the case may be), and on the making of the order itself. Not only does this protect the landlord against an inadvertent waiver, but it also allows him to act at the earliest opportunity, on the presentation of a petition, in order to recover the premises before the insolvency proceedings are brought fully into operation.

However, it must be established how each insolvency event affects the right of the landlord to forfeit the lease.

32.5.1 Individual insolvency

At any time after the presentation of a petition in bankruptcy (or a petition for an interim order in bankruptcy), the court may, on application, order a stay on any action, execution or other legal process against the property of the debtor (s 285(1) of the Insolvency Act 1986). Once a bankruptcy order (or an interim order) has been made, no creditor may have a remedy against the property of the bankrupt in respect of a debt provable in the bankruptcy without the leave of the court (s 285(3) of the Insolvency Act 1986). There is, however, a suggestion in *Ezekiel v Orakpo* [1976] 3 WLR 693 (which was decided in relation to similar provisions contained in the Bankruptcy Act 1914) that forfeiture does not come within the scope of the latter provision. This case was followed in *Razzaq v Pala* [1997] 38 EG 157. If this proposition is correct, and leave is not required to obtain possession by forfeiture after the bankruptcy order has been made, it is difficult to see how the court could be justified in restraining a forfeiture before the order is made.

32.5.2 Corporate insolvency

After the presentation of a winding up petition, the court may, on application, order a stay on any existing forfeiture proceedings. Once the winding up order is made, forfeiture proceedings cannot be continued without leave of the court although peaceable re-entry is probably still possible. If the company is in voluntary liquidation, application can be made to the court for a stay on forfeiture proceedings at any time after the commencement of the winding up, as if the company were being wound up by the court.

Once a petition for an administration order has been lodged at court, and during the period of administration, whilst there are no restrictions on the landlord's ability to serve a s 146 notice, the landlord cannot forfeit the lease by court proceedings without leave of the court or consent of the administrator. Again, peaceable re-entry is probably permissible without leave.

The court will grant leave as a matter of course in liquidation cases (and presumably also in bankruptcy cases) since the landlord, in enforcing a forfeiture, is only seeking to recover his own property. In administration cases, leave should not be refused unless it would seriously impede the achievement of the purposes of the administration, or inflict a loss upon others which is substantially greater than the loss to be inflicted upon the landlord if leave were denied.

If the tenant company is in receivership, the landlord's ability to forfeit is unaffected.

32.6 INSOLVENCY AND CLAIMS FOR RENT OR DAMAGES

As an alternative to forfeiting the lease (or possibly in addition) the landlord may pursue other remedies. For instance, if the tenant fails to pay the rent, the landlord may bring a civil action for the arrears, exercise his right to distrain for the arrears, or, if the tenant has created a sub-tenancy, he may serve notice on the sub-tenant under s 6 of the Law of Distress Amendment Act 1908 requiring the sub-tenant to pay rent direct to the head landlord until rent arrears under the head-lease have been paid off. If the tenant is in breach of any of the other covenants under the lease, the landlord may bring an action for damages against the tenant.

If the tenant company is in receivership, the landlord's remedies for non-payment of rent or breach of covenant are unaffected, although he may find that the only time any judgment he obtains is met by the receiver is when the receiver applies to the landlord for licence to assign. The landlord would be likely to impose a condition on assignment that all arrears of rent, and any sums in respect of loss arising out of any other breaches of covenant are paid to the landlord before consent is given. The receiver incurs no personal liability for the company's debts, unless, being an administrative receiver, he specifically adopts any of the liabilities of the company.

Once a petition for an administration order has been presented, leave of the court or consent of the administrator is required before any action for damages or arrears of rent (including distress) is taken against a corporate tenant. It also seems that leave or consent will also be required in respect of the service of a notice on any sub-tenant of the insolvent tenant under s 6 of the Law of Distress Amendment Act 1908. Leave or consent is unlikely to be granted while the purpose of the administration proceedings may still be achieved. An administrator incurs no personal liability for the company's debts.

In a compulsory liquidation, on the making of the winding up order, no actions may be commenced or proceeded with against the company without leave of the court. This general stay on proceedings prevents the landlord from distraining for rent, but would not, it appears, prevent him from serving a s 6 notice on any sub-tenants. In a voluntary liquidation, the court may stay any proceedings upon application by the liquidator. Insofar as the landlord is a creditor of the company, he must prove for his debt in the liquidation as an ordinary unsecured creditor. However, if the liquidator decided to retain possession of the premises for the purposes of the winding up, rent accrued since the commencement of the winding up will be payable in full by the liquidator as an expense of the liquidation.

In a bankruptcy, since the trustee-in-bankruptcy incurs personal liability, he is likely to disclaim the lease unless it has a capital value. Any actions the landlord may have against the individual tenant may be stayed on application by the trustee in those proceedings, although the landlord is still permitted to distrain for arrears of rent accrued due in the 6 months preceding the date of the bankruptcy order.

32.7 LANDLORD'S INSOLVENCY

In many cases the insolvency of the landlord will not greatly affect the tenant since the landlord's receiver, liquidator, administrator or trustee-in-bankruptcy will be keen to continue receiving the income generated by the lease. Problems will arise where the tenant wishes to take action for breach of covenant against an insolvent landlord, or where the landlord ceases to perform services in accordance with service charge provisions, or apply advance service charge payments made by the tenants. These problems are beyond the scope of this book.

Chapter 33

METHODS OF TERMINATION

Chapter 33 contents

33.1 INTRODUCTION

There are a number of ways at common law in which a lease may be ended. Before looking at these in detail, it is important to appreciate that if the tenant enjoys the protection of the security of tenure provisions under Part II of the LTA 1954, the lease may only be ended in one of the ways specified by that Act. For example, a protected fixed term will not come to an end on the expiry of that term; a protected periodic tenancy will not come to an end by the service of a landlord's common law notice to quit. Such tenancies can only be terminated in one of the ways specified in the Act. These restrictions on termination are dealt with in Chapter 34. The methods of termination to be considered here are:

(1) expiry;
(2) notice to quit;
(3) operation of break clause;
(4) forfeiture;
(5) surrender;
(6) merger.

33.2 EXPIRY

A fixed-term tenancy will terminate at the end of that term; there is no need for either party to take any steps at all. If the tenant remains in possession beyond the expiry date with his landlord's consent, he holds over as a tenant at will, ie on terms that either party may end the tenancy at any time. A tenancy at will may be converted into an implied periodic tenancy by the payment and acceptance of rent.

33.3 NOTICE TO QUIT

A periodic tenancy may be determined by service of a notice to quit by either party. There are many technical rules surrounding the drafting and service of such notices and reference should be made to one of the standard works on landlord and tenant law for a consideration of these. What follows is only intended as a reminder of some of the more important rules.

In the absence of contrary agreement, the minimum length of notice required is as follows:

(1) yearly tenancy: half a year's notice (or two quarters if the tenancy expires on a quarter day);
(2) monthly tenancy: one month's notice;
(3) weekly tenancy: one week's notice.

Not only must the length of notice be correct, it must also expire at the end of a completed period of the tenancy. In the case of a yearly tenancy, this means that the notice must expire on the anniversary of the commencement of the tenancy or on the day before the anniversary. For example, with a yearly tenancy beginning on the 1 January in one year, the notice should expire on the 1 January or 31 December in any subsequent year. A similar rule applies to other periodic tenancies.

At common law, no particular form of notice is required but it must be unambiguous and, for the avoidance of doubt, in writing.

As a general rule, unless the lease provides to the contrary, a notice to quit must relate to all of the land in the lease and not just part.

33.4 OPERATION OF BREAK CLAUSE

The lease may contain an option by which one or both parties may determine the lease, at a particular time or on the happening of a specified event, before it has run its full term. This is known as a break clause. If there are any conditions precedent to the exercise of the option, these must be strictly observed (*Bairstow Eves (Securities) Ltd v Ripley* [1992] 2 EGLR 47). If, for example, the option is only exercisable provided the tenant has performed all of his obligations, he will not be able to exercise it whilst in arrears or in breach of his repairing covenant. However, the exact wording of the option should be examined to see whether such conditions have to be satisfied at the date the notice exercising the option is served, or at the date when it expires. Whilst great care should always be taken in drafting the break notice, minor errors which would not mislead a reasonable recipient may not render the notice invalid (see *Mannai Investment Co Ltd v Eagle Star Life Assurance Co Ltd* [1997] 24 EG 122).

The exercise of a break clause in a head-lease may operate to terminate any sub-lease which has been created (this is certainly the case in the event of exercise by the superior landlord). However, the sub-tenant may have the right to remain in possession if he is protected under Part II of the LTA 1954.

33.5 FORFEITURE

Forfeiture is the landlord's right to re-enter the premises and determine the lease on breach by the tenant of any of his covenants, or upon the happening of certain specified events. However, the right to forfeit is not automatic; it only exists where the lease expressly includes such a right (or if the lease is made conditional upon the performance of the covenants). The drafting of an appropriate provision is dealt with in Chapter 26.

Before the landlord proceeds to forfeit the lease, he should consider carefully the consequences of so doing. In a rising market the landlord should have no difficulty in subsequently re-letting the premises, possibly at a higher rent. If, however, the landlord is faced with a falling market, re-letting the premises may not be so easy. As a result of forfeiture the landlord may be left with an empty property on his hands for a long time. This will lead to a loss of income and may have a detrimental effect on any adjoining property of the landlord, for example, other shops in a parade.

The right of forfeiture is enforced by the landlord in one of two ways. First, the landlord may issue and serve proceedings for recovery of possession or, secondly, the landlord may peaceably re-enter the premises. Landlords are sometimes reluctant to adopt the second alternative because an offence will be committed if any violence is used or threatened and the landlord knew that there was someone on the premises opposed to the entry (Criminal Law Act 1977, s 6). There are further statutory restrictions on the right of peaceable re-entry where the premises are let as a dwelling (Protection from Eviction Act 1977).

33.5.1 Waiver of the right to forfeit

A landlord will be prevented from forfeiting a lease if he has expressly or impliedly waived the right to forfeit. The landlord will still be able to pursue his other remedies but will have lost his right to forfeit. Waiver will be implied where the landlord, knowing of the breach, does some unequivocal act which recognises the continued existence of the lease. It is not, however, a question of intention. So long as the act is inconsistent with an intention to determine the lease, the motive for the act is irrelevant. Thus, a demand for rent, or receipt of rent falling due *after* the right to forfeit has arisen, will amount to waiver notwithstanding a clerical error by the landlord's agent, receipt of rent paid under a standing order, or that the rent is demanded or received 'without prejudice to the landlord's right to forfeit'.

Waiver only operates in respect of past breaches of covenant. Where the landlord waives a 'once and for all' breach (eg breach of a covenant against sub-letting) his right to forfeit is lost for ever. If, however, the breach is of a continuing nature (eg breach of a repairing covenant) the right to forfeit, though waived on one occasion, will arise again, as the property continues to be in disrepair (see *Greenwich London Borough Council v Discreet Selling Estates Ltd* [1990] 48 EG 113; as to the need for a fresh s 146 notice).

33.5.2 Forfeiture for non-payment of rent

That the tenant owes rent to his landlord may seem a necessary pre-condition of the landlord's right to forfeit. Yet, exceptionally, this may not be the case. If, on an assignment of the reversion, the tenant is in arrears with payment of the rent, the 'old' and 'new' landlords often come to some arrangement as to who has the right to sue for the outstanding arrears. Such was the situation in *Kataria v Safeland plc* [1998] 05 EG 155, where it was agreed that, on completion, the right to receive the arrears of rent and all rights of action relating thereto were vested in the 'old' landlord. Notwithstanding this, it was held that the 'new' landlord, following completion, was entitled to forfeit the lease for non-payment of rent (even though the arrears were owed to the 'old' landlord). Hence it becomes important to distinguish the right to forfeit from the right of action in respect of the arrears.

The landlord must make a formal demand for the rent before forfeiting unless the lease exempts him from this obligation. To avoid the technicalities of a formal demand, most leases will provide for forfeiture if the tenant is, for example, 21 days or more in arrears 'whether the rent is formally demanded or not' (see also s 210 of the Common Law Procedure Act 1852). If the rent falls into arrears, the landlord may proceed to forfeit either by court proceedings, or by peaceable re-entry.

However, the tenant may have the right to apply to court for relief from forfeiture which, if granted, will mean that the tenant continues to hold under the existing lease. Where the landlord is proceeding by way of court action, those proceedings will be stayed if the tenant pays all the arrears plus the landlord's costs before the hearing. In certain cases, the tenant may also apply for relief within 6 months from the landlord's recovery of possession, although the rules differ between the High

Court and county court. Where the landlord is proceeding by way of peaceable re-entry, the tenant may still apply to the court for relief. Again, the tenant will have to pay the arrears and must, as a general rule, apply within 6 months of re-entry by the landlord (although in exceptional circumstances the court may be prepared to grant relief outside this period: *Thatcher v CH Pearce & Sons (Contractors) Ltd* [1968] 1 WLR 748).

33.5.3 Forfeiture for breach of other covenants

Before a landlord is able to forfeit for a breach of covenant, other than for the payment of rent, the landlord must normally serve a notice on the tenant under s 146 of the LPA 1925. Where there has been an unlawful assignment, the notice should be served on the unlawful assignee.

A s 146 notice must:

(1) specify the breach;
(2) require it to be remedied within a reasonable time, if it is capable of being remedied; and
(3) require the tenant to pay compensation for the breach, if the landlord so requires.

As far as the second requirement is concerned, the notice will be invalid if the landlord wrongly takes the view that the breach is irremediable and, therefore, does not require the tenant to remedy it within a reasonable time. Whether a breach is remediable is a question of fact in each case. As a general rule, breach of a positive covenant is usually remediable by the tenant doing that which he has left undone. Thus, for example, it has been held that breach of a covenant requiring the tenant to reconstruct the premises by a stated date, was capable of being remedied by the tenant carrying out the work within a reasonable time (*Expert Clothing Service & Sales Ltd v Hillgate House Ltd* [1986] Ch 340). With negative covenants the issue is less clear. Views have been expressed in the past that breaches of negative covenants can never be remedied; once the forbidden act has been done it cannot be undone. However, current thinking is that the breach of some negative covenants can be remedied. Where, for example, the tenant has erected advertisement hoardings in breach of covenant, the removal of them would, it is submitted, remedy the breach. On the other hand, it has been held that certain breaches of negative covenants cannot be remedied. Thus, the breach of an alienation covenant, a covenant against immoral user and a covenant against trading without the appropriate licences have all been held to be irremediable (see generally *Expert Clothing Service & Sales Ltd v Hillgate House Ltd* above, and *Scala House & District Property Co Ltd v Forbes* [1974] QB 575). If the landlord is in any doubt about whether a particular breach can be remedied, the notice should require the tenant to remedy the breach 'if it is capable of remedy'.

If the tenant does not comply with the requirements of a valid s 146 notice, the landlord may proceed to forfeit the lease by court proceedings or peaceable re-entry. In either case the tenant may be able to seek relief from forfeiture but there is a vital difference between the two methods. If the landlord takes court proceedings, the tenant can seek relief at any time before the landlord actually re-enters the premises: no relief can be granted afterwards. However, if the landlord re-enters peaceably, the tenant can seek relief even after the landlord has re-entered, though the court will take into account all the circumstances including any delay by the tenant in seeking relief (*Billson v Residential Apartments Ltd* [1992] 1 AC 494).

In deciding whether or not to grant relief, the court will have regard to the conduct of the parties and all other relevant circumstances. If relief is granted, it will be granted on such terms as the court thinks fit (LPA 1925, s 146(2)). This gives the court a very wide discretion and the House of Lords has refused to lay down any rigid rules on its exercise. Relief is usually granted where the breach has been remedied and is unlikely to re-occur.

Where the s 146 notice relates to internal decorative repairs, the tenant has a special right to apply to the court for relief under s 147 of the LPA 1925. This is separate from the general right to apply for relief under s 146. Under s 147, the court may wholly or partially relieve the tenant from liability for internal decorative repairs if, having regard to all the circumstances of the case and in particular the length of the tenant's term still unexpired, it thinks the notice is unreasonable. However, s 147 does not apply:

(1) where the liability is under an express covenant to put the property in a decorative state of repair which has never been performed; or
(2) to any matter necessary or proper for keeping the property in a sanitary condition, or for the maintenance or preservation of the structure; or
(3) to any statutory liability to keep a house fit for human habitation; or
(4) to any covenant to yield up the premises in a specified state of repair at the end of the term.

Three special cases

(1) Where the breach by the tenant is of a repairing covenant, a special procedure may apply. If the lease was granted for 7 or more years and still has 3 or more to run, the s 146 notice must also contain a notice of the tenant's right to serve a counter-notice within 28 days. If this is served, the landlord cannot proceed to forfeit without leave of the court. Such leave is only granted on specified grounds (Leasehold Property (Repairs) Act 1938, see **31.1.2**).
(2) A lease will usually give the landlord the right to forfeit upon the tenant's bankruptcy (or liquidation) or having the lease taken in execution. If the landlord wishes to forfeit, he need only serve a s 146 notice and the tenant may only apply for relief during the first year following the bankruptcy or taking in execution. However, there is an important exception to this rule. If, during that first year, the trustee or liquidator sells the lease, the s 146 protection lasts indefinitely. Without such an exception, it would be difficult for the trustee or liquidator to find a buyer for the lease because of the risk of forfeiture taking place after the expiration of the first year without the service of a s 146 notice and with no right to seek relief.
(3) Exceptionally, there is no need for the landlord to serve a s 146 notice following bankruptcy, liquidation or taking in execution, and the tenant has no right to apply for relief if the lease is of:
    (a) agricultural land;
    (b) mines or minerals;
    (c) a public house;
    (d) a furnished house;
    (e) any premises where the personal qualifications of the tenant are important for the preservation of the nature or character of the premises or on the ground of neighbourhood to the landlord or anyone holding under him.

33.5.4 Position of sub-tenants and mortgagees on forfeiture

If the head-lease is forfeited, this will automatically end any sub-lease. This is unfair to sub-tenants who stand to lose their interest through no fault of their own. In order to protect sub-tenants in this situation, s 146(4) enables them to apply for relief against forfeiture of the head-lease even in those cases where the head tenant is unable to do so. The granting of relief is entirely at the discretion of the court which can impose such conditions as it thinks fit and may, for example, require the sub-tenant to comply with the terms of the head-lease. If the court grants relief, the sub-tenant will become the immediate tenant of the landlord but cannot be granted a longer term than that remaining under the sub-lease. Difficult problems can arise where the sub-lease is of part only of the premises comprised in the head-lease. The view has sometimes been expressed that the sub-tenant may, as a condition of granting relief, have to take a new lease of all the property comprised in the head-lease or pay the arrears of rent relating to the whole.

An important example of the operation of s 146(4) arises in the case of a mortgagee of a lease. Lenders (whether by sub-demise or legal charge) are sub-tenants for the purposes of the sub-section and can thus apply for relief from forfeiture of the lease (see *United Dominion Trust Ltd v Shellpoint Trustees* [1993] EGCS 57, as to the time within which relief must be sought by lenders).

33.6 SURRENDER

Surrender occurs where a tenant relinquishes his lease to his immediate landlord, with his landlord's consent. The lease will merge in the reversion and be extinguished. Surrender can be express or by operation of law. An express surrender must generally be made by deed. Surrender by operation of law occurs where the parties act in a way which is inconsistent with the continuance of the lease. For example, a surrender will occur if the parties agree a new lease to commence during the currency of the existing lease. A similar situation occurs if the tenant gives up possession and returns the key to the landlord and the landlord accepts this as surrender. However, surrender requires the agreement of both parties. If the key is merely left with the landlord, this in itself will not amount to surrender unless the landlord accepts it as surrender, for example, by re-letting the premises.

If a lease protected under Part II of the LTA 1954 requires the tenant to offer to surrender the lease before seeking consent to assign, the landlord's acceptance of that offer may be void under s 38 (*Allnatt London Properties Ltd v Newton* [1984] 1 All ER 423, and see **34.1.5**).

33.6.1 Effect of surrender

A surrender will release the tenant from any future liability under the lease but not in respect of past breaches. A well-advised tenant should, therefore, seek a release from all breaches.

The surrender of a head-lease will not affect any sub-lease. The sub-tenant will become the immediate tenant of the head landlord on the terms of the sub-lease. Sometimes, a head tenant will agree to surrender his head-lease with a view to taking a new fixed term from his landlord; this may happen where the head-lease is coming to the end of its fixed term. In this situation, any new head-lease granted following the surrender will be subject to the sub-lease (LPA 1925, s 150).

33.7 MERGER

Merger occurs where a tenant acquires his immediate landlord's reversion or a third party acquires both the lease and the immediate reversion. In such a case the lease will end. However, merger will only take place where the person acquiring both the lease and immediate reversion holds both estates in the same capacity and intends merger to take place.

As with surrender, merger of a lease will not affect the position of any sub-tenant.

Chapter 34

THE LANDLORD AND TENANT ACT 1954, PART II

Chapter 34 contents

34.1 INTRODUCTORY MATTERS

34.1.1 The protection of the Act

The principal Act conferring security of tenure on business tenants and regulating the manner in which business tenancies can be terminated is Part II of the LTA 1954 (statutory references in this chapter are to this Act, unless otherwise stated). The protection given to tenants covered by the Act is twofold. First, a business tenancy will not come to an end at the expiration of a fixed term, nor can a periodic tenancy be terminated by the landlord serving an ordinary notice to quit. Instead, notwithstanding the ending of the contractual term, the tenancy will be automatically continued under s 24 until such time as it is terminated in one of the ways specified in the Act. Secondly, upon the expiration of a business tenancy in accordance with the Act, business tenants normally have a statutory right to apply to court for a new tenancy and the landlord may only oppose that application on certain statutory grounds. Any new tenancy granted will also enjoy the protection of the Act.

34.1.2 The application of the Act

Section 23(1) provides that:

> 'this Act applies to any tenancy where the property comprised in the tenancy is or includes premises which are occupied by the tenant and are so occupied for the purposes of a business carried on by him or for those and other purposes.'

This involves a number of elements.

There must be a 'tenancy'

Tenancy includes an agreement for a lease and an underlease (even an unauthorised one). However, licences are not protected. The lease/licence distinction is further considered at **10.4**. In view of the danger for landlords in inadvertently creating a protected tenancy, the use of licences as a means of avoiding the Act needs very careful consideration. Certain tenancies are specifically excluded from the protection of the Act and these are dealt with at **34.1.3**.

The premises must be occupied by the tenant

Occupation need not be by the tenant personally. It has been held that occupation may be sufficient where it is conducted through the medium of a manager or agent provided that such representative occupation is genuine and not a sham arrangement. If, however, the premises are occupied by a company owned by the tenant, this will not be sufficient because it is the company, a separate legal entity, which is the occupier rather than the tenant. Occupation need not be continuous provided that the 'thread of continuity' of business user is not broken (*Hancock & Willis v GMS Syndicate Ltd* (1982) 265 EG 473).

Problems may arise where a business tenant sub-lets part of the property to a business sub-tenant. In such a situation, they cannot both qualify for protection in respect of the sub-let part; there can be no dual occupation for the purposes of the Act. In normal circumstances, it will be the sub-tenant who enjoys the protection of the Act although in an exceptional case the head tenant may reserve sufficiently extensive rights over the sub-let part that he remains the occupier (see *Graysim Holdings Ltd v P & O Property Holdings Ltd* [1996] 03 EG 124).

Special rules on occupation apply where a tenancy is held on trust, vested in partners as trustees or held by a member of a group of companies (ss 41, 41A and 42).

The premises must be occupied for the purposes of a business carried on by the tenant

'Business' is widely defined in s 23 to include a 'trade, profession or employment and includes any activity carried on by a body of persons, whether corporate or unincorporate'. Where the business is carried on by an individual, it must amount to a trade, profession or employment; but where it is carried on by a body of persons (corporate or unincorporate) 'any activity' may suffice. Thus, it has been held that the organising of a tennis club and the activities of the governors in running a hospital, both amounted to a business use (*Addiscombe Garden Estates v Crabbe* [1958] 1 QB 513 and *Hills (Patents) Ltd v University College Hospital Board of Governors* [1956] 1 QB 90). This does not mean however that the Act will apply whenever the tenant is a body of persons; the 'activity' must be correlative to the conceptions involved in the words 'trade, profession or employment'.

Two problem areas may arise with this requirement:

(1) The demised premises will sometimes be used for two purposes, only one of which is a business user. For example, the letting may consist of a shop on the ground floor with living accommodation above. Does the Act still apply? In cases of mixed user the Act will apply provided the business activity is a significant purpose of the occupation and not merely incidental to the occupation of the premises as a residence (*Cheryl Investments Ltd v Saldhana* [1978] 1 WLR 1329 and *Gurton v Parrot* [1991] 1 EGLR 98). In the example mentioned, the Act is likely to apply. If, however, a residential tenant occasionally brought work home with him this would not result in his tenancy being protected under the Act.

(2) The business user may be in breach of a covenant of the lease. How does that affect the tenant's rights? If the lease merely forbids a specific business use (eg not to use the shop as a newsagents), or any use except the business use specified (eg not to use the premises for any purpose other than as a newsagents), a business use in breach of such a provision will not deprive the tenant of the protection of the Act. However, s 24(3) does exclude from protection any tenancy where the use of the premises for business purposes is in breach of a general prohibition preventing all business use (eg not to carry on any business, trade, profession or employment) although if the landlord had consented to or acquiesced in the breach, the Act would still apply.

34.1.3 Exclusions from the Act

Apart from those tenancies which fail to satisfy the requirements of s 23, there are other tenancies which are not protected by the Act. These include:

(1) tenancies at will. In *Javad v Aqil* [1991] 1 WLR 1007, a prospective tenant who was allowed into possession while negotiations proceeded for the grant of a new business lease was held, on the facts, to be a tenant at will, and thus excluded from protection;
(2) tenancies of agricultural holdings: these have their own form of protection under the Agricultural Holdings Act 1986;
(3) a farm business tenancy;
(4) mining leases;
(5) service tenancies. These are tenancies granted to the holder of an office, appointment or employment from the landlord and which continue only so long as the tenant holds such office etc. For the exclusion to apply the tenancy must be in writing and express the purpose for which it was granted;
(6) fixed-term tenancies not exceeding 6 months. These tenancies are excluded unless the tenancy contains provisions for renewing the term or extending it beyond 6 months, or the tenant (including any predecessor in the same business) has already been in occupation for a period exceeding 12 months;
(7) 'contracted out' tenancies (see **34.1.5**).

34.1.4 Two important definitions

The competent landlord

It is between the tenant and the competent landlord that the procedure under the Act must be conducted. It is important, therefore, that the tenant identifies his competent landlord and deals with him. Where a freeholder grants a lease, there is no cause for concern as the tenant's competent landlord can be no other than the freeholder. However, where the tenant is a sub-tenant, the statutory definition of competent landlord means that the sub-tenant's immediate landlord may not be his competent landlord. Using s 44 of the Act, the sub-tenant must look up the chain of superior tenancies for the first person who either owns the freehold or who has a superior tenancy which will not come to an end within 14 months. The following examples may assist:

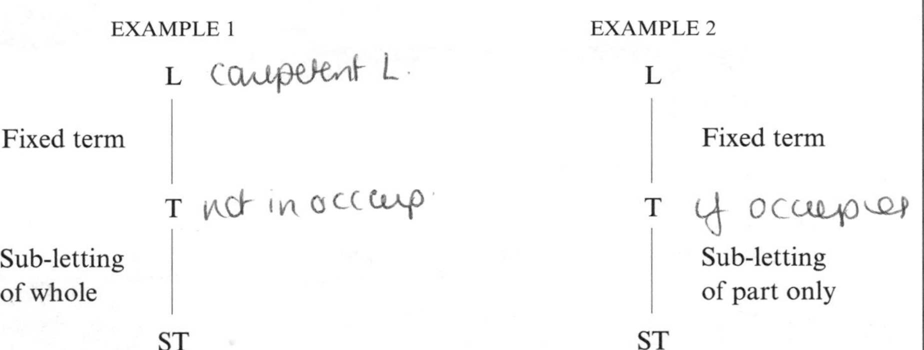

As the first example involves a sub-letting of the whole of the premises, T will not be in occupation, and will not, therefore, enjoy the protection of the Act. This means that the head-lease will come to an end on its contractual expiry date, with the result that as soon as the head-lease has entered the last 14 months of its contractual term, ST's competent landlord will be the freeholder. However, in the second example, because it is a sub-letting of part only, then provided T occupies the remaining part for business purposes, the head-lease will be protected. Therefore, it will not expire by effluxion of time. So even if the head-lease has entered the last 14 months of its contractual term, the sub-tenant's competent landlord will still be T (unless, eg the freeholder has served an appropriate notice terminating the head-lease within 14 months, see **34.2.1**).

It is, therefore, very important for sub-tenants to identify their competent landlord and this can be done by serving a notice on their immediate landlord under s 40 of the Act seeking information about the landlord's interest. A s 40 notice should always be served by a sub-tenant before taking any other steps under the Act.

The 'holding'

The definition of the holding is important because the tenant's right to a new lease normally only extends to that part of the premises known as the 'holding'. Further, many of the landlord's grounds of opposition refer to the holding. This term is defined in s 23(3) of the Act as being the property comprised in the current tenancy excluding any part which is not occupied by the tenant or a person employed by the tenant for the purposes of the tenant's business. In practice, in the majority of cases, it is correct to describe the holding as comprising all the premises originally let except those parts which the tenant is currently sub-letting.

34.1.5 Contracting out

As a general rule, s 38(1) forbids any contracting out of the Act. This means that any agreement purporting to exclude or modify the tenant's security of tenure is void. However, under s 38(4) of the Act the court is empowered to make an order excluding the security of tenure provisions, provided certain conditions are satisfied:

(1) the proposed letting must be for a term of years certain (the definition of a term of years certain does not include a tenancy for 12 months and thereafter from year to year: *Nicholas v Kinsey* [1994] 16 EG 145); and
(2) there must be a joint application to court by both parties.

Further, and most importantly, the court's approval must be obtained before the tenancy is granted (*Essexcrest Ltd v Evenlex Ltd* [1988] 1 EGLR 69).

Section 38(1) also renders void an agreement to surrender a business tenancy in the future, without the court's approval. Thus, where the terms of the lease require the tenant to offer to surrender the lease before seeking consent to assign, any resulting agreement to surrender will be void and unenforceable (*Allnatt London Properties Ltd v Newton* [1984] 1 All ER 423).

34.1.6 Continuation tenancies

A business tenancy protected by the Act will not come to an end on the expiry of the contractual term. Instead, s 24 continues the tenancy on exactly the same terms (except those relating to termination) and at exactly the same rent until it is terminated in accordance with the Act. However, the landlord may be able to obtain an increased rent by asking the court to fix an interim rent under s 24A (see **34.4**).

If the tenant wishes to leave and thus does not want his tenancy to be continued in this manner, he can prevent this happening by serving an appropriate notice upon his landlord under s 27 of the Act (see **34.2**).

Section 24 continues the tenancy, but does it also continue the liability of the original tenant (or any previous assignees who have given direct covenants) for breaches committed by an assignee during the continuation tenancy? This was the question which arose in *City of London Corporation v Fell* and *Herbert Duncan Ltd v*

Cluttons [1993] 04 EG 115. In both these cases the original tenant was sued by the landlord for arrears of rent that had accrued during the continuation tenancy due to non-payment by an assignee. The court decided that if the original tenant had covenanted to pay rent during the contractual term only, the landlord was unable to recover from him any rent accruing after that date. However, had the covenant been worded so that the original tenant was liable to pay rent during any statutory extension of the contractual term, the landlord would have been able to recover accordingly. Further, even if the lease had been drafted so that the tenant was bound to pay rent during the statutory continuation, this did not extend to any interim rent ordered by the court. Landlords must bear these points in mind when defining the term of the lease.

34.2 TERMINATION UNDER THE ACT

A tenancy protected under the Act will not end automatically at the expiration of a lease for a fixed term nor, if it is a periodic tenancy, can it be ended by an ordinary notice to quit given by the landlord. Instead, such a tenancy can only be terminated in one of the ways prescribed by the Act:

(1) by the service of a landlord's statutory notice (a 's 25 notice');
(2) by the tenant's request in statutory form (a 's 26 request');
(3) forfeiture (or forfeiture of a superior tenancy);
(4) surrender. To be valid the surrender must take immediate effect;
(5) by the tenant giving the landlord a notice to quit, unless this was given before the tenant has been in occupation for a period of one month;
(6) where the lease is for a fixed term, by written notice under s 27 of the Act, served by the tenant upon the landlord at least 3 months before the contractual expiry date. If the time for serving this notice has already passed, then the tenant will have to give 3 months' written notice expiring on any quarter day. However, the case of *Esselte AB v Pearl Assurance plc* [1997] 02 EG 124 shows that if the tenant ceases to occupy the premises for business purposes on or before the contractual expiry date, the lease will come to an end by effluxion of time and a s 27 notice is not needed.

It is the first two of the above methods, the s 25 notice and s 26 request, which are the usual methods of terminating a protected business tenancy.

34.2.1 Section 25 notices

Form

If such a notice is to be effective, it must be in the prescribed form and be given to the tenant by the competent landlord not less than 6 months, nor more than 12 months, before the date of termination specified in it. The prescribed form is contained in the Landlord and Tenant Act 1954, Part II (Notices) Regulations 1983 as amended by the Landlord and Tenant Act 1954, Part II (Notices) (Amendment) Regulations 1989, although a form 'substantially to the like effect' can be used instead.

A tenant will often seek to attack the validity of his landlord's notice on the ground that it is not in the correct form. The task of the court in these circumstances is to ascertain whether the notice served is substantially the same as the prescribed form. In doing this, any omission from the notice of matters irrelevant to the tenant's rights or obligations may not affect the validity of the notice. However, if the court decides that the notice is not the same as, or substantially to the same effect as, the prescribed form, it is irrelevant that the recipient did not suffer any prejudice: the notice will be invalid (*Sabella Ltd v Montgomery* [1998] 09 EG 153).

In *Smith v Draper* [1990] 2 EGLR 69, it was held that a landlord who had served what turned out to be an invalid notice, could withdraw it and serve a second valid notice.

Content

The notice must comply with the following requirements:

(1) The notice must state the date upon which the landlord wants the tenancy to end. The specified termination date must not be earlier than the date on which the tenancy could have been terminated at common law (and, as mentioned above, the notice must be given not less than 6 months, nor more than 12 months, before this specified termination date).

For a periodic tenancy or a fixed term with a break clause, the specified termination date cannot be earlier than the date upon which the landlord could have ended the tenancy with an ordinary common law notice. If there is a break clause, it would appear that a separate contractual notice is unnecessary provided the s 25 notice states a date for termination no earlier than the date the break clause would operate (*Scholl Manufacturing Ltd v Clifton (Slim-Line) Ltd* [1967] Ch 41). If the tenancy is for a fixed term without a break clause, the specified termination date cannot be earlier than the last day of the contractual term. If, however, the contractual tenancy has already expired and the tenancy is being continued under the Act, the s 25 notice need only comply with the 6–12-month rule mentioned above.

(2) The notice must require the tenant within 2 months after the giving of the notice to notify his landlord, in writing, whether or not he is willing to give up possession of the premises on the specified termination date. Thus, the service of a s 25 notice always requires a response from the tenant. This is in the form of a tenant's 'counter-notice'.

(3) The notice must state whether or not the landlord will oppose an application to court by the tenant for the grant of a new tenancy and, if so, on which statutory ground(s). The tenant has the right to apply to court for a new tenancy but the landlord can oppose that application on one or more of the seven grounds of opposition set out in s 30 of the Act (see **34.5**). If this is the landlord's intention, he must state in his s 25 notice the ground(s) upon which he intends to rely. As there is no provision in the Act allowing the landlord to amend his notice, the choice of ground(s) is a matter which must be given very careful consideration.

It will not be in every case that the landlord states a ground of opposition. Often the landlord will be quite happy with the tenant's presence and is seeking to end the current tenancy simply with a view to negotiating a new tenancy upon different terms, for example, at an increased rent. In this type of situation the landlord should consult a valuer and obtain expert advice before proceeding further.

(4) The notice must relate to the whole of the premises contained in the lease. A s 25 notice cannot relate to part only of the demised premises (*Southport Old*

Links Ltd v Naylor [1985] 1 EGLR 66, and see also *M & P Enterprises (London) Ltd v Norfolk Square Hotels Ltd* [1994] 1 EGLR 129).

(5) The notice must be given and signed by, or on behalf of, the landlord. If there are joint landlords, all their names must be given (*Pearson v Alyo* [1990] 1 EGLR 114).

34.2.2 Section 26 requests

Rather than wait for the landlord to serve a s 25 notice, the tenant can sometimes take the initiative and request a new tenancy from his landlord under s 26 of the Act. However, the tenant must remember that the sooner there is a new tenancy, the sooner the new rent will be payable, which may be higher than the rent payable under the old tenancy. Nevertheless, there are situations where the service of a request by the tenant has tactical advantages for him.

Not all tenants can request a new tenancy. A request cannot be served if the landlord has already served a s 25 notice. Further, a request is only possible where the tenant's current lease was granted for a term of years exceeding one year (or during its continuance under s 24). This will exclude both periodic tenants and those with fixed terms of one year or less; although these tenants still enjoy security of tenure.

Form

To be valid, the request must be in the prescribed form as laid down in the Landlord and Tenant Act 1954, Part II (Notices) Regulations 1983 and served on the competent landlord. As with the s 25 notice, a form 'substantially to the like effect' can be used instead.

Content

The request must comply with the following requirements:

(1) it must state the date on which the new tenancy is to begin. The current tenancy will terminate on that date. This date must not be more than 12 months nor less than 6 months after the making of the request, and cannot be earlier than the date on which the tenancy could have been terminated at common law;

(2) it must give the tenant's proposals as to:

  (a) the property to be comprised in the new tenancy, which must be either the whole or part of the property comprised in the current tenancy;

  (b) the proposed new rent. This issue requires the advice of a valuer;

  (c) the other terms of the tenancy (eg as to duration);

(3) the request must be signed by or on behalf of all the tenants.

A landlord who is unwilling to grant a new tenancy must, within 2 months of receipt of the request, give notice to the tenant that he will oppose any application to court for a new lease stating on which statutory ground(s) of opposition he intends to rely. This is effected by means of a landlord's counter-notice (see **34.2.3**).

As with a s 25 notice, the landlord must choose his ground(s) of opposition with care because he will be confined to those stated in his counter-notice.

If the tenant serves a valid s 26 request and then fails to apply to court for a new tenancy within time (see **34.3**), he will not be allowed to withdraw it and serve a new one with a view to complying with the time-limit the second time since the effect of the s 26 request was to fix the date of termination of the tenancy (*Stile Hall Properties Ltd v Gooch* [1979] 3 All ER 848).

Reasons for making a request

Usually a tenant is best advised not to make a request because it is not always in a tenant's interest to bring his current tenancy to an end. However, there are some situations in which it might be advisable. For example:

(1) if the rent payable under the current tenancy is more than that presently achievable in the open market. In a falling market like this the landlord is unlikely to serve a s 25 notice, as it is in his interests to let the existing tenancy continue under the Act. Therefore, the tenant should give careful consideration to ending the current tenancy and obtaining a new one at a reduced rent;

(2) if, as is more often the case, the current rent is less than the present market rent, it is in the tenant's interest to prolong the tenancy for as long as possible. In this case the tenant may be able to make what is sometimes called a pre-emptive strike. Say the lease is contractually due to expire on 30 September. In the previous March the landlord is considering serving a s 25 notice with a view to bringing the tenancy to an end on 30 September and negotiating a new tenancy at an increased rent. If the tenant knows or suspects the landlord's plans, he can, before the landlord has acted, serve a request specifying sometime in the following March as the date for the new tenancy. The tenant has thus achieved an extra 6 months at the old rent;

(3) if the tenant has plans to improve the premises, he may prefer the certainty of a new fixed term as opposed to the uncertainty of a statutory continuation;

(4) if the tenant has plans to sell the lease, a buyer would prefer the security of a new fixed term rather than the uncertainty of a statutory continuation.

34.2.3 Counter-notices

The tenant's counter-notice

Within 2 months of receipt of the landlord's s 25 notice the tenant must notify the landlord in writing whether or not he is willing to give up possession by service of a counter-notice. There is no prescribed form: a letter will suffice. A tenant who has served a counter-notice, stating his willingness to give up possession, is irrevocably bound by it.

If the tenant fails to serve a counter-notice within 2 months, he loses the right to apply to court for a new tenancy and, therefore, it must be served even where the landlord has stated that he would not oppose any application to court for a new tenancy. If no counter-notice is served, the tenant's occupation beyond the specified termination date would depend entirely on the willingness of the landlord to grant a new tenancy on such terms as the landlord pleases. However, cases like *Kammins Ballrooms Co Ltd v Zenith Investments (Torquay) Ltd* [1971] AC 850) and *JT Developments v Quinn* [1991] 2 EGLR 257 suggest that in appropriate circumstances it may be possible for a tenant to contend that the landlord's conduct has amounted to a waiver of strict adherence to the time-limit. Notwithstanding cases like this, it is of the utmost importance that tenants always serve a proper counter-notice. Failure to do so may lead to an action by the tenant against his solicitor in negligence.

The landlord's counter-notice

The service of a s 26 request by the tenant will require a counter-notice by the landlord if he wishes to oppose the tenant's application to court for a new tenancy. This must state any ground(s) of opposition that the landlord intends to rely on to oppose the tenant's application (see **34.5**). If the landlord fails to serve a counter-notice within 2 months of receipt of the tenant's request, he will lose his right to raise any ground of opposition to the tenant's application to court for a new tenancy although he will be allowed to raise issues relating to the terms of the new tenancy.

A landlord who has served a counter-notice stating that he will not oppose the tenant's application for a new tenancy will be bound by that decision. Similarly, the landlord cannot later amend his stated grounds of opposition.

There is no prescribed form of counter-notice but it should be unequivocal and in writing.

34.2.4 Service of notices and requests

Notices and requests given under the Act require service. Section 23(1) of the LTA 1927 provides for personal service or by leaving the notice at the last known place of abode (which includes the place of business of the person to be served, *Price v West London Investment Building Society* [1964] 2 All ER 318), or by sending it through the post by registered or (as now applies) recorded delivery. Service on a company may be effected at its registered office (s 725 of the Companies Act 1985). The effect of complying with one of the methods of service laid down in the LTA 1927 is that there is a presumption of service so that it does not matter that the recorded delivery letter may not have been received by the intended recipient because it went astray in the post. Other methods of service may be effective (eg the ordinary post) if in fact the notice is received by the person to whom it has been given. But the risk is that the letter may be lost in the post, in which case, notice will not have been given. The question also arises as to the date on which the notice is treated as having been served. In *Railtrack plc v Gojra* [1998] 08 EG 158 it was held that if the registered or recorded delivery method is used (both being methods laid down in the LTA 1927), the notice (or request) is served on the date on which it is posted. When, however, notice is sent through the ordinary post it is served on the date of receipt.

34.3 THE TENANT'S APPLICATION TO COURT

34.3.1 The need for an application

It will become apparent after service of a s 25 notice or counter-notice to a s 26 request, whether or not the landlord is willing to grant a new tenancy. Where a s 25 notice has been served, the contents will have told the tenant whether or not the landlord intends to oppose his application. If the tenant initiated the termination procedure with a s 26 request, the landlord will have responded with a counter-notice if he is not prepared to grant a new tenancy.

If the tenant wants a new tenancy the next stage is for him to apply to court not less than 2 months, nor more than 4 months after the service of the landlord's s 25 notice or tenant's s 26 request, as the case may be. Where a s 25 notice has been served, the tenant will only be able to make an application if he has served a valid counter-notice stating that he is unwilling to give up possession. The need to make this application applies even where the landlord has indicated his willingness to grant a new tenancy and the parties are near to agreement. Unless the parties have already entered into a binding lease the tenant must always apply to court at the appropriate time otherwise he will lose the right to a new tenancy. Often the proceedings are adjourned and there will only be a hearing if the negotiations break down. If, on the other hand, the landlord has stated his opposition to the grant of a new tenancy, clearly the tenant must apply to court as this is the only way he may obtain a new lease.

34.3.2 The application

The High Court and County Courts Jurisdiction Order 1991 confers unlimited jurisdiction on the county court in respect of the tenant's application. Thus, applications may be commenced in either the High Court or, as is more usual, in the county court.

The application must be made not less than 2 months, nor more than 4 months after the service of the landlord's s 25 notice or tenant's s 26 request, as the case may be. Commencement in the first or second month is bad as being too early. Similarly, commencement in the fifth or sixth month is bad as being too late. The tenant must apply in either the third month or the fourth month after the notice or request was served. It is very important that the tenant complies strictly with these time-limits because the court has no power to extend them. However, it has been held that because the time-limits are procedural in nature the parties may themselves waive them (*Kammins Ballrooms Co Ltd v Zenith Investments (Torquay) Ltd* [1971] AC 850 and *Saloman v Akiens* [1993] 14 EG 97). If, therefore, the tenant fails to apply to court in time, his ability to make an out-of-time application will depend on him being able to show waiver on the landlord's part. An analysis of the relevant case-law shows that this will not always be easy for the tenant to establish and emphasises the importance of applying at the correct time (see, eg *Stevens & Cutting Ltd v Anderson* [1990] 11 EG 70, where the issue of estoppel was also discussed).

In 1981, The Law Society recommended a form of agreement which a landlord and tenant might enter into if they wished to defer commencement of proceedings, for example, pending negotiations (see the Law Society *Gazette* [1981] 853, and [1989] 10). Notwithstanding this possibility, many practitioners take the view that the safest course of action is for the tenant always to apply to court within the statutory time-limit. If such an agreement is made, it should not defer proceedings beyond the date specified in the s 25 notice or s 26 request.

Following the tenant's application to court it is advisable to protect the application by registration of a pending land action under the Land Charges Act 1972. This will make the tenant's application binding on a buyer of the reversion. Where the landlord's title is registered the application may be an overriding interest under the Land Registration Act 1925, s 70(1)(g), but it would nevertheless be prudent to register a caution against the reversionary title.

34.3.3 Service of process and the landlord's response

The originating summons (High Court) or originating application (county court) must be served on the competent landlord within 2 months of issue (RSC Ord 97, r 6; CCR Ord 43, r 6). The relevant court can extend the period for service but this power is exercised sparingly.

In the county court, the landlord must file an answer to the application within 14 days after service upon him. Failure to do so may lead to the landlord being unable to oppose the grant of a new tenancy although he may still be heard on its terms (see *Desbroderie Ltd v Segalov* (1956) 106 LJ 764).

34.4 INTERIM RENTS

34.4.1 The need for an interim rent

Where the tenant has validly applied to court for a new tenancy, his current tenancy will not terminate on the date specified in the s 25 notice or s 26 request. Instead, s 64 of the Act provides that the current tenancy will be continued at the old contractual rent until 3 months after the proceedings are concluded. As the Act was originally drafted there was thus an incentive for tenants to delay proceedings as much as possible, because the longer the current tenancy lasted the longer the old rent (which was usually below current market rents) remained payable. This was unfair to landlords particularly in those cases where, due to the effects of inflation, there was a substantial difference between the old contractual rent and the rent presently achievable in the open market. As a result of this unfairness, s 24A was inserted into the Act by the Law of Property Act 1969. This gives the court a discretion, on the application of the competent landlord, to determine an 'interim rent' to be substituted for the old contractual rent until such time as the current tenancy ceases. This interim rent is payable from the date on which the landlord applies for it or the termination date specified in the s 25 notice or s 26 request, whichever is the later.

34.4.2 Amount

The interim rent is an open market rent which is assessed by the court in the same way as the rent under the new tenancy. However, there are reasons why the interim rent is usually less than the open market rent:

(1) Section 24A requires the court to assess the interim rent on the basis of a yearly tenancy, whilst the rent payable under the new lease is usually assessed on the basis of a term of years. And market rents under yearly tenancies are usually less than under fixed terms, since the latter guarantee tenants a more substantial period of occupation.

(2) The court is obliged to have regard to the rent payable under the current tenancy. This is so that the court can exercise a discretion to 'cushion' the tenant from too harsh a blow in moving from the old out-of-date contractual rent to the new rent (see *English Exporters (London) Ltd v Eldonwall Ltd* [1973] Ch 415). However, a 'cushion' does not have to be provided in every case. The court has a discretion which it may use to specify the full market rent, especially in those cases where the tenant has already benefited from a low contractual rent for a long time (see, eg *Department of the Environment v Allied Freehold Property Trust Ltd* [1992] 45 EG 156).

In a falling market, landlords should give careful consideration to the possibility of the interim rent being less than the contractual rent. In such a situation, landlords should seek specialist valuation advice before making the application.

34.4.3 Avoiding s 24A

Whilst the introduction of interim rents has been a step in the right direction for landlords, many still feel that the application of the 'cushion' can produce unfairness. Accordingly, the landlord may be able to avoid s 24A altogether by including a penultimate day rent review in the lease. This would revise the contractual rent just before the contractual term expired. In such a case the harshness of changing from the old rent to the new rent would be suffered during the contractual term without the imposition of any 'cushion'. Tenants, on the other hand, will wish to resist such a clause.

Another way of avoiding s 24A would be for the landlord, at the lease-drafting stage, to make it clear that the contractual rent review provisions are to continue to apply notwithstanding the ending of the contractual term. Careful drafting would be required to achieve this but the case of *Willison v Cheverell Estates Ltd* [1996] 26 EG 113 indicates that this is another possibility for the landlord.

34.5 GROUNDS OF OPPOSITION

When the landlord serves his s 25 notice or counter-notice in response to the tenant's s 26 request, he must, if he is intending to oppose the grant of a new tenancy, set out one or more of the seven grounds of opposition in s 30 of the Act. The landlord can only rely on the stated ground(s); no later amendment is allowed.

If the landlord has stated a ground of opposition and the tenant's application proceeds to a hearing, a 'split trial' will usually be ordered with the question of opposition being dealt with first as a preliminary issue. Only if the ground is not made out will the terms of the new tenancy be dealt with.

The statutory grounds of opposition are all contained in s 30(1) of the Act and, as will be seen, some of the grounds ((a), (b), (c) and (e)), confer a discretion on the court whether or not to order a new tenancy even if the ground is made out.

34.5.1 Ground (a): tenant's failure to repair

The landlord can oppose the tenant's application for a new tenancy on the ground of the tenant's failure to repair the holding. To succeed, the landlord will have to show that the tenant was under an obligation to repair or maintain them and that the tenant is in breach of that obligation. Problems can arise where the repairing obligation is divided between the landlord and tenant, for example, where the landlord is responsible for the exterior and the tenant for the interior of the premises. In such cases, an inspection will be necessary to determine the party in breach. The ground only applies to failure to repair the holding (see **34.1.4**), and not to the disrepair of another part of the demised premises not forming part of the tenant's holding (eg where the tenant has sub-let part and it is that part which is in disrepair).

This is one of the discretionary grounds and the landlord is only likely to succeed if the tenant's breaches are both serious and unremedied at the date of the hearing.

As an alternative, the landlord may be able to commence forfeiture proceedings to terminate the tenancy; this being one of the permitted methods of termination under the Act. This remedy may be available throughout the term and while the tenant may apply for relief, this will usually only be granted if the tenant rectifies the breach.

34.5.2 Ground (b): persistent delay in paying rent

The requirement of 'persistent delay' suggests that the tenant must have fallen into arrears on more than one occasion. However, the rent need not be substantially in arrears nor need the arrears last a long time. Indeed, there need not be any arrears at the date of the hearing; the court will look at the whole history of payment. Again, this is one of the discretionary grounds and the court is entitled to take into account the likelihood of future arrears arising should a new tenancy be ordered. The tenant should, therefore, consider offering to provide a surety for any new lease ordered.

34.5.3 Ground (c): substantial breaches of other obligations

Discretionary ground (c) requires other substantial breaches by the tenant of his obligations in the lease, or some other reason connected with the tenant's use or management of the holding. Any breach of an obligation may be relied upon by the landlord (eg breach of the user covenant) but the breach must be substantial and this will be a question of fact and degree. The ground also extends to reasons connected with the tenant's use or management of the holding and this has been held to include carrying on a use in breach of planning control.

34.5.4 Ground (d): alternative accommodation

The landlord must have offered and be willing to provide or secure alternative accommodation for the tenant. The accommodation must be offered on reasonable terms having regard to the terms of the current tenancy and all other relevant circumstances. Further, the accommodation must be suitable for the tenant's requirements, (including the requirement to preserve goodwill) bearing in mind the nature and type of his business and the location and size of his existing premises. It seems that offering the tenant part only of his existing premises may qualify as alternative accommodation.

This ground, unlike the three previously mentioned, is not discretionary. If the landlord proves the requirements of the ground, the court must refuse the tenant's application.

34.5.5 Ground (e): current tenancy created by sub-letting of part only of property in a superior tenancy

Ground (e) is the least used ground because the necessary requirements are seldom fulfilled. It only applies where the current tenancy was created by a sub-letting of part of the property in a superior tenancy, and the sub-tenant's competent landlord is the landlord under the superior tenancy. The competent landlord will succeed if he can show that the combined rents from the sub-divided parts of a building are substantially less than the rent to be obtained on a single letting of the whole building, and that he requires possession to let or dispose of the whole.

This is the last of the discretionary grounds.

34.5.6 Ground (f): demolition or reconstruction

Ground (f) is the most frequently used ground. The landlord must show that on termination of the tenancy:

(1) he has a firm intention;
(2) to demolish or reconstruct the premises in the holding (or a substantial part of them), or to carry out substantial work of construction on the holding (or part of it); and
(3) that he could not reasonably do so without obtaining possession of the holding.

Each of these elements is considered in turn.

The landlord's intention

The landlord must prove a firm and settled intention to carry out relevant work. It has been said that the project must have 'moved out of the zone of contemplation . . . into the valley of decision' (per Asquith LJ in *Cunliffe v Goodman* [1950] 2 KB 237, approved in *Betty's Cafes Ltd v Phillips Furnishing Stores Ltd* [1959] AC 20). Not only must the landlord have made a genuine decision to carry out relevant work, he must also show that it is practicable for him to carry out his intention. This will be a question of fact in each case but the landlord's position will be strengthened if he has:

(1) obtained planning permission and building regulation approval (if necessary);
(2) instructed professional advisers;
(3) prepared the necessary drawings and contracts;
(4) obtained quotations and secured finance; and
(5) obtained the consent of any superior landlord (if necessary).

Where the landlord is a company, intention is normally evidenced by a resolution of the board of directors. Similarly, local authority landlords should pass an appropriate resolution and have it recorded in their minutes.

The landlord's intention must be established at the date of the hearing (*Betty's Cafes Ltd v Phillips Furnishing Stores Ltd*, above). It is thus irrelevant that the s 25 notice (or s 26 counter-notice) was served by the landlord's predecessor who did not have the necessary intention.

If the court is not satisfied that the landlord's intention is sufficiently firm and settled at the date of the hearing, a new tenancy will be ordered. In such cases, however, the court, in settling the terms of the new tenancy, may take into account the landlord's future intentions, and limit the duration of the new tenancy so as not to impede development later when the landlord is able to fully establish intention and the ability to carry it out (see **34.7.2**).

The nature of the works

The landlord must prove an intention to do one of six things:

(1) demolish the premises comprised in the holding (see *Coppin v Bruce-Smith* [1998] EGCS 45);
(2) reconstruct the premises comprised in the holding. For the works to qualify as works of reconstruction it has been held that they must entail rebuilding and involve a substantial interference with the structure of the building but need not necessarily be confined to the outside or loadbearing walls (*Romulus Trading Co Ltd v Henry Smith's Charity Trustees* [1990] 2 EGLR 75);
(3) demolish a substantial part of the premises comprised in the holding;
(4) reconstruct a substantial part of the premises comprised in the holding;
(5) carry out substantial work of construction on the holding. It has been held that such works must directly affect the structure of the building and must go beyond what could be more properly classified as works of refurbishment or improvement (*Barth v Pritchard* [1990] 1 EGLR 109);
(6) carry out substantial work of construction on part of the holding.

The need to obtain possession

The landlord must show that he could not reasonably execute the relevant work without obtaining possession of the holding. This means the landlord must show that he needs 'legal' (not just 'physical') possession of the holding. He has to show that it is necessary to put an end to the tenant's interest, and this may not always be the case. Accordingly, if the lease contains a right of entry for the landlord which is sufficiently wide to enable him to carry out the relevant work, his ground of opposition will fail. In such a situation, the tenant will be able to argue that the work can be carried out under the terms of the lease and there is thus no need to end it.

Even if the lease does not include a right of entry, the landlord may still fail in his opposition if the tenant is able to rely on s 31A of the Act. This provides that the court shall not find ground (f) to be established if the tenant will either:

(1) agree to a new lease which includes access and other rights for the landlord, which enable the landlord to reasonably carry out the relevant work without obtaining possession and without substantially interfering with the use of the holding for the tenant's business; or
(2) accept a new lease of an economically separable part of the holding with, if necessary, access rights for the landlord.

34.5.7 Ground (g): landlord's intention to occupy the holding

Ground (g) is another frequently used ground. The landlord must prove that on the termination of the current tenancy he intends to occupy the holding for the purposes, or partly for the purposes, of a business to be carried on by him, or as his residence. There are a number of elements to this ground which will be considered in turn.

The landlord's intention

As with ground (f), the landlord's intention must be firm and settled, and many of the matters discussed at **34.5.6** will be equally relevant here. Therefore, not only must the landlord be able to show a genuine intention to occupy the holding, he must also show that he has a reasonable prospect of being able to do so. It is, therefore, necessary for the court to take into account, for example, whether planning permission would be required to use the premises for the landlord's business and, if so, whether it would be likely to be granted. In some cases, the court has accepted as evidence of intention to occupy, an undertaking to do so given by the landlord. Such an undertaking is not conclusive but it is a relevant consideration when the court is determining the issue (see, eg, *London Hilton Jewellers Ltd v Hilton International Hotels Ltd* [1990] 1 EGLR 112). As with ground (f), the landlord's intention must be shown to exist at the date of the hearing.

The court will not assess the viability of the landlord's proposed business venture provided his intention to occupy is genuine. Thus, the court has held the ground to be established even where they thought the landlord's business plans to be ill thought out and likely to fail; his intention was nevertheless genuine.

The purpose of occupation

Occupation must be for the purpose of the landlord's business or as his residence. The landlord need not intend to occupy all the holding immediately, provided that within a reasonable time of termination he intends to occupy a substantial part of the holding for one of these purposes.

The wording of this ground refers to a business to be carried on by the landlord. However, the landlord need not physically occupy the premises and it will be sufficient if occupation is through a manager or agent provided that the arrangement is genuine. Further, the ground is still available where the landlord intends to carry on the business in partnership with others. Where the landlord has a controlling interest in a company, any business to be carried on by the company, is treated as a business carried on by the landlord. The landlord has a controlling interest for this purpose, either if he beneficially holds more than half of the company's equity share capital, or if he is a member and able, without consent, to appoint or remove at least half of the directors (s 30(3)). Where the landlord is a company in a group of companies, it may rely on ground (g) where another member of the group is to occupy the premises (s 42). If the landlord is a trustee, he may be able to rely on an intention to occupy by a beneficiary (s 41).

The 5-year rule

The most important limitation on the availability of this ground of opposition is the '5-year rule' in s 30(2) of the Act. A landlord cannot rely on ground (g) if his interest was purchased or created within 5 years before the end of the current tenancy, ie the termination date specified in the s 25 notice or s 26 request. However, the restriction only applies if, throughout those 5 years, the premises have been subject to a tenancy or series of tenancies within the protection of the Act.

The idea behind the provision is to stop a landlord buying a reversion within 5 years of the end of the lease, and then using this ground to obtain possession for himself at the end of the term. Thus, a landlord will not be able to rely on this ground if he purchased the premises subject to the tenancy within the last 5 years. However, the restriction does not apply where a landlord buys premises with vacant possession, grants a lease, and then seeks to end the lease within 5 years relying on this ground.

The wording of the provision refers to the landlord's interest being 'purchased' and this is used in its popular sense of buying for money (*Bolton Engineering Co Ltd v Graham & Sons Ltd* [1957] 1 QB 159). Thus, it will not cover a freeholder who has accepted the surrender of a head-lease without payment, and then seeks to use this ground against the sub-tenant.

Finally, a landlord who is unable to rely on ground (g) because of this restriction, may be able to rely on ground (f) if he intends to demolish or reconstruct the premises. This remains so even if the landlord then intends to use the reconstructed premises for his own occupation.

34.5.8 'Near miss' cases

Sometimes the landlord will be unable to make out his ground of opposition at the date of the hearing but can show that he would have been able to do so had the termination date in the s 25 notice or s 26 request been a little later. This is sometimes referred to as a 'near miss' for the landlord and notwithstanding the landlord's failure to make out his ground, the tenant may not be granted a new tenancy. This arises where the landlord unsuccessfully opposes on ground (d), (e) or (f) but the court is satisfied that he would have been successful, had the specified date of termination been up to 12 months later. In such a situation the court must refuse the tenant's application for a new tenancy. However, the tenant can ask the court to substitute that later date for the termination date originally specified in the notice or request which will mean that the current tenancy will continue until that later substituted date.

34.6 COMPENSATION FOR FAILURE TO OBTAIN A NEW TENANCY

On termination, a tenant may be entitled to compensation for any improvements he has made (see **22.6**). Additionally, if the tenant is forced to leave the premises he may lose the goodwill which he has built up and he will be faced with all the costs of relocation. This is particularly unfair to those tenants who are forced to leave the premises through no fault of their own, ie if the landlord establishes one of the grounds of opposition (e), (f) or (g). In certain circumstances, therefore, the tenant may be entitled to compensation for failing to obtain a new tenancy where the landlord establishes one of these 'no fault' grounds.

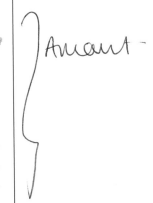

34.6.1 Availability

Compensation is only available on quitting the premises in one of the following situations:

(1) where the landlord serves a s 25 notice or counter-notice to a s 26 request stating one or more of the grounds of opposition (e), (f) or (g) but no others, and the tenant either:

  (a) does not apply to court for a new tenancy or does so but withdraws his application; or
  (b) does apply to court for a new tenancy, but his application is refused because the landlord is able to establish his stated ground;

(2) where the landlord serves a s 25 notice or counter-notice to a s 26 request specifying one or more of the grounds (e), (f) or (g) and others; the tenant applies to court for a new tenancy but the court refuses to grant a new tenancy solely on one or more of the grounds (e), (f) or (g). Here the tenant must apply to court for a new tenancy and ask the court to certify that a new tenancy was not ordered solely because one of these three 'no fault' grounds has been made out.

34.6.2 Amount

The amount of compensation is the rateable value of the holding multiplied by the 'appropriate multiplier' which is a figure prescribed from time to time by the Secretary of State, and is currently 1. In some cases, the tenant will be entitled to double compensation.

34.6.3 Double compensation

Sometimes the appropriate multiplier is doubled. This happens when the tenant or his predecessors in the same business have been in occupation for at least 14 years prior to the termination of the current tenancy. These provisions are summarised in the following illustration.

Single or double compensation

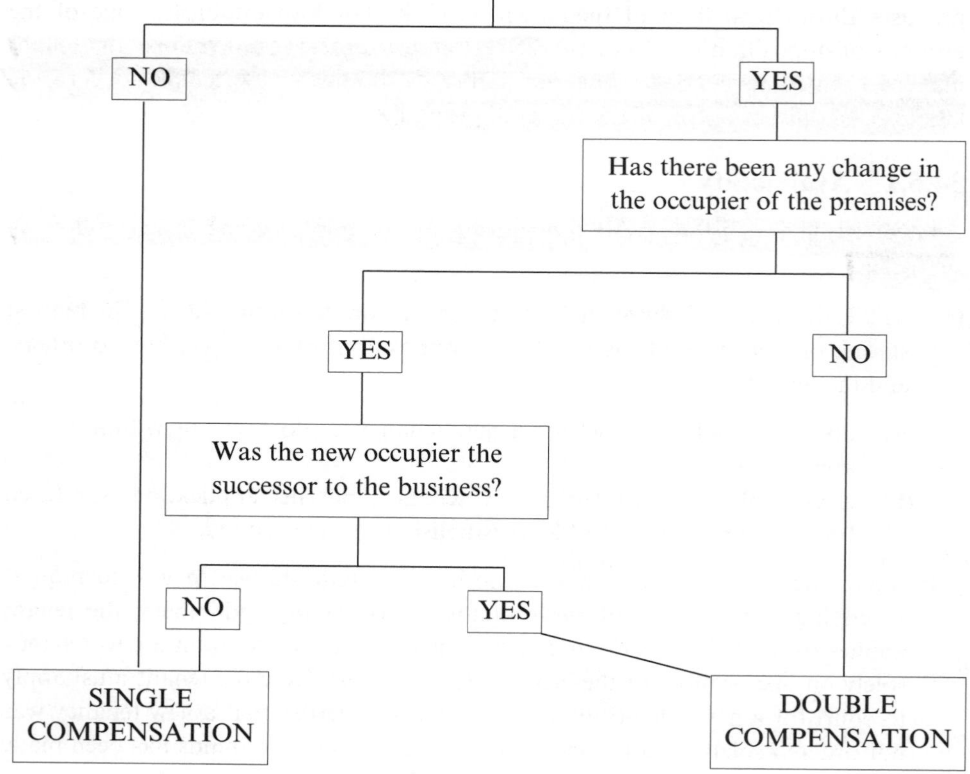

34.6.4 Contracting out

In some situations the tenant's right to compensation can be excluded by agreement between the parties. This agreement is often in the lease itself. However, s 38(2) of the Act provides that where the tenant or his predecessors in the same business have been in occupation for 5 years or more prior to the date of quitting, any agreement to exclude or reduce the tenant's right to compensation is void.

34.7 THE RENEWAL LEASE

If the tenant follows all the correct procedures and properly applies to court for a new tenancy, the court will make an order for a new lease in two situations:

(1) if the landlord fails to make out his s 30 ground of opposition; or
(2) if the landlord did not oppose the tenant's application for a new tenancy.

The terms of this new lease are usually settled by agreement between the parties and it is only in default of such agreement that the court will be called upon to decide the terms. In either event, any new lease will also enjoy the protection of the Act.

The court has jurisdiction over the premises, duration, rent and the other terms.

34.7.1 The premises

The tenant is only entitled to a new tenancy of the holding as at the date of the order. This term was defined in **34.1.4**, and excludes any part of the premises which have been sub-let. However, the landlord (but not the tenant), has the right to insist that any new tenancy to be granted shall be a new tenancy of the whole of the demised premises including those parts sub-let.

The court may grant a new lease of less than the holding under s 31A, where the landlord establishes ground (f), the redevelopment ground, but the tenant takes a new lease of an 'economically separable part' of the holding (see **34.5.6**).

The new lease may also include appurtenant rights enjoyed by the tenant under the current tenancy.

34.7.2 The duration

The length of any new lease ordered by the court will be such as is reasonable in all the circumstances but cannot exceed 14 years (often it is much less than this). In deciding this issue the court has a very wide discretion and will take into account matters such as:

(1) the length of the current tenancy;
(2) the length requested by the tenant;
(3) the hardship caused to either party;
(4) current open market practice;
(5) the landlord's future proposals.

It may be that the landlord was unable to rely on ground (f) because he could not prove that his intention to demolish or reconstruct was sufficiently firm and settled at the date of the hearing (see **34.5.6**). If, however, the court is satisfied that he will be able to do so in the near future, it may order a short tenancy so as not to impede development later. Similarly, if the premises are shown to be ripe for development, the new lease may be granted subject to a break clause (*National Car Parks Ltd v The Paternoster Consortium Ltd* (1990) 15 EG 53). In the same way, where the landlord has narrowly missed being able to rely on ground (g) because of the 5-year rule, the court may be prepared to grant a short tenancy.

34.7.3 The rent

The amount of rent to be paid is the greatest source of disagreement between the parties and specialist valuation advice will be essential. If the question of rent comes before the courts, they will assess an open market rent having regard to the other terms of the tenancy. However, in assessing the rent the court is obliged to disregard certain factors which may otherwise work to the detriment of the tenant, ie:

(1) any effect on rent of the fact that the tenant or his predecessors have been in occupation. The classic landlord's argument would be that the tenant, being a sitting tenant, would pay more in the open market for these premises simply to avoid relocation. This would inflate an open market rent and is thus to be disregarded;
(2) any goodwill attached to the holding due to the carrying on of the tenant's business. The tenant should not have to pay a rent assessed partly on the basis of goodwill he generated;
(3) any effect on the rent of improvements voluntarily made by the tenant (certain conditions must also be satisfied);

(4) where the holding comprises licensed premises, any addition in value due to the tenant's licence.

Where the premises are in disrepair due to the tenant's failure to perform his repairing obligation, conflicting views have been expressed on whether the court should disregard this in setting the rent of the new tenancy. One view is that the premises should be valued in their actual condition. This will probably produce a lower rent but the landlord may be able to sue the tenant for breach of his repairing obligation.

The other view is that the premises should be valued on the basis that the tenant has complied with his obligation, thus preventing the tenant benefiting from his own breach. This view is supported by cases such as *Crown Estate Commissioners v Town Investments Ltd* (1992) 08 EG 111.

In *Fawke v Viscount Chelsea* [1980] QB 441, the premises were in disrepair because the landlord was in breach of his repairing obligation. The court decided that the premises should be valued in their actual condition and, therefore, fixed a new rent which was below open market value but which increased once the landlord had complied with his obligation.

Under s 34(3) the court has power to insert a rent review clause in the new lease whether or not the previous lease contained such a provision. The frequency and type of review is at the discretion of the court which may be persuaded by the tenant to make provision for downward revisions as well as upward (see *Forbouys plc v Newport Borough Council* [1994] 24 EG 156).

As to the effect of the LTCA 1995, see **34.7.4**.

Finally, the court does have power to require the tenant to provide guarantors.

34.7.4 Other terms

It will only fall to the court to decide other terms in the absence of agreement between the parties. In fixing the other terms the court must have regard to the terms of the current tenancy and all other relevant circumstances. For that reason the terms will be much the same as before. The leading case in this area is *O'May v City of London Real Property Co Ltd* [1983] AC 726 which held that if one of the parties seeks a change in the terms, it is for that party to justify the change. Further, the change must be fair and reasonable and 'take into account, amongst other things, the comparatively weak negotiating position of a sitting tenant requiring renewal, particularly in conditions of scarcity' (per Lord Hailsham in *O'May*). Therefore, the tenant should be on his guard against any attempt by the landlord to introduce more onerous obligations into the new lease (eg a more restrictive user covenant). In the *O'May* case the landlord was, in effect, trying to transfer the responsibility for the repair and maintenance of office premises to the tenant. This would have increased the value of the reversion by more than £1m but the House of Lords held that the landlord was not entitled to do this. Notwithstanding the effect of the *O'May* case, variations may be made in the renewal lease to reflect the changes introduced by the LTCA 1995. The renewal lease will, of course, be subject to the provisions of that Act. This will often mean that under the current lease (granted before 1 January 1996) the original tenant was liable for the entire duration of the term through privity of contract; whereas for the renewal lease, privity of contract will not apply. This change is one of the circumstances to which the court must have regard in fixing the rent and other terms of the new lease. For example, the landlord may wish to alter the terms of the alienation covenant to balance the effect of the loss of privity of contract (see **20.2.5**).

34.8 THE ORDER FOR THE NEW LEASE

Any new lease ordered by the court will not commence until 3 months after the proceedings are 'finally disposed of'. This is when the time for appeal has elapsed, and for appeals to the Court of Appeal the time-limit is 4 weeks from the date of the order. The tenant continues to occupy under his old tenancy during this period. Either party may appeal.

If the court makes an order for a new tenancy upon terms which the tenant finds unacceptable (eg as to rent), the tenant may apply for revocation of the order within 14 days. In such a case the existing tenancy will continue for such period as the parties agree or the court determines as necessary to enable the landlord to re-let the premises.

Chapter 35

SELLING THE REVERSION

Chapter 35 contents

35.1 CIRCUMSTANCES OF A SALE

Although the heading to this chapter indicates that a sale of the reversion is being contemplated, the chapter also deals with the implications of a situation where the reversion is transferred to a funding institution as part of the funding arrangements between the developer and the provider of finance. There are, therefore, three situations contemplated by this chapter:

(1) where a developer does not intend retaining the reversion once development has been completed, and the premises have been fully let. Rather than receiving the income to be generated by the development, the developer prefers an immediate capital return on his investment by selling the reversionary interest;
(2) where the developer has received development finance to fund the development of the site, and it is a term of the funding agreement that the reversion is to be transferred to the funding institution, once the development has been completed and the building is fully let, or has been pre-let (ie is subject to agreements for lease);
(3) where, in other cases, one investment fund is simply disposing of part of its investment property portfolio (eg an old established building) to another.

In some cases, the transferee of the reversion may be a buyer; in others it may be more appropriate to call him an investor, or a lender. For consistency, he is called an investor, unless the context dictates otherwise.

In all cases, however, the investor will need to satisfy himself about the following matters:

(1) the terms of the lease(s) granted, or to be granted in respect of the premises;
(2) the condition of the building, and the availability of warranties in respect of defective condition;
(3) other matters affecting the building which may be revealed by searches and enquiries;
(4) the terms of the transfer;
(5) the title to the reversion;
(6) the taxation implications of the transfer.

35.2 TERMS OF THE LEASE

The investor will need to be satisfied that the terms of the leases by which the premises are demised are in an acceptable form. The building may not yet be occupied, although agreements for lease may have been entered into, but equally, the investor needs to be satisfied that the agreed form of leases are acceptable.

What the investor will be looking for is an institutionally acceptable form of lease. Traditionally, an institutional lease is one which is granted for a term of 25 years (or shorter, in recessionary times) containing a rent review clause allowing upward revisions of rent only, at every 5th year of the term. It places full responsibility for repairing the premises upon the tenant, and obliges the tenant to reimburse the landlord the costs he incurs in insuring the premises. If the lease relates to part only of a building, it contains comprehensive service charge provisions to enable the landlord to recover all costs and expenses incurred in respect of the provision of services to the tenants, and the repair and maintenance of those parts of the building in respect of which tenants are not responsible. It guarantees to the landlord that the rent payable under the lease will be a clear income, which is not subject to fluctuations caused by expenditure on the building. In a falling market, when tenants have greater bargaining power as regards the terms of a lease, the traditional form of institutional lease may come under threat (eg tenants may insist on shorter-length terms or the presence of break clauses).

The investor has to be satisfied that the lease does not contain any clauses which would have an adverse impact on the rental value of the premises, since this will necessarily have an effect on the capital value of the reversion. For example, if some of the clauses in the lease are too restrictive from a tenant's point of view (eg user is narrowly defined, or alienation is severely restricted), the landlord is likely to be prejudiced in rent review negotiations, since the open market rent in respect of the premises would be reduced to reflect the harshness of the lease terms. Whilst the investor may be able to take account of the adverse effect of certain clauses by reducing his purchase price (or level of investment) at the time of acquisition, there would still remain an element of uncertainty about the rental and capital value of the building. On the other hand, if the clauses are too wide, so that the tenant is allowed too much freedom, then although the landlord might have the edge in review negotiations, he could still lose out if the tenant altered the premises, or changed the use of them in such a way that they became a less attractive investment property.

The following points are of particular concern.

35.2.1 Liability of the tenant

The institutional form of lease was designed by property lawyers as a species of investment which produces a guaranteed income, with capital growth, over a fixed duration. Of primary importance, therefore, to the institutional investor is the guarantee of rental income throughout the term. There are now two forms of institutional lease in the commercial property market. First, there are those leases granted under the old privity regime (ie granted before 1 January 1996), where the investor will want to be satisfied that the covenant given by the original tenant (and any contractual guarantors) is of sufficient strength (having regard to the extent of his obligations under the lease). If the tenant is of poor financial standing, the development will appear unattractive to investors. The investor will also want to ensure that there are no provisions in such a lease curtailing the original tenant's continuing liability. Further, the investor would like to ensure that the lease term is defined to include any statutory extension under Part II of the LTA 1954, to prolong the original tenant's liability beyond the contractual termination date, although this point is not fundamentally important.

Secondly, there are those leases granted under the new privity regime. In such cases, whilst the investor will still be keen to vet the covenant strength and financial standing of the original tenant (and any contractual guarantors), as the tenant (and his guarantor) will be obtaining a release from covenants on assignment, the investor will want to make sure that the lease obliges an outgoing tenant to enter into an AGA, and that the alienation covenant imposes stringent conditions to be satisfied by an incoming tenant, to ensure that the incoming tenant is also of sufficient financial standing (see **20.2.5** and **20.2.8**).

35.2.2 Liability of any contractual guarantor

The investor will want the obligations of the tenant to be guaranteed by a third party for the same reasons as did the original landlord. He will want to ensure that the obligation of the guarantor is co-extensive with the tenant whose performance is being guaranteed, and that there is an obligation to take a new lease from the landlord in the event of disclaimer.

In the same way that the investor examined the financial strength of the tenant, so too should he examine the standing of the guarantor. If the guarantor is a company, it is prudent to make a company search against the guarantor to check the financial status of the company and that it is acting within its powers in providing a guarantee.

Insofar as the guarantor guarantees obligations of the tenant which touch and concern the demised premises, the guarantor's own covenant is one which touches and concerns the reversion and, therefore, the benefit of it will pass to a buyer of the reversion without an express assignment. If the guarantor's obligations are expressed to be personal, or extend to covenants which do not touch and concern, the buyer should obtain an express assignment (see *P & A Swift Investments v Combined English Stores Group plc* [1988] 2 All ER 885). It may be considered wise in any case to obtain an express assignment to avoid any argument that a particular covenant does not touch and concern.

As mentioned at **35.2.1**, the lease (if it is a new lease) should make provision for outgoing tenants to enter into an AGA.

35.2.3 Rent and rent review

The investor's favoured length of term is a 25-year term with a 5-yearly review pattern although in recent recessionary times, a 15-year lease has become more common. The manner in which the rent review clause was drafted can have a substantial effect upon the amount of rent recoverable throughout the term and, therefore, upon the capital value of the reversion. If there is a defect in the drafting, the impact at each review can be so severe as to dissuade potential investors from investing in the reversion.

Rent review clauses were dealt with in Chapter 18 in the context of the drafting of the lease. The investor must bear in mind similar considerations. The primary purpose of the investor in analysing the review provisions is to ensure that the landlord is able to maximise the rent receivable under the lease at each review, by the use of upward-only open market revaluations. It is, therefore, important to check that the review periods are constant, and that the hypothetical letting is upon terms, and contains assumptions and disregards that do not work to the disadvantage of the landlord. Valuation advice as to the effect on rent of the terms of the review clause, and the lease terms in general is essential.

As regards the implementation of the review, the investor should ensure that the landlord is able to implement and force the process, and that time is not of the essence of any part of the clause. If that were the case, there would be a danger of the landlord losing his ability to increase the rent by reason of a delay. The review should provide for an independent third party determination in default of agreement. The nature of investment property is such that huge sums may be at stake and, therefore, a determination by an arbitrator is often preferred.

35.2.4 Recovery of interest

The investor should ensure that there are sufficient provisions in the lease enabling interest to be recovered from the tenant on all sums paid late.

35.2.5 The repair covenant

It is one of the fundamental characteristics of an institutional lease that the tenant bears all of the cost of repairing the demised premises. If the lease is of the whole of a building, the investor will expect the tenant to be under a covenant to repair the whole of the building (damage by insured risks only excepted). The investor may be discouraged from investing in a development where liability for damage caused by inherent defects falls upon the landlord, even if collateral warranties from the development team have been procured.

If the building is the subject of several leases, the investor will accept that each tenant will only covenant to repair the premises demised to him, and that liability to repair and maintain the structure and exterior, and the common parts of the building will fall upon the landlord. However, the investor will expect the lease to contain comprehensive service charge provisions enabling the landlord to recover all of his repair and maintenance costs (and the costs of providing services, where the lease obliges the landlord so to provide). Again, the investor may be discouraged from investing in a development where ultimate liability for inherent defects does not fall upon the tenants.

35.2.6 Arrangements for insurance

Most commercial leases oblige the landlord to maintain insurance. An investor's main concerns will be to check that he can maintain sufficient insurance cover under the lease, and at the tenant's expense. He will need to be sure that any increased premiums that may become payable as a result of the activities of the tenant are recoverable in full.

The investor should analyse the provisions in the lease for reinstatement of damage caused by an insured risk to ensure that the provisions are fair and operate sensibly, giving the landlord the opportunity to reinstate, but with a right to terminate the lease if reinstatement proves to be impossible. Since the tenant is likely to have the benefit of a rent abatement clause, the investor should make sure that there is provision in the lease allowing the landlord to insure against loss of rent at the expense of the tenant.

35.2.7 Restrictions on alienation

The identity and status of the person in occupation of the premises often has an effect on the capital value of the landlord's reversion. An investor, therefore, invariably requires extensive control over all forms of alienation. He will often want to ensure that the lease contains an absolute covenant against any form of dealing which may result in a sub-division of the premises or shared occupation of them, and a qualified covenant against any other kind of dealing. As regards assignment, it should again be remembered that there are two types of lease in the commercial property market: those granted under the old regime, where, although the original tenant is caught by privity of contract, a covenant against assigning without consent is subject to s 19(1)(a) of the LTA 1927, and s 1 of the LTA 1988, without further qualification; and those granted under the new regime, where the tenant is released upon assignment, but the landlord is freely able to stipulate in advance conditions which need to be satisfied before consent to assignment is given. If sub-lettings are to be permitted, the investor will want the terms of the head-lease to give the landlord control over the terms of any proposed sub-lease. He will also want the ability to oblige sub-tenants to enter into direct covenants with the landlord.

35.2.8 Restrictions on alterations and change of use

The investor will want to see control balanced with the marketability of the tenant's lease. On the one hand, an investor will want to be able to restrain certain alterations and changes of use, in case the tenant were to make a change which affected the capital value of the reversion (although, of course, the ability to control improvements is limited). On the other hand, he will want the tenant to have a degree of flexibility since, if the user or alterations covenant is too tight, this may affect the open market rental value of the tenant's interest, work to the detriment of the landlord at review and, therefore, decrease the value of the reversion. Valuation advice will often be required as to the rental and capital value implications of these clauses.

35.2.9 Provision of services and payment of service charge

If the lease obliges the landlord to provide services for the tenants, an investor will want to ensure that he is able to add to, withhold or vary those services with relative freedom throughout the term, and that he is able to recover all of the costs incurred in providing services. Any provision in the lease which might lead to the landlord having to bear irrecoverable expenditure may dissuade an investor from purchasing.

35.2.10 The forfeiture clause

An investor will want to ensure that he has a comprehensive right to re-enter the tenant's premises on the occurrence of any tenant default, or the happening of one of a number of insolvency events. An investor may avoid buying the reversion if the landlord's ability to forfeit has been significantly restricted.

35.2.11 The effect of the LTA 1954

The fact that the tenant may enjoy the protection of Part II of the LTA 1954 will not greatly concern an investor. However, the investor must bear in mind when analysing the terms of the tenant's lease that those terms are likely to be repeated in any renewal lease granted under the Act. Under s 35 of the Act, the court, in fixing the terms of the new lease, has to have regard to the terms of the old lease (and to the effect of the LTCA 1995). The investor should, therefore, be advised that if he is prepared to accept the presence of an unfavourable provision in the current lease, he is also likely to have to accept its presence in any renewal lease granted to the tenant.

35.2.12 VAT provisions

The investor will want to be sure that there are no provisions in the lease which prevent the landlord from adding VAT to the rent and other sums payable under the lease, should he elect to waive the VAT exemption.

35.3 ENQUIRIES TO BE MADE

35.3.1 Condition of the building

If the investor is investing in the freehold of an established building, he will instruct surveyors to conduct a full structural survey. If the building is a new development, the investor will need to be satisfied that the development has been constructed to a sufficient standard, with good quality materials, and is free from construction or design defects. With this in mind, he too may commission a full structural survey of the development. However, the very nature of construction or design defects is that they are unlikely to manifest themselves until several years after completion of the development, and may not therefore be apparent on an initial survey.

The ability of a successor in title to the developer to pursue an action against the developer's construction and design team in respect of poor workmanship, or poor quality materials is remote (see **8.3**). The successor has no contractual relationship with the development team, and an action in tort is unlikely to bear fruit. The investor, therefore, needs some protection against inherent defects.

Whilst it has already been made clear at **35.2** that an institutionally acceptable form of lease is one which places all repairing costs on the tenant (including the cost of repairing damage caused by an inherent defect) and, therefore, the investor might not expect to incur repairing costs in respect of design and construction defects, nevertheless, the investor will need protection. This is because there is no guarantee that the investor will always be able to fix a tenant with liability to repair. For example, circumstances may arise in which the investor decides to forfeit the tenant's lease. If a defect were then to become apparent, the cost of repair would have to fall upon the investor. Alternatively, the tenant may go into liquidation, and the liquidator may disclaim the lease. Even if the tenant's liability under his repair covenant has not come to an end, the tenant may be insolvent and, therefore, unable to meet his obligations. In other cases, the defect which exists may be in need of remedy, but may not have caused any disrepair, and so the tenant would not be obliged to repair under his covenant.

For these reasons, where the building is still relatively new, the investor will require protection in one of the following forms:

(1) collateral warranties from the development team;
(2) latent defects insurance;
(3) an assignment by the developer of all and any of the rights he may have against the development team.

These matters are dealt with in greater detail in Chapter 8.

35.3.2 Conveyancing searches and enquiries

An investor would want the benefit of all the usual conveyancing searches and enquiries before either contracting to purchase the reversion, or entering into funding arrangements. His enquiries of the owner may focus upon the following additional matters.

Deleterious materials

In attempting to discover matters relating to the physical condition of the property, it is common to ask whether any deleterious materials have been used in the construction of the premises. These are materials the use of which is either unlawful, or considered dangerous (eg asbestos, urea formaldehyde, high alumina cement).

Collateral warranties/assignment of rights
For the reasons referred to above, in respect of new buildings, the investor will ask what form of protection against inherent defects will be made available. If collateral warranties are to be provided, the investor will need to see a copy of the building contract between the developer and the building contractor, and the terms of engagement of the developer's professionals, since collateral warranties have to be read in conjunction with the contractual documentation. The development team will warrant that they have performed their contractual duties to the standard required by the building contract or terms of engagement. Similarly, if the developer's rights are to be assigned to the investor, the investor will need to see the building contract and terms of engagement so that he may ascertain what those rights are.

Professional indemnity insurance
Where rights against the development team are to be assigned to the investor, or collateral warranties are to be procured for the investor's benefit, the investor will want to inspect indemnity insurance policies taken out by the development team to ensure that sufficient cover is available should the investor ever wish to pursue claims against the development team.

Copyright in architect's drawings
Copyright in any drawings prepared by the developer's architect will remain with the architect, the developer having either an implied or express licence to use such drawings for the purpose of the development (eg in conjunction with an application for planning permission). The investor will want to ensure that he also has a licence to use the drawings for whatever purpose he requires.

Insurance arrangements
In all probability, the seller of the reversion, as landlord, will be maintaining insurance in respect of the property. It may be wise for the investor to take over the seller's insurance policy as from completion, instead of taking out his own policy. If he were to take out a new policy, he is likely to encounter difficulties in recovering his insurance premiums from tenants who have already contributed to the payment of the seller's premium for the current year. If the buyer is to take over the seller's policy, it will need to be inspected, and if the *Standard Conditions of Sale* (3rd edn) are being used, Standard Condition 5.1.3 will need to be reversed by special condition. Some institutional investors have block policies which cover their entire property portfolios, in which case it is not possible for the investor to take over the seller's policy. The contract should provide, therefore, for the seller to cancel his policy from completion, and to pay any premium refund to the investor.

Copy of the lease, agreement for lease, and all other related documents
The investor will want to see a copy of the lease, or leases, by which the premises are demised so that he can satisfy himself as to their terms. However, he must make sure that he also inspects all other documents relating to the lease, such as licences to assign, sub-let, alter or change use, deeds of variation, memoranda of revised rents, side letters or undertakings exchanged between the parties, and the agreement for lease itself, as all of these documents may have an effect on the liabilities of the parties to the lease. Furthermore, as collateral agreements (as defined in s 28(1) of the LTCA 1995), the obligations contained in them may be binding upon successors in title, where the lease is a new lease for the purposes of the LTCA 1995.

Information regarding the service charge

In respect of established buildings, the investor will be taking over the liability to provide services, and the right to receive service charge payments, but he must ensure that he receives all relevant information, for example:

(1) service charge accounts from previous years;
(2) details of interim service charge payments already received from the tenants in the current financial year;
(3) details of any reserve fund maintained by the seller;
(4) details of items of expenditure incurred in respect of services in the current year, and already paid by the seller out of funds received;
(5) details of items of expenditure incurred, but not yet paid by the seller. (The investor should check that the seller has not incurred expenditure which, under the service charge provisions, cannot be recovered from the tenants);
(6) any estimates already obtained by the seller in respect of items of expenditure about to be incurred.

It should be remembered that at the end of the financial year, the landlord will have to perform a balancing act whereby he sets service charge income against actual service charge expenditure, and if there is a shortfall in income, he will call upon the tenants to contribute to it. However, to enable the investor to do this, he must be in possession of all the relevant information.

Rent arrears

The buyer should always ask the seller whether any sums due from the tenant under the lease are in arrear, and if so, who is to be entitled to recover those sums after completion (see **35.4.2**). Assuming rent is not in arrear, it will be apportioned at completion, and the seller will be expected to hand over written rental authorities to the buyer instructing the tenant in future to pay his rent to the buyer.

Rent deposit

The investor should enquire whether a rent deposit was taken on the grant of the lease and whether the benefit and burden of the agreement is to be passed on to him. Under leases granted before 1 January 1996, unless specific provision has been made to the contrary, a rent deposit agreement is a personal arrangement between the original contracting parties. The benefit and burden of rent deposit agreements in respect of leases granted on or after that date will pass to successors in title unless expressed to be personal (s 3 of the LTCA 1995 and see **14.5**).

Planning matters

The investor should seek to ascertain the authorised use of the premises before exchange since, although the premises may be tenanted, enforcment action can be taken against either owner or occupier. Sellers frequently include a special condition in the contract intended to negate any implied warranty or representation that the current use of the premises is authorised under the planning acts.

Environmental matters

The buyer should raise enquiries designed to ensure that the building being acquired was not constructed on a contaminated site, and is not being used for contaminative uses.

Fire certificate

If the building should have a fire certificate, the buyer should ask to see a copy of it.

35.4 TERMS OF A SALE

The contract to sell the freehold reversion can be made by incorporating a set of conditions of sale (eg the *Standard Conditions of Sale* (3rd edn)), since most of the standard conditions are appropriate for use in the transaction contemplated. However, several special conditions may be required to deal with the following matters.

35.4.1 Disclosure of leases

In the contract, the seller should disclose details of the leases subject to which the sale is to be made. Copies of the leases should be supplied to the buyer before exchange of contracts, together with all other documents which may have an effect on the lease terms (eg licences, supplemental deeds, memoranda). The seller can rely upon Standard Condition 3.3.2(a), and should also have regard to Standard Condition 3.3.2(c).

35.4.2 Assignment of rent arrears

As regards leases under the old regime, it is not clear from *Re King, Robinson v Gray* [1963] 1 All ER 781 whether under s 141 of the LPA 1925 the right to sue for arrears of rent and other sums due under the lease passes to the buyer on a sale of the reversion, or remains with the seller. It is, therefore, prudent for the seller in respect of such leases to make provision in the contract (whether or not any arrears exist when the contract is drafted) for any arrears to be assigned, by way of a separate deed of assignment, to the seller at completion. The buyer must ensure that the deed of assignment contains a covenant by the seller not to engage in any insolvency proceedings against the tenant when pursuing the arrears (as this may result in the bankruptcy or liquidation of the tenant, followed by disclaimer of the lease), nor against any guarantor.

The relative bargaining strengths of the parties may be such that the buyer is able to negotiate a reduced purchase price as consideration for the assignment of the right to recover arrears or, alternatively, he may succeed in persuading the seller to assign any rights he may have in respect of the arrears to the buyer, either as part of the agreed sale, or for an additional consideration.

As regards leases granted under the new regime, the right to sue for arrears of rent (and other breaches) remains with the assignor of the reversion (s 23(1) of the LTCA 1995), although that right can be assigned to the assignee (s 23(2) of the LTCA 1995). A prudent buyer would always seek to take an assignment of the right to sue to avoid his seller taking action which places the tenant in liquidation.

35.4.3 Conduct of rent reviews

If a rent review is scheduled for the period between exchange and completion, the buyer should insist on a special condition preventing the seller from taking any steps in connection with the review (eg service of review notices, agreeing a new rent, making a reference to the expert or arbitrator under the review clause) without the prior written consent of the buyer. The seller may require that the buyer's consent is not to be unreasonably withheld or delayed. If the buyer is willing to consent, he will want the ability to take over the conduct of review negotiations. Often, a rent review will not be settled until after completion but may relate, in part, to a period when the property was still vested in the seller. The seller will want to ensure that the contract enables him to claim an apportioned part of the increase, and that it obliges the investor to pursue the review actively, and not to settle upon a revised rent without the seller's consent.

35.4.4 Conduct of LTA 1954 proceedings

Similarly, if LTA 1954 proceedings are likely to occur between exchange and completion, the buyer would want a special condition in the contract preventing the seller from taking any steps in any negotiations for a new lease, or in any proceedings commenced by the tenant without the consent of the buyer. The buyer will want the ability to conduct any lease renewal negotiations, and will want the seller to co-operate in ensuring that the buyer is able to be substituted as the respondent in respect of any court application the tenant may make. Use may be made of Standard Condition 3.3.2(b) although the parties are likely to prefer to deal with this matter by way of a more extensive special condition.

35.4.5 Conduct of applications for licence to assign, alter, etc

The buyer may require a special condition preventing the seller from giving consent under any of the provisions of the lease after exchange of contracts without first obtaining the buyer's approval. Use may be made of Standard Condition 3.3.2(b).

35.4.6 Assignment of reserve fund

If, under the service charge provisions, the seller has built up a reserve or sinking fund, to be used to cover the cost of future items of expenditure, the buyer should ensure that the contract provides for the assets comprised in the fund to be transferred to the buyer at completion. If the assets are simply cash at the bank, no formal assignment will be necessary. However, if the reserve fund has been invested (eg in stocks and shares), the buyer should ensure that the contract provides for the assets to be assigned to the buyer at completion, and that the seller is obliged to do all other things necessary to perfect the buyer's title to the assets.

35.4.7 Rent deposit agreements

Under the old regime, the obligation to return a rent deposit to the original tenant is one which affects the original landlord only (see *Hua Chaio Commercial Bank v Chiaphua Industries Ltd* (1986) 130 SJ 923). However, it is common for the tenant to insist that the rent deposit agreement provides that, on a transfer of the reversion by the landlord, the landlord must ensure that the buyer either enters into a fresh deposit agreement with the tenant, or takes an assignment of the benefit and burden of the existing agreement. Therefore, depending upon the terms of the original agreement, appropriate provision may need to be made in the special conditions of the contract.

Under leases granted on or after 1 January 1996, the obligation to return the deposit is one which binds successors in title, who must therefore ensure that they have control of the relevant fund (although see **14.5** as to the reluctance of original landlords to do this).

35.4.8 Assignment of benefit of surety covenant

The benefit of a surety covenant will usually pass to the buyer of the reversion without express assignment (*P & A Swift Investments v Combined English Stores Group plc* [1988] 2 All ER 885) but it still seems that one will be necessary if there is any evidence that the covenant is expressed to be personal (ie with the original landlord alone) or insofar as the covenant is intended to guarantee performance of tenant's covenants which are purely personal. The same principles apply in relation to covenants given by a former tenant under an AGA.

35.4.9 Collateral warranties

If warranties are to be procured for the benefit of the buyer, and have not already been executed by the development team, a form of collateral warranty should be attached to the contract, and the seller should be obliged by special condition to procure warranties in that form. If, alternatively, the buyer is to take an assignment of whatever rights the seller may have against the development team, the contract should include an appropriate provision.

35.4.10 Indemnity covenant

Since, under the old regime, the original landlord remains liable on his covenants throughout the duration of the lease, he will require an indemnity covenant from his buyer in respect of future breaches of covenant. Standard Condition 4.5.4 may be relied upon, although many solicitors prefer to use their own form of covenant and, therefore, include a special condition obliging the buyer to enter into a covenant in a specified form. Under the new regime, a landlord who has not obtained a release remains jointly and severally liable on the landlord covenant with his assignee.

35.4.11 VAT

The contract should deal with the VAT consequences of the sale of the reversion. The sale of a tenanted building is often viewed by HM Customs & Excise as a transfer of a business as a going concern which, provided that certain procedural requirements are met, will not give rise to any VAT liability. There are special rules governing these transactions which are outside the scope of this book.

35.4.12 Landlord's release

If the lease is one to which the LTCA 1995 applies and, on an assignment of the reversion, the landlord fails to obtain a release from his covenants, the landlord should ensure that the contract to sell the reversion obliges the buyer to notify him of a sale on, so that he may again apply to be released from his covenants (see **14.2.2** for the procedure to be followed in such a case).

35.5 AN ALTERNATIVE TO INVESTIGATING TITLE

If the traditional method of conveyancing is adopted in respect of the sale of the freehold reversion, the seller will deduce title to the reversion, and the buyer will investigate title, and raise requisitions on it in the usual way, whilst attempting to discover other information about the property by making the normal conveyancing searches and enquiries.

However, there are cases where greater speed is required. Commercial property transactions are sometimes required to be completed in a matter of days after instructions are received. In such a transaction, the traditional method of conveyancing will not conform with the timescale expected by the client, and some other procedure will be required. In other cases, the seller may be disposing of a number of properties to the buyer, each one being the subject of a commercial letting, and the parties may consider it more appropriate to dispense with the traditional procedure. In funding transactions, where commercial investment property is being offered as security for a loan, and on the sale of the share capital of a property-owning company, the lender's and buyer's solicitors often dictate that the usual method of deduction and investigation is dispensed with.

The usual alternative to an investigation is for the seller's or borrower's solicitor to prepare a 'certificate of title' (and other matters) where, instead of producing evidence of title to be examined by the buyer (or lender), and leaving the buyer (lender) to conduct the usual searches and enquiries, the seller's solicitor issues a comprehensive certificate relating to all matters of title, and all other matters affecting the property which would concern the buyer (lender).

The exact form of the certificate is a matter for negotiation between the parties, but it is usual for the party who requires the certificate (ie the buyer or lender) to insist that it is given in the form prepared by that party's solicitor. The buyer's (lender's) solicitor will prepare a certificate in seemingly unconditional terms, requiring the seller's (borrower's) solicitor to certify several important facts, for example, that the title to the property is owned solely and beneficially by the seller (borrower) and is unincumbered and good for all purposes, and that the current use of the property is an authorised use, and that there are no entries relating to the property on any public registers, etc. The solicitor giving the certificate will qualify its unconditional nature by making a series of qualifications to the certified facts, so that, for instance, if there are incumbrances on the title, the certificate is qualified accordingly. The certificate is often further qualified by the solicitor by way of a disclaimer which states that the solicitor does not assume any responsibility in respect of information supplied by the company itself, and not obtained, for example, from an inspection of title documents or from the usual searches.

The purpose of the certificate is to put the recipient into the same position as if a thorough investigation and enquiry had been conducted. The benefit of the certificate from the recipient's point of view is that the seller's (borrower's) solicitor will owe a duty of care in respect of the unqualified content of the certificate.

35.6 ASSET ACQUISITION OR SHARE ACQUISITION?

The transactions so far contemplated by this chapter assume that a transfer of the reversion to the investor will take place, so that, after making careful enquiry and investigation, the investor will acquire the landlord's asset, and step into his shoes. The investor may only wish to acquire the landlord's freehold (or leasehold) reversionary interest. However, it may be that, where the landlord is a company, the acquisition of the reversionary interest is simply a part of a company take over. The detail of company acquisitions is outside the scope of this book, but insofar as such transactions have a bearing on the commercial property lawyer, they are considered here.

There are two basic ways in which the business of a company may be acquired. The first involves the acquisition of the assets of the company (eg freehold and leasehold premises, plant and machinery, stock, book debts, goodwill, etc). The second involves the acquisition of the shares in the company. In this way, the assets of the company (including the reversionary interest of the property-owning landlord-company) remain vested in the company. Therefore, instead of acquiring the company's assets, the investor acquires the company itself.

If the transaction is to be conducted by way of a share acquisition, the investor's concerns as regards properties owned by the company, are much the same as if he were acquiring the assets themselves (eg check the terms of any leases granted by the landlord; make the enquiries and investigations referred to at **35.3**). There are, however, several important differences between the two kinds of business acquisitions:

(1) on an asset acquisition, the landlord-company will be the seller. On a share acquisition, the shareholders in the landlord-company will be the sellers;
(2) if the landlord-company is the subject of an asset acquisition, title to its property will need to be conveyed or assigned to the investor, whereas if the transaction is a share acquisition, there will be a transfer of shares, but no need for formal conveyances of property. It should be noted that in acquiring assets of the landlord-company, the investor will take over any liabilities that attach to that property (eg an obligation to pay rent, or to perform covenants, or possible clean-up liability under the Environment Act 1995). However, on a share acquisition, the investor will be taking over all of the liabilities of the landlord company (eg its tax history, any present and possible future litigation, any continuing liability in respect of leasehold property no longer owned by the landlord-company);
(3) if properties which are the subject of an asset acquisition are leasehold, it is almost certain that licence to assign will have to be obtained from each landlord, whereas on a share acquisition, the identity of the tenant will remain the same. However, if, following the sale, the investor changes the nature of the operating business, there is a risk that the user covenant might be breached. It should be noted that, occasionally, alienation covenants are drafted to require the consent of the landlord if beneficial ownership of the tenant-company is transferred (such consent not to be unreasonably withheld);
(4) on an asset acquisition, stamp duty of one, two or three per cent will be payable on the consideration for the freehold or leasehold properties (subject to usual certificates of value), whereas on a share acquisition, stamp duty on the consideration is levied at one half per cent;
(5) a share acquisition does not attract VAT as the transfer of shares is an exempt supply. The acquisition of the whole or part of the business of a company by way of a transfer of its assets is outside the scope of VAT (as a transfer of a going concern). Care should be taken where all that is acquired from the company is its reversionary interest in an investment property. Provided certain conditions (which are outside the scope of this book) are satisfied, HM Customs & Excise is prepared to treat the transaction as the transfer of part of a business as a going concern. However, if those conditions are not satisfied, the transfer will be either an exempt supply (subject to the option to tax), or a standard-rated supply if the building is new;
(6) land registry fees are likely to become payable as a result of an asset acquisition, whereas on a share acquisition, as there is no transfer of title, there will be no application for registration of title;
(7) searches conducted prior to the completion of the transaction carry certain benefits (eg an erroneous local search may give compensation for undisclosed local land charges; a Land Charges Act search gives the benefit of a priority period, and is conclusive according to its tenor; a land registry search will give a priority period). However, these benefits are only available to purchasers (meaning, specifically, purchasers of land, and their mortgagees), and they are not therefore available to a purchaser of shares. For land registry purposes,

there is a specific form of 'search without conferring priority' for use in such acquisitions (Form 94C);

(8) deduction and investigation of title. The same options as those mentioned at **35.5** (ie the traditional conveyancing method, or use of certificates of title) are available to the parties to a share acquisition. However, see **35.7** as to the use of warranties and disclosures in corporate acquisitions.

35.7 CORPORATE SUPPORT

A commercial property lawyer invariably plays an important part in assisting the firm's corporate department in a company acquisition or disposal, whether the transaction is an asset or share sale. In virtually every company take over, there are property implications. The company which is the subject of the take over may primarily be a property-owning company. However, even if it is not, it is likely to own various properties (either freehold or leasehold), for example, its administrative offices, factories, or warehouses. In an asset sale, the buyer needs to be sure that the properties he is to acquire have good marketable titles which are not subject to onerous incumbrances. In a share sale, the buyer needs to be satisfied that he is acquiring a company which owns properties with good marketable titles which are not subject to onerous incumbrances.

In either form of transaction, the buyer may conduct a traditional investigation of title (accompanied by searches, enquiries, surveys and inspections), or may require the seller's solicitor to give a certificate of title and other matters (see **35.5**). Frequently, however, he will require the seller to make certain unqualified warranties about the title and condition of the properties. These warranties are several amongst many relating to all aspects of the company's business and which are contained in the business agreement which deals with the sale and purchase of the shares (or assets) of the company. The property warranties relate to matters which would ordinarily be discovered from a thorough investigation of title, or from usual searches and enquiries. Buyers often insist on warranties dealing with (inter alia) the following matters:

(1) that the company has good title to each of the properties, and has possession or control of all deeds and documents necessary to prove title;
(2) that each property is held free from mortgage, charge, lien, notice, caution, land charge, local land charge or other incumbrance of any kind;
(3) that the current use of each property is authorised under the Planning Acts;
(4) that all covenants, conditions, restrictions or other obligations relating to each property have been complied with;
(5) that the company has vacant possession of each of the properties;
(6) that each of the properties is in good and substantial repair and condition and fit for the purpose for which it is currently used.

The buyer's main purpose in requiring warranties is to elicit information from the seller without having to make enquiry, and as the buyer often has the upper hand in a company take over, he usually insists that warranties are given. If the seller wishes to avoid liability for breach of warranty, he must qualify his warranties by disclosing all material information relating to the properties (eg if vacant possession is not available because all or some of the properties have been let). Qualifying warranties is done by way of a disclosure letter given by seller to buyer, subject to which the warranties have effect.

The role of the commercial property lawyer, asked to assist in a corporate disposal, seems relatively straightforward, but carries a great deal of risk. He is usually presented with property warranties from the business agreement (drafted by the buyer's solicitor), and asked to make whatever disclosures of information are necessary to qualify satisfactorily the client's warranties, and asked either to approve the form of warranties, or make appropriate amendments. The buyer's commercial property lawyer role is to check to see whether any amendments to the warranties can be accepted, and to make sure that he has full details of all disclosed matters to enable a report to be given to the client, so that an informed view can be taken.

Property warranties give the buyer similar protection to certificates of title, save that liability rests with the seller, not his solicitor. Some would say there is no substitute for a buyer's thorough investigation. As to which method to choose, it depends upon available time, and the relative bargaining positions of the parties. A thorough investigation will give the buyer's solicitor a lot to do and will therefore increase the buyer's legal fees, whereas the requirement of a certificate of title will increase the seller's fees. The use of warranties and disclosures is likely to spread the cost more evenly, since the warranties will be the subject of much negotiation, and there will be much disclosed documentation to wade through. A further consideration relates to which solicitor is to take the greater risk; the seller's solicitor in giving a certificate, or allowing his client to give warranties, or the buyer's solicitor for carrying out a thorough investigation?

35.8 TAXATION IMPLICATIONS

The taxation implications of a sale of a reversionary interest are dealt with briefly at **12.2.3**. The VAT consequences of the sale of a tenanted building are outside the scope of this book.

PART III

RESIDENTIAL TENANCIES

Chapter 36

INTRODUCTION TO RESIDENTIAL TENANCIES

36.1 RESIDENTIAL OCCUPIERS

A person may be occupying residential accommodation in one of various capacities. He may, of course, be an owner-occupier or, at the other extreme, a squatter or trespasser. Between those two extremes the residential occupier is likely to be either a tenant occupying under a periodic tenancy or fixed-term lease or a licensee lawfully occupying the property under a contract or some other arrangement with the owner which does not amount to a tenancy/lease.

This part of the book is concerned with both short-term and long-term lettings of residential property. It deals with the following potential problem areas:

- What happens at the end of a tenancy? Does the landlord have a right to possession?
- Who is responsible for repairs?
- Does the tenant have a right to compel the landlord to sell him the freehold or grant him a new lease?

Tenants with long leases (exceeding 21 years) are often given rights to compel the sale of the freehold; all residential tenants may have security of tenure, ie the right to stay on in possession even after the end of the contractual term.

All of these matters are significant, not only from the point of view of the tenant, but also from the point of view of the landlord or a potential purchaser of the freehold, who might have plans for redevelopment which may be affected by the tenant's rights.

In dealing with or advising upon a residential landlord and tenant matter, the question of the status or intended status of the residential occupier is of paramount importance in determining the relevant law.

It is necessary first of all to determine whether the occupier is a tenant or a licensee. The rights and obligations of the parties and the appropriate statutory provisions will, in many cases, hinge on this distinction. The distinction between a lease or tenancy on the one hand and a licence on the other is dealt with primarily by the common law rather than by statute. If a residential occupier is merely a licensee, he has no proprietary interest in the property that he occupies so that, in general terms, when the licence terminates or expires or when the owner dies or transfers ownership of the property, the occupier's right to occupy ceases. Further, there is very little statutory protection (or 'security of tenure') for residential licensees. Most legislation is aimed at the protection of tenants. A tenancy confers on the tenant an estate in the property which is capable of subsisting notwithstanding the death of the landlord or any alienation by him. A tenancy is a recognised 'proprietary interest', capable of binding future owners, which can be terminated only by certain recognised methods. In addition, many residential tenants enjoy security of tenure so that, even if the tenancy is terminated by one of the methods recognised at common law, the tenant is entitled to remain in occupation notwithstanding this termination.

In order to obtain possession, the landlord will usually have to prove that one of the 'grounds' for possession set out in the legislation exists. Further, the extent to which a landlord can increase the amount of rent payable is also controlled by statute for some types of tenancy. Thus, the distinction between a tenancy/lease and a licence is of fundamental importance. This distinction is considered in detail in Chapter 37.

Having dealt with the question of the status of the occupier as between tenant and licensee, it is then necessary to look at the relevant law affecting the tenancy or licence. It will normally be a mixture of common law and statute.

36.2 THE COMMON LAW

All licences, leases and tenancies are, to some extent, governed by common law. The law of contract, land law and the law of torts each play an important part, and must be the starting point when considering any problem that concerns leases, licences or tenancies. The relevant common law is dealt with where appropriate in later sections of the book. However, it must be appreciated that the common law is frequently modified or supplemented by statute.

36.3 THE STATUTES

The major statutory provisions are contained in the Leasehold Reform Act 1967 (LRA), the Rent Act 1977 (RA 1977), the Protection from Eviction Act 1977 (PEA 1977), the Housing Act 1985 (HA 1985), the Landlord and Tenant Act 1985 (LTA 1985), the Landlord and Tenant Act 1987 (LTA 1987), the Housing Act 1988 (HA 1988), the Leasehold Reform, Housing and Urban Development Act 1993 (LRHUDA) and the Housing Act 1996 (HA 1996). These will be looked at in detail in later chapters. In should be appreciated at the outset, however, that most of this legislation was introduced on an ad hoc basis to deal with a particular problem and does not form part of an integrated consistent whole. So the qualifying conditions for each statute need to be looked at carefully to see whether any particular tenant is or is not protected.

36.4 PUBLIC SECTOR LETTINGS

Most tenants of local authorities (and certain others in the public sector) enjoy protection as secure tenants under the HA 1985. They have substantial security of tenure. If the landlord wishes to regain possession it must usually comply with the procedure and the established grounds for possession laid down in that Act. However, there is no statutory control over the amounts of rent that local authorities can charge. In relation to repairs, harassment or unlawful eviction, there is generally no difference between public sector tenants and private sector tenants. Similarly, the rights given to long leaseholders under LRHUDA also apply to local authority tenants (see Chapter 45). However, the rights of secure tenants are otherwise outside the scope of this book.

36.5 PRIVATE SECTOR LETTINGS

The rights of short-term tenants of private landlords often depend upon when the tenancy was originally entered into. As regards security of tenure and rent control in the private sector, a clear distinction must be made between tenancies granted prior to 15 January 1989 and those granted on or after that date. The former are usually governed by the RA 1977 under which tenants enjoy substantial security of tenure and significant statutory control over the amount of rent that the landlord can charge. As regards tenancies granted on or after 15 January 1989 the rules are quite different and are contained in the HA 1988. This established the concept of the 'assured tenancy', with full security of tenure, and the 'assured shorthold tenancy', under which the landlord has an absolute right to possession at the end of the letting. However, in relation to tenancies under both the RA 1977 and the HA 1988, the rules relating to repairs, harassment and unlawful eviction are the same.

36.6 THE NEXT STEP

Having considered the question of residential status and, where appropriate, which statutory regime applies, it is then necessary to look at the detail of the relevant law and procedures and to apply them to the facts of the case and to the client's specific instructions.

Chapter 37

CREATION OF A RESIDENTIAL TENANCY

37.1 LEGAL REQUIREMENTS

A lease must be granted by deed unless it takes effect in possession for a term not exceeding 3 years and is at the best rent which can reasonably be obtained without taking a fine (s 54 of the Law of Property Act 1925 (LPA 1925)). If such conditions are complied with, no formalities are required and so the tenancy could be granted orally. It is obviously desirable, however, to have at least a written tenancy agreement to avoid any disputes as to the terms of the letting. A possible method of resolving disputes as to the terms of an oral letting is discussed at **39.3.4**.

Most residential lettings will be for less than 3 years and so a deed may not always be necessary, but care should be taken. Lettings will normally be at the best rent but may not take effect in possession. A tenancy entered into on one date which is not to commence until a later date does not take effect in possession and so must be granted by deed if a legal estate is to be created. A fine may also be taken which again would dictate the use of a deed in order to create a legal lease. A fine, or premium as it is often called, is a non-returnable lump sum payable at the start of the letting in addition to (or instead of) rent; it should not be confused with a deposit. A deposit is a returnable payment often required by landlords as a form of security in the case of damage to the property or non-payment of rent. See **37.3.12** as to deposits.

If a deed is not used where it should be, the letting would still be valid and binding between the parties in equity if the requirements of s 2 of the Law of Property (Miscellaneous Provisions) Act 1989 (LP(MP)A 1989) are complied with, ie the agreement is signed by both landlord and tenant. If, as sometimes happens, only the tenant signs the agreement, neither a legal nor equitable lease will be created. On payment and acceptance of rent, however, an implied legal periodic tenancy will arise.

Under Rule 6 of the Solicitors' Practice Rules 1990, it is generally not possible to act for both landlord and tenant on the grant of a lease. Even where the exceptions within Rule 6(2) potentially apply, there will most probably be a conflict of interest between the parties which will prevent acting for both of them.

37.2 THE LEASE/LICENCE DISTINCTION

37.2.1 Why is the distinction so important?

As outlined in Chapter 36, the distinction between a lease and a licence is of vital importance. A lease creates an interest in land. It is capable of existing as a legal estate in land; a term of years absolute is one of the two legal estates which can exist since 1925. As an interest in land it is capable of binding successors in title to the freehold. Further, most of the security of tenure legislation which has been enacted only protects tenants. Occupiers who have a licence, on the other hand, will find that they have limited statutory protection (principally against eviction without a court order, see Chapter 41) but no security of tenure. Also, as a licence does not create an interest in land, it is generally not binding upon a successor to the original grantor. Because licences have no security of tenure, there is an incentive for property owners to grant licences to occupy property rather than tenancies. The courts, however, will be astute to detect sham arrangements and may declare an arrangement to be a tenancy, and thus capable of having security of tenure, no matter that the parties may have called it a licence. So what is the distinction?

37.2.2 The need for exclusive possession

It is an essential requirement of a lease that the tenant should be given exclusive possession of the property. If the 'tenant' does not have exclusive possession then the arrangement cannot be a lease; it can only amount to a licence. Exclusive possession involves the right to be able to exclude all others, including the landlord, from the premises. It does not follow, however, that if exclusive possession is given, that the arrangement will then necessarily be a lease. It is also possible for a licence to confer exclusive possession. However, in the circumstances where this has been held to be the case there has been something in the circumstances, such as a family arrangement, or an act of friendship or generosity to negative the intention to create a tenancy. Normally, in a commercial arrangement where rent is being paid, the deciding factor is whether or not exclusive possession is actually being given to the occupier. See, for example, *Street v Mountford* [1985] AC 809. In deciding whether exclusive possession is being conferred on the occupier, the courts will look at the substance and effect of the agreement rather than just the wording used. So in *Street v Mountford*, the House of Lords declared the arrangement to amount to a tenancy even though the agreement itself stated that it was a licence. The 'label' placed on the arrangement by the parties is not conclusive.

37.2.3 Sharing arrangements

It was clear in *Street v Mountford* that the tenant had exclusive possession of her flat as she was the sole occupant. But what of the common situation where a group of people, often students, are given the right to share a flat or house. Do these give rise to licences or are they to be construed as tenancies? In *Antoniades v Villiers* [1988] 3 WLR 1205, a young couple were looking for accommodation together. They each signed a separate agreement, described as a 'licence agreement', to share a one-bedroomed flat. Each agreement provided that the 'licensor' also had the right to occupy the premises and that he might licence others to share occupation with the 'licensees'. The House of Lords held that the arrangement was clearly a lease and that the young couple were joint tenants of the flat even though they had signed separate agreements. The terms allowing occupation by the landlord or others were clearly shams, not intended to be operative. It would be ridiculous to contemplate that the landlord intended to share the one bed in the flat with the young couple or that he intended to send in others to do so. The young couple jointly had exclusive possession of the flat.

On the other hand, their Lordships heard the case of *AG Securities v Vaughan* [1988] 3 WLR 1205 at the same time as *Antoniades v Villiers*. In the *AG Securities* case the premises comprised a flat which had four bedrooms plus bathroom, kitchen, etc. The flat was occupied by four people who were selected by the owner and who did not previously know one another. Each had arrived at a different time and each paid a different amount for the use of the flat. Each was given the right to share the flat with the other three. Exclusive possession of no part of the flat was given, not even a bedroom. The owner did not dictate which bedroom each was to occupy. This was left to be decided amongst the current occupiers. These arrangements were held to constitute genuine licences.

37.2.4 Conclusions

It can be seen that property owners can only validly make use of licences so as to avoid the security of tenure legislation in the *AG Securities* kind of situation. The premises must be capable of being shared by a group of people. So a licence could not be used in the case of a self-contained one-person flat (*Street v Mountford*). Even so, great care must be taken. The licence agreement must be carefully drafted to ensure that exclusive possession of no part of the premises is given. If, for example, the exclusive right to occupy one bedroom is given, together with the right to share the remainder of the house, this will give rise to a tenancy of the bedroom, which would be capable of being an assured tenancy, with full security of tenure, under the HA 1988. Equally, if the occupants are friends or others seeking accommodation together it is likely that even separate well-drafted agreements would be construed together as a joint tenancy as in the *Antoniades v Villiers* case. Due to the uncertainties involved, and the risk that if an arrangement was construed as a tenancy, it would be an assured tenancy with full security of tenure, most landlords use assured shorthold tenancies instead (see Chapter 39). These give a landlord an absolute right to possession at the end of the letting, provided he follows the correct notice procedure.

However, in the case of an arrangement entered into on or after 28 February 1997, if it was to be construed as a tenancy, it would be as an assured shorthold anyway. Thus, it may well be that there is now less risk than before in attempting to use licences. Licences have the advantage that there is no right for the tenant to query the rent (see **39.4** as to such rights in assured shorthold tenancies). Further, a landlord must give 2 months' notice of requiring possession under a shorthold (see **39.7**), whereas a fixed-term licence will expire without any notice at all, and only 28 days' notice need be given for a periodic licence.

37.3 THE TERMS OF THE AGREEMENT

Many residential lettings are entered into quite informally but the landlord's instructions should be taken, and advice given, as to the desirability of the inclusion of terms dealing with the following matters.

37.3.1 Description of the property

The property should be clearly defined, including, for example, the number or precise location of the flat, should this be appropriate. Any necessary easements for the tenant, for example for access, should be included and any easements required by the landlord over the property to be leased should be reserved.

37.3.2 Inventory of contents and schedule of condition

If the house is being let furnished, a detailed inventory of all the contents should be drawn up and annexed to the tenancy agreement.

If the tenant is to be responsible for internal repairs and decoration, a schedule of condition should be drawn up and annexed to the tenancy agreement. This will ensure that there can be no doubt at any later stage of the exact state of the property at the commencement of the tenancy.

37.3.3 Payment of rent

Express provision should be made for payment of rent in advance. Otherwise, the common law implication is that rent is payable in arrears. The intervals for payment must also be stated. If weekly intervals are chosen, the landlord must provide the tenant with a rent book: LTA 1985, s 4(1). The intervals should be weekly, fortnightly, monthly, quarterly or yearly. If any other intervals are chosen, and the tenancy is an assured tenancy, mandatory Ground 8 may not be available to the landlord (see **38.10.3**). In the case of arrears of rent, the landlord will not be entitled to interest unless and until he commences proceedings. It is advisable, therefore, to include an express term in the agreement allowing the landlord to add interest to any arrears.

37.3.4 Water charges

Provision should be made as to who is to be responsible for the payment of water charges. The implication in the absence of express provision is that the tenant must pay them. Often, in short-term lettings the landlord will accept responsibility for them. If so, there should be some provision in the agreement allowing the landlord to increase the rent to take account of any increase in water charges during the continuance of the tenancy.

37.3.5 Council tax

Council tax is payable from 1 April 1993 on 'dwellings', ie houses or self-contained units such as flats. Liability for the tax generally falls on the person in occupation, ie the tenant. However, if the property is in multiple occupation it is the landlord who will be responsible. The definition of 'multiple occupation' includes any dwelling inhabited by persons who do not constitute a single household, all of whom either only have the right to occupy part of the house or who are mere licensees paying no rent. The tenancy agreement should contain provisions stating that the rent is exclusive of council tax and requiring the tenant either to pay it to the local authority or to reimburse the landlord should he become responsible for payment. If the landlord is to be reponsible, there should also be a provision allowing the landlord to increase the rent to take account of any increase in council tax during the term.

37.3.6 Repairs

It is likely that s 11 of the LTA 1985 will apply to the letting. This imposes an obligation on the landlord to repair, inter alia, the structure and exterior where the tenancy is for a term of less than 7 years (see **42.4**). However, provision needs to be included allocating responsibility for non-structural internal repairs and decoration which will not be covered by the landlord's implied obligation. Apart from such an express provision, neither landlord nor tenant would be under an obligation to attend to such matters. Often, in a short letting the landlord would retain the obligation; in a longer lease, it may be appropriate to impose the obligation on the tenant.

37.3.7 User

It is usual to restrict the use of the property to that of a single private dwelling house and also to impose obligations on the tenant not to cause nuisance or annoyance to the neighbouring occupiers and not to damage the house or contents in any way.

37.3.8 Insurance

In a short lease, the landlord will normally insure the premises as he has the most valuable interest in the house. However, the activities of the tenant could affect the validity of the insurance policy or the amount of premium payable by the landlord and so terms should be included obliging the tenant not to do or omit to do anything which might have such effects on the insurance.

37.3.9 Assignment

It is essential that the landlord retains control over who is permitted to occupy his house. At common law, a tenant can freely assign the tenancy to whomsoever he wishes. Although there is an implied term in most periodic assured tenancies prohibiting assignment without consent (see **38.6**), this should not be relied upon. It is not always implied and will not be implied in fixed-term lettings. An absolute prohibition on assignment is advisable rather than a qualified restriction so avoiding the implied proviso under s 19 of the LTA 1927 that the landlord cannot withhold his consent unreasonably.

37.3.10 Sub-letting

As with assignment, an absolute prohibition on sub-letting is desirable. In the case of a shorthold it is essential. In the absence of such a provision, a shorthold tenant could grant a sub-lease which could be an ordinary assured tenancy and which would then be binding as such upon the head landlord. The prohibition on sub-letting implied by s 15 of the HA 1988 will not be implied into a fixed-term shorthold (see **38.6**).

37.3.11 Address for service

Under s 48 of the LTA 1987, no rent is lawfully due from a tenant unless and until the landlord has given to the tenant notice in writing of an address in England and Wales at which notices (including notices in proceedings) can be served upon him. For many years, it was not clear whether merely stating the landlord's address in the tenancy agreement was sufficient and so the practice arose of specifically stating an address for service, either in the agreement or in a separate notice. However, in *Rogan v Woodfield Building Services Ltd* [1994] EGCS 145, the Court of Appeal decided that if the landlord's name and address in England and Wales was stated on the tenancy agreement without any qualification or limitation, then this would be sufficient to comply with s 48. There was no need in such a case for a separate notice to be given or for the address to be specifically designated as an address for service. Obviously, however, if the landlord's address changes during the currency of the tenancy, for example on a change of landlord, then a separate s 48 notice will be needed. This s 48 notice need not be in any prescribed form nor need the address be the landlord's home address (or registered office, in the case of a limited company); it could be, for example, the address of a solicitor or other agent.

37.3.12 Deposit

It is usual for a landlord to take a deposit from a tenant to provide security against non-payment of rent or damage to the property or its contents. The amount is often the equivalent of one or 2 months' rent, but could be more in the case of furnished lettings due to the higher risk involved. The tenancy agreement should clearly state the occasions on which the landlord can have resort to it and when it would become repayable to the tenant. Provision should also be made as to what is to happen to the deposit on a change of landlord, ie is it to be returned to the tenant or handed over to the new landlord? Other matters to be dealt with include the question of interest. Is this to be held for the benefit of the tenant or the landlord? If the landlord has to have resort to the deposit for any purpose, provision should be included requiring the tenant immediately to make up the deficit. The provisions of the Unfair Terms in Consumer Contracts Regulations 1994 (see **37.3.20**) should also be considered in relation to deposits.

37.3.13 Rent review

In a fixed-term tenancy which is for longer than (say) 12 months, it is essential to include a provision allowing the landlord to increase the rent to take account of the effects of inflation. Without such a provision an increase in rent will not be possible without the tenant's agreement during the continuance of the tenancy. In the case of a periodic assured tenancy, the common law rule that the landlord cannot change the rent during the subsistence of the tenancy is subject to the provisions of ss 13 and 14 of the HA 1988 (see **38.5.3**). Although these allow a landlord to increase the rent without bringing the tenancy to an end, the procedure is complex and time consuming and the tenant has the right to refer the rent to the Rent Assessment Committee. It is preferable, therefore, not to rely on these statutory provisions and include instead an express term allowing the landlord to increase the rent on giving (say) 28 days' notice to the tenant.

37.3.14 Break clauses

In the case of fixed-term tenancies (including shortholds) a break clause in favour of either the landlord or the tenant may be appropriate in the circumstances. A break clause is a provision allowing the lease to be terminated prior to the expiry of the fixed term. Where there are joint tenants, provision should be included as to whether it is necessary for all of the joint tenants to concur in the exercise of the break clause. The provisions of the Unfair Terms in Consumer Contracts Regulations 1994 (see **37.3.20**) should also be considered where a right to break is being given to a landlord but not to the tenant.

37.3.15 Children and pets

If children and/or pets are to be prohibited, then an express provision will be required.

37.3.16 Service of notices

Provision should be included allowing service of notices under ss 8 and 21 of the HA 1988 in accordance with the provisions of s 196 of the LPA 1925. This will facilitate service of these notices by allowing service by registered or recorded delivery post or by simply leaving them at the premises.

37.3.17 Mandatory grounds for possession

Where the landlord is intending to rely on one of the mandatory grounds for possession which require service of a warning notice on the tenant no later than the grant of the tenancy, eg in the case of an owner occupier using Ground 1, this can be included in the agreement (see generally **38.10.3**).

37.3.18 Forfeiture

Although it is not possible to forfeit an assured tenancy, a forfeiture clause is still essential in any fixed-term assured tenancy, including a shorthold. The tenancy may at some time cease to be assured, in which case the forfeiture clause could then be operated in the normal way to terminate the tenancy. More importantly, some of the grounds for possession are exercisable during the subsistence of the fixed term, but only if the tenancy agreement makes specific provision for this. This provision can take any form and so the forfeiture clause should make it clear that termination can be made using Grounds 2 or 8 of the mandatory grounds and Grounds 10 to 15 of the discretionary grounds (see **38.10.2**).

37.3.19 Costs

If it is intended that the tenant should be responsible for the landlord's costs and disbursements (eg stamp duty) in relation to the preparation and grant of the tenancy agreement, a provision to this effect should be inserted in the agreement in order to comply with the Costs of Leases Act 1958.

37.3.20 The Unfair Terms in Consumer Contracts Regulations 1994

The Unfair Terms in Consumer Contracts Regulations, SI 1994/3159, apply to all contracts between a business supplier and a consumer entered into on or after 1 July 1995. They will thus apply to all residential lettings between a landlord and a private individual but *not* to a letting of residential accommodation to a company. The regulations declare void any term in the agreement which has not been individually negotiated and is 'unfair' to the tenant. A term is deemed to be unfair if 'contrary to the requirement of good faith it causes a significant imbalance in the parties' rights and obligations to the detriment of the consumer', ie the tenant. All terms in a standard-form tenancy agreement must thus be looked at in the light of these regulations. In particular, provisions requiring payment of a deposit by the tenant and allowing the landlord to terminate the tenancy early must be looked at carefully if these cause a 'significant imbalance in the parties' rights and obligations.

37.4 COMPLETION OF THE AGREEMENT

Although many residential lettings are entered into quite informally, the tenancy agreement should be prepared in duplicate as on the grant of any other lease. The landlord should then sign the original which will be handed to the tenant, the tenant signing the counterpart which will be retained by the landlord.

37.5 STAMP DUTY

Stamp duty is payable on both the tenancy agreement and the counterpart. The duty is assessed on the amount of the rent payable as well as on any premium paid.

The rates are subject to change and an up-to-date table of stamp duties should be consulted.

It is not unusual for short-term tenancy agreements to remain unstamped, but this practice is not to be recommended. If a tenancy agreement does not bear the correct amount of stamp duty, not only are there financial penalties, but the agreement cannot be produced as evidence in court. This lack of admissibility is something the court should raise of its own motion and potentially could cause problems for landlords seeking a court order for possession. However, it has to be said that the lack of stamps is in practice very rarely raised. Even if it was raised, the court has jurisdiction to waive the insufficiency of stamps in return for an undertaking to get the document stamped as soon as possible.

As from 6 May 1994, no lease shall be treated as duly stamped unless:

(a) it contains a certificate that there is no agreement to which it gives effect; or
(b) it is stamped with a stamp denoting:
    (i) that there is an agreement to which it gives effect, but that it is not chargeable to duty; or
    (ii) the amount of the duty paid on the agreement.

Chapter 38

ASSURED TENANCIES

38.1 INTRODUCTION

The concept of assured tenancies and assured shorthold tenancies was introduced by the HA 1988. This came into force on 15 January 1989, and virtually all new lettings by private landlords after that date will be one or the other (but see **38.4**). Lettings entered into before that date will generally remain subject to the provisions of the RA 1977, see **38.3.1**.

An assured tenancy gives the tenant extensive security of tenure; at the end of the contractual term the tenant has a statutory right to remain in possession. If the landlord wishes to obtain possession, he must not only follow the prescribed procedure but also establish one of the prescribed grounds for possession. However, there is no statutory control over the amount of the rent which the landlord can charge; the rent is left to be decided by the ordinary operation of market forces. There is, however, some protection given to a tenant where the landlord wishes to increase the rent payable under an existing tenancy.

In the case of lettings entered into on or after 28 February 1997 (the commencement date of the Housing Act 1996), most will be assured shorthold tenancies (see generally Chapter 39) and *not* assured tenancies. However, a shorthold is merely a type of assured tenancy and so must comply with the definition of an assured tenancy as well as the extra requirements which make it a shorthold (see **39.2.1**).

Tenancies which do *not* satisfy the definition of an assured tenancy (and so cannot be shortholds either) will not be subject to the provisions of the HA 1988 as set out in this chapter. Instead, ordinary common law rules as to termination etc will apply. They will, however, be subject to the protection from eviction protections set out in Chapter 41.

38.2 WHAT IS AN ASSURED TENANCY?

The definition of an assured tenancy is set out in s 1 of the HA 1988. A tenancy under which a dwelling house is let as a separate dwelling will be an assured tenancy, if and so long as all of the following requirements are met:

(1) the tenant or each of joint tenants is an individual; and
(2) the tenant or at least one of joint tenants occupies the dwelling house as his only or principal home; and
(3) the tenancy is not specifically excluded by other provisions of the Act.

Each of these requirements must be looked at in detail.

38.2.1 Tenancy

There must be a 'tenancy'; licences to occupy dwelling houses are excluded from protection. For the distinction between a tenancy and a licence, see Chapter 37.

38.2.2 Dwelling house

There is no statutory definition of 'dwelling house', and it will be a question of fact whether premises are a house or not, but any building designed or adapted for living in is capable of forming a dwelling house for these purposes. As well as including lettings of whole houses and self-contained flats, lettings of single rooms in a house will also be included, as will converted barns, windmills, etc.

38.2.3 Let as a separate dwelling

The premises, as well as being a dwelling house, must be let *as* a dwelling. So the purpose of the letting is relevant; thus, if a building that would otherwise qualify as a dwelling house is let for business purposes, the tenant cannot claim that it is let on an assured tenancy merely because he decides to move in and live there.

There must be a letting as *a* dwelling. It has been established that this only permits of a singular construction (notwithstanding the Interpretation Act 1978). So if the let property comprises two or more residential units, each intended for separate occupation (eg the letting of the whole of a house converted into several flats), that tenancy cannot be an assured tenancy. The sub-letting of each of the individual flats could, however, be within the definition.

There must be a *separate* dwelling. This is intended to exclude lettings of accommodation which lacks some essential feature of a dwelling, such as a kitchen. However, s 3 of the HA 1988 makes special provision for the situation where the tenant shares some of the essential features of a dwelling with others. Such a letting is deemed to be an assured tenancy (assuming that all the other conditions are met) even though the absence of essential facilities in the demised property would normally prevent the tenancy from fulfilling the statutory requirements. The tenant must, however, have the exclusive occupation of at least one room (otherwise it cannot be a tenancy), and if the other accommodation is shared with the landlord, the tenancy will be excluded from the definition of an assured tenancy for different reasons (see **38.9**). However, the provisions of s 3 mean that arrangements whereby each tenant is given exclusive occupation of his own bed-sitting room, but shares bathroom and kitchen with other tenants, will be deemed to be capable of being assured tenancies. Such an arrangement must be contrasted, however, with the situation where each member of a group of people is given a right to share the occupation of the whole of the house with the others. No one has the right to exclusive possession of any part of the house, and the arrangement can only give rise to a licence (see Chapter 37).

38.2.4 'If and so long as'

The status of the tenancy is not to be determined once and for all at the commencement of the letting. Whether a tenancy is an assured tenancy can fluctuate according to changed circumstances. For example, one requirement of the definition is that the tenant must be occupying the house as his only or principal home. This may have been the case at the start of the tenancy, and so the tenancy would be assured, but if subsequently the tenant ceases to reside, the tenancy will no longer be assured. The tenant will thus lose his security of tenure.

38.2.5 The tenant must be an individual

Lettings to companies are excluded from the definition, even though an individual (eg a director or employee of the company) may be in occupation of the house.

Lettings to limited companies are often used by landlords as a way of avoiding the grant of an assured tenancy with its security of tenure implications. Any sub-letting by the company tenant could qualify as an assured tenancy, however, and so this should be expressly prohibited in any lettings to a company designed to take advantage of this rule.

38.2.6 The tenant must occupy as his 'only or principal home'

It is possible for a person to have more than one 'home'. If that is the case, then it is a question of fact as to which is the tenant's principal home. This could be a significant question, for example, for the person working in the City who has a flat nearby in which he lives during the week, and a house in the country in which he lives at weekends. Which is his principal home? Only a tenancy of the principal home can be an assured tenancy. Although the provision requires 'occupation', this does not mean continuous occupation. A mere temporary absence will not deprive a tenancy of its status as an assured tenancy.

38.3 TENANCIES WHICH CANNOT BE ASSURED

Various lettings which satisfy the basic definition of an assured tenancy will, in fact, not be protected if they fall within one of the following exceptions. Equally, as they cannot be assured tenancies, they cannot be assured shorthold tenancies either.

38.3.1 Tenancies entered into before the commencement of the HA 1988

The HA 1988 came into force on 15 January 1989; it is not retrospective. Only lettings entered into on or after that date can be assured tenancies. Any pre-existing tenancy will, if it has any protection at all, still remain subject to the provisions of the RA 1977 (see Chapter 40). There are, however, exceptions to this rule in some cases where a succession has taken place in relation to a pre-existing tenancy (see **40.5**). With regard to lettings on or after 15 January 1989 to a person with a subsisting RA 1977 tenancy, see **38.4**.

38.3.2 High value properties

Because of the abolition of domestic rates, a distinction has to be drawn between those tenancies granted before 1 April 1990 and those granted on or after that date. For tenancies granted before 1 April 1990, a tenancy of a dwelling house with a rateable value in excess of £750 (£1,500 in Greater London) cannot be an assured tenancy. If the tenancy was granted on or after 1 April 1990, it cannot be an assured tenancy if the rent payable is £25,000 or more per annum.

38.3.3 Tenancies at a low rent

This exclusion has also been affected by the abolition of domestic rates. Lettings made before 1 April 1990 cannot be assured if the annual rent is less than two-thirds of the rateable value of the property. For tenancies granted on or after 1 April 1990, the exclusion applies to tenancies in which the rent does not exceed £250 per annum (£1,000 per annum in Greater London).

38.3.4 Business tenancies

A tenancy to which Part II of the LTA 1954 applies cannot be an assured tenancy. This Act applies to lettings in which the premises are occupied for the purposes of a business. This means that mixed-user lettings, ie lettings of property used partly for business and partly for residential purposes cannot be assured tenancies, despite being occupied by the tenant as his only or principal home, etc. They will, however, have some protection under the LTA 1954. However, it is possible to contract out of the LTA 1954 with the consent of the court and certain types of tenancy will also be excluded from protection under that Act. Lettings contracted out, or otherwise outside the LTA 1954, will still not be within the definition of an assured tenancy.

38.3.5 Licensed premises

Premises licensed for the sale of alcohol for consumption *on* the premises, eg a public house, are excluded from the definition of an assured tenancy even if the tenant is residing on the premises. This exception was originally required as licensed premises were also outside the protection of the LTA 1954. However, they are now protected by that Act and so the exception is now redundant.

38.3.6 Tenancies of agricultural land

A tenancy under which agricultural land exceeding 2 acres is let together with the house, cannot be an assured tenancy.

38.3.7 Tenancies of agricultural holdings

A tenancy under which a dwelling house is comprised in an agricultural holding (within the meaning of the Agricultural Holdings Act 1986 (AHA 1986)) and is occupied by the person responsible for the control of the farming of the holding, cannot be an assured tenancy.

Agricultural holdings (ie farms) have their own system of security of tenure under the AHA 1986 and the Agricultural Tenancies Act 1995.

38.3.8 Lettings to students

Lettings to students by specified educational bodies are outside the definition of an assured tenancy. This exception does not apply to lettings to students by landlords other than the specified universities and colleges; these are capable of being assured tenancies, subject to the normal requirements being fulfilled.

38.3.9 Holiday lettings

A letting for the purpose of a holiday cannot be an assured tenancy. Some landlords have tried to exploit this exception by purportedly granting holiday lettings in non-holiday areas and for excessively long periods of time. Such arrangements, however, will be open to attack as 'shams' if they do not represent the true intention of the parties.

38.3.10 Lettings by resident landlords

A tenancy will have a resident landlord where the landlord lives in another part of the same building in which the accommodation let to the tenant is situated. In the case of a letting by a resident landlord, it is likely that the landlord and the tenant will be living in such close proximity to each other that it might be unwise to give the tenant security of tenure. This would result in the landlord and the tenant being forced to continue living under the same roof, which might lead to unpleasantness. Such lettings are excluded from the definition of an assured tenancy provided that certain conditions are complied with (for details, see **38.9**).

38.3.11 Crown, local authority and housing association lettings

Although Crown, local authority and housing association lettings are excluded from the definition of an assured tenancy, lettings by local authorities and housing associations may have other protections (see **36.4**).

38.4 TRANSITIONAL PROVISIONS

Provisions were inserted in the HA 1988 to ensure that any existing RA 1977 tenants were not deprived of their existing protections under that Act by landlords granting them new tenancies after the coming into force of the HA 1988. Thus, a tenancy granted to a person who was a protected or statutory tenant under the RA 1977 by that person's landlord (or one of joint landlords) will still be a protected tenancy even though it is granted on or after 15 January 1989. This will still be the case even if the new letting is of a different property to that comprised in the previous tenancy. The only exception to this provision is if the tenant was a protected shorthold tenant under the RA 1977. Protected shortholds were the precursors of assured shortholds and like them gave no security of tenure. Any new letting to a protected shorthold tenant will be an *assured* shorthold whether or not it complies with the normal shorthold requirements (HA 1988, s 34(3)). For further details as to assured shortholds, see Chapter 39, and as to protected shortholds, see Chapter 40.

38.5 RENTS UNDER ASSURED TENANCIES

38.5.1 The initial rent

There is no restriction on the amount of rent which can initially be charged on the grant of an assured tenancy. This is so even if there is a subsisting registration of a fair rent for the purposes of the RA 1977 (see Chapter 40). However, if the landlord subsequently wishes to increase the rent, he may not be able to do so unless he follows the correct procedure.

38.5.2 Contractual increases

Under normal contractual principles, a landlord cannot unilaterally vary the terms of a tenancy after it has been granted. He cannot, therefore, change the amount of the rent payable without the consent of the tenant or without bringing the existing letting to an end and then granting a new one to the tenant at the higher rent. As the tenant under an assured tenancy has security of tenure, bringing the tenancy to an end might not be possible. It is essential, therefore, for a provision to be inserted in any tenancy agreement likely to subsist for some length of time, allowing the landlord to increase the rent, should he wish to do so. Many informally granted tenancies, however, contain no such provisions and so the HA 1988 contains provisions enabling a landlord to increase the rent even though this is not permitted by the terms of the agreement (see **38.5.3**). These provisions apply only to periodic tenancies, however, and the procedure is somewhat complex. It is, therefore, still advisable to include a provision for rent increase even in a periodic tenancy. This express provision will then prevail over the statutory rules.

38.5.3 Statutory increases for assured periodic tenancies

Statutory increases for assured periodic tenancies are governed by ss 13 and 14 of the HA 1988 which lay down a complicated procedure requiring the landlord to serve a notice (in the prescribed form) on the tenant. This can then be referred to the Rent Assessment Committee for arbitration if agreement as to the new rent cannot be reached between the parties. There is no suggestion, however, that the rent would in any way be less than the open market rent for the house. The Rent Assessment Committee is specifically directed to determine the rent at which the premises might reasonably be let in the open market. This is not a return to the old 'fair rent' system under the RA 1977 under which a rent lower than an open market rent is frequently assessed (see Chapter 40). If there is an express term in the tenancy agreement permitting rent increases, this will avoid the need to rely on the statutory procedure.

38.5.4 Rent increases for fixed-term assured tenancies (including shortholds)

There are no statutory provisions allowing an increase for fixed-term assured tenancies. In the absence of any express provision in the tenancy agreement, the landlord will be unable to increase the rent during the fixed term without the agreement of the tenant. Once the fixed term has ended and the tenant continues in possession as a statutory periodic tenant (see **38.10.1**) then the above provisions of ss 13 and 14 of the HA 1988 will apply to enable the landlord to increase the rent, even if there is no express provision in the lease. However, it is essential that fixed-term leases of longer than (say) 12 months' duration should contain an express term permitting the landlord to increase the rent in order to counter the possible effects of inflation during the period of the tenancy.

38.6 PROHIBITION ON ASSIGNMENT WITHOUT CONSENT

At common law, a tenant under a lease can freely assign it, sub-let, or take in lodgers, etc. This is unlikely to be acceptable to a landlord; there is little point in a landlord carefully checking the references etc, of a tenant, to find that the tenant can then assign the tenancy to a person who would have been an unacceptable tenant. It is sensible, therefore, for the tenancy agreement to contain an express prohibition on assignment without consent. However, if there is no such express provision, s 15 of the HA 1988 may be of some assistance to the landlord. The section only applies to periodic assured tenancies (including statutory periodic tenancies); like the provisions allowing increases of rent, it does not apply to fixed-term assured tenancies (including shortholds). Thus, in the absence of an express contractual prohibition, fixed-term tenants will be able to assign or sub-let at will.

The term implied into a periodic assured tenancy is that the tenant must not without the consent of the landlord:

(1) assign the tenancy; or
(2) sub-let or part with possession of all or part of the property.

One advantage for the landlord of this implied term over an express term is that the protections given to tenants by s 19 of the LTA 1927 do *not* apply. Section 19, which applies only to qualified covenants against assignment, ie covenants not to assign without the landlord's consent, prevents a landlord from withholding such consent unreasonably. As this provision does not apply, the landlord can be as unreasonable as he likes in withholding consent under this implied term.

In the case of a periodic tenancy which is not a statutory periodic tenancy, these prohibitions do not apply if a premium was paid on the grant or renewal of the tenancy. 'Premium' is defined to include any pecuniary consideration in addition to rent and also includes returnable deposits exceeding one-sixth of the annual rent. Because of the possibility that a premium might have been paid, it is always advisable for a landlord to include an express prohibition on assignment in his tenancy agreement. As previously stated, it is essential to include such a provision in a fixed-term letting. If there is an express provision dealing with assignment etc, the terms of this will prevail over the statutory provisions. This express term should be an absolute bar on assigning etc, so avoiding the reasonableness proviso under s 19 of the LTA 1927. Even with this absolute prohibition, it would always be open to a landlord to agree to a particular assignment, etc should be wish to do so. As the reasonableness proviso of s 19 is not applicable, however, he can be as arbitrary as he likes in making this decision. Note that the provisions of s 22 of the Landlord and Tenant (Covenants) Act 1995 (which allow a landlord and tenant to agree in advance terms or circumstances in which a landlord will or will not consent to an assignment) do *not* apply to lettings of residential premises.

38.7 SUCCESSION ON DEATH

On the death of a tenant, his tenancy does not die with him; it is a proprietary right and will pass in the same way as the deceased's other property. On the death of one of joint tenants, the tenancy will vest in the survivor(s). On the death of a sole tenant the tenancy will pass under his will or intestacy. The HA 1988, however, contains specific provisions (s 17) dealing with the succession to an assured periodic tenancy on the death of a sole tenant which will override these normal rules.

On the death of a sole periodic tenant the tenancy will vest in the tenant's spouse, notwithstanding the terms of the deceased's will, provided that immediately before the deceased tenant's death the spouse was occupying the dwelling house as his or her only or principal home. 'Spouse' is defined to include a person who was living with the tenant as his or her wife or husband as well as persons who were lawfully married. There can be no succession, however, in favour of a person of the same sex who may have been co-habiting with the deceased tenant. This provision will not apply if the deceased tenant was himself a 'successor', as defined, ie the tenancy became vested in him:

(1) by virtue of this section; or
(2) under the will or intestacy of a former tenant; or
(3) he is the sole survivor of joint tenants; or
(4) he succeeded to the tenancy under the provisions of the RA 1977 (see Chapter 40).

Thus, only one statutory succession is possible. If there is no statutory succession, eg because there is no qualifying 'spouse', or there has already been a succession, or the tenancy is for a fixed term, the tenancy will then pass under the will or intestacy of the deceased in the normal way. However, on the death of a periodic assured tenant in such a situation, the landlord would be able to make use of one of the mandatory grounds in order to obtain possession (see Ground 7 at **38.10.3**).

38.8 SUB-LETTINGS

As between the particular landlord and tenant it is irrelevant whether the landlord owns the freehold interest in the property or merely a leasehold interest. If the conditions are complied with for the creation of an assured tenancy, then the tenant will have the benefit of security of tenure and the other assured tenancy provisions against his landlord, whether or not that landlord owns the freehold or is himself a tenant.

The question arises as to whether an assured sub-tenant has protection against the owner of the freehold reversion. The normal rule at common law is that if a head lease comes to an end then any sub-lease derived out of it will also determine. This, however, is varied by the provisions of s 18 of the HA 1988. This provides that in the case of a house lawfully sub-let on an assured tenancy, that on the ending of the head lease, the sub-tenancy will still continue. The assured sub-tenant will then become the direct tenant of the head landlord with full security of tenure. It is because of this rule that it is essential for a prohibition on sub-letting to be included in the terms of an assured shorthold tenancy. Even though the head tenant (the assured shorthold tenant) will have no security against the head landlord, the sub-tenant might if the sub-letting amounts to an ordinary assured tenancy. However, this only applies to lawful sub-lettings. A sub-letting will not be lawful if it is in breach of an express or implied prohibition on sub-letting contained in the head lease (eg by virtue of s 15 of the HA 1988, see **38.6**). In the case of an unlawful sub-letting, the sub-tenant will have no security once the head lease has been determined and the head landlord will thus have an absolute right to possession.

38.9 LETTINGS BY RESIDENT LANDLORDS

As stated in **38.3.10**, most lettings by resident landlords will be excluded from the definition of an assured tenancy. Because of this, they cannot be shortholds either. Such lettings will thus have no security of tenure, and may also only have limited protection under the protection from eviction legislation (see Chapter 41). However, for the resident landlord exception to apply various conditions must be fulfilled.

38.9.1 Qualifying conditions

The following qualifying conditions apply:

(1) the dwelling house which is let forms only part of a building; and
(2) the building is not a purpose-built block of flats; and
(3) the tenancy was granted by an individual (ie not a limited company) who at the time of the grant occupied another part of the same building as his only or principal home; and
(4) at all times since the tenancy was granted, the interest of the landlord has continued to belong to an individual who continued so to reside.

Continuity of residence

It is not sufficient for the landlord merely to have been in residence at the commencement of the tenancy; he must be in occupation throughout the tenancy. If he ceases to reside then the exception will cease to apply and the letting will once again be capable of being an assured tenancy with full security of tenure. However, if the letting is entered into on or after 28 February 1997 (the commencement date of the Housing Act 1996), then the letting will become an assured shorthold tenancy. The landlord will still have an absolute right to possession but must then follow the correct shorthold procedure. Note that, if the interest of the landlord is vested in two or more individuals, only one of those persons need be in residence at any one time.

Periods of absence disregarded

Further, certain periods of absence will be disregarded when deciding whether the landlord's occupation has been continuous:

(1) a period of 28 days beginning with the date on which the interest of the landlord becomes vested at law and in equity in a new owner. If, during this 28 days, the new owner notifies the tenant in writing of his intention to occupy another part of the building as his only or main home, the disregard will be extended up to 6 months from the change of legal etc, ownership; and
(2) any period not exceeding 2 years during which the interest of the landlord becomes and remains vested in:
    (a) trustees as such; or
    (b) the Probate Judge under s 9 of the Administration of Estates Act 1925 (AEA 1925); or
    (c) personal representatives of a deceased person acting in that capacity.

Throughout any period during which absence is so disregarded (except in a situation where the house is vested in personal representatives), no order for possession can be made except one which might have been made if the tenancy were an assured tenancy. In other words, during these periods of deemed residence the letting becomes a quasi-assured tenancy and possession can only be obtained against the tenant if assured tenancy grounds can be established. However, as an exception to that rule, personal representatives of a deceased resident landlord will be able to recover possession without proving assured tenancy grounds, provided that the contractual term can be terminated.

Purpose-built blocks of flats

This resident landlord exception does not apply if the building is a purpose-built block of flats and the landlord occupies one flat in the block and lets one (or more) of the others. Such lettings are therefore capable of being assured tenancies. With a purpose-built block of flats, as opposed to a house etc, converted into flats, there is not likely to be the close proximity between landlord and tenant which dictated that security of tenure should not be given to the tenant. So what is a 'purpose-built' block of flats?

A building is a purpose-built block of flats if *as constructed* it contained, and still contains, two or more flats.

'Flat' means a dwelling house which forms only part of a building and is separated horizontally from another dwelling house which forms part of the same building.

The HA 1988 makes it clear, however, that if the landlord occupies one flat in a purpose-built block and lets part of that flat, then the resident landlord exception can still apply. In that situation there will once again be potential problems if the parties are compelled to continue living in the same flat.

38.9.2 Exceptions

The HA 1988 lays down an exception to this resident landlord rule, ie a situation which looks as though it will be outside the definition of an assured tenancy because of the resident landlord exception, but which will in fact still be capable of being an assured tenancy. A tenancy will be excluded from the resident landlord provisions if two conditions are both fulfilled:

(1) it was granted to a person who immediately before the grant was an assured tenant of the same house or of another house in the same building; and
(2) the landlord under the new tenancy and under the former tenancy is the same person. If either of the tenancies was granted by two or more persons, it is sufficient for this condition that the same person is the landlord or one of the landlords under each tenancy.

This is an anti-avoidance provision designed to ensure that a landlord does not deprive existing tenants of their protection as assured tenants by taking up possession himself and then granting a new tenancy to those existing tenants.

38.10 SECURITY OF TENURE

38.10.1 Restriction on termination by landlord

An assured tenancy cannot be brought to an end by the landlord otherwise than by obtaining a court order for possession. Thus, in the case of a periodic assured tenancy, a notice to quit is of no effect. On the ending of a fixed-term assured tenancy (including a shorthold) otherwise than by an order of the court or by surrender, the tenant is entitled to remain in possession as a statutory periodic tenant. This statutory periodic tenancy will be on the same terms as the previous fixed-term tenancy (although there is a little used procedure for changing those terms: see s 6 of the HA 1988). However, any provision which provides for termination of the tenancy by the landlord or the tenant shall not have effect while the tenancy remains an assured tenancy.

38.10.2 Obtaining a court order

The landlord will only obtain a court order for possession if he follows the correct procedure and can establish one or more of the grounds for possession set out in Sch 2 to the HA 1988. Further, although some of these grounds are mandatory grounds, ie the court must order possession if the ground is established, many of them are discretionary grounds. With these, the court, on proof of the ground, may order possession only if it considers it reasonable to do so. The procedure for obtaining possession involves the landlord serving a notice on the tenant (a 's 8 notice'), in the prescribed form. The s 8 notice must specify the ground(s) upon which the landlord intends to rely and must give 2 weeks' notice of the landlord's intention to commence possession proceedings. (Sometimes 2 months' notice has to be given depending upon the ground used.) However, if Ground 14 is specified (whether or not with any other ground) then the proceedings can be commenced as soon as the s 8 notice has been served. The proceedings must then be commenced not earlier than the date specified and not later than 12 months from the date of service of the notice. It is possible for the court to dispense with the requirement for a s 8 notice (unless Ground 8 is being relied upon), but only if it considers it 'just and equitable' to do so.

In the case of a fixed-term assured tenancy, the landlord cannot normally obtain possession until after the end of the contractual fixed term (assuming that a ground for possession can then be established). However, as an exception to this, certain of the grounds for possession will be available to the landlord during the fixed term provided that the tenancy agreement contains a provision for it to be brought to an end on the ground in question. This provision can take any form at all, including a proviso for re-entry or a forfeiture clause. The grounds on which the landlord can obtain possession in this way during the fixed term are grounds 2, 8 and 10 to 15.

38.10.3 The grounds for possession: mandatory grounds

The mandatory grounds are set out in Sch 2 to the HA 1988, the full text of which is set out below. Part 1 of the Schedule contains the mandatory grounds, ie those, on proof of which, the court must make an order for possession in the landlord's favour.

Ground 1 (owner-occupier etc)

> 'Not later than the beginning of the tenancy the landlord gave notice in writing to the tenant that possession might be recovered on this ground or the court is of the opinion that it is just and equitable to dispense with the requirement of notice and (in either case)—
>
> (a) at some time before the beginning of the tenancy, the landlord who is seeking possession or, in the case of joint landlords seeking possession, at least one of them occupied the dwelling house as his only or principal home; or
>
> (b) the landlord who is seeking possession or, in the case of joint landlords seeking possession, at least one of them requires the dwelling house as his or his spouse's only or principal home and neither the landlord (or, in the case of joint landlords, any one of them) nor any other person who, as landlord, derived title under the landlord who gave the notice mentioned above acquired the reversion on the tenancy for money or money's worth.'

This ground is sometimes referred to as the 'owner-occupier' ground, but it really consists of two separate situations entitling the landlord to possession, only one of which requires prior occupation by the landlord. For both, though, it is necessary for the landlord to have given a written notice to the tenant 'not later than the beginning of the tenancy' that possession might be recovered under this ground. Due to this wording, such a notice would be valid if contained in the tenancy agreement itself. If the notice was not served, then it can be dispensed with if the court thinks that it is 'just and equitable' to do so. This might be the case where the landlord told the tenant orally that he was an owner-occupier but omitted to give written notice as required by the ground. Obviously, this dispensation should not be relied upon.

Paragraph (a) of the ground merely requires the landlord to prove that at 'some time' before the tenancy was granted he occupied the house as his only or principal home. This residence by the landlord need not be immediately prior to the letting; it could be several years before. Once having established this, he does not have to give or prove any reason as to why he might want possession; it does not have to be because he now wishes to live in the house again, although this might often be the case. Possession is available whatever his reasons.

If paragraph (b) of this ground is being relied upon, there is no need for the landlord to have resided in the property at any time in the past. In this situation, however, the landlord will need to show that the house is required as his (or his spouse's) only or principal home. This will be a question of fact in each particular case. There is an obvious danger here that an unscrupulous person might buy the reversion in the house subject to a tenancy, perhaps at a very low price because of the sitting tenant, and then use this ground to obtain possession from the tenant. This is prevented by the proviso that the ground will not be available to a landlord who has acquired the reversion to the tenancy for money or money's worth. There is no time-limit within which this acquisition must have taken place; even if it occurred (say) 5 years ago, this ground will still not be available. The ground will be available, however, to a landlord who has inherited the reversion from a deceased landlord, or who acquires the reversion by way of a gift.

This is one of the grounds for which s 8 requires 2 months' notice of impending proceedings being given.

Ground 2 (mortgagee exercising power of sale)

> 'The dwelling house is subject to a mortgage granted before the beginning of the tenancy; and
>
> (a) the mortgagee is entitled to exercise a power of sale conferred on him by the mortgage or by section 101 of the Law of Property Act 1925; and
> (b) the mortgagee requires possession of the dwelling house for the purpose of disposing of it with vacant possession in exercise of that power; and
> (c) either notice was given as mentioned in Ground 1 above or the court is satisfied that it is just and equitable to dispense with the requirement of notice;
>
> and for the purposes of this ground "mortgage" includes a charge and "mortgagee" shall be construed accordingly.'

Sometimes a mortgagee will be able to obtain possession against a tenant without the need to prove any ground for possession. Although a mortgagor in possession has limited powers to grant leases under s 99 of the LPA 1925, this is normally excluded by the terms of the mortgage deed. Any tenancy granted by the mortgagor without the consent of the mortgagee will thus not be binding upon the mortgagee. Accordingly, although the mortgagor/landlord would not be able to obtain possession without proving assured tenancy grounds, the mortgagee (eg a building society) will have an absolute right to possession. If the mortgagee were to give consent to a letting during the continuance of the mortgage, it is likely that it would require this ground to be available to it in order to protect its position should it need to realise its security. There is some confusion over the precise meaning of the requirement that for this ground to apply, a notice 'as mentioned in Ground 1' needs to have been given. It is probable that this means that as long as a Ground 1 notice has been given, then the mortgagee can use Ground 2, should it need to do so. However, many mortgagees, as a condition of giving consent to the letting will require the mortgagor/landlord to give a separate notice stating that Ground 2 will be available against the tenant. Although this is probably superfluous, giving such a notice does no harm, *provided* that a Ground 1 notice is given as well; it is likely that it is the service of the Ground 1 notice that triggers the availability of Ground 2, as previously stated. This is one of the grounds which are available during the subsistence of a fixed term if there is an appropriate provision in the tenancy agreement (see **37.3.18** and **38.10.2**).

As with Ground 1, 2 months' notice of proceedings must be served.

Ground 3 (out-of-season holiday accommodation)

> 'The tenancy is a fixed term tenancy for a term not exceeding eight months and—
>
> (a) not later than the beginning of the tenancy the landlord gave notice in writing to the tenant that possession might be recovered on this ground; and
>
> (b) at some time within the period of twelve months ending with the beginning of the tenancy, the dwelling house was occupied under a right to occupy it for a holiday.'

Here it is clear that the notice which must be served 'not later than the beginning of the tenancy' must specifically state that this ground will be available against the tenant. Unlike Grounds 1 and 2, there is no discretion given to the court to dispense with this notice, even though it might be just and equitable to do so. This ground will not be available unless the notice is served in writing in accordance with the above requirements.

This ground is designed to be used by landlords who let their property for holiday purposes during the summer months, but who make it available for ordinary residential use during the winter months. These are frequently referred to as 'winter lets', and the landlord needs to be able to ensure that he will be able to obtain vacant possession before the accommodation is once more required for holiday-makers. One possibility would be to make use of an assured shorthold tenancy, but this ground has the advantages that only 2 weeks' notice of impending possession proceedings is required, and there is no restriction on obtaining possession within 6 months of the grant; as to the position with assured shorthold tenancies, see Chapter 39. For this ground to apply, the letting must be for a fixed term (not exceeding 8 months); this ground will not be available in the case of a periodic tenancy, even if the correct notice was given.

Ground 4 (out of term student accommodation)

> 'The tenancy is fixed-term tenancy for a term not exceeding twelve months and—
>
> (a) not later than the beginning of the tenancy the landlord gave notice in writing to the tenant that possession might be recovered on this ground; and
>
> (b) at some time within the period of twelve months ending with the beginning of the tenancy, the dwelling house was let on a tenancy falling within paragraph 8 of Schedule 1 to this Act.'

Paragraph 8 of Sch 1 applies to tenancies granted to students by a specified educational institution and which are outside the definition of an assured tenancy. Many educational institutions, however, let their accommodation during non-term times to non-students (eg for conferences); this ground enables them to ensure that they will be certain of recovering possession at the end of the letting, provided that the requirements of the ground as to serving notice etc, are complied with. As with

Ground 3, there is no power for the court to dispense with the requirements as to notice.

Ground 5 (minister of religion's house)

> 'The dwelling house is held for the purpose of being available for occupation by a minister of religion as a residence from which to perform the duties of his office and—
>
> (a) not later than the beginning of the tenancy the landlord gave notice in writing to the tenant that possession might be recovered on this ground; and
>
> (b) the court is satisfied that the dwelling house is required for occupation by a minister of religion as such a residence.'

Two months' notice of proceedings is required for this ground, which is again dependent upon service of a notice in writing which cannot be dispensed with.

Ground 6 (demolition etc)

> 'The landlord who is seeking possession or, if that landlord is a registered housing association or charitable housing trust, a superior landlord intends to demolish or reconstruct the whole or a substantial part of the dwelling house or to carry out substantial works on the dwelling house or any part thereof or any building of which it forms part and the following conditions are fulfilled—
>
> (a) the intended work cannot reasonably be carried out without the tenant giving up possession of the dwelling house because—
>
> (i) the tenant is not willing to agree to such a variation of the terms of the tenancy as would give such access and other facilities as would permit the intended work to be carried out, or
>
> (ii) the nature of the intended work is such that no such variation is practicable, or
>
> (iii) the tenant is not willing to accept an assured tenancy of such part only of the dwelling house (in this sub-paragraph referred to as "the reduced part") as would leave in the possession of his landlord so much of the dwelling house as would be reasonable to enable the intended work to be carried out and, where appropriate, as would give such access and other facilities over the reduced part as would permit the intended work to be carried out, or
>
> (iv) the nature of the intended work is such that such a tenancy is not practicable; and
>
> (b) either the landlord seeking possession acquired his interest in the dwelling house before the grant of the tenancy or that interest was in existence at the time of that grant and neither that landlord (or, in the case of joint landlords, any of them) nor any other person who, alone or jointly with others, has acquired that interest since that time acquired it for money or money's worth; and
>
> (c) the assured tenancy on which the dwelling house is let did not come into being by virtue of any provision of Schedule 1 to the Rent Act 1977, as amended by Part I of Schedule 4 to this Act or, as the case may be, section 4 of the Rent (Agriculture) Act 1976, as amended by Part II of that Schedule.
>
> For the purposes of this ground, if, immediately before the grant of the tenancy, the tenant to whom it was granted or, if it was granted to joint tenants, any of them was the tenant or one of the joint tenants of the dwelling house concerned

> under an earlier assured tenancy or, as the case may be, under a tenancy to which Schedule 10 to the Local Government and Housing Act 1989 applied, any reference in paragraph (b) above to the grant of a tenancy is a reference to the grant of that earlier assured tenancy or, as the case may be, to the grant of the tenancy to which the said Schedule 10 applied.
>
> For the purposes of this ground "registered housing association" has the same meaning as in the Housing Associations Act 1985 and "charitable housing trust" means a housing trust, within the meaning of that Act, which is a charity, within the meaning of the Charities Act 1960.
>
> For the purposes of this ground, every acquisition under Part IV of this Act shall be taken to be an acquisition for money or money's worth; and in any case where—
>
> (i) the tenancy (in this paragraph referred to as "the current tenancy") was granted to a person (alone or jointly with others) who, immediately before it was granted, was a tenant under a tenancy of a different dwelling house (in this paragraph referred to as "the earlier tenancy"), and
> (ii) the landlord under the current tenancy is the person who, immediately before that tenancy was granted, was the landlord under the earlier tenancy, and
> (iii) the condition in paragraph (b) above could not have been fulfilled with respect to the earlier tenancy by virtue of an acquisition under Part IV of this Act (including one taken to be such an acquisition by virtue of the previous operation of this paragraph),
>
> the acquisition of the landlord's interest under the current tenancy shall be taken to have been under that Part and the landlord shall be taken to have acquired that interest after the grant of the current tenancy.'

This long and complex ground is quite simple in its basic intent; the complications come from detailed rules which are designed to prevent unscrupulous landlords from attempting to use this ground when the circumstances do not really justify it. The ground is that the landlord intends to demolish or reconstruct the house (or the building of which it forms a part) or a substantial part of it. Unlike the previous mandatory grounds, there is no requirement for any warning notice to have been served prior to the grant of the tenancy. Paragraph (a) makes it clear that if the works can be carried out 'around the tenant' without possession being obtained, then the ground will not apply, unless the tenant refuses to agree to the necessary arrangements. Paragraph (b) prevents a landlord who has acquired his interest for money or money's worth since the date of the grant of the tenancy from using the ground. This is included for the same reason as the similar provision in Ground 1. Another 'anti-avoidance' device prevents a landlord from circumventing this restriction by purchasing the reversion subject to a tenancy and then granting a new tenancy to the same tenant (or one of joint tenants). The purchase subject to the original tenancy prevents this ground from being used.

The references in para (c) exclude from the operation of this ground those former RA 1977 tenancies which are converted to assured tenancies on a succession taking place following the death of the original tenant (for details of these, see Chapter 40).

Two months' notice of proceedings must be served by the landlord for this ground to be available.

If this ground is established, the landlord must pay the tenant's reasonable removal costs.

Ground 7 (death)

> 'The tenancy is a periodic tenancy (including a statutory periodic tenancy) which has devolved under the will or intestacy of the former tenant and the proceedings for the recovery of possession are begun not later than twelve months after the death of the former tenant or, if the court so directs, after the date on which, in the opinion of the court, the landlord or, in the case of joint landlords, any one of them became aware of the former tenant's death.
>
> For the purposes of this ground, the acceptance by the landlord of rent from a new tenant after the death of the former tenant shall not be regarded as creating a new periodic tenancy, unless the landlord agrees in writing to a change (as compared with the tenancy before the death) in the amount of the rent, the period of the tenancy, the premises which are let or any other term of the tenancy.'

In certain circumstances, on the death of an assured tenant, the deceased's spouse will be entitled to succeed to the tenancy (see **38.7**), in which case this ground will not be available. If the succession provisions do not apply, for example, if there is no spouse entitled to succeed, then the tenancy will vest in the deceased's personal representatives and pass according to his will or intestacy. However, in such a case, this mandatory ground for possession will be available against whomsoever might be entitled under the will etc. The possession proceedings themselves must be commenced within 12 months of the death. However, landlords need to be careful as the s 8 notice still needs to be served before the proceedings are commenced and, for this ground at least 2 months' notice must be given. So, in effect, the landlord has less than 10 months from the death in which to serve the notice if proceedings are to be commenced within the 12-month time-limit. It may be that the landlord does not become aware of the death of the tenant until some time after it occurs. In that situation, the requisite 12-month period runs from the date upon which the landlord, in the opinion of the court, became aware of the death. This will be a question of fact in each particular case. The mere fact that the landlord has accepted rent from a third party (eg a relative of the deceased) after the death will not serve to create a new periodic tenancy in that person's favour. Depending upon the circumstances of the case, such payment may or may not give notice to the landlord of the death of the original tenant.

Ground 8 (substantial rent arrears)

> 'Both at the date of the service of the notice under section 8 of this Act relating to the proceedings for possession and at the date of the hearing—
>
> (a) if rent is payable weekly or fortnightly, at least eight weeks' rent is unpaid;
> (b) if rent is payable monthly, at least two months' rent is unpaid;
> (c) if rent is payable quarterly, at least one quarter's rent is more than three months in arrears; and
> (d) if rent is payable yearly, at least three months' rent is more than three months in arrears;
>
> and for the purpose of this ground "rent" means rent lawfully due from the tenant.'

One frequent ground for complaint by landlords of RA 1977 tenants was the difficulty of obtaining possession against tenants who defaulted in their rental payments. Under RA 1977, rent arrears is a discretionary ground for possession (see Chapter 40) and often the court will exercise its discretion and refuse to order possession despite proof of arrears. For assured tenancies, however, Ground 8 makes rent arrears a mandatory ground for possession, but only in the limited circumstances laid down in the ground.

As originally drafted, the ground was only available, in the case of weekly or monthly payments, if 13 weeks' or 3 months' arrears were established. However, as from 28 February 1997, the commencement date of the HA 1996, this was reduced to 8 weeks' or 2 months' arrears in an attempt to satisfy complaints from landlords that 13 weeks' arrears was too long to have to wait before possession could be guaranteed. The amended version of the ground applies to all lettings, whenever created, and not just those entered into after the commencement of the HA 1996.

Note, however, that these arrears must exist *both* at the time of the service of the s 8 notice *and* at the date of the hearing. Thus, a partial payment by the tenant before the hearing so that only (say) 7 weeks' arrears existed, would be sufficient to prevent the ground from applying.

As to the significance of the requirement that the rent must be 'lawfully due', see **37.3.11** and the provisions of s 48 of the LTA 1987.

It is not possible for the court to dispense with the requirement for the service of a notice under s 8 of the HA 1988 if this ground is being relied upon.

For discretionary grounds for possession based on arrears of rent, see Grounds 10 and 11 at **38.10.4**. In view of the possibility of a tenant making a partial payment by the date of the hearing and so preventing this ground from being relied upon, it would be usual for a landlord to serve a s 8 notice and commence proceedings based on these discretionary grounds as well as Ground 8.

Ground 8 (and also grounds 10 and 11) can be used during the subsistence of a fixed term tenancy provided this is permitted by the terms of the tenancy agreement (see **37.3.18** and **38.10.2**).

38.10.4 Grounds for possession: discretionary grounds

Proof of the following grounds for possession will not inevitably result in a possession order being made against a tenant. The court can only make such an order if it considers it 'reasonable to do so'. This will be a question of fact in each case, but this proviso will enable the court to consider the prospective hardship likely to be suffered by both the landlord and the tenant, depending upon whether it makes a possession order or not. The conduct of the parties during the tenancy will also be relevant to the question of 'reasonableness'.

Ground 9 (alternative accommodation)

> 'Suitable alternative accommodation is available for the tenant or will be available for him when the order for possession takes effect.'

The 'suitable alternative accommodation' need not be provided by the landlord, although the landlord must be able to prove to the court that it will be available for the tenant when the order takes effect. Part III of Sch 2 to the HA 1988 sets out the circumstances to be taken into account in deciding whether the alternative accommodation will be 'suitable' or not. If the landlord can obtain a certificate from the local housing authority to the effect that it will provide alternative accommodation for the tenant, the certificate is deemed to be conclusive evidence that the accommodation will be 'suitable' for the needs of the tenant. In practice, however, it is most unlikely that such a certificate would be forthcoming from the housing authority due to other pressures on the limited amount of accommodation available to it. It may well be that, if a possession order was obtained, the housing authority would be obliged to rehouse the tenant because of its responsibilities to homeless persons under the HA 1985, but that is not to say that the authority will facilitate the making of the possession order by issuing such a certificate.

Alternatively, the landlord will have to show that the proposed alternative accommodation is 'reasonably suitable' to the needs of the tenant and his family as far as location, size and rent. Further, it must be available for letting on an assured tenancy, but not an assured shorthold, nor one to which mandatory Grounds 1 to 5 might apply.

To avail himself of this ground, 2 months' notice of proceedings is required. As with mandatory Ground 6, the landlord must pay the tenant's reasonable removal expenses if possession is ordered on this ground.

Ground 10 (rent arrears)

> 'Some rent lawfully due from the tenant—
>
> (a) is unpaid on the date on which the proceedings for possession are begun; and
>
> (b) except where subsection (1)(b) of section 8 of this Act applies, was in arrears at the date of the service of the notice under that section relating to those proceedings.'

This is the first of the two discretionary grounds based on rent arrears (see also Ground 11). Unlike the mandatory Ground 8, which requires at least 8 weeks' rent to be in arrears both at the date of the service of the s 8 notice and at the date of the hearing, for this ground to be established there is no minimum amount that needs to be outstanding. Indeed, as long as some rent was in arrears at the date of the s 8 notice and at the start of the possession proceedings, it does not matter whether or not there is any rent in arrears at all when the hearing day arrives. It is sensible, therefore, for a landlord to use this ground in addition to Ground 8 to cover the possibility of a tenant paying off some or all of the arrears prior to the hearing date. Although it will be easier for the landlord to establish this ground rather than Ground 8, it is a discretionary ground. Even though the ground is established, the court can only make an order for possession if it considers it reasonable to do so.

The reference in the ground to subsection (1)(b) of s 8, relates to the court's power to dispense with the service of a s 8 notice if it considers it just and equitable to do so. See **37.3.18** as to the use of this ground during the subsistence of a fixed term.

Ground 11 (persistent delay)

> 'Whether or not any rent is in arrears on the date on which proceedings for possession are begun, the tenant has persistently delayed paying rent which has become lawfully due.'

For this ground, there is no need for any rent to be in arrears at all, whether at the date of service of the s 8 notice, or when the possession proceedings are commenced, or at the date of the hearing; all that must be established is that the tenant has 'persistently delayed paying rent'. What amounts to a persistent delay will be a question of fact in each case. Again it is usual to plead this ground as an alternative to Grounds 8 and 10. See **37.3.18** as to the use of this ground during the subsistence of a fixed term.

Ground 12 (breach of covenant etc)

> 'Any obligation of the tenancy (other than one related to the payment of rent) has been broken or not performed.'

This 'obligation of the tenancy' can be an express obligation or an implied one: for example, the implied term against assigning or sub-letting, see **38.6**. The ground will still be established even if the breach has been remedied by the date of the hearing (although this might be relevant as to whether it is reasonable for the court to order possession). This ground can be used during the subsistence of a fixed term (see **37.3.18**).

Ground 13 (waste or neglect etc)

> 'The condition of the dwelling house or any of the common parts has deteriorated owing to acts of waste by, or the neglect or default of, the tenant or any other person residing in the dwelling house and, in the case of an act of waste by, or the neglect or default of, a person lodging with the tenant or a sub-tenant of his, the tenant has not taken such steps as he ought reasonably to have taken for the removal of the lodger or sub-tenant.'

Breach of this ground may also result in a breach of Ground 12 (eg there could be a breach of the tenant's implied obligation at common law to use the property in a tenant-like manner). However, this implied obligation is ill-defined and uncertain in its operation and this ground might be easier to establish. This ground also extends to the acts etc, not just of the tenant personally, but of any other person residing in the house, for example, a spouse, or child or lodger. If the deterioration is caused by someone other than the tenant, the ground is only established if the tenant has failed to take such steps as 'he ought reasonably to have taken for the removal of the lodger or sub-tenant'. This gives rise to several unresolved problems. What steps would it be reasonable for the tenant to take to 'remove' a lodger who has caused the house to deteriorate? Is it necessary to commence possession proceedings against such a person? And what if the damage is caused by a member of the tenant's family: is that family member a 'lodger' whose removal the tenant should seek? And if so, what steps would it be reasonable to expect a tenant to take to evict his spouse or son? See **37.3.18** as to the use of this ground during a fixed term.

Ground 14 (nuisance etc)

The original wording of this ground as enacted in the HA 1988 was:

> 'The tenant or any other person residing in the dwelling house has been guilty of conduct which is a nuisance or annoyance to adjoining occupiers, or has been convicted of using the dwelling house or allowing the dwelling house to be used for immoral or illegal purposes.'

From 28 February 1997 (the commencement date of HA 1996), it was amended to read:

> 'The tenant or a person residing in or visiting the dwelling house—
>
> (a) has been guilty of conduct causing or likely to cause a nuisance or annoyance to a person residing, visiting or otherwise engaging in a lawful activity in the locality, or
>
> (b) has been convicted of—

(i) using the dwelling house or allowing it to be used for immoral or illegal purposes, or

(ii) an arrestable offence committed in, or in the locality of, the dwelling house.'

One of the changes brought about by HA 1996 was an attempt to combat anti-social behaviour by tenants by making it easier for landlords to obtain possession from them.

It can be seen that the extended ground is now much wider than previously. So it is no longer just the activities of the tenant or others residing in the house which are relevant; the conduct of visitors to the premises is also relevant. Further, the conduct in question need not actually cause a nuisance; it is sufficient if it is likely to cause a nuisance. The nuisance etc need no longer be caused to an adjoining occupier; the word 'locality' will imply a much wider area around the house. Note also the extension to cover convictions for an arrestable offence in the locality.

As far as illegal or immoral use of the house is concerned, this on its own is not sufficient to establish part (b) of the ground; there has to have been a conviction for such use. However, it may well be possible to show that illegal or immoral use is conduct causing or likely to cause a nuisance within part (a) of the ground.

Although this ground could be seen to be somewhat draconian in its implications, it should be remembered that it is only a discretionary ground, so the mere fact that on one occasion one visitor to the house caused a nuisance to someone walking their dog in the neighbourhood, will not necessarily lead to possession being ordered against the tenant. However, the importance placed by the Government on anti-social behaviour is emphasised by the s 8 notice requirements. Normally, under s 8 of the HA 1988, 2 weeks' (or sometimes even 2 months') notice of the commencement of proceedings has to be given to a tenant; in the case of this ground, whether pleaded alone or with other grounds, proceedings can be commenced as soon as the s 8 notice has been served (see **38.10.2**). This ground is one of those available during a fixed term (see **37.3.18**) and the new version of the ground applies to all lettings, whether entered into before or after the commencement of the HA 1996.

Ground 14A (domestic violence)

'The dwelling house was occupied (whether alone or with others) by a married couple or a couple living together as husband and wife and—

(a) one of the partners is a tenant of the dwelling house,

(b) the landlord who is seeking possession is a registered social landlord or a charitable housing trust,

(c) one partner has left the dwelling house because of violence or threats of violence by the other towards —

(i) that partner, or

(ii) a member of the family of that partner who was residing with that partner immediately before the partner left, and

(d) the court is satisfied that the partner who has left is unlikely to return.

For the purposes of this ground "registered social landlord" and "member of the family" have the same meaning as in Part I of the Housing Act 1996 and "charitable housing trust" means a housing trust, within the meaning of the Housing Associations Act 1985 which is a charity within the meaning of Charities Act 1993.'

This is a new ground introduced by HA 1996 and is only available from the commencement date of that Act (28 February 1997). It again relates to a tenant's anti-social behaviour, but it is not available to all landlords. Only charitable housing trusts or registered social landlords can make use of it. A registered social landlord is a non-profit making body registered with the Housing Corporation (or Housing for Wales) which has as, or amongst, its objects or powers the provision of housing available for letting.

The ground covers cases of domestic violence which have lead to one partner being forced to leave the house. The violent partner who remains in the house can now be evicted because of this behaviour. It does not matter in establishing the ground which one of the partners is the actual tenant, nor need it be the case that the landlord intends to allow the partner who has been forced to leave back into the house again.

This ground is one of those available during a fixed term and can be used in relation to all lettings, whether entered into before or after the commencement of the HA 1996.

Ground 15 (damage to furniture etc)

> 'The condition of any furniture provided for use under the tenancy has, in the opinion of the court, deteriorated owing to ill-treatment by the tenant or any other person residing in the dwelling house and, in the case of ill-treatment by a person lodging with the tenant or by a sub-tenant of his, the tenant has not taken such steps as he ought reasonably to have taken for the removal of the lodger or sub-tenant.'

This ground will only be available where the dwelling house is let furnished. For comments on the uncertain position where the damage is caused by someone living with the tenant, see the comments on the similarly worded Ground 13 (above). This ground can also be used during a fixed term (see **37.3.18**).

Ground 16 (former employee)

> 'The dwelling house was let to the tenant in consequence of his employment by the landlord seeking possession or a previous landlord under the tenancy and the tenant has ceased to be in that employment.'

This ground is relevant with reference to what are sometimes called 'service tenancies'; situations where an employee is housed by his employer. If the employment ceases, for whatever reason, then this ground will be available. It is not necessary for the landlord to prove that he requires the accommodation to house a new employee, although this may be a relevant factor when deciding the question as to whether it is reasonable for the court to order possession. Not all employees housed by their employers will have tenancies. If it is essential for the employee to occupy the house in order for him to carry out the terms of his employment, then he will be a 'service occupant', a mere licensee, and thus the arrangement could not amount to an assured tenancy. In such a case, the landlord would have an absolute right to possession on termination of the employment.

Ground 17 (false statement by tenant)

> 'The tenant is the person, or one of the persons, to whom the tenancy was granted and the landlord was induced to grant the tenancy by a false statement made knowingly or recklessly by—

(a) the tenant, or
(b) a person acting at the tenant's instigation.'

This is a new ground introduced by the HA 1996 and only available from the commencement date of that Act (28 February 1997), although it does apply to all lettings whether entered into before or after the commencement of that Act.

Prospective tenants are sometimes so desperate to obtain accommodation that they are less than truthful in the statements they make to landlords. So, they might state that they are in employment when they are not or that they have no children when they have in order to deceive the landlord who, had he known the truth, would not have granted them a tenancy. The landlord grants the tenancy and when he finds out the truth it is then too late to do anything about it; the tenant has security of tenure and the landlord has no ground to obtain possession – until now. Note, that the ground covers statements made, not only by the tenant, but by persons at his instigation. It would thus also cover false statements made in references supplied by friends, etc, of the tenant.

This is, however, a discretionary ground, so presumably the nature of the statements made to the landlord would be relevant in deciding whether or not to order possession, so as to prevent a landlord using this ground as an excuse to obtain possession when no other ground was available.

Chapter 39

ASSURED SHORTHOLD TENANCIES

Chapter 39 contents

39.1 INTRODUCTION

A distinction must first of all be drawn between 'old' shortholds, ie those entered into before 28 February 1997, the commencement date of the HA 1996, and 'new' shortholds, ie those entered into on or after that date.

An old shorthold is a fixed-term tenancy of at least 6 months' duration with no security of tenure. Thus, once the fixed term has expired the landlord has an absolute right to recover possession, provided that he complies with the correct procedure. Prior to the grant of the tenancy, however, the landlord must have served a notice on the tenant, in the prescribed form, warning him of the lack of security of tenure. This notice cannot be dispensed with.

Because of the lack of security, shortholds became very popular with landlords and most lettings purported to be shortholds. However, sometimes a purported shorthold would fail due to non-compliance with the conditions, leading to an assured tenancy with full security of tenure (see Chapter 38). From 28 February 1997, however, all new lettings (with certain exceptions, see **39.3.2**) are deemed to be shortholds. The old conditions need no longer be complied with; the letting need not be for a fixed term, there is no need for a warning notice etc. However, the landlord still has the same absolute right to possession as in an old shorthold.

Note that 'old' shortholds continue as before and if one fails due to the conditions not have being complied with, eg no warning notice was served, the tenancy will still become a fully protected assured tenancy. This means that the conditions for the grant of an old shorthold are still of considerable practical importance even after the introduction of new shortholds.

The only disadvantage of a shorthold (whether new or old) from a landlord's point of view is the right given to the tenant to refer the rent initially payable to the Rent Assessment Committee. However, the Committee can only reduce the rent if it is 'significantly higher' than the rents under other comparable assured tenancies.

39.2 OLD SHORTHOLDS

39.2.1 Definition

Section 20 of the HA 1988 sets out the qualifying conditions for shortholds entered into before 28 February 1997. It provides that an assured shorthold tenancy is an assured tenancy which:

(1) is a fixed-term tenancy granted for a term of not less than 6 months; and
(2) contains no power for the landlord to terminate it during the first 6 months; and
(3) was preceded by the giving to the tenant of the prescribed shorthold notice.

An assured tenancy

An assured shorthold tenancy is merely a type of assured tenancy. It must, therefore, comply with all the requirements of an assured tenancy (see Chapter 38). There must be a letting of a dwelling house to an individual who occupies the house as his only or principal home. Equally, none of the specific exclusions from the definition of an assured tenancy must apply (see **38.3**). For example, high rental tenancies and lettings by resident landlords cannot be assured shortholds as they fall outside the definition of an assured tenancy.

A shorthold cannot be granted to an existing tenant under an ordinary assured tenancy (or to one of joint tenants), if it is granted by the landlord under that existing tenancy. This is so even if the lettings are not of the same premises. This is an anti-avoidance device to prevent landlords from depriving their existing tenants of security of tenure by purportedly granting them a shorthold. Similarly, as with all assured tenancies, a shorthold cannot be granted to an existing RA 1977 protected or statutory tenant. (But see **38.4** as to protected shorthold tenants.)

Minimum 6-month fixed term

The initial grant of a shorthold could not be for a periodic term. It had to be for a fixed term and for a minimum duration of 6 months. A letting for '6 months and then from month to month' is not a letting for a term certain and so cannot be a shorthold, even though it is for longer than the minimum 6 months. There is, however, no maximum length, despite the implication from the expression 'shorthold'. It is legally possible to have a shorthold granted for (say) 21 years or more; there are, however, practical reasons connected with rent control (see **39.3.2**) why long shortholds would not be a good idea from a landlord's point of view. Many shortholds are granted for the minimum 6-month period and, in such a case, care must be taken to ensure that the tenant is given a right to occupy for the minimum period. The 6-month period will run from the date on which the tenancy is entered into; it cannot be backdated. So a tenancy granted 'from and including 1 January 1997 until 30 June 1997' but not actually executed until 15 January 1997 would not give the tenant the requisite 6 months' occupation from the date of grant and so could not be a shorthold.

Problems are likely to arise where a tenancy agreement is drawn up containing a fixed termination date and there is then a delay in the agreement being executed so that by the time that it is executed there then remains less than 6 months until the prescribed termination date. Such a letting would amount to an ordinary assured tenancy giving the tenant full security of tenure.

No power for landlord to terminate during first 6 months

Even if a minimum period of 6 months is granted, any power, however expressed, which would or might allow the landlord to terminate the tenancy within the first 6 months of the tenancy will prevent the tenancy from amounting to a shorthold. Break clauses exercisable outside that period are not prohibited, but care must be taken with such clauses to ensure that they are only exercisable outside the initial 6 months; otherwise an ordinary assured tenancy will be created giving the tenant full security of tenure. Note, however, that a forfeiture clause or a clause allowing termination on assured tenancy Grounds 2, 8 and 10 to 15 will not breach this requirement even though it is exercisable during the first 6 months of the term. A term allowing the tenant to terminate during the first 6 months can be validly included. Such a provision, however, will not be implied. A tenant entering into a shorthold will, therefore, be contractually bound to pay the rent and perform the

Housing Act 1988 section 20

Notice of an Assured Shorthold Tenancy

- Please write clearly in black ink.
- If there is any thing you do not understand you should get advice from a solicitor or a Citizens' Advice Bureau, before you agree to the tenancy.
- The landlord must give this notice to the tenant before an assured shorthold tenancy is granted. It does not commit the tenant to take the tenancy.
- **This document is important, keep it in a safe place**

To: [ ] *Name of proposed tenant. If a joint tenancy is being offered enter the names of the joint tenants.*

1. *You are proposing to take a tenancy of the dwelling known as:*

from / /19 *to* / /19 *The tenancy must be for a term certain of at least six months.*

day month year day month year

2. This notice is to tell you that your tenancy is to be an assured shorthold tenancy. Provided you keep to the terms of the tenancy, you are entitled to remain in the dwelling for at least the first six months of the fixed period agreed at the start of the tenancy. At the end of this period, depending on the terms of the tenancy, the landlord may have the right to repossession if he wants.

3. The rent for this tenancy is the rent we have agreed. However, you have the right to apply to a rent assessment committee for a determination of the rent which the committee considers might reasonably be obtained under the tenancy. If the committee considers (i) that there is a sufficient number of similar properties in the locality let on assured tenancies and that (ii) the rent we have agreed is significantly higher than the rent which might reasonably be obtained having regard to the level of rents for other assured tenancies in the locality, it will determine a rent for the tenancy. That rent will be the legal maximum you can be required to pay from the date the committee directs. [If the rent includes a payment for council tax, the rent determined by the committee will be inclusive of council tax.]

[4. This notice was served to you on 19]

To be signed by the landlord or his agent (someone acting for him). If there are joint landlords each must sign, unless one signs on behalf of the rest with their agreement.

Signed

Name(s) of landlord(s)

Address of landlord(s)

Tel:

If signed by agent, name and address of agent

Tel:

Date: 19

Special note for existing tenants

- Generally if you already have a protected or statutory tenancy and you give it up to take a new tenancy in the same or other accommodation owned by the same landlord, that tenancy cannot be an assured tenancy. It can still be a protected tenancy.

- But if you currently occupy a dwelling which was let to you as a protected shorthold tenant, special rules apply.

- If you have an assured tenancy which is not a shorthold under the Housing Act 1988, you cannot be offered an assured shorthold tenancy of the same or other accommodation by the same landlord.

other obligations under the tenancy agreement for the full term entered into. This is not always appreciated by tenants who should beware of entering into lengthy fixed-term lettings when there is a possibility that they might wish to move on part way through the term.

Preceded by the giving of the prescribed shorthold notice

As the tenant under an assured shorthold has no security of tenure, he had to be served with a notice prior to the grant of the tenancy warning him of this fact. This notice must be in the prescribed form. The content of the necessary form has changed twice since the introduction of assured shortholds on 15 January 1989 and care must be taken to ensure that the shorthold notice served was the correct one as at the date of service. The specimen notice set out above is intended to be a composite notice covering all three variations. The variable matters are enclosed in square brackets. For notices served before 17 August 1990 the original form must have been used. This includes paragraph 4, but excludes the final sentence of paragraph 3. For notices on or after 17 December 1990, paragraph 4 must be excluded, as again must the final sentence of paragraph 3. For notices served on or after 17 August 1990 but before 17 December 1990 either of these versions could be used, ie with or without paragraph 4. For notices served on or after 1 April 1993, paragraph 4 must be excluded and the final sentence of paragraph 3 included.

The notice must have been served before the tenancy agreement was entered into and not at the same time. Thus, it cannot be included in the tenancy agreement itself. It was thought best to ensure that there was an adequate interval between the service of the notice and the signing of the tenancy agreement to give the tenant the opportunity of digesting the contents of the notice. However, it appears from *Bedding v McCarthy* [1994] 41 EG 151 that an interval of a few hours between the service of the s 20 notice and the tenancy agreement being entered into would be sufficient. In the case of joint tenants, all of the prospective tenants should be served. Common law rules as to service will apply (and not s 196 of the LPA 1925) and so it is necessary to show that the notice actually came into the tenant's hands. Correct service of the current version of the shorthold notice is vital. The court has no power to dispense with these notice requirements even though it might be just and equitable to do so. The regulations do allow service of a form 'substantially to the same effect' as the prescribed form, but this is not a provision to be relied upon except in an emergency.

Relevance of old shorthold rules

Although an old shorthold can no longer be created after 28 February 1997, it is still relevant to consider the application of these old shorthold rules in the case of shortholds granted before that date which are still subsisting. In the case, for example, of a purported old shorthold granted on 1 January 1997, if the old shorthold rules were not fully complied with, that tenancy would be a fully protected assured tenancy, as would any further letting on or after 28 February 1997 by the same landlord to the same tenant.

39.3 NEW SHORTHOLDS

39.3.1 Definition

Shortholds entered into on or after 28 February 1997 (otherwise than pursuant to a contract made before that date) are governed by s 19A of the HA 1988 (as inserted by the HA 1996). This provides that *any* assured tenancy entered into on or after the commencement date will be a shorthold *unless* it falls within one of the specified exceptions.

So there is no longer any need for a shorthold to be preceded by a prescribed form of notice. There is no need for a shorthold to be for a fixed term, it can be periodic; there is no need for a minimum period of 6 months; it can be for any period, no matter how short. However, although there is no prohibition on the landlord being able to terminate during the first 6 months, no order for possession using the shorthold ground can be made earlier than 6 months from the start of the tenancy, whether the tenancy is for a fixed term or it is a periodic tenancy (see **39.7**). However, this does not stop possession being obtained during the first 6 months using an assured tenancy ground eg Ground 14; a new shorthold, like an old shorthold, is merely a type of assured tenancy, see **39.2.1**.

As a new shorthold is a type of assured tenancy, it must still comply with all the requirements of an assured tenancy, (see Chapter 38). A tenancy which falls outside of the definition of an assured tenancy (eg due to the resident landlord rule) cannot be a shorthold either. Such a tenancy will be subject to ordinary common law rules as to termination.

39.3.2 Which lettings will not be new shortholds?

As previously stated (see **39.3.1**), all new assured tenancies granted on or after 28 February 1997 (other than those granted pursuant to a contract made before that date) will be shortholds subject to certain exceptions. These exceptions are set out in Sch 2A to the HA 1988 as inserted by the HA 1996. The following lettings will be excluded and will thus take effect as ordinary assured tenancies.

(1) Tenancies excluded by notice

The Schedule allows the landlord to serve a notice on the tenant either before or after the grant of the tenancy stating that the letting is not to be a shorthold. There is no prescribed form for this notice.

It is rather strange that a landlord can change the status of a tenancy *after* it has been entered into. In most cases this will be to the advantage of the tenant in that it will give him greater security of tenure than before; it will, however, take away from the tenant his right to refer the rent if he considers it excessive (see **39.4**).

(2) Tenancies containing a provision stating that the tenancy is not to be a shorthold

Similarly, if the tenancy agreement itself states that it is not to be a shorthold, it will then take effect as an ordinary assured tenancy.

(3) Lettings to existing assured tenants

A letting to an existing ASSURED (ie not shorthold) tenant (whether alone or with others) by a person who is the landlord (or one of the landlords) under the existing tenancy, will *not* be a shorthold *unless* the TENANT serves notice on the landlord, in the prescribed form, before the new tenancy is entered into that he wants it to be a shorthold.

The requirements that this notice must be served *before* the new tenancy is entered into will give rise to similar considerations as already exist with regard to the service of s 20 notices for old shortholds; see **39.2.1**.

Of course, this provisions begs the question as to *why* should a tenant want to serve such a notice when it will result in him losing the security of tenure he had before? One possible advantage would be for a tenant who had no security as an assured tenant (eg because of Ground 1) and was unhappy about the rent under the new letting. By serving a notice stating that the tenancy was to be a shorthold, he would then have the right to refer the rent to the Rent Assessment Committee as being excessive. See **39.4** as to references of the rent to the Rent Assessment Committee.

The existence of this procedure, allowing a tenant to elect to have a shorthold, does give rise to worries as to whether there is a danger of undue pressure being placed on tenants by landlords anxious to take advantage of the provisions of the HA 1996.

39.3.3 What are the practical implications of new shortholds?

Under the old law, all tenancies of houses would be assured tenancies with full security of tenure unless the conditions for shortholds were complied with. That rule has now been reversed; every tenancy will be a shorthold unless it is within one of the exceptions or it falls outside the definition of an assured tenancy, (as to which, see **38.2**).

From a landlord's point of view, this removes the main risk of letting property using an old shorthold, ie that he might accidentally not comply with all of the conditions and thus end up with a fully protected assured tenant. It may be, therefore, that more landlords will now be encouraged to bring property into the letting market.

From the point of view of a tenant, it may be seen as the virtual end of private sector lettings with security of tenure. Although there are some exceptions (see **39.3.2**), the introduction of the rules on new shortholds means that virtually all new lettings will have no security of tenure, thus putting the clock back to what the position was before the passing of the RA 1977.

In practice, it has to be said that most tenants will probably find little difference. Most lettings already purported to be shortholds under the old rules and it was very difficult for a tenant to find accommodation to let on anything other than a shorthold.

Perhaps the HA 1996 can thus best be seen as merely a natural progression from the HA 1988. If landlords are given the choice of letting without security of tenure, it goes without saying that most of them will take up that opportunity, and once most landlords have done so, the 1996 Act can be seen as merely recognising the existing state of affairs.

39.3.4 Duty of the landlord to provide a statement of the terms of a shorthold tenancy

Under s 20A of the HA 1988 (as inserted by the HA 1996), the landlord is placed under a duty, in certain circumstances to provide a tenant with details of some of the more important terms of the tenancy. The tenant must make a request in writing and the landlord must provide a written statement of the terms.

The landlord must provide details of the following terms provided that they are not already evidenced in writing:

(1) the commencement date of the tenancy;
(2) the rent payable and the dates on which it is payable;

(3) any terms providing for rent review;
(4) the length of a fixed-term tenancy.

It is a criminal offence to fail to provide the information within 28 days, unless the landlord has reasonable excuse. On summary conviction, the penalty is to be a fine not exceeding level 4.

Note that the right only exists where the terms are not already evidenced in writing. So the provision will only apply to tenancies granted orally, or those granted in writing which makes no reference to one or more of the specified matters.

It is a well known problem that when tenancies are granted orally, there is often uncertainty as to the precise terms of the letting. But at first sight this seems a very strange provision. It seems to allow the landlord to dictate the terms of the tenancy, whereas the terms should (in theory) be agreed by both parties and one party to a contract cannot unilaterally change them.

However, the Act does go on to provide that a statement provided by the landlord is not to be regarded as conclusive evidence as to what was agreed between the parties. So the contractual niceties are preserved. The statement is the landlord's version of what was agreed; it is still open to the tenant to allege that any particular term was not agreed to by him.

These provisions only apply to new shortholds, ie those to which s 19A of the HA 1988 applies. They do not apply to old shortholds. However, on the ending of an old shorthold any new letting between the same parties will be a new shorthold, and these provisions will then apply.

39.4 RENT CONTROL

39.4.1 What protection is given?

The protection given differs slightly depending upon whether the tenant has a new shorthold or an old shorthold, but the general principles are the same for both.

On the granting of the tenancy, the landlord can charge such rent for the premises as the market will bear. There is no statutory restriction on the amount of rent chargeable. Any existing registration of a 'fair rent' under the provisions of the RA 1977 (see Chapter 40) can be ignored, as can any rental figure previously determined by the Rent Assessment Committee under these provisions. However, an assured shorthold tenant can apply to the local Rent Assessment Committee for the determination of the rent which, in the Committee's opinion, the landlord might reasonably be expected to obtain under the shorthold tenancy.

If the tenant has an old shorthold, he can apply at any time during the first tenancy entered into between the parties; no application can be made during any subsequent letting. See **39.4.3**.

If the tenant has a new shorthold, whether for a fixed term or a periodic letting, he cannot apply if more than 6 months have elapsed since the beginning of the tenancy. If the tenancy is a 'replacement tenancy', ie a second or subsequent shorthold between the same parties and of the same property, the application cannot be made if more than 6 months have elapsed from the commencement of the first shorthold between the parties.

In all cases, the Committee cannot make a determination as to the rent unless there is a sufficient number of similar dwelling houses in the locality let on assured tenancies and the rent payable under the shorthold is significantly higher than the rent which the landlord might reasonably be expected to obtain having regard to the level of rents payable under these other tenancies. There is no question of the rent which is assessed being in any way lower than the market rent for the premises; this is not a return to the 'fair rent' system as used under the RA 1977, which frequently results in a rent of less than the market value being fixed. Thus a landlord is only at risk of a lower rent being fixed if he is charging 'significantly' more than the market rent for the house.

39.4.2 What is the effect of a determination by the Rent Assessment Committee?

If a rent is determined by the Committee, the effect again differs slightly between old and new shortholds.

In the case of old shortholds and fixed-term new shortholds, the rent as assessed will become the maximum rent chargeable for the property throughout the remainder of the fixed term. This is despite anything to the contrary in the tenancy agreement. There is no provision for this figure to be increased during the fixed term, no matter how long the unexpired term of the tenancy. It is for this reason that landlords are still best advised to avoid the grant of long shortholds. In the case, for example, of a 21-year shorthold, a rent fixed in the first year would continue to apply for the remainder of the term, despite any contractual provisions to the contrary.

In the case of a new shorthold which is a periodic tenancy, again the rent once fixed will, in theory, remain fixed throughout the tenancy. However, in practice, once 12 months have expired, the landlord will then be able to make an application under ss 13 and 14 of the HA 1988 to increase the rent (see **38.5**).

With both old and new shortholds, once the rent has been determined by the Committee no further application for the fixing of a different figure can be made by either landlord or tenant. However, the rent determined by the Committee only has relevance to the particular tenancy in question. It will not limit the amount of rent chargeable under any subsequent letting, even if this is between the same parties. Further, in the absence of a further grant, on the ending of a fixed-term shorthold (whether old or new) a statutory periodic tenancy will arise and the provisions of ss 13 and 14 of the HA 1988 will again apply to allow the landlord to increase the rent.

39.4.3 When is an application to the Rent Assessment Committee not possible?

The restrictions on tenants with new shortholds applying have been dealt with in **39.4.1**.

As far as old shorthold tenants are concerned, it is not possible for the tenant to refer the rent to the Rent Assessment Committee once the original term of the shorthold has expired. This is so even if a new letting is entered into between the same parties and irrespective of whether an application was made during the original shorthold.

Note also that, with both old and new shortholds, only one application to the Committee can be made. Once the rent has been determined by the Committee, it cannot be resubmitted for a further determination, even if the original determination was many years before and open market rents have fallen in the meantime.

39.5 WHAT HAPPENS WHEN A SHORTHOLD EXPIRES?

On the ending of a fixed term, the tenant is allowed to remain in possession as a statutory periodic tenant. However, the tenant still has no security of tenure. Under s 21(1) of the HA 1988 the court must still make an order for possession if the landlord follows the correct procedure. This involves the service on the tenant of not less than 2 months' notice stating that the landlord requires possession (see **39.7**).

39.6 WHAT HAPPENS IF A NEW TENANCY IS GRANTED?

Although there are, again, slight differences between new and old shortholds, the basic principle remains the same; if the parties are the same, any new tenancy of the same (or substantially the same) premises will be deemed to be a shorthold unless the landlord serves notice on the tenant that the new letting is not to be a shorthold.

In the case of an old shorthold, the effect of this deeming provision is that the new tenancy will be a shorthold even though it does not comply with the normal requirements for an old shorthold. So the shorthold notice need not have been served, the letting need not be for a fixed term, ie a periodic shorthold is permissible, and any fixed term need not be for a minimum period of 6 months. However, the new tenancy must still comply with the normal requirements for an assured tenancy, eg the tenant must still be occupying the house as his only or main home.

A further feature of a deemed shorthold following an old shorthold is that there is no right to refer the rent to the Rent Assessment Committee. This is the case whether or not an application was made to the Committee during the initial shorthold term. In the case of a tenancy following a new shorthold, the second tenancy will be a 'replacement tenancy' (see **39.4.1**) and an application to the Rent Assessment Committee cannot be made more than 6 months from the commencement of the original tenancy. So in the unlikely event of a new shorthold granted for 3 months, followed by a replacement tenancy granted for (say) 6 months, an application to the Rent Assessment Committee could be made during the first 3 months of that replacement tenancy.

In any event, if a rent was determined by the Committee during the initial term this will not limit the amount of rent chargeable by the landlord under the new tenancy agreement.

39.7 HOW DOES THE LANDLORD OBTAIN POSSESSION?

Unless the tenant leaves voluntarily, the landlord must apply to the court and obtain an order for possession. The court must order possession provided that the landlord follows the correct procedure. This involves the landlord serving a notice on the tenant (the 's 21 notice') giving the tenant at least 2 months' notice that he requires possession. Note, however, that possession cannot be obtained using this shorthold procedure during the continuance of a fixed term; possession is only available after its expiry (although the procedure can be set in motion during the fixed term so that possession can be obtained as soon as it has ended). Note also, that in the case of a new shorthold, possession cannot be obtained within 6 months of the commencement of the term using the shorthold procedure. This is so whether the tenancy is for a fixed term or is periodic.

39.8 ARE THERE ANY OTHER GROUNDS FOR POSSESSION?

A shorthold is a type of assured tenancy and so, during the term, the mandatory and discretionary grounds which apply to ordinary assured tenancies can also apply. For full details of these see **38.10.3** and **38.10.4**, but it does mean, for example, that mandatory Ground 8 and discretionary Grounds 10 and 11 (all of which relate to rent arrears) can be used during the subsistence of the shorthold should the landlord be faced with a defaulting tenant. However, in the case of a fixed term letting, as with other assured tenancies, these grounds can be used during the fixed term only if the tenancy agreement so provides. In the case of a shorthold which is a periodic tenancy, these ordinary assured tenancy grounds will be available to a landlord without the need for any such provision in the tenancy agreement.

In the case of a fixed-term shorthold, however, it is always sensible to insert a provision allowing the landlord to terminate the tenancy on the specified grounds. In the case of an old shorthold, this is permissable despite the usual rule that there must be no power for the landlord to terminate within the first 6 months of the tenancy. This rule does not apply to termination because of a breach of the terms of the tenancy, eg non-payment of rent. Similarly, in the case of new shortholds, although possession cannot be obtained using the shorthold procedure within 6 months of the commencement (see **39.7**), possession can be obtained during that period using the ordinary assured grounds should they be satisfied.

When the landlord is seeking to obtain possession on one of the ordinary assured grounds, then the procedure relevant to an ordinary assured tenancy should be followed, and *not* the shorthold procedure. In particular, this will mean that a s 8 notice will have to be served on the tenant before proceedings can be commenced, and *not* a s 21 notice.

Chapter 40

THE RENT ACT 1977

Chapter 40 contents

40.1 INTRODUCTION

The RA 1977 applies to lettings entered into prior to 15 January 1989. Although the HA 1988 made some minor changes to the protections given to such lettings, they basically remain subject to the same system as before. There are still many thousands of such tenancies in existence today, although their numbers are likely to decline as the years go by and tenants leave. Further, it is also still possible for new RA 1977 tenancies to be created today, albeit in very limited circumstances (see **38.4**). Tenancies within the RA 1977 are given wide-ranging security of tenure, in many ways similar to that given to assured tenancies. The main difference from assured tenancies, though, is that they are also subject to rent control, the 'fair rent' system which tends to keep rents below those which would prevail in the open market. On the death of a tenant there are succession rights which tend to be more generous than those applying to assured tenancies. Sometimes, following a succession, the new tenant will lose his RA 1977 protection and become an assured tenant under the HA 1988 (see **40.5**).

40.2 PROTECTED TENANCIES

There will be a protected tenancy within the RA 1977 where a dwelling house is 'let as a separate dwelling' (RA 1977, s 1). See the discussion of the similarly worded requirement for an assured tenancy under the HA 1988 (at **38.2.3**). Unlike the HA 1988, there is no need for the letting to be to an individual, nor does the house need to be the tenant's only or principal home. There are various exceptions which are generally very similar to those for assured tenancies, for example, lettings by resident landlords, holiday lettings, tenancies at a low rent (see **38.3**). Also excluded from the definition are lettings where the rent includes payment for board or attendance; this would exclude from the definition of a protected tenancy lettings where meals are provided or the landlord cleans the rooms. There is no similar exclusion for assured tenancies. Protected tenancies will have rent control and succession rights, but not necessarily security of tenure.

40.3 STATUTORY TENANCIES

The statutory tenancy is the device by which security of tenure is given. At the end of the contractual protected tenancy, the tenant is given security of tenure and is allowed to remain in possession only 'if and so long as he occupies the dwelling house as his residence'. Only an individual can occupy as a residence, so a company tenant can be a protected tenant but not a statutory tenant. There is no requirement that the dwelling house should be occupied as the tenant's only or main residence; for RA 1977 purposes it is accepted that a person can have two homes and that there can be a statutory tenancy of either or both of them. In order to obtain possession against a protected tenant, therefore, a landlord must first of all terminate that protected tenancy, for example, by serving notice to quit. If the tenant does not qualify as a statutory tenant, the landlord will be immediately entitled to a court order for possession. If a statutory tenancy does arise, the landlord will have to establish one (or more) of the grounds for possession laid down in the Act. As with assured tenancies, some of these grounds are mandatory and so the court must order possession on proof of the ground, but many are discretionary where the court can only order possession if it considers it reasonable to do so. Many of the assured tenancy grounds for possession were based on RA 1977 grounds and reference should be made to the equivalent assured tenancy ground where relevant. The RA 1977 grounds are called 'cases' and are set out in Sch 15 to the RA 1977.

40.3.1 Discretionary grounds for possession

Case 1

> 'Where any rent lawfully due from the tenant has not been paid, or any obligation of the protected or statutory tenancy . . . has been broken or not performed.'

This case should be compared with Grounds 8, 10, 11 and 12 (see **38.10**) for assured tenancies. Note, in particular, that non-payment of rent is only a discretionary ground, no matter how great the amount of the arrears.

Case 2

> 'Where the tenant or any person residing or lodging with him or any sub-tenant of his has been guilty of conduct which is a nuisance or annoyance to adjoining occupiers, or has been convicted of using the dwelling house or allowing the dwelling house to be used for immoral or illegal purposes.'

This case is identical in effect to the old version of assured tenancy Ground 14. It has not been amended so as to have the same effect as the new version of assured tenancy Ground 14.

Case 3

> 'Where the condition of the dwelling house has, in the opinion of the court, deteriorated owing to acts of waste by, or the neglect or default of, the tenant or any person residing or lodging with him or any sub-tenant of his and, in the case of any act of waste by, or the neglect or default of, a person lodging with the tenant or a sub-tenant of his, where the court is satisfied that the tenant has not, before the making of the order in question, taken such steps as he ought reasonably to have taken for the removal of the lodger or sub-tenant, as the case may be.'

This is virtually the same as assured tenancy Ground 13 (see **38.10.4**) and shares its problems. Unlike Ground 13, though, it does not extend to damage etc caused to the common parts of the building.

Case 4

> 'Where the condition of any furniture provided for use under the tenancy has, in the opinion of the court, deteriorated owing to ill-treatment by the tenant or any person residing or lodging with him or any sub-tenant of his and, in the case of any ill-treatment by any person lodging with the tenant or a sub-tenant of his, where the court is satisfied that the tenant has not, before the making of the order in question, taken such steps as he ought reasonably to have taken for the removal of the lodger or sub-tenant, as the case may be.'

See assured tenancy Ground 15 at **38.10.4**.

Case 5

> 'Where the tenant has given notice to quit and, in consequence of that notice, the landlord has contracted to sell or let the dwelling house or has taken any other steps as the result of which he would, in the opinion of the court, be seriously prejudiced if he could not obtain possession.'

This case has no equivalent under assured tenancies. It is necessary for RA 1977 tenancies as s 2 imposes a statutory tenancy, with security of tenure, no matter how the protected tenancy may end. So even if a tenant gives notice to quit a protected tenancy, a statutory tenancy will still arise in his favour giving him security of tenure and the landlord will not be entitled to possession unless he can prove one of the grounds laid down by the Act. This could place him in difficulty if, thinking that the tenant is about to vacate the property, he enters into a contract to sell etc, with vacant possession. Apart from this case, the landlord would have no right to possession if the tenant should subsequently change his mind and decide not to vacate after all. The case will only apply if the landlord has entered into a contract to sell or let, or would otherwise be seriously prejudiced. There is no need for an equivalent ground for assured tenancies, as s 5(2) of the HA 1988 makes it clear that if an assured tenancy comes to an end by virtue of a tenant's notice to quit, then there is no security of tenure for the tenant and the landlord will have an absolute right to possession without proof of anything more.

Case 6

> 'Where, without the consent of the landlord, the tenant has, . . . assigned or sub-let the whole of the dwelling house . . .'

This case will apply whether or not there is any express prohibition on assignment or sub-letting in the tenancy agreement. It has no direct equivalent in assured tenancies, but it is an implied term of every periodic assured tenancy that the tenant will not assign or sub-let without consent (HA 1988, s 15). A breach of this implied term would then render the tenant liable to possession being ordered against him under Ground 12 (breach of the terms of the tenancy).

Case 7

Case 7 has now been repealed.

Case 8

> 'Where the dwelling house is reasonably required by the landlord for occupation as a residence for some person engaged in his whole-time employment, or in the whole-time employment of some tenant from him or with whom, conditional on housing being provided, a contract for such employment has been entered into, and the tenant was in the employment of the landlord or a former landlord, and the dwelling house was let to him in consequence of that employment and he has ceased to be in that employment.'

This is similar to assured tenancy Ground 16 (see **38.10.4**), the main difference being that for this case to apply, the landlord has to prove that he reasonably requires the house for accommodation by another employee; there is no such requirement under Ground 16.

Case 9

> 'Where the dwelling house is reasonably required by the landlord for occupation as a residence for–
>
> (a) himself, or
> (b) any son or daughter of his over 18 years of age, or
> (c) his father or mother, or
> (d) . . . the father or mother of his wife or husband,
>
> and the landlord did not become landlord by purchasing the dwelling house or any interest therein . . .'

Part III of Sch 15 to the RA 1977 prevents a court from ordering possession under this case if, having regard to all the circumstances, the court is satisfied that greater hardship would be caused by granting the order than by refusing to grant it. The question of hardship will be a question of fact in each particular case, but factors such as the availability of alternative accommodation to the respective parties will be relevant to this.

This case will be available to a landlord whether or not he has resided in the property prior to the letting and there is no need for any warning notice to have been served on the tenant prior to the letting (cf Case 11 and assured tenancy Ground 1 at **38.10.3**). Unlike those grounds, it is only a discretionary ground, so that even if the landlord overcomes the greater hardship test, the court will still order possession only if it considers it reasonable to do so.

Case 10

Case 10 allows possession to be claimed if the tenant has sub-let part of the house at a rent greater than that legally allowed (see the fair rent system, at **40.4**).

Suitable alternative accommodation

Although not allocated a case number, s 98(1)(a) of the RA 1977 allows the court to order possession on this ground if it considers it reasonable to do so. As to what amounts to 'suitable alternative accommodation', see the discussion on assured tenancy Ground 9 at **38.10.4**.

40.3.2 Mandatory grounds for possession

Case 11

> 'Where a person who (in this Case referred to as "the owner-occupier") let the dwelling house on a regulated tenancy had, at any time before the letting, occupied it as his residence and—
>
> (a) not later than [the date of the commencement of the tenancy] the landlord gave notice in writing to the tenant that possession might be recovered under this Case, and
> (b) the dwelling house has not . . . been let by the owner-occupier on a protected tenancy with respect to which the condition mentioned in paragraph (a) above was not satisfied, and
> (c) the court is of the opinion that of the conditions set out in Part V of this Schedule one of those in paragraphs (a) and (c) to (f) is satisfied.'

The conditions referred to above, set out in Sch 15, Part V, para 2, are as follows:

'(a) the dwelling house is required as a residence for the owner or any member of his family who resided with the owner when he last occupied the dwelling house as a residence;

(b) . . .

(c) the owner has died and the dwelling house is required as a residence for a member of his family who was residing with him at the time of his death;

(d) the owner has died and the dwelling house is required by a successor in title as his residence or for the purpose of disposing of it with vacant possession;

(e) the dwelling house is subject to a mortgage, made by deed and granted before the tenancy, and the mortgagee . . . is entitled to exercise a power of sale . . . and . . . requires possession of the dwelling house for the purpose of disposing of it with vacant possession . . .; and

(f) the dwelling house is not reasonably suitable to the needs of the owner, having regard to his place of work, and he requires it for the purpose of disposing of it with vacant possession and of using the proceeds of that in acquiring, as his residence, a dwelling house which is more suitable to those needs.'

This case must be distinguished from the superficially similar Case 9. Unlike Case 9, it is dependent upon the service of a warning notice prior to the letting and the landlord must have resided in the house at some time prior to the letting. However, if the court is of the opinion that it is just and equitable to make an order for possession, it has the power to dispense with the notice requirement. Apart from this, however, the court has no discretion. Possession must be ordered whether or not it is reasonable to do so and without any consideration of the question of greater hardship. This case also deals with the possibility that possession might be required after the death of the owner, either for sale or as a residence. Possession is also recoverable to enable a sale with vacant possession to take place either by a mortgagee or if the landlord has changed his place of work.

Case 12

Case 12 allows possession to be claimed by a landlord who has purchased a house as a prospective retirement home, but lets it in the meantime. There is no need for prior residence (cf Case 11), but the availability of the case is again dependent upon the service of a warning notice no later than the commencement of the tenancy. This notice can, however, be dispensed with in the same circumstances as in Case 11. The landlord will then be entitled to possession on retirement or in the circumstances set out in paragraphs (c) to (f) of Case 11.

Case 13

'Where the dwelling house is let under a tenancy for a term of years certain not exceeding 8 months and—

(a) not later than [the commencement of the tenancy] the landlord gave notice in writing to the tenant that possession might be recovered under this Case; and

(b) that dwelling house was, at some time within the period of 12 months ending on [the date of the commencement of the tenancy], occupied under a right to occupy it for a holiday.'

This is virtually identical with assured tenancy Ground 3 (see **38.10.3**). As with that ground, the prior warning notice cannot be dispensed with: cf Cases 11 and 12.

Case 14

'Where the dwelling house is let under a tenancy for a term of years certain not exceeding 12 months and—

(a) not later than [the commencement of the tenancy] the landlord gave notice in writing to the tenant that possession might be recovered under this Case; and
(b) at some time within the period of 12 months ending on [the commencement of the tenancy], the dwelling house was subject to such a tenancy [granted by a specified educational institution to a student].'

This case is almost identical to assured tenancy Ground 4 (see **38.10.3**).

Case 15

'Where the dwelling house is held for the purpose of being available for occupation by a minister of religion as a residence from which to perform the duties of his office and—

(a) not later than [the commencement of the tenancy] the tenant was given notice in writing that possession might be recovered under this Case; and
(b) the court is satisfied that the dwelling house is required for occupation by a minister of religion as such a residence.'

This case is identical in effect to assured tenancy Ground 5 (see **38.10.3**).

Cases 16, 17 and 18

Cases 16, 17 and 18 relate to lettings of farm houses and lettings of houses to persons employed in agriculture where the house is required for occupation by a new employee.

Case 19

This is the case which gave the landlord of a protected shorthold tenancy (see **40.6**) a mandatory right to possession. As it is unlikely that there are still any protected shorthold tenancies in existence, this case is now no longer of practical significance.

Case 20

This case allows members of the armed forces who acquired houses during their service and let them in the meantime to obtain possession in similar circumstances to owner-occupiers under Case 11. Although a warning notice needs to have been served on the tenant no later than the commencement of the tenancy, there is no need for the landlord ever to have occupied the house prior to the letting. The warning notice can be dispensed with in the same circumstances as under Case 11.

40.4 THE FAIR RENT SYSTEM

40.4.1 The system

Both protected and statutory tenancies are subject to control as to the amount of the rent the landlord can charge for the property. The RA 1977 set up a register of 'fair rents' for dwelling houses. Once a rent has been registered in relation to a property then that becomes the maximum chargeable under any protected or statutory tenancy of that property. The rent is assessed by the rent officer, a local authority official, in accordance with criteria laid down by the Act. These are designed to exclude from the calculation of the rent the scarcity element. Under normal market forces, the scarcity of accommodation to let tends to push up the amount of rent chargeable beyond the means of many people. By requiring the rent officer to assume that there is no shortage of accommodation to let (even though there might be), the rent assessed is often considerably lower than it otherwise would be in the open market. However, in many parts of the country there is no longer a shortage of accommodation to let, and if this can be established to the satisfaction of the rent officer, it may well be that the rent fixed will not be significantly lower than the open-market rent.

40.4.2 Applying for a fair rent

Assuming that no fair rent is registered in respect of the property, on the grant of a tenancy the landlord can charge whatever rent the market will bear. However, at any time during the continuance of the tenancy the tenant can apply for a fair rent to be assessed. Once assessed this then becomes the maximum payable, despite the existence of a higher agreed figure in the tenancy agreement. The fair rent cannot then be exceeded in any new letting of the house, whether to the same or to a different tenant. The only way in which the landlord can increase the rent is by applying himself to the rent officer for the assessment of a higher fair rent. However, he normally cannot make such an application within 2 years of an earlier fair rent having been assessed. On the fixing of a fair rent, therefore, a tenant is thus assured of a minimum period of 2 years before an increase in rent can take place. If, after that 2-year period, the landlord applies for a new fair rent and that is higher than the rent being currently paid (and there is no guarantee that it will be) the landlord is not entitled to the whole of the increase at once. Even though the rent officer has assessed a higher rent, the landlord must serve a 'notice of increase' on the tenant in order to recover any of it.

40.5 SUCCESSION TO RENT ACT TENANCIES

On the death of a statutory or a protected tenant, that person's spouse (or a person living with the tenant as husband or wife) will become the statutory tenant of the house and thus entitled to the benefits of security of tenure and rent control. If there is no surviving spouse (or person who had lived with the tenant as husband or wife), then the succession rules differ depending upon the date of death of the tenant.

40.5.1 Deaths prior to 15 January 1989

In this case any member of the tenant's family who was living with him at the time of death and had lived with him for at least 6 months prior to the death would succeed as a statutory tenant.

40.5.2 Deaths on or after 15 January 1989

Now, for a family member to succeed, he needs to have resided for 2 years prior to the death. Further, in such cases the family member will only become entitled to an assured tenancy on the succession and *not* a statutory tenancy.

40.5.3 Second transmissions

On the death of the 'first successor', it is sometimes possible for a second 'transmission' to a 'second successor' to occur. In the situation where the first successor died before 15 January 1989, a second transmission was always possible in favour of the first successor's spouse or family member, using the same succession rules as applicable to the first succession. However, in the case of the death of a first successor after 15 January 1989, a second transmission is only possible in very limited circumstances. A person is entitled to a second succession only if he or she was both a member of the original tenant's family and a member of the first successor's family and had also resided with the first successor for at least 2 years prior to the first successor's death. There is no requirement for this second successor to have lived with the original tenant at all; it is sufficient for he or she to be a member of the original tenant's family. This complicated formula is designed, however, to cover the situation where the original tenant was (say) a man living in the house with his wife and child. On the death of that original tenant, a first transmission will occur in favour of the spouse; on the death of the spouse, a second transmission is then possible in favour of the child. This second successor will always take the tenancy as an assured tenant.

40.6 PROTECTED SHORTHOLD TENANCIES

Protected shorthold tenancies were introduced by the HA 1980 but it is unlikely that there will still be any subsisting nowadays. They were the precursors of assured shortholds and shared some of their characteristics. Thus, they had to be for a fixed period and be preceded by the service of a warning notice. Unlike assured shortholds, however, they had to be for at least 12 months in duration. At the end of the fixed term the landlord had a mandatory right to possession, as with assured shortholds. However, the procedure for obtaining possession was very complex and had to be approached with care if the landlord was to be successful. The HA 1988 provided that any new letting on or after 15 January 1989 to a protected shorthold tenant would be an assured shorthold (whether or not the normal assured shorthold requirements were complied with). It is this provision coupled with the short duration of most protected shortholds that ensured their rapid demise after the implementation of the HA 1988.

Chapter 41

PROTECTION FROM EVICTION

41.1 INTRODUCTION

The most traumatic experience that residential tenants or licensees may have to face is the peremptory eviction from, or harassment in, their homes by their landlords. Landlords sometimes resort to threats and violence because they think it is a cheaper and quicker method of eviction than taking court proceedings for possession, which may not in any event be successful due to the security of tenure legislation. Tenants suffering such unacceptable actions on the part of their landlords may have civil remedies against them. There may also be criminal sanctions. The tenant's basic remedy will be damages, although an injunction will often be available to restrain future actions and to restore a dispossessed tenant to the property. The statutory protections apply not only to tenants but also to licensees, although there is a category of excluded licences and tenancies where the protection is more limited. Apart from these excluded tenancies, the protections will apply whether or not the tenant has security of tenure. For tenants not governed by the HA 1988, the requirements of a valid notice to quit must also be considered.

Chapter 41 contents

41.2 CRIMINAL SANCTIONS: THE PROTECTION FROM EVICTION ACT 1977

41.2.1 Protection from eviction

The offence

It is an offence unlawfully to evict a residential occupier unless it is reasonably believed that he no longer lives in the premises (PEA 1977, s 1).

Except in the case of an excluded licence or tenancy (see **41.6**), eviction will be unlawful if a residential occupier is evicted otherwise than by means of a court order.

Residential occupier

Protection is given to residential occupiers as defined in s 1(1) of the PEA 1977. These are persons occupying the premises as a residence 'whether under a contract or by virtue of any enactment or rule of law giving him the right to remain in occupation or restricting the right of any other person to recover possession of the premises'. The definition thus includes all tenants, whether they are protected tenants under the RA 1977, assured or assured shorthold tenants under the HA 1988, secure tenants under HA 1985 or whether they have no statutory protection at all. The use of the term 'contract' will also include contractual licensees within these protections.

41.2.2 Protection from harassment

The offences

There are two offences of harassment laid down by PEA 1977: one requires intent on the part of the offender and is set out in s 1(3); the other is contained in s 1(3A) and requires only knowledge or belief. In both cases, protection is given to residential occupiers as defined in s 1(1) of the PEA 1977 (see **41.2.1**). The actions amounting to harassment would include, for example, removing doors and windows, disconnecting services, and acts and threats of violence.

Section 1(3) harassment

It is an offence to do acts likely to interfere with the peace or comfort of a residential occupier or to withhold services reasonably required for the occupation of the premises with intent to cause the residential occupier to give up the occupation of the premises. Problems are caused by the need to prove intent although it might be possible to infer intent if the particular result could be foreseen as the natural consequence of the actions in question.

Section 1(3A) harassment

It is an offence for a landlord to do acts likely to interfere with the peace and comfort of a residential occupier, or withhold services reasonably required for the occupation of the premises, if he knows or has reasonable cause to believe that the conduct is likely to cause the residential occupier to give up the occupation of the premises. As no specific intent is required for this offence, it may be easier to establish than s 1(3) harassment; this was certainly the intention of the legislature. It is a defence to the withholding of services if this can be justified on 'reasonable grounds'.

41.3 CRIMINAL SANCTIONS: THE CRIMINAL LAW ACT 1977

Under s 6(1) of the Criminal Law Act 1977, any person who 'without lawful authority' uses, or threatens to use, violence to secure entry to premises commits an offence if there is someone present on those premises at the time who is opposed to the entry.

41.4 BRINGING CRIMINAL PROCEEDINGS

The local authority will normally be responsible for commencing proceedings under the PEA 1977. The Crown Prosecution Service are responsible for prosecutions under the Criminal Law Act 1977. A private prosecution might also be possible.

41.5 COMPENSATION IN CRIMINAL PROCEEDINGS

Under s 35 of the Powers of Criminal Courts Act 1973, magistrates have the power to order compensation for 'personal injury, loss or damage resulting' from an offence. These powers are available in relation to all the above offences no matter who brings the prosecution. If compensation is awarded, however, it will be deducted from any damages subsequently awarded in civil proceedings.

41.6 EXCLUDED LICENCES AND TENANCIES

Certain types of licence and tenancy are 'excluded' from some of the protections enacted by the PEA 1977. Section 3A of the PEA 1977 defines 'excluded' licences and tenancies for the purposes of these provisions. A tenancy or licence will be 'excluded', inter alia, if:

(1) the occupier shares accommodation with the landlord or licensor who occupies as his only or principal home, the premises of which the shared accommodation forms part;
(2) the occupier shares accommodation with a member of the landlord's or licensor's family who occupies as his only or principal home, the premises of which the shared accommodation forms part;
(3) it confers the right to occupy for the purpose of a holiday;
(4) it was granted otherwise than for money or money's worth.

It can be assumed that these licences and tenancies are within the protection of a particular provision of the PEA 1977, unless it is stated otherwise.

41.7 CIVIL PROCEEDINGS

41.7.1 Why take civil proceedings?

Criminal sanctions will often not be an adequate remedy for a dispossessed or threatened occupier. The occupier may want an injunction to restrain future actions on the part of the landlord or to restore the tenant to possession of the property; compensation awarded in criminal proceedings is often not as much as would be ordered in civil proceedings. Damages and injunctions are available in civil proceedings in the county court and often provide a more effective and speedy remedy; if need be, emergency procedures can be followed in order to obtain immediate relief.

41.7.2 Causes of action

Alternative causes of action

Various causes of action are available to dispossessed or harassed tenants, some statutory, and some based upon the common law, depending upon the precise facts of the case in question. It is sensible to plead as many alternative causes of action as reasonably present themselves in the circumstances. Actions in both contract and tort may be possible.

Actions for breach of contract

BREACH OF THE COVENANT FOR QUIET ENJOYMENT

It is an implied term of every tenancy that the landlord will allow his tenant 'quiet enjoyment' of the premises. The obligation is for the landlord to allow the tenant peaceable, uninterrupted enjoyment of the property. Unlawful eviction and most actions of harassment will be a breach of this covenant. Thus, knocking on the tenant's door and shouting threats would be a breach of this implied term. It may be possible to argue that a similar term should be implied into a contractual licence. Courts are prepared to imply terms into contracts in order to give proper effect to what has been agreed.

BREACH OF CONTRACT IN GENERAL

Any other breach of a term of the tenancy or licence agreement will be actionable by the occupier. So if a landlord evicts a tenant before the ending of the tenancy, he is in breach of contract. Similarly, if the landlord agrees to provide gas and electricity to a house and then withdraws these facilities, he is again liable for a breach of contract.

Actions in tort

TRESPASS TO LAND

A tenant has the right to the exclusive possession of the demised premises. If the landlord enters onto those premises without permission, he is liable as a trespasser. Licensees who do not have the right to exclusive possession probably cannot sue in trespass.

TRESPASS TO THE PERSON

Harassment and unlawful eviction are frequently accompanied by violence or threats of violence. These may well amount to the torts of assault and battery. A battery is the infliction of physical violence on another without lawful excuse; assault is any act which puts a person in immediate and reasonable fear of a battery. This cause of action will be available both to tenants and to licensees.

TRESPASS TO GOODS

In the process of harassing or evicting an occupier, a landlord frequently damages the occupier's furniture or other personal belongings. This would amount to trespass to goods. If the landlord detains or otherwise deprives the occupier of the use of the goods, this might amount to the tort of conversion. Both tenants and licensees can use this cause of action.

PEA 1977, s 3

Section 3 of the PEA 1977 provides that when a tenancy or licence which is not 'statutorily protected' comes to an end, but the former tenant continues to reside in the premises, he cannot be evicted without a court order. Any eviction of such a tenant will give rise to an action in tort for breach of statutory duty. The definition of 'statutorily protected tenancy' excludes from the protection of this section assured and assured shorthold tenancies under the HA 1988 and protected tenancies under the RA 1977. Also outside the protection of this section will be excluded tenancies and licences (see **41.6**).

Breach of the HA 1988, s 27

Section 27 of the HA 1988 creates a statutory tort if a landlord:

(1) attempts unlawfully to deprive a residential occupier of his occupation; or
(2) knowing or having reasonable cause to believe that the conduct is likely to cause a residential occupier to give up his occupation, does acts likely to interfere with the peace or comfort of the residential occupier or members of his household,

and (in either case) as a result the residential occupier gives up his occupation.

For definition of 'residential occupier' see **41.2.1**. Note in particular that it will include licensees. This tort is only satisfied if the residential occupier actually gives up occupation; this cause of action cannot be used for harassment that does not cause the occupier to leave. Further, there will be no liability under s 27 if the occupier is reinstated in the property either by the landlord or on an order of the court. It is a defence to this action if the landlord can prove that he believed and had reasonable cause to believe that the occupier had ceased to reside in the premises, or that he had reasonable grounds for doing the acts complained of. There is a special measure of damages for this tort (see **41.7.3**).

41.7.3 Remedies

Damages

The basic remedy for breach of contract or tort will be damages, but the measure of damages will differ depending upon which cause of action is pleaded.

MEASURE FOR s 27 ACTIONS

For actions under s 27 of the HA 1988 a special measure of damages is laid down in s 28. Normally, damages are assessed on the basis of the loss to the plaintiff; under s 28 the damages are to be assessed on the basis of the gain to the landlord. This is a deliberate attempt to deprive landlords of the benefit of their wrongdoing. The damages are to be the difference between the value of the premises with a sitting tenant and the value with vacant possession. This difference in value could be substantial (over £30,000 in one decided case) and both plaintiff and defendant must be prepared to bring valuation evidence where a claim under s 27 is being brought. The amount of the damages payable can be reduced by the court if:

(a) the prior conduct of the occupier was such that it would be reasonable to mitigate the damages; or
(b) the occupier has unreasonably refused an offer of reinstatement.

It is not unknown for tenants to harass and assault landlords and so the defence to s 27 might be available to such a landlord who decides to take the law into his own hands by way of retaliation. As far as other actions are concerned, it is likely that many offers of reinstatement could be refused quite reasonably by the occupier. If the occupier has suffered a series of unpleasant events, it cannot be unreasonable for him to refuse reinstatement when, in his mind at least, that might carry the risk of further similar conduct.

MEASURE IN OTHER ACTIONS

In tort, damages are intended to put the plaintiff in the position he would have been in had the tort in question not been committed. In contract, on the other hand, damages will be assessed to put the plaintiff into the position he would have been in had the contract been fulfilled. There are various types of damages (see the LPC Resource Book *Civil Litigation* (Jordans) for the difference between special and general damages. Particularly relevant in unlawful eviction cases (see below) will be exemplary and aggravated damages).

EXEMPLARY DAMAGES

Exemplary damages are only available for actions in tort. They will be awarded only where the defendant's conduct has been calculated to make a profit over and above any damages he would have otherwise had to pay to the plaintiff. They are available in unlawful eviction cases 'to teach wrongdoers that tort does not pay'. It is not necessary to show that the landlord actually did make a profit in order to claim exemplary damages, nor are they limited to the amount of the profit actually made. They must, however, be specifically pleaded in the particulars of claim. Although not available in contract actions, see the special measure of damages under s 27 of the HA 1988 which have a similar objective.

AGGRAVATED DAMAGES

Aggravated damages are again only available in relation to actions in tort, but unlike exemplary damages need not be specifically pleaded. They are in many respects similar to exemplary damages but there is no need to show the element of calculation on the defendant's part. They will thus be available in cases of particularly unpleasant conduct on the landlord's part to express the outrage and indignation of society at such behaviour.

Injunctions

Awarding damages in harassment and unlawful eviction cases will often not provide the occupier with a full remedy. An occupier who remains in occupation will want protection and reassurance that the harassment will not be repeated; an occupier who has been unlawfully evicted may want to be reinstated in the property; an occupier who has been deprived of his personal belongings will want them restored to him. The appropriate remedy in these cases will be an injunction. If an occupier fears that he may suffer unlawful eviction in the future, he may also seek an injunction to restrain the landlord from such conduct. Unlike damages, an injunction is a discretionary equitable remedy; even if the plaintiff's case is proved there is no right to insist on the granting of an injunction and the usual equitable bars to relief will apply. Thus, an applicant who delays in coming to court may fail to obtain an injunction, as may an applicant who does not 'come to equity with clean hands', for example, who has been guilty of violence against the landlord.

Types of injunction

An injunction can be made by the court as a final order or as an interim order. A final order is made on the final determination of the case, which may be several months after the commencement of the proceedings. In harassment cases, such delay will inevitably be unacceptable and so an interlocutory injunction should be applied for. An interlocutory injunction is one awarded during the continuance of the action and will normally be an interim injunction, ie it will not be the final determination of the issues between the parties, but will remain in force only until some specified date. Normally, an injunction is ordered by the court only after hearing both sides to the action. However, in an emergency, an ex parte order can be obtained, ie an order made on the hearing of evidence from the plaintiff only. In many harassment and unlawful eviction cases the occupier will require a speedy remedy and so an ex parte injunction will need to be sought.

When will an interlocutory injunction be available?

Interlocutory relief is not available as of right; various conditions must be satisfied. However, in harassment cases this should not cause an undue problem. The requirements which must be satisfied are:

(1) that there is a serious question to be tried; and
(2) that damages would not be adequate compensation; and
(3) that the balance of convenience is in favour of granting the injunction rather than awaiting the outcome of the full trial (see *American Cyanamid Co v Ethicon Ltd* [1975] AC 396).

The applicant will usually be required to give an undertaking to compensate the landlord if it is later found that the order should not have been made. The fact that the applicant is legally aided (and so unable to give a financially worthwhile undertaking) should not prevent the making of an interlocutory order in appropriate cases.

41.8 NOTICES TO QUIT

Notices to quit can only be used to determine periodic tenancies, not fixed-term tenancies. However, although they are an effective common law method of terminating a periodic tenancy, they are often not required to terminate a tenancy of a dwelling house due to the effect of the security of tenure legislation. Where they are required, special formalities have to be complied with under s 5 of the PEA 1977. In the case of a periodic licence, a notice will normally be required. This is often referred to as a 'notice to determine'.

41.8.1 When is a notice to quit required?

Notices to quit are only potentially relevant to periodic tenancies. At common law, a fixed-term tenancy will expire by effluxion of time; there is no need for the service of a notice to quit. Due to the security of tenure legislation, notices are not always necessary even for periodic tenancies. Thus, assured tenancies under the HA 1988 can only be brought to an end by the landlord by the obtaining of a court order. Section 5(1) of the HA 1988 specifically provides that the service by the landlord of a notice to quit shall be of no effect. A periodic assured tenancy can, however, be terminated by a tenant's notice to quit. In the case of protected tenancies under the RA 1977, a notice to quit is necessary to terminate a periodic tenancy. Service of a valid notice may, however, give rise to a statutory tenancy (see **40.3**) in which case the service of a further notice to quit would not be necessary prior to the landlord commencing possession proceedings. In the absence of any agreement to the contrary, a periodic tenancy which is outside any of the security of tenure provisions will require the service of a notice to quit before it can be ended. In the cases where a notice to quit is required, a periodic tenancy will continue to run unless and until a valid notice to quit has been served by one party on the other. So if a tenant vacates the premises, this will not of itself be sufficient to end the tenancy and so the tenant's liability for rent will continue. To be valid, a notice to quit must be of the correct length (see **41.8.2**), expire on the correct day (see **41.8.3**) and often contain prescribed information (see **41.8.4**). At common law, the termination of contractual licences is governed by the terms of the contract. In the absence of an express provision, a periodic licence will be terminable by reasonable notice, but see **41.8.2**.

41.8.2 Length of notice

At common law, a notice, whether given by landlord or tenant, must be of a length equivalent to the period of the tenancy. So one month's notice is required for a monthly tenancy, but only one week for a weekly tenancy. Yearly periodic tenancies, as an exception to this rule, require only half a year's notice. However, under s 5 of the PEA 1977, a notice to quit a dwelling house must be of not less than 4 weeks' duration. This applies whether the notice is given by the landlord or by the tenant. The notice must also be in writing and contain prescribed information. This provision also applies in relation to notices to determine periodic licences of dwelling houses, but does not apply to excluded licences and tenancies as defined in **41.6**.

41.8.3 Expiry of the notice

It is not sufficient that the correct length of notice is served; to be valid at common law a notice must also expire on the correct day. This involves the application of the corresponding day rule. This dictates that the notice must expire either on the first day or the last day of a period. So in the case of a weekly tenancy which commenced on a Monday, the notice (4 weeks, in writing etc) must expire on a Monday or a Sunday; if it expires on any other day of the week it will be ineffective and the tenancy will continue to run. Similarly, with a monthly tenancy commencing on the 15th of a particular month, the notice must expire on the 14th or 15th of some succeeding month and not, for example, on the 31st. It can sometimes be unclear precisely when a tenancy commenced and so it is sensible when serving a notice to include some kind of saving clause to operate just in case the wrong termination date has been specified. So the notice will be expressed to expire on a date at least 4 weeks later 'or the day on which a complete period of your tenancy expires next after the end of 4 weeks [one month] from the service of this notice on you'. It is, of course, always open to the parties to agree in the tenancy agreement as to the length and expiry date of a notice to quit. Provided that this agreement does not conflict with s 5 of the PEA 1977 (see **41.8.2**), it can be agreed that the notice can expire on any day and not just the corresponding day.

41.8.4 Prescribed information

In order to be valid, a notice to quit a dwelling house (whether let on a tenancy or a licence) must not only be of the correct length and expire on the correct day, it must also be in writing and contain the prescribed information. The prescribed information is:

> '(1) if the tenant or licensee does not leave the dwelling, the landlord or licensor must get an order for possession from the court before the tenant or licensee can lawfully be evicted. The landlord or licensor cannot apply for such an order before the notice to quit or notice to determine has run out;
>
> (2) a tenant or licensee who does not know if he has any rights to remain after a notice to quit or notice to determine runs out can obtain advice from a solicitor. Help with all or part of the cost of legal advice and assistance may be available under the legal aid scheme. He should also be able to obtain information from a citizens' advice bureau, a housing aid centre or a rent officer.'

These provisions do not apply to excluded licences and tenancies as defined in **41.6**.

Chapter 42

REPAIRS TO RESIDENTIAL PROPERTIES

Chapter 42 contents

42.1 INTRODUCTION

The issue of repairs may arise in various contexts. The most common is where the tenant complains that work needs doing to the house or flat, for example, that a leaking roof or defective gutter is causing dampness. The question may also arise in a rent arrears case where the tenant has refused to pay rent because of an alleged disrepair; or in a personal injury case where the tenant (or a visitor) has been injured by reason of defective premises. It may also arise because a local authority has instituted criminal proceedings under public health/environmental protection legislation. Clearly, the question of liability or responsibility for carrying out repairs and the consequences of disrepair must be viewed in the context in which the particular legal problem arises. However, in this chapter the emphasis is on civil liability for repairs as between landlord and tenant (although some of the wider aspects are considered briefly).

The first question to be considered is the meaning of the word 'repair'. The basic definition of 'repair' is not affected by the nature of the property involved and so reference should be made to the chapter on repairs in the Commercial Leases part of the book (Chapter 19).

42.2 WHO IS LIABLE FOR REPAIR?

42.2.1 Position at common law

In the absence of any express provisions in the lease or tenancy agreement, the landlord gives no warranty that the premises will be fit for habitation or that he will repair them.

There are two exceptions:

(1) Furnished lettings: where there is a furnished letting, the landlord impliedly warrants that the premises are fit for habitation at the commencement of the term. This is a very limited exception based on the case of *Smith v Marrable* [1843] 11 M&W 5, where a furnished house was infested with bugs. It was held that the tenant could repudiate the tenancy and recover damages for loss suffered. However, there is no continuing obligation on the part of the landlord to keep the premises fit for habitation during the term.

(2) Common parts: in certain cases, the courts may imply a covenant to give business efficacy to a lease or tenancy. For example, if the premises consist of a tower block containing lifts, staircases, rubbish chutes and other common parts and the tenancy agreements of the individual flats do not impose obligations on either the tenant or landlord to maintain the common parts, the court may hold that, since the terms of the tenancy agreement are obviously incomplete, and that the premises cannot function without such common parts being maintained, the landlord must have impliedly taken responsibility to keep them in reasonable condition: see *Liverpool City Council v Irwin* [1977] AC 239. However, such implied term is not automatic and depends on the facts of each

particular case and is based on the contractual principle that the courts may imply a term to make a contract function. If the lease or tenancy agreement expressly deals with these matters there is clearly no room for an implied term.

As regards the tenant, there are no implied repairing obligations on his part at common law so that, in the absence of an express agreement, the tenant, is not responsible for repair as such. However, a tenant must not commit waste. A tenant under a fixed-term lease is liable for both voluntary and permissive waste. This means that he must not carry out alterations or allow the property to fall into serious disrepair. A yearly periodic tenant is, however, only liable to keep the premises 'wind and water tight'. A weekly tenant on the other hand is not liable for permissive waste but must use the premises in 'a tenant-like manner'. This means that he must take proper care of them, for example, by unblocking drains, cleaning chimneys, mending fuses and doing the little jobs around the house that a reasonable tenant would do. The position at common law is not satisfactory from either the landlord's or the tenant's point of view. The question of repairing liability is, therefore, usually either dealt with expressly by the terms of the tenancy agreement or covered by some statutory provision. If a matter is covered both by an express obligation and also by a statutory provision, and the express obligation is in conflict with the statutory obligation, the statutory obligation prevails.

42.2.2 Express covenants

In many cases the lease or tenancy agreement will expressly set out the repairing obligations of the parties. Subject to the statutory provisions mentioned below, the parties are free to agree who should be liable for which repairs. For example, it may have been agreed that the landlord will be liable for exterior repairs and that the tenant will be liable for interior repairs and decoration. If the lease or tenancy agreement sets out these obligations expressly, those provisions will override the common law and will be enforceable, subject only to statutory intervention.

42.2.3 Modification by statute

Despite the presence or absence of express repairing obligations, the LTA 1985 implies certain repairing obligations on the part of the landlord which cannot be excluded except with leave of the court. These statutory implied terms are important and must now be considered.

42.3 LANDLORD AND TENANT ACT 1985, s 11

42.3.1 Leases to which s 11 applies

Section 11 of the LTA 1985 applies to any lease or agreement for lease of a dwelling house, granted on or after 24 October 1961, if the term is less than 7 years. This includes periodic tenancies even if the tenant has been in occupation for more than 7 years. It also applies to a fixed-term lease granted for more than 7 years if the landlord can determine the term within the first 7 years, ie there is a break clause in the landlord's favour. However, s 11 does not apply to a lease for less than 7 years if it contains an option for renewal by the tenant where the term can be extended to more than 7 years. No contracting out is allowed unless sanctioned by the county court. This includes indirect contracting out, for example, by placing an obligation on the tenant to pay money in lieu of repairs.

42.3.2 The implied terms

There is an implied covenant by the landlord:

(1) to keep in repair the structure and exterior of the dwelling house (including drains, gutters and external pipes); and
(2) to keep in repair and proper working order the installations in the dwelling house for the supply of water, gas and electricity and for sanitation (including basins, sinks, baths and sanitary conveniences but not other fixtures, fittings and appliances for making use of the supply of water, gas or electricity); and
(3) to keep in repair and proper working order the installations in the dwelling house for space heating and heating water.

42.3.3 'Structure and exterior'

The word 'structure' is not defined by the Act but would clearly include the main fabric of the building such as the main walls, roof, timbers and foundations as distinguished from decorations or fittings. The word 'exterior' is not defined either, but has been held to include paths or steps which form an essential means of access (*Brown v Liverpool Corporation* [1969] 3 All ER 1345) but not paving in the back yard (*Hopwood v Cannock Chase District Council* [1975] 1 WLR 373) nor a footpath at the rear of the house (*King v South Northamptonshire District Council* [1992] 06 EG 152). The words 'structure and exterior' can cause particular problems where a tenant in a block of flats is seeking to force the landlord to do repairs in respect of common parts or to the entire block rather than just the particular flat occupied by the complaining tenant.

It was held in *Campden Hill Towers v Gardner* [1977] QB 823 that the landlord's implied covenant extends only to the flat in question and not to the entire block; it extends to the outside of the inner party wall of the flat, the outer side of the horizontal division between the flat and the flats below and above but does not extend to the entire building. This problem has now been resolved by an amendment made by the HA 1988 but only in respect of leases or tenancies granted on or after 15 January 1989. The position now is that reference to 'dwelling house' in s 11 is extended to include any part of the building in which the landlord has an estate or interest and that any references to 'installations' in the dwelling house include installations directly or indirectly serving the house forming part of the same building or which are owned or under the control of the landlord. Thus, for leases granted on or after 15 January 1989 where the landlord owns the entire block, the landlord will be under an obligation to maintain the structure and exterior of the entire block including common parts and the stipulated facilities. However, it is expressly provided that the landlord is not liable unless the disrepair is such as to affect the tenant's enjoyment of the flat or common parts in question. As to the position with regard to common parts in the case of tenancies granted before 15 January 1989, see **42.2.1**.

42.3.4 'Installations in the dwelling house'

The landlord is also obliged to repair and keep in working order the installations for the supply of water, gas, electricity, sanitation, space heating and water heating. The section does not oblige the landlord to provide these facilities but simply to maintain such as exist at the commencement of the tenancy. Thus, if the house does not have these facilities to begin with there is no obligation on the part of the landlord to provide the necessary installations. Further, it applies only to installations that are actually within the house. If a fault occurs in a supply installation outside the house this is not within the section. However, in the case of flats, where the tenancy was granted on or after 15 January 1989, the obligation extends to installations within the entire building which the landlord owns or to installations within the building over which the landlord has control. Thus, if a flat is centrally heated by a communal boiler in the basement and the boiler breaks down, liability under the section will depend on when the tenancy commenced. If the tenancy commenced prior to 15 January 1989, the landlord will not be liable (under the section) whereas if the tenancy was granted on or after that date the landlord will be liable.

42.3.5 Standards of repair

The section provides that in determining the standards of repair regard must be had to the age, character and prospective life of the dwelling and the locality in which it is situated (LTA 1985, s 11(3)). Thus, a house in a poor condition at the commencement of the tenancy, in an area of poor quality housing, does not need to be comprehensively repaired under s 11. 'Patching' repairs may satisfy the section depending on the circumstances of each particular case.

42.3.6 Exceptions

There are some specific exceptions to liability under s 11.

Under s 11(2) the covenant does not extend to:

(1) repairs for which the tenant is liable by virtue of his duty to use the premises in a tenant-like manner;
(2) rebuilding or reinstating the premises in the case of destruction or damage by fire or by tempest or other accident;
(3) keeping in repair or maintaining anything that the tenant is entitled to remove from the dwelling house (tenant's fixtures).

Further, the landlord is not liable unless he has notice of the need for repair. Thus, in *O'Brien v Robinson* [1973] AC 912 the plaintiffs were injured when the ceiling of their flat fell on them. This was found to be the result of a latent defect. The landlords were not liable for the personal injuries caused to the plaintiffs since there had been no breach of the duty of repair under s 11 in that the landlord did not know of this latent defect at the material time. However, this requirement for notice only applies to those premises or parts of premises actually demised to the tenant. There is no need for notice in respect of those parts of the premises which remain in the possession or control of the landlord. This will be particularly relevant in relation to the extension of the landlord's liability to the whole of a building made by the HA 1988 (see **42.3.3**).

42.4 REMEDIES FOR BREACH BY THE LANDLORD OF AN EXPRESS OR IMPLIED TERM AS TO REPAIRS

42.4.1 The need for notice

A landlord is not in breach of his repairing obligation in respect of the demised premises unless he has notice of the need for repair and has failed to repair within a reasonable time of the notice being given. The notice need not be a formal notice nor need it necessarily come from the tenant direct. The notice could be oral or could arise because a landlord's inspection revealed the defect. Alternatively, it may arise because a local authority environmental health officer or surveyor has inspected the premises and has reported the defects to, or served notice on, the landlord for other purposes, for example, under the Environmental Protection Act 1990 or under a tenant's application under the right to buy scheme for council houses.

Sometimes, problems can arise because the tenant does not know the precise identity of his landlord. This most commonly happens where the letting has been by an agent. Obvious problems can arise with giving notice of the need for repair and with regard to enforcement if the landlord's identity is not known and for this reason there are various statutory provisions which may assist.

First, under s 1 of the LTA 1985, the person who is collecting the rent must disclose the landlord's identity within 21 days if requested to do so by the tenant. Further, by s 3 of the LTA 1985, on any assignment of the landlord's interest the new landlord shall give notice of his name and address within 2 months. There are criminal sanctions for breach of these sections. Perhaps of more practical use to a tenant is the fact that in case of a breach of s 3, the former landlord will still remain liable upon the terms of the lease and thus any repairing obligation until notice of the new landlord's name and address is given. This liability expressly extends to breaches which did not arise until after the transfer of ownership. Additionally, use might be made of the provisions of s 48 of the LTA 1987 (see **37.3.11**) which requires a landlord to give a tenant an address for service.

Assuming that the landlord's identity is known and that he has failed to effect repairs within a reasonable time of notice having been given, the tenant has a choice of remedies.

42.4.2 Damages

Breach of a repairing covenant is a breach of contract. The tenant will be entitled to damages on normal contractual principles. The rules in *Hadley v Baxendale* (1834) Exch 341 will apply. The object of the damages is to place the plaintiff, so far as money can do so, in the same position he would have been in had the breach not occurred. Each case must be looked at on its own merits and will depend on what has actually happened. For example, the tenant may have been forced to pay to have the repairs done himself and possibly have been driven into finding alternative accommodation whilst the repairs were being carried out. General damages could include loss of enjoyment or loss of use and occupation, reduction in rental income or compensation for ill health or personal injuries. Special damages could include money actually laid out by the tenant in doing repairs or the cost of medical treatment. A good illustration of the court's approach is set out in the case of *Calabar Properties Ltd v Stitcher* [1984] 1 WLR 287, CA.

42.4.3 Specific performance

Section 17(1) of the LTA 1985 provides as follows:

> '(1) In proceedings in which a tenant of a dwelling alleges a breach on the part of his landlord of a repairing covenant relating to any part of the premises in which the dwelling is comprised, the court may order specific performance of the covenant whether or not the breach relates to a part of the premises let to the tenant and notwithstanding any equitable rule restricting the scope of the remedy, whether on the basis of a lack of mutuality or otherwise.'

Specific performance is a discretionary remedy. It is available to a tenant suing the landlord for breach of a landlord's repairing covenant and not usually vice versa.

The landlord's covenant may be express or implied. Thus, if the tenancy is one to which s 11 of the LTA 1985 applies (see **42.3**), specific performance of the landlord's implied covenant for repair may be granted.

Although s 17 is not confined to flats (and is available in all residential lettings where the landlord is contractually liable for repairs), it is particularly useful in the context of flats. If there is a defect in the common parts of the building such as a shared staircase (which the landlord has an express or implied duty to repair under a repairing covenant) an individual tenant of one of the flats may not have the incentive or the right himself to repair the defect. It will be seen, however, that under s 17 specific performance may be ordered 'whether or not the breach relates to a part of the premises let to the tenant'. Thus, specific performance of the covenant to repair the common parts could be ordered.

42.4.4 Self-help: deduction from rent

It is possible, in certain circumstances, for the tenant to have the repairs done and to reimburse himself as to the cost from future rental payments. This will, of course, only assist the tenant who has the necessary means with which to pay for the repairs in the first place. If he has, and so chooses, he can then deduct the repair bill from rent that would otherwise be payable to the landlord.

The leading case in this area is *Lee-Parker v Izzet* [1971] 1 WLR 1688. In that case, Goff J stated:

> 'I do not think this is bound up with technical rules of set off. It is an ancient common law right. I therefore declare that so far as the repairs are within the express or implied covenants of the landlord, the [third and fourth] defendants are entitled to recoup themselves out of future rents and defend any action for payment of rent. It is a question of fact in every case whether and to what extent the expenditure was proper.'

For this right of reimbursement to be exercised, it is again a prerequisite that the landlord has notice of the disrepair and has been allowed a reasonable period in which to comply with the repairing obligation. It is advisable for the tenant to obtain three estimates for the cost of repairs and to submit copies to the landlord and inform him of the tenant's intentions if the work is not done. In order to mitigate his loss the tenant should use the lowest estimate and, if the landlord failed to reimburse the tenant, the tenant would be entitled to stop paying rent to the landlord and to use the rent by way of reimbursement.

There is, however, the danger that the landlord may then start possession or forfeiture proceedings based upon alleged rent arrears. For the landlord to succeed in establishing rent arrears he must show that the rent is 'lawfully due'. It can be argued, on the tenant's behalf, that the appropriation of the rent to reimburse the cost of repairs, in the circumstances outlined, is another way of lawfully paying the rent. In the Court of Appeal in *Televantos v McCulloch* [1991] 19 EG 118, a tenant set off unpaid rent against landlord's repairs. The Court of Appeal held that since the landlord was relying upon a discretionary ground for possession, (in that case under the RA 1977), it was not reasonable for an order for possession to be made. However, the Court of Appeal, without deciding the point, were of the opinion that in these circumstances the rent may not be lawfully due for the purposes of establishing arrears as the money had been lawfully used to pay for the landlord's repairing obligation. It was arguable that the rent was not lawfully due. This point may be of crucial importance in a possession case on Ground 8 of the HA 1988 (2 months' rent arrears). This is a mandatory ground, and not a discretionary ground, but the rent must be 'lawfully due' at the relevant time. If the rent has been lawfully set off against repairs, it can be argued that the rent is not lawfully due, to that extent, and this could make Ground 8 inappropriate by reducing the amount of the arrears below the crucial 2-month figure.

42.5 LANDLORD'S TORTIOUS LIABILITY

42.5.1 Defective Premises Act 1972, s 4

Section 4 of the Defective Premises Act 1972 states:

'(1) Where the premises are let under a tenancy which puts on the landlord an obligation to the tenant for the maintenance or repair of the premises, the landlord owes to all persons who might reasonably be expected to be affected by defects in the state of the premises a duty to take such care as is reasonable in all circumstances to see that they are reasonably safe from personal injury or from damage to their property caused by a relevant defect.

(2) The said duty is owed if the landlord knows (whether as the result of being notified by the tenant or otherwise) or if he ought in all circumstances to have known of the relevant defect.

(3) In this section "relevant defect" means a defect in the state of the premises existing at or after the material time and arising from, or continuing because of, an act or omission by the landlord which constitutes or would if he had had notice of the defect, have constituted a failure by him to carry out his obligation to the tenant for the maintenance or repair of the premises; and for the purposes of the foregoing provision "the material time" means—

(a) where the tenancy commenced before this Act, the commencement of this Act; and

(b) in all other cases, the earliest of the following times, that is to say—

(i) the time when the tenancy commences;

(ii) the time when the tenancy agreement is entered into;

(iii) the time when possession is taken of the premises in contemplation of the letting.

(4) Where the premises are let under a tenancy which expressly or impliedly gives the landlord the right to enter the premises to carry out any description of maintenance or repair of the premises, then, as from the time when he first is, or by notice or otherwise can put himself, in a position to exercise the right and so long as he is or can put himself in that position, he shall be treated for the purposes of subsections (1) to (3) above (but for no other purpose) as if he were under an obligation to the tenant for that description of maintenance or repair of the premises; but the landlord shall not owe the tenant any duty by virtue of this subsection in respect of any defect in the state of the premises arising from or continuing because of a failure to carry out an obligation expressly imposed on the tenant by the tenancy.

(5) For the purposes of this section obligations imposed or rights given by an enactment in virtue of a tenancy shall be treated as imposed or given by the tenancy.

(6) This section applies to a right of occupation given by contract or any enactment and not amounting to a tenancy as if the right were a tenancy, and "tenancy" and cognate expressions shall be construed accordingly.'

No contracting out is allowed.

Since this liability is tort-based the plaintiff must show damage, ie personal injury or damage to property. However, in *Barrett v Lounova* [1989] 2 WLR 137, Kerr LJ suggested that 'there is no reason of principle or jurisdiction, why an injunction to enforce obligations under s 4(1) of the Act of 1972 should not issue in appropriate circumstances'. The term 'appropriate circumstances' is vague but, if the plaintiff is in imminent danger of suffering personal injury by reason of a breach of s 4, this may possibly be such a circumstance.

The landlord may be liable for matters which are not his liability under the tenancy agreement. Section 4(4) states that a right of entry to do repairs carries with it a deemed obligation to repair a defect which the exercise of the right ought to have revealed. In *McCauley v Bristol City Council* [1991] 23 HLR 586, the Court of Appeal gave judgment in favour of a tenant who broke her ankle after falling on some steps in the back garden. It was accepted that there was no obligation on the landlord to repair the steps, whether express or implied. However, the fact that the landlord had a right to enter and carry out repairs brought into operation subsection (4) of s 4. There was deemed to be an obligation on the landlord to effect any repairs which the exercise of the right ought to have revealed. The landlord was thus in breach of a duty of care with regard to the step and was liable to compensate the tenant for the injury suffered.

42.5.2 Occupiers' Liability Act 1957, s 2

If the landlord retains occupation of any part of the premises (eg common parts) the landlord owes a common duty of care to all visitors to take such care as in all the circumstances of the case is reasonable to see that the visitors are reasonably safe in using the premises.

Thus, if the members of the tenant's family or persons visiting the property are injured by defects in, for example, a shared staircase retained by the landlord, the landlord may be liable if he is in breach of the common duty of care.

42.5.3 Common law

Apart from the above statutory provision, a landlord is not generally liable in tort to the tenant in respect of defective premises.

However, exceptionally the landlord may be liable for the torts of nuisance or negligence.

Liability in nuisance

Where the landlord retains parts of the building (as in a block of flats) he may be liable if defects occur in the parts retained which interfere with the tenant's reasonable enjoyment of the part let. For example, in *Cockburn v Smith* [1924] 2 KB 119 the landlord retained a roof over flats. Lack of maintenance caused severe dampness to one of the flats. In consequence, the tenant became ill. The landlord was held to be liable.

Liability in negligence

If the landlord is also the builder or developer of the premises, he may owe a common law duty of care for damage arising from defective construction or design. Similarly, if a landlord does work to the premises after letting them, there is duty to exercise reasonable care so as to avoid defects or causing damage to persons or property. However, these are exceptional cases and, as a general rule, there is immunity for a landlord who lets defective, dangerous or unsafe property on which he has done no work. For example, in *McNerny v Lambeth Borough Council* [1989] 21 HLR 188 the landlord let premises which were severely damp by reason of condensation, but the landlord had not built or designed the property. It was held that the landlord was not liable, at common law, for the tort of negligence. However, there may be liability under the Environmental Protection Act 1990 for a statutory nuisance or under the Housing Act 1985 if the house is unfit for human habitation. The detail of these provisions is outside the scope of this book.

Chapter 43

ENFRANCHISEMENT: LONG LEASES OF HOUSES

43.1 INTRODUCTION

The Leasehold Reform Act 1967 (LRA 1967) confers on certain tenants holding long leases of houses the right to acquire the freehold (and superior leasehold reversions) on their properties. Alternatively, they can acquire an extended lease. For these rights to apply, various conditions must be fulfilled.

43.2 THE QUALIFYING CONDITIONS IN OUTLINE

There are four major requirements:

(1) there must be a 'house';
(2) let on a 'long lease';
(3) at a low rent;
(4) tenanted by a 'qualifying tenant'.

43.2.1 'A house'

The LRA 1967 applies only to houses and not to flats.

Section 2(1) of the LRA 1967 defines a house as:

> 'For the purposes of this Part of this Act, "house" includes any building designed or adapted for living in and reasonably so called, notwithstanding that the building is not structurally detached, or was not or is not solely designed or adapted for living in, or is divided horizontally into flats or maisonettes.'

This definition includes ordinary purpose-built houses, and it can include buildings which were not originally houses (eg barns, warehouses, stables, etc) later converted or adapted as houses.

The main problem area is deciding what is a house 'reasonably so called'. This definition can cause problems in relation to shops with living accommodation above and also with properties which have been converted into flats.

As regards shops with living accommodation, the leading authority is the House of Lords decision in the case of *Tandon v Trustees of Spurgeons Homes* [1982] AC 755, which concerned a purpose-built shop with a flat above. Approximately 75 per cent of the property was attributed to the shop and 25 per cent to the living accommodation. By a majority decision it was held that the premises were a house reasonably so called even though it was also reasonable to call them something else, ie a shop! It is a question of law whether it is reasonable to call a building a house, but if the building is designed or adapted for living in, in exceptional circumstances only will a judge be justified in holding that it is not reasonable to call it a house.

Another problem concerns buildings which are converted into flats. Many properties which were originally houses have been converted into flats. An individual flat cannot be a house but, nevertheless, the whole building may retain its characteristics as a house. For example, if a house is converted into two self-contained flats by the owner of a long lease who continues to occupy one of the flats, sub-letting the other, the long leaseholder may be in a position to enfranchise. The building looked at as a whole may still reasonably be called a house notwithstanding the internal sub-division.

43.2.2 'Long lease'

Section 3 of the LRA 1967 defines a long lease as a 'tenancy granted for a term of years certain exceeding 21 years'. It is the length of the original term that matters. The fact that less than 21 years remains unexpired when the rights are exercised is not relevant to this particular issue. Further, the fact that the lease may be terminated before it runs 21 years (eg by forfeiture, break clause, etc) is to be ignored. If the long lease has expired but the tenant holds over under another tenancy of the property, the new tenancy is deemed to be a long lease (subject to exceptions).

43.2.3 'Low rent'

The general rule is that the rent must not exceed two-thirds of the rateable value on the appropriate day. The detailed rules are complex and depend (inter alia) on the date when the tenancy was granted. Reference should be made to the LRA 1967 for the detailed rules. If, however, the tenancy was granted on or after 1 April 1990 'low rent' means £1,000 per annum or less if the property is in Greater London or £250 or less if the property is elsewhere.

Under s 106 of the HA 1996, a further right to enfranchise is given in cases where the low rent test is not satisfied. If the tenancy, although not at a low rent, was originally granted for a term certain exceeding 35 years, then the tenant will be given the same right to enfranchise as if the tenancy were at a low rent. Such a tenant, however, is only given the right to enfranchise; he is not given a right to an extended lease.

43.2.4 'Qualifying tenant'

The LRA 1967 does not use the expression 'qualifying tenant' but it does impose certain minimum residence requirements which must be satisfied before the tenant 'qualifies' for enfranchisement or an extended lease. The tenant must, at the date when he serves the appropriate notice (see **43.3.1**) exercising his rights, be occupying the house (or part of it) as his only or main residence and have done so for the last 3 years or for an aggregate of 3 years out of the last 10 years.

The occupation need not be exclusively for residential purposes. For example, if the house has been used partly for business purposes, the business user may not disqualify the tenant. Moreover, sub-letting of part of the property does not disqualify the tenant provided he retains occupation of some other part as his only or main residence for the relevant period.

Trust property

A beneficiary's occupation of the house under a trust or strict settlement counts as occupation for this purpose even though the legal estate is held by trustees or a tenant for life. If the beneficiary is entitled absolutely to the house, he can, after the relevant period, exercise the rights himself.

If he is not absolutely entitled, the trustees or a tenant for life can exercise the rights on his behalf.

Succession on death

If the tenant dies before exercising rights under the Act and the tenancy passes to a member of his family, the successor can, in certain circumstances, add his own qualifying period of residence as tenant to the length of time he lived with the deceased tenant in order to make up the 3-year minimum. This only applies, however, where the deceased tenant dies while occupying the house as his only or main residence and the successor also resided in the house with the deceased tenant as his only or main residence and is still so resident at the date of death. 'Member of the family' is defined in s 7(7) of the LRA 1967 and includes spouse, step-children, parents or parents-in-law.

43.3 ENFRANCHISEMENT OR EXTENDED LEASE

The tenant who satisfies the above conditions will normally wish to enfranchise. This means that the landlord must convey the fee simple to the tenant at a price, and on the terms, referred to in the LRA 1967. Alternatively, the tenant may elect to take an extended lease. Here, the landlord must grant the tenant a new lease for the unexpired residue of the term of the existing lease plus a further 50 years. The new lease will be, broadly, on the same terms as the existing lease and the rent will be the same until the expiry date of the existing lease, but thereafter, the rent will be replaced by a modern ground rent (reviewed after 25 years of the extra 50 years).

43.3.1 Desire notice

The tenant must serve written notice of his desire ('the desire notice') in the prescribed form to have either the freehold or an extended lease. This desire notice is normally the first step in the procedure to obtain the rights granted by the Act. The desire notice is deemed to be an estate contract and it should, therefore, be protected by an appropriate registration under the Land Charges Act 1972 or the LRA 1925 as the case may be. The landlord must, within 2 months, serve a Notice in Reply admitting or objecting to the tenant's claim. For the detailed procedure, reference should be made to the Act and the regulations made under it.

Although the desire notice is deemed to create an estate contract, it is generally personal to the tenant and is not assignable to third parties. However, if the tenant assigns the lease, he can assign the benefit of the desire notice at the same time to the assignee of the lease. The assignee could then proceed with the acquisition of the freehold or an extended lease even though the assignee does not qualify under the Act (LRA 1967, s 5).

43.4 TERMS OF THE CONVEYANCE OF THE FREEHOLD

The conveyance (or transfer if the landlord's title is registered) will be subject to:

(1) the tenancy; and
(2) tenant's incumbrances but free from other incumbrances.

The broad effect of this is that the tenant will be bound by any mortgages or charges which have been created in respect of the leasehold interest, but will take free from mortgages or charges created by the landlord over the freehold interest.

The conveyance will grant and reserve, broadly, the same easements as existed under the lease.

Disputes about the terms of the conveyance (other than as to price) are resolved by the court.

43.5 THE PRICE OF THE FREEHOLD

The LRA 1967 lays down the principles and formulae for ascertaining the price and the appeals machinery if it cannot be agreed between the parties.

There are two methods of ascertaining the price depending on the value of the house and premises. They are dealt with by s 9(1) and s 9(1A) of the LRA 1967 respectively.

The valuation under s 9(1) is very favourable to the tenant. It must be assumed for valuation purposes that the landlord is selling the freehold subject to the lease and on the assumption that this had been extended for a further 50 years under the Act and assuming the tenant is not the buyer. It is thus looked at as if the freehold is being bought largely for its investment income (which, by definition is likely to be fairly small). The fact that the tenant can, on acquisition, merge the freehold and leasehold interests is ignored. This 'marriage value', as it is sometimes called, is not taken into account under s 9(1).

The valuation under s 9(1) only applies to lower value properties. For higher value properties, a much less favourable formula has to be used. This not only requires marriage value to be taken into account, but also requires an assumption that the tenant has no right to extend the lease under LRA 1967. Both these assumptions will result in a considerably higher price being paid than if the lower value formula were to be used. The method of deciding whether a house falls into the lower or higher value bands depends upon whether the house had a rateable value on 31 March 1990. If it did (and most houses in existence at that date would have had a rateable value), then the rule is that houses with rateable values of £500 or less (£1,000 or less if the house is in Greater London) will be classed as lower value. Any other houses will be classed as higher value. Owing to the abolition of domestic rates, it is not possible to use rateable value as a deciding factor for houses not rated on 31 March 1990, ie basically houses built since that date. For these houses, a complex formula is applied based on the premium originally paid on the grant and the length of the term, for which, see s 1(1)(a)(i) of the LRA 1967 (as amended).

In addition to the purchase price, the tenant must pay all reasonable legal and valuation fees incurred by the landlord. Disputes as to price are dealt with by the Leasehold Valuation Tribunal.

Chapter 44

LANDLORD AND TENANT ACT 1987

Chapter 44 contents

44.1 INTRODUCTION

Under the LTA 1987, if a landlord of a building composed of flats wishes to dispose of his freehold reversion he is obliged, subject to the conditions specified in the Act, to offer it first to the relevant tenants.

Further, in the case of 'bad management' by the landlord the court can, in certain circumstances, compel the landlord to transfer his interest to the tenants.

However, the main impact of the Act is the so-called 'tenant's right of first refusal'. The relevant law is contained in Part I of the Act. This has been almost entirely substituted by the HA 1996, with the object of making it easier for tenants to enforce their rights. Criminal sanctions have also been imposed for landlords who evade the Act.

44.2 THE TENANT'S RIGHT OF FIRST REFUSAL

There are four major conditions before tenants can claim the pre-emption rights conferred by Part I of the Act:

(1) the premises must come within the Act;
(2) the landlord must not be an exempt landlord;
(3) the tenant must be a qualifying tenant; and
(4) there must be a proposed 'relevant disposal'.

44.2.1 The premises

The premises must consist of a building divided into at least two flats occupied by 'qualifying tenants' where not more than 50 per cent of the floor area is used for non-residential purposes. Thus, if there are shops on the ground floor with flats above, the Act will not apply if the floor area of the shops exceeds the floor area of the flats.

44.2.2 The landlord

Certain landlords are excluded from the Act. These are mainly public sector landlords, for example, local authorities, the Housing Corporation and certain housing associations. In the private sector, resident landlords are excluded. A resident landlord is a landlord who lives in part of the building (not being a purpose-built block of flats) and who occupies a flat in the premises as his only or principal home and who has occupied it for at least 12 months.

Subject to the above, the landlord is the tenant's immediate landlord but if that landlord does not own the freehold or a reversion of at least 7 years then the superior landlord is also regarded as a landlord for the purposes of the Act.

44.2.3 Qualifying tenants

A tenant is a qualifying tenant unless his tenancy falls into one of the following categories:

(1) a protected shorthold tenancy;
(2) a business tenancy under Part II of the LTA 1954;
(3) a tenancy terminable on cessation of employment;
(4) an assured tenancy under the HA 1988.

So which tenancies will be qualifying? Although there is no requirement for a qualifying tenant to have a long lease, the exclusion of assured tenancies in practical terms dictates that most qualifying tenants will be long leaseholders at low rents. However, any surviving RA 1977 tenants will also qualify, as these are not excluded from the definition.

44.2.4 Relevant disposal

A relevant disposal is the disposal of any estate or interest in the premises which is not excluded from the Act. The exclusions consist of the following:

(1) the grant of a tenancy of a single flat;
(2) the grant of a mortgage, although a sale by a lender in exercise of his power of sale would be a relevant disposal;
(3) a disposal to a trustee in bankruptcy or liquidator;
(4) transfers ordered by the court in connection with matrimonial or succession proceedings;
(5) a disposal following a compulsory purchase order;
(6) a gift to a member of the landlord's family or to a charity;
(7) the surrender of a lease in pursuance of a provision in the lease to that effect;
(8) a disposal to the Crown;
(9) a disposal within a group of companies which have been associated for at least 2 years.

If the landlord proposes to make a relevant disposal (as defined above), he must serve notice on the qualifying tenants detailing the proposed terms, including the price, and stating that the notice constitutes an offer to dispose of the property and certain other particulars. If more than 50 per cent of the qualifying tenants decide to accept the offer, they must do so within the period stated by the notice which must be not less than 2 months. The purchasing tenants are then given a further 2 months in which to nominate a person who will purchase the landlord's interest on the tenants' behalf, for example, a limited company formed for that purpose. If the tenants do not elect to purchase within the first 2 months or do not make a nomination within the second 2 months or if the tenants fail to complete within 3 months, the landlord is free to proceed with the disposal elsewhere.

If the landlord makes a disposal without complying with the Act, the tenants have a right of acquisition against the buyer. Thus, a buyer from a landlord falling within the Act should always ensure the requisite notices have been served and the time-limits complied with before the relevant disposal proceeds.

44.2.5 Anti-avoidance measures – HA 1996

As originally drafted, the 1987 Act did not impose any real sanctions for landlords who failed to comply with its provisions and some freeholders sought to exploit ways round the legislation. The HA 1996 attempts to solve these omissions.

A new s 10A is inserted into the 1987 Act which makes it a criminal offence not to notify the tenants of a proposal to make a relevant disposal. New provisions are also inserted making it clear that a contract to make a relevant disposal is itself a relevant disposal and making it easier for tenants to enforce their rights both against a disposing landlord and against a person who takes the property under a disposal not complying with the Act.

44.3 COMPULSORY ACQUISITION OF THE REVERSION

Part I of the Act applies where the landlord wishes to dispose of his reversion, but under Part III of the Act the landlord can, in certain circumstances, be forced to sell his interest to the tenants against his wishes. Part III applies where there has been a history of bad management by the landlord. The detailed rules are complex and are beyond the scope of this book.

Chapter 45

LEASEHOLD REFORM, HOUSING AND URBAN DEVELOPMENT ACT 1993

Chapter 45 contents

45.1 INTRODUCTION

Tenants of flats have traditionally been excluded from the benefits of enfranchisement afforded to other long leaseholders (see Chapter 43). One major problem has always been the need to ensure the proper management and repair of a block of flats. This might prove difficult between freehold flat-owners. There is also the question as to who would own the common parts of the block. The LRHUDA 1993 has now given to flat-owners a collective right to enfranchise, the freehold in the whole block being acquired by a nominee on behalf of the individual tenants. It also contains an alternative right for individual tenants to purchase a new lease running until 90 years after the term date of their original lease. Tenants under long leases of flats (and houses) do, in any event, have a right under the LTA 1954, Part I (as amended) to remain in possession following the ending of their leases, basically as assured tenants under the HA 1988. Although flat tenants do thus have security of tenure at the end of their long leases, this is only at a price. As an assured tenant, they will be required to pay the full open market rent for their flat. This will be fixed, without taking into account any premium which was paid on the acquisition of the lease.

45.2 COLLECTIVE ENFRANCHISEMENT

45.2.1 The right

Collective enfranchisement consists of the tenants in a block of flats acquiring the freehold in the block, the freehold being conveyed into the name of a nominee on their behalf. This conveyance can take place without the landlord's consent, although there are limited grounds on which the landlord can resist a claim (see **45.2.4**). For the right to exist, various conditions must also be fulfilled. In particular, the tenants must be 'qualifying tenants' of 'flats' which are themselves in 'premises', all as defined by the Act.

For the right to be available, 'qualifying tenants' must hold at least two-thirds of the total number of flats in the premises. The premises in question, therefore, need not be let exclusively to tenants on long leases; some of the flats might be let to HA 1988 tenants, for example. Equally, the premises need not be let exclusively for residential purposes, but see **45.2.16**.

45.2.2 Nature of the collective right

The right to collective enfranchisement is the right to have the freehold in the premises acquired on behalf of the participating qualifying tenants by a person or persons appointed by them at a price to be determined in accordance with the Act.

45.2.3 Exercise of the collective right

As stated in **45.2.1**, at least two-thirds of the flats in a block must be held by 'qualifying tenants' before the collective right arises. However, it is not necessary for all of the qualifying tenants in the block to be involved in the enfranchisement. The right to enfranchise is exercised by the service of the appropriate notice on the reversioner and to be valid this must be given by at least two-thirds of the qualifying tenants. At least one half of the qualifying tenants who serve the notice must have occupied their flat as their only or principal home for the previous 12 months or for periods totalling 3 years out of the previous 10 years. Further, to prevent only a minority of tenants seeking to enfranchise, the tenants serving the notice must occupy at least one half of the flats in the block.

45.2.4 Landlord's grounds for opposition

A landlord can dispute the right to enfranchise if he can establish that one or more of the qualifying conditions have not been complied with by the applicants, for example, if two-thirds of the flats in the block are not held by qualifying tenants. Apart from this, his only ground of opposition will be if he can establish that he intends to redevelop the whole or a substantial part of the premises. Such a ground for opposition will only be possible, however, where not less than two-thirds of the long leases in the block are due to terminate within 5 years and the landlord cannot reasonably carry out his redevelopment without obtaining possession.

45.2.5 Qualifying tenants

A person will be a 'qualifying tenant' for collective enfranchisement if he is a 'tenant' of a 'flat' under a 'long lease' at a 'low rent'. Alternatively, now the HA 1996 is in force, a tenant will be a qualifying tenant, if he does not satisfy the definition of a tenant at a low rent as long as he has a 'particularly long lease'. Companies and other non-human persons can be qualifying tenants and participate in an enfranchisement, but see **45.2.3** as to the need for at least half of the participating qualifying tenants to satisfy a residence requirement.

'Tenant' is defined to include a person holding a lease or tenancy or an agreement for a lease or tenancy; and lease and tenancy includes a sub-lease and a sub-tenancy. Joint leaseholders are treated together as a single tenant.

'Flat' means a separate set of premises, whether or not on the same floor, which forms part of a building, and is constructed or adapted for use as a dwelling, and either the whole or some material part lies above or below some other part of the building. The emphasis in the definition is to at least part of the flat being above or below some other part of the building. Thus, flats above shops etc will be included in this definition, but 'granny flats', or similar premises, which consist of an extension to an existing building, but are not above or below part of that building, will not be within the definition. This part of the definition ties in with the definition of a house for the purposes of the LRA 1967 (see Chapter 43).

'Long lease' is defined to mean:

(1) a lease granted for a term of years certain exceeding 21 years. Any provisions for determination within that period, whether by landlord or by tenant, and whether by forfeiture or otherwise, will not prevent the lease from being a long lease;

(2) a perpetually renewable lease, other than a sub-lease out of a superior lease which is not a long lease. (These are converted into leases for 2,000 years by s 145 of the LPA 1922);

(3) a lease terminable on death or marriage. (These are converted into fixed terms of 99 years by s 149(6) of the LPA 1925.) Such a lease will not be treated as a long lease, however, if:

  (a) notice to terminate can be served at any time after the death or marriage; and
  (b) the notice period is 3 months or less; and
  (c) the terms of the lease preclude both sub-letting of the whole and assignment;

(4) a lease granted in pursuance of the right to buy or the right to buy on rent to mortgage terms conferred by Part V of the HA 1985. (This relates to rights granted to tenants from local authorities and other public bodies);

(5) a shared ownership lease where the tenant's total share is 100 per cent;

(6) a new tenancy granted expressly or impliedly to a tenant on the expiry of a long lease at a low rent will itself be deemed to be a long lease irrespective of its length. Similarly, where a lease is being continued under the terms of Part I of the LTA 1954 or under Sch 10 to the Local Government and Housing Act 1989 (LGHA 1989), it will be included in the definition of a long lease;

(7) Where a lease was granted for a term not exceeding 21 years but has been renewed without payment of a premium on one or more occasions under an option for renewal so that the total of the terms granted exceeds 21 years, then the original lease is to be treated as exceeding 21 years, ie it will be treated as a long lease;

(8) If the same person holds, from the same landlord, separate leases of two or more parts of a single flat, or separate leases of a flat or part of one and land or other premises occupied with it, then such of those leases as are 'long leases' as defined above are to be treated as a single long lease for the purposes of the Act. This might apply, for example, where a tenant has been granted separate long leases of a flat and a garage to be used with the flat, or has acquired two adjacent flats under separate leases and has subsequently converted them into a single flat.

Whether the rent payable under a lease is a 'low rent' is decided by reference to the rent payable in the initial year of the lease, ie in the year beginning with the date of commencement of the lease. Thus, the rent presently payable under the lease is irrelevant and may well not be a low rent. In deciding upon the amount of rent payable at any time, any payments to be made in respect of services, repairs, maintenance or insurance, even though reserved as rent, are to be excluded. Whether the rent payable in the initial year is a low rent then depends upon when the lease was granted:

(1) lease granted before 1 April 1963: the rent must not have exceeded two-thirds of the letting value of the flat on those lease terms on the date of commencement of the lease;

(2) lease granted on or after 1 April 1963 but before 1 April 1990, or, if the property had a rateable value on 31 March 1990, leases granted on or after 1 April 1990 in pursuance of a contract made before that date: the rent must not have exceeded two-thirds of the rateable value of the flat on the day of commencement of the lease;

(3) for all other leases, the rent in the initial year must not have exceeded £1,000 if the flat is in Greater London, or £250, if elsewhere.

Where a lease is deemed to be a long lease because of one or more renewals (see (7) above), then for the purpose of deciding whether that lease is let at a low rent, the amount of the rent for the year following the last renewal will be the relevant rental figure to be considered.

The requirement that a qualifying tenant had to have a long lease at a low rent, caused many problems. In particular the need to prove what the letting value of a flat was when it was first granted many years ago caused great difficulties to potential claimants. The HA 1996 attempts to remedy these problems. It provides that if a tenant has a lease for a 'particularly long term' then he will be a qualifying tenant even though the lease is not at a low rent. Obviously, the other requirements for a qualifying tenant (eg a lease of a flat) must still be fulfilled.

A particularly long term is defined to mean:

(1) a lease granted for a term certain exceeding 35 years; or
(2) a perpetually renewable lease; or
(3) a lease terminable on death or marriage; or
(4) it is a lease granted for less than 35 years which has been renewed on one or more occasions without payment under an option to renew, so that the total of the terms exceeds 35 years.

45.2.6 Qualifying tenants: exclusions

A person will not be a qualifying tenant if:

(1) his lease is within Part II of the LTA 1954 (business tenancies);
(2) his immediate landlord is a charitable housing trust and the flat forms part of the accommodation provided by it for its charitable purposes;
(3) the lease is an unlawful sub-lease out of a superior lease which is not itself a long lease at a low rent.

45.2.7 Interests included in the collective right

The acquisition will cover not only the freehold of the premises in which the flats are situated, but also:

(1) Certain other freehold property owned by the same freeholder: this must be appurtenant property demised with at least one of the flats, or any property which at least one qualifying tenant is entitled to use in common with the occupiers of other premises.

'Appurtenant property' means any garage, outhouse, garden or yard belonging to or usually enjoyed with the flat. This will, therefore, cover the situation where a flat lease also demises a separate garage or car-parking space to the tenant. This appurtenant property must be demised by the flat lease, but sometimes there will be separate leases of the flat and the garage. See **45.2.5** as to the two leases being deemed to be a single lease, thus ensuring that this requirement is fulfilled.

Also covered is the common situation where easements of way or to park cars are granted to a flat owner over the grounds adjoining the block of flats. The freehold in the land over which such rights are granted will be included in the acquisition rights (assuming it is owned by the same freeholder as the flats) even if the occupiers of other buildings have rights over it as well. This latter factor could well cause problems for landlords, and so they are given the choice of excluding such property from enfranchisement provided that permanent rights are granted over the property equivalent to those enjoyed under the terms of the lease.

(2) The acquisition rights will also include any intermediate leasehold interests between the freehold and the leases held by the qualifying tenants. The qualifying tenants are required to acquire all superior leases which include the flat of a qualifying tenant. If the superior lease consists of any common parts of the premises or any 'appurtenant property' (as defined above), the qualifying tenants may acquire such leasehold interests where the acquisition is reasonably necessary for the proper management of the common parts or appurtenant property on behalf of the qualifying tenants.

45.2.8 Interests excluded from the collective right

The freeholder can retain the title to any underlying minerals, provided that proper provision is made for the support of the premises.

45.2.9 Interests to be leased back

The freeholder can also retain, by means of a lease-back arrangement, certain parts of the acquired premises. The following must be leased back:

(1) flats let by the freeholder on secure tenancies;
(2) flats sub-let on secure tenancies where the freeholder and all mesne landlords are public sector landlords;
(3) flats let by housing associations on tenancies other than secure tenancies.

The following are to be leased back if the freeholder so requires:

(1) units which are not flats let to qualifying tenants. This could include any part of the premises which are let on a business tenancy, or on tenancies which are not long leases at a low rent; it will also include unlet flats;
(2) a flat occupied by a resident landlord.

45.2.10 Terms of the lease back

There are detailed provisions dealing with the terms of any lease to be granted back to the freeholder (see Sch 8 to the Act). Basically, unless the parties agree otherwise, or the Leasehold Valuation Tribunal otherwise directs, they are to be 999-year leases at a peppercorn rent with appropriate appurtenant rights, landlord's covenant for repair, rebuilding and insurance and service charge provisions. There is to be no restriction on assignment or sub-letting, except in the case of lease-backs of business units where qualified covenants against dealings and change of use are to be inserted.

45.2.11 Enfranchisement price (Sch 5)

The price to be paid for the freehold will be the total of three separate elements:

(1) market value;
(2) half of the marriage value;
(3) compensation.

Where the freehold and intermediate leases are being acquired, each interest is to be valued and paid for separately, so the market value, marriage value and any compensation for each individual interest being acquired will need to be calculated and paid over to the respective owner. In addition, the reasonable costs of each respective owner will be payable.

45.2.12 Market value

Market value is the price which might be expected to be realised if the property was sold on the open market by a willing seller, with neither the nominee buyer nor any participating tenant seeking to buy. Any defects in the landlord's title will thus serve to reduce the value of his interest as they would on any other sale. As an anti-avoidance device, it is provided that the value is not to be increased by any transaction entered into after the date of the passing of the Act. The following assumptions (inter alia) are also to be made in arriving at the market value of the interest:

(1) on the assumption that the seller is selling the fee simple:

 (a) subject to any leases subject to which the freeholder's interest is to be acquired by the buyer; but
 (b) subject also to any intermediate or other leasehold interests in the premises which are to be acquired by the buyer;

(2) on the assumption that the Act confers no rights to acquire the premises or to acquire a new lease;
(3) on the assumption that any increase in value caused by improvements carried out by any participating tenant is to be disregarded.

45.2.13 Marriage value

Marriage value is a complex valuation principle and follows from the fact that when both leasehold and freehold interests in a property become vested in the same person then the value of those interests to that person will be more than the combined value of the interests when held by different persons. It is, of course, generally the case that a freehold subject to a tenancy will be worth a lot less than the same freehold when vacant possession is available. So, to give an example, if the freehold when held by X is worth £30,000 and the leasehold interest when held by Y £40,000, it may well be that when Y also acquires the freehold the value of the property may now be £110,000, ie £40,000 more than the sum total of freehold and leasehold interests when owned by different people. This £40,000 is the marriage value and the landlord is entitled to one half of it or such greater share as may be agreed by the parties or determined by a leasehold valuation tribunal. In the relatively few cases so far decided by Leasehold Valuation Tribunals, landlords are generally being awarded the basic one half of the marriage value.

45.2.14 Compensation

The third element in assessing the price is compensation to the freeholder for any loss or damage he may suffer by result of the enfranchisement. This will include any diminution in the value of any other property owned by the landlord, including loss of development value. This is to cover the situation, for example, where the landlord is now unable to redevelop his adjoining property due to the fact that he no longer is the owner of the enfranchised premises.

45.2.15 Premises: definition

The flats must be in premises, as defined. Premises are defined as a self-contained building or as a self-contained part of a building and, as originally drafted, all of this building or part had to be owned by the same person. This proved an attractive avoidance device to landlords wishing to avoid the operation of the Act. It was simply necessary to vest a part of the block of flats (eg one or two floors) into the name of a different owner and the Act would not apply. The HA 1996 has now closed this loophole.

Under the HA 1996, the Act applies to premises even if there are multiple freeholders, unless the part in separate ownership is itself a self-contained part of a building. In that case, the flat tenants will be able to enfranchise each self-contained part separately.

A building is a self-contained building if it is structurally detached; part of a building is a self-contained part if it consists of a vertical division of the building and its structure is such that that part could be redeveloped independently of the remainder. In addition, the services provided for the occupiers (by pipes, cables etc) are or could be provided independently of the services provided for the rest of the building.

45.2.16 Premises: exclusions

The 'premises' need not be used exclusively for residential purposes, provided that any parts occupied or intended to be occupied for non-residential purposes do not exceed 10 per cent of the internal floor area of the premises as a whole. In making this calculation, any common parts of the building are to be ignored.

Premises will not be included within the definition if they have a resident landlord. There will be a resident landlord if, at any time, the freeholder or an adult member of his family occupies a flat in the premises as his only or principal home and has done so for at least the previous 12 months. However, this exclusion does not apply if the premises contain more than four units or are a purpose-built block of flats. In these cases, the Act will still apply even though there is a resident landlord.

45.3 INDIVIDUAL ACQUISITION OF A LONG LEASE

45.3.1 Nature of the right

The right given is the right to be granted a new lease to expire 90 years after the expiry date of the tenant's existing lease. This new lease is to be at a peppercorn rent, but the tenant must pay a premium to be calculated as laid down by the Act. The new lease is to take effect immediately in substitution for the tenant's existing lease. This right is available whether or not the right to collective enfranchisement is also available. The new lease will be binding upon the landlord's lenders even if the existing lease was granted in breach of the terms of the mortgage.

45.3.2 Entitlement to a new lease

Entitlement to a new lease is given to a tenant if:

(1) he is a qualifying tenant; and
(2) he has occupied the flat as his only or main residence for the past 3 years or for periods totalling 3 years in the last 10 years.

The definition of qualifying tenant is the same as for the purposes of enfranchisement (see **45.2.5**). The residence requirement effectively limits this right to one flat only and excludes companies and other non-human persons. In the case of joint tenants, the 3-year residence requirement need only be fulfilled by one of them. Note that this residence requirement is longer than that required for collective enfranchisement.

45.3.3 Refusal of new lease

The landlord can obtain a court order declaring that the tenant's right to a new lease is not exercisable, where the court is satisfied that:

(1) the tenant's existing lease is due to terminate within 5 years from the date of the tenant requesting a new lease; and
(2) the landlord intends, once the existing lease has expired, to demolish or reconstruct the whole or a substantial part of the premises and he could not reasonably do so without obtaining possession of the flat.

45.3.4 Terms of the new lease

The new lease is to be on the same terms as the existing lease except as to:

(1) the rent, which will be a peppercorn;
(2) the term, which will be for a period to end 90 years after the term date of the existing lease;
(3) the omission of property comprised in the existing lease but not comprised in the flat. However, for these purposes, 'flat' includes any garage, outhouse, garden or yard let to the tenant with the flat;
(4) the inclusion, where the existing lease is inadequate, of provisions for variable service charges in respect of repairs, services, maintenance and insurance;
(5) the inclusion of a statement that the lease has been granted under these provisions;
(6) the omission of any options or pre-emptions contained in the existing lease;
(7) limitation of the landlord's liability under his covenants to breaches for which he is personally responsible;
(8) modifications to reflect defects in the existing lease or other provisions which it would be unreasonable to include without modification;
(9) the reservation of a right for the landlord to apply to the court for possession for redevelopment purposes during the last 12 months of the term of the original lease or during the last 5 years of the new lease, subject to compensation being payable.

45.3.5 The amount of the premium

Complex provisions are laid down for the calculation of the premium. Briefly, the premium is to be the aggregate of:

(1) the diminution in the market value of the landlord's interest, comparing the value before and after the grant of the new lease, and ignoring the tenants' rights under this Act; and
(2) the landlord's share of the marriage value. Here, marriage value is the difference between the aggregate values of the existing lease and all superior interests compared with the aggregate values of the new lease and all superior interests. The landlord's share of the marriage value is 50 per cent or such

higher figure as may be fixed by agreement or by a leasehold valuation tribunal; and

(3) reasonable compensation to the landlord for loss or damage resulting from the grant of the new lease in respect of other property, including loss of development value.

In addition, the tenant will be responsible for the landlord's costs in granting the new lease.

45.3.6 The effect of the grant of a new lease

Once a new lease has been granted, this will not preclude a subsequent exercise of the right to collective enfranchisement. Equally, a further claim to another new lease under these provisions can be brought in relation to any new lease granted. However, that is the only security of tenure applicable to such lease; no other security of tenure provisions are to apply to the lease nor to any sub-tenancies granted out of it once the term date has passed. This means that neither the tenant nor any sub-tenant (whether lawful or otherwise) can claim protection after the end of the 90-year extended term, whether under the LTA 1954 (Part I or II), RA 1977, HA 1988 or any similar legislation.

INDEX

References in the right-hand column are to paragraph numbers.